# THEORETICAL FRAMEWORKS FOR PERSONAL RELATIONSHIPS

Edited by

**Ralph Erber**
*DePaul University*

**Robin Gilmour**
*University of Lancaster*

**LEA** LAWRENCE ERLBAUM ASSOCIATES, PUBLISHERS
1994   Hillsdale, New Jersey                           Hove, UK

Lawrence Erlbaum Associates, Inc., Publishers
365 Broadway
Hillsdale, New Jersey 07642

**Library of Congress Cataloging-in-Publication Data**

Theoretical frameworks for personal relationships / edited by Ralph
  Erber, Robin Gilmour.
     p.     cm.
  Includes bibliographical references (p.      ) and indexes.
  ISBN 0-8058-0573-7 (c : acid-free paper)
  1. Interpersonal relations.  2. Man-woman relationships.
3. Intimacy (Psychology).  I. Erber, Ralph.  II. Gilmour, Robin.
HM132.T45  1994
306.7—dc20                        93-42465
                                        CIP

Printed in the United States of America
10  9  8  7  6  5  4  3  2  1

This volume is dedicated to *Maureen* and *Brian*, my most important personal relationships (RE); to *MC* and the *menagerie* (RG); and to *George Levinger* whose life-long contributions to the area of personal relationships make it possible for both of us to be here today.

# Contents

# Preface

The past two decades have seen a tremendous increase in research and scholarship devoted to personal relationships. From rather scattered beginnings, a recognizable and recognized field has emerged, whose strength and health is reflected in a wide variety of indicators. At ground level, there is the sheer volume of published journal articles and books. At a second and more organizational level, there is the emergence of two major journals devoted to the field, the *International Journal of Personal Relationships* and the *Journal of Social and Personal Relationships*, along with the now firmly established International Society for the Study of Personal Relationships and the long-running series of International Conferences on Personal Relationships. Beyond all this solid evidence there is an interesting form of additional validation in the way many writers, commentators, and editors point out almost as a matter of course how satisfactorily the young field has grown. Indeed, perhaps the most telling sign of all is the fact that dwelling on such an observation is now regarded as hackneyed and trite.

So to use a developmental metaphor, the infant has grown up, the young adult has emerged and is clearly thriving. It is not our intention to go over old ground here. Instead, we wish to pursue the argument a step further by proposing that relationship research has reached a certain stage of maturity that is reflected in the title of this volume. Our contention is that, although the vigor of a field is often shown in the diversity and innovation of its research, it is in the theoretical domain that we find evidence of a real coming of age. The early years of any new scientific endeavor generally require careful empirical work to map out the terrain and its boundaries. Maturity, on the other hand, is characterized by the development of theoretical structures that enable us to consolidate research work to further understand the issues and to give direction to our empirical work.

This volume provides grounds for arguing that the diversity of theorizing is particularly healthy at this point. We believe that it manifests itself in several ways. There is a diversity in the type of issues that were tackled by our contributors, the approaches that were taken, and the disciplinary background from which the different frameworks emerged. Chapters 1 and 2 are concerned with distinctions. Levinger makes one with regard to microanalytic and macroanalytic approaches; Mills and Clark talk about the unique norms that distinguish personal relationships from more casual relationships. The inception and development of close relationships is the focus of chapters 3 and 4 by Huston and Lane and Wegner. Reis (chapter 5) and Kenny (chapter 6) present theories regarding new methodologies developed to understand processes in close relationships. Attachment is the focus of the next three chapters. Kerns (chapter 7) and Sharabany (chapter 8) offer some speculations about the "missing links" between infant attachment and adult romantic attachment. Davis, Kirkpatrick, Levy, and O'Hearn (chapter 9) compare the relative contributions of attachment theory and love styles theory to our understanding of personal relationships. The final two chapters apply theories to close relationships that were intially not formulated with that goal in mind. Specifically, in chapter 10, Erber and Tesser introduce self-evaluation maintenance theory and contrast it with other approaches to close relationships. In chapter 11, Dykstra and de Jong Gierveld take the rather generic theory of mental incongruity and apply it to the understanding of loneliness among the widowed.

The reader will notice that there is some diversity in terms of how much theory and research is contained in each chapter. Whereas some are purely theoretical, others complement theory with original pieces of empirical research. Finally, the editors and contributors are from different countries—yet another way in which the diversity of this volume manifests itself.

We view the diversity of the frameworks presented in this volume as a strength, as building on established strengths elsewhere to feed into relationship research and enhance its vitality. We believe that each chapter has its own contribution to make to thinking and research about personal relationships. As a group, they add up to an exciting collection that not only reflects a richness of conceptual backing, but also a wide range of usable theoretical structures—usable both in helping us explain relationship phenomena and enabling us to generate additional empirical research.

## ACKNOWLEDGMENTS

Numerous people and institutions have helped make this volume possible. We are especially indebted to George Levinger and Sheldon Cotler, the chairpeople of the DePaul University Psychology Department, for their support during the final stages of this project. We also thank Antoinette D'Ambrosio, Lucinda Rapp, Nancy Rospenda, Kimberly Ross, Julie Rybarski, and Mark Schuster for providing the backup support for this project, and Maureen Wang Erber for her patience and continued intellectual stimulation.

*Ralph Erber*
*Robin Gilmour*

# Chapter 1

# Figure Versus Ground:
# Micro- and Macroperspectives
# on the Social Psychology
# of Personal Relationships

George Levinger
*University of Massachusetts, Amherst*

In this chapter, I examine both micro- and macroaspects of personal relationships, because I believe recent research progress has neglected the influence of broad trends in the sociocultural environment. Social psychological research has usually focused on the figure of pair interaction at the expense of its ground—on its immediate or proximal influences, rather than on its distal social determinants. Although personal relations researchers tend to focus narrowly on individuals or close pairs, it is evident that broad social forces affect how people relate to each other, as well as how investigators frame their research problems. Thus, traditional society has stifled studies into interpersonal relations, but modern society encourages such inquiry, which helps people answer questions about a world in flux. Therefore, I attend to the wider context that affects both the study of personal relationships and their phenomena.

This chapter has two main parts. In the first part, I examine how the study of personal relationships developed over the past half century, focusing especially on some of my own ideas and research on this topic. In the second part, I consider several recent microanalytic analyses of dyadic interaction and relationship, and then contrast their emphases with macroanalytic appraisals of social structural influences on relationships in our culture, after which I discuss some interconnections between micro- and macroapproaches.

## DIALECTIC TENSIONS

To set the backdrop to my discussion, let me begin with some dialectic images from Raush's (1977) reflections on the first published conference on the topic of close relationships, held in 1974 (Levinger & Raush, 1977). Reviewing what the contributors had said, Raush wrote about the dialectic tensions among the personal, interpersonal, and societal orientations to relationships. He suggested that these different orientations are frames through which both outside observers and inside participants view relationships (Raush, 1977). For instance, he reviewed the changing conceptions of intimacy over a 300-year span of U.S. history. To capture those changes, he employed the metaphor of the dance. Talking about the Colonial Era in America 300 years ago, Raush saw couples performing a set dance pattern in the context of the group: "Couples join and separate, but the pattern is fixed and it is the community that surrounds and controls the dance. Individual skill and grace may be called for but never individual self-expression" (p. 179). In the Jacksonian Era, 150 years later, "the formalities of popular dance structures begin to disintegrate. . . . The dance 'caller' appears for the first time. The once fixed sequence of patterns is no longer given communally, and it is the 'caller' who sets the sequence" (p. 180). Still later, in the early 20th century, "the dance becomes that of a couple as the unit. Each couple dances in close physical contact, apart from other couples, and with little or no sense of social community. The male leads, the female follows. The dance steps, however, are patterned to the music, and some elements of a formal sequence are maintained" (p. 181). Finally today, or in the 1970s when Raush was writing, the "formation is still one of pairs, and the music provides the background. [But T]here is no defined sequence of steps; the partners are in minimal and momentary contact with each other, and each does as he or she wishes; the emphasis is on individual autonomy . . . while meeting in transit" (p. 183). However, Raush noted that there have been recent countertrends, as in the revival of folk dancing and even ballroom dancing among both older and younger people.

In each of these eras, individuals and couples have made personal decisions about dancing: Will they dance at all? With whom? How enthusiastically and for how long? People are aware of such personal decisions, but they are often unaware how the alternatives from which they choose are governed by societal scripts. As for the social scientists: Some study the dancers, others study dancing and dance patterns, and still others attend to the music; but we too are frequently uncognizant of our historical and cultural context.

## WHAT IS FIGURE AND WHAT IS GROUND?

Let me consider figure and ground in other ways. In his opening address to the first international conference on personal relationships in 1982, Kelley (1986) spoke about the daunting task of personal relationships research. In doing so, he presented a picture of the interpersonal relationship caught between the individual person on one side, and society on the other side.

Kelley's (1986) image was a variant of other social systems models, including Hinde's (1987) recent multiple causation model or the organizing model from the book *Close Relationships* (Kelley et al., 1983). The Kelley et al. model (see Fig. 1.1a) spotlighted microanalytic pair events and interactions between Person (P) and Other (O), but it also acknowledged the broad causal conditions that reside in each partner's personal characteristics (P and O), in the cumulative properties of the P–O relationship (P × O), in the social and the physical environment (E soc and E phys), and in the multiple links among those many variables. Each of these foci is a legitimate approach to the study of a relationship system,[1] but the total array of events and causal conditions is hardly possible to examine all at once; single studies usually limit themselves to only one or two aspects.

The diagram in Fig. 1.1a was influenced in turn by earlier images, for example, the illustration Huston and Levinger (1978) used in a review of the literature on attraction and relationships, which showed changing Person–Other relations embedded in both partners' social networks, which are nested in subcultural and cultural environments, all subject to change over time (see Fig. 1.1b). That figure was influenced by pictures that Lewin (1940/1948) drew way back in 1940 of a husband–wife pair nested in a larger family, embedded in a community, and so forth.

## A SELECTIVE HISTORICAL OVERVIEW

Before comparing a micro- with a macroanalytic perspective, I review the historical context that helped shape social psychological research on personal relationships.

### The 1940s

I begin this overview by going back half a century to Lewin's 1940 paper, which he titled "The Background of Conflict in Marriage." In it, he described marriage as a "very small group" that touches "central regions" of both members who have "intimate relations" with each other. His paper contained images of pair and group fields, and of the embeddedness of small systems in larger systems. Although Lewin focused on the immediate ecology of the life space, he elsewhere cautioned readers that a complete psychological analysis must

---

[1]Note that family systems theorists and therapists (e.g., Hoffman, 1981; Kaslow, 1991; Minuchin, 1974) have also emphasized the importance of examining all these variables in their complex interplay. This chapter focuses primarily on academic work in social psychology.

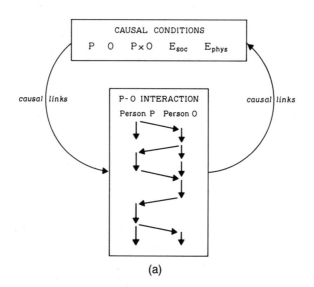

(a)

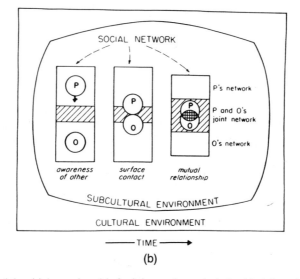

(b)

FIG. 1.1. (a) A causal model of pair interaction and relationship (adapted from Kelley et al., 1983). (b) The Person–Other relationship in its sociocultural context (Huston & Levinger, 1978).

account for a person's wider nonpsychological environment (Lewin, 1943/ 1951).

However, aside from Lewin's provocative paper, the 1940s showed little social psychological interest in interpersonal relationships. For example, the influential social psychology textbook by Krech and Crutchfield (1948) considered only the individual, group, and institutional levels as alternative perspectives on social phenomena. After all, the 1940s were concerned with World War II and its aftermath—with teamwork and cooperation, and with society's readjustments to peace-time life.

## The 1950s

When I entered the Michigan social psychology program in 1951, I was attracted to the Research Center for Group Dynamics, which at that time took seriously the study of groups. For us, the group was the primary environment to which individual behavior mattered. This was typical of that time. "Human relations" had become a field of study, but mainly in industry and other work contexts. Pair relationships were generally ignored and, when they were studied, socioemotional functions usually were subordinated to task functions.

When interpersonal attraction was studied, it was considered either as an attitude toward whole categories of persons, as in the Social Distance Scale (Bogardus, 1925), or in group settings, as in sociometric studies of classrooms or living groups (e.g., Jennings, 1943; Moreno, 1934). Even later in the 1950s, when the study of groups faltered and attention began to center on more individualistic conceptions, such as Festinger's (1954, 1957) theories of social comparison or cognitive dissonance, there was still little in the way of interpersonal analysis.

Important exceptions began to emerge, however. Although Heider's (1946) balance theory was conceived from the standpoint of the individual, Newcomb's (1953) balance theory, which he later applied to studying acquaintance processes (Newcomb, 1961), focused on communication in dyadic systems. Important problems in group psychology, especially the study of social power (Cartwright, 1959), were soon formulated in dyadic terms (e.g., French & Raven, 1959). For instance, in my own doctoral dissertation (Levinger, 1959) on the genesis of social power relationships, I transposed a problem drawn from a group setting in a summer camp to a pair setting in the university laboratory.

Also in the 1950s, mathematical game theory emerged as a lens for viewing social situations, and the two-person Prisoner's Dilemma matrix became a popular paradigm for examining mixed-motive conflicts. In 1959, Thibaut and Kelley's important book *The Social Psychology of Groups* used such outcome matrices for analyzing social interdependence. Ironically, their analysis was far more suited to understanding relations in pairs than in groups, and thus their model served to shift attention from the multiperson group to the dyad.

What about the personal relationship? Aside from sociological survey research, such as Burgess and Wallin's (1953) ambitious studies of engagement and marriage or Goode's (1956) inquiry into the determinants and consequences of divorce, there were some notable theoretical developments in the 1950s. One was Herbst's (1952) creative application of Lewin's life-space topology to the measurement of husband–wife relations. He used field theory to compare families with regard to differing activity patterns, decision-making dominance, and degrees of marital tension. A few years later, Herbst's ideas strongly influenced Blood and Wolfe's (1960) survey study of marital task division and power. In turn, their work influenced later sociological analyses of marriage, as well as Huston and others' (e.g., this volume) recent longitudinal studies.

Another development in the 1950s was the rediscovery of Simmel's (1908/1950) distinction between the dyad and the larger group. Simmel had noted a strain toward intimacy in two-person groups and had theorized that its members often feel intense responsibility for one another, because in the dyad—in contrast with larger groups—either partner alone can end the group's existence. He said that the dyad is the locus of "sentimentalism," in that its members are especially sensitive to each other's actions and needs. Simmel's theoretical notions were confirmed empirically in Bales and Borgatta's (1955) small-group research, which found that members of pairs adopt a gentler approach to each other than do members of larger groups. This research also found that the pair's reluctance to voice disagreement is associated with greater interpersonal tension.

Nevertheless, only a few years later, Slater (1963), one of Bales' students, expressed provocative worries about the threat that "dyadic withdrawal"—as well as individual withdrawal—poses to families and the wider social community. It was also in the 1950s that Fromm (1956), in his book on *The Art of Loving*, argued that love is not primarily a relationship toward one particular person, but "an orientation of character which determines the relatedness of a person toward the world as a whole, not toward one 'object' of love." He wrote that, ". . . If I truly love one person I love all persons, I love the world" (p. 46). Note the huge difference between this perspective on love from that of the 1970s and 1980s (Rubin, 1970; Sternberg & Barnes, 1988), when the study of love became directed almost exclusively toward romantic and companionate forms of dyadic relationships.

## The 1960s

I began studying close relationships in the late 1950s through my initial research on family groups. My immediate influence was my first teaching job in a social work doctoral program, where I decided to apply group-dynamic ideas to the study of families. I had compared the interaction of clinic families, consisting of two parents and one 11-year-old child, with similarly composed school families. However, in 1960 I decided to focus on problem solving in the parental dyad, the family's most powerful pair. Although at the time I was mainly aware of my own professional environment, I was surely affected by distal trends toward an increasingly impersonal society putting increasing emphasis on nuclear family units.

At that time, academic research on marriage was dominated by sociological ideas and findings (e.g., Blood & Wolfe, 1960; Burgess & Locke, 1945; Goode, 1956; Hill, 1958; Parsons & Bales, 1955; Winch, 1958). In contrast, my students and I employed group-dynamic analyses that soon extended from marital problem solving to task and socioemotional behavior; to similarity and complementarity; to power; and to marital satisfaction, cohesiveness, and dissolution (e.g., Levinger, 1964a, 1964b, 1965; Levinger & Breedlove, 1966).

However, in 1965, I moved to a psychology department in a small town where there was little opportunity to study families, but definite interest in interpersonal attraction among college students. One year earlier, Secord and Backman (1964) had reviewed the attraction literature, tying together Newcomb's (1961) balance theory and research, need complementarity theories (e.g., Schutz, 1958; Winch, 1958), exchange theories (Thibaut & Kelley, 1959), as well as their own ideas of interpersonal congruency. Byrne (1961) started experimental work on a reinforcement model of attraction. Between 1965 and 1969, social psychologists published at least five further reviews of the attraction literature (Berscheid & Walster, 1969; Byrne, 1969; Cartwright, 1968; Lott & Lott, 1965; Marlowe & Gergen, 1968). Nevertheless, most attraction research neglected the relation between the perceiver and target, so that in 1968 Bennis, Schein, Steele, and Berlew noted that "the scientific study of interpersonal relations lags woefully behind other areas of social research" (p. 3).

In planning my new research, I looked for ways to integrate the current interest in the similarity-leads-to-attraction hypothesis with my own interest in established pairs. I became fascinated with Kerckhoff and Davis's (1962) longitudinal study of courtship among Duke University students, which had found evidence for the validity of both similarity and complementarity theories and had explicitly suggested under what conditions each theory seemed applicable. Therefore, with David Senn at Massachusetts and, soon after, Keith Davis's collaboration at Colorado, I undertook in 1966–1967 a large-scale extension of the Duke study. We added numerous questions and more than quadrupled the size of the 1959–1960 Duke sample. But, despite prolonged statistical analyses, neither our results from Massachusetts nor Colorado could confirm the earlier findings (Levinger, Senn, & Jorgensen, 1970). Neither value similarity nor need complementarity was related to progress in our 1966–1967 courting relationships.

*An Instructive Failure.*    In interpreting our results, we tried hard to explain our failure to confirm Kerckhoff and Davis's (1962) filter theory. As our major conclusion, we proposed the conjunction of "two supplementary processes . . . in deep-going attachments," the second of which had apparently overridden the first process. I quote from our conclusion:

> One process entails encounter, disclosure, and the discovery of co-orientation [as previously proposed by others]. . . . A second process, not previously formulated, is the development of the relationship *per se*. The first process governs [how two] partners discover one another; the second pertains to their subsequent build-up of a joint enterprise.

> Pairs that form *in vivo* [outside the lab] may construct a common property that cannot be indicated by reference to the members' separate individual properties. To the extent that both [!!] partners invest their efforts and resources in the intersection of their relationship, the product will supersede indices that focus only on the partners' individualities. Therefore [we need indices] that specifically assess the extent of this investment. Such an intersection might be called "pair communality," in contrast to "member similarity" which refers to the overlap of individual orientations. In closely knit relationships, the effects of pair commonality would eventually transcend those of member similarity. (Levinger et al., 1970, p. 441)

*Pair Communality.*    In other words, we concluded what happens inside the relationship is more important than what the individual members bring to it, which led to my later interest in the idea of pair communality. It first led me, together with Diedrick Snoek, to conceive an "intersection model" of pair relatedness, and to construct indices for measuring pair interdependence (Levinger, 1974, 1980), which were improved on by others' work in the 1980s (e.g., Berscheid, Snyder, & Omoto, 1989; Kenny, 1988).

*Vastly Changed Need Scores.*    But there was another, less noted aspect of our failure to replicate Kerckhoff and Davis's need complementarity findings. In 1966, we got dramatically different patterns of need scores from those obtained by Kerckhoff and Davis in 1959. Both our Massachusetts and Colorado data showed that "both males' and females' scores on the needs for Inclusion (or connection) and for Affection (love) were far higher than the norms standardized by William Schutz in the 1950s, while scores on the need 'to-*be*-controlled' were substantially lower" (1970, pp. 436–437). Schutz (personal communication, 1968) was amazed by our dramatically different mean scores, but my colleague Diedrick Snoek soon obtained similarly skewed scores on the Schutz scales from engineering students at Carnegie-Mellon (see Levinger et al., 1970).

At the time, I was merely frustrated at our replication failure. Today, I see that these need-score changes paralleled more general cultural shifts in the

United States, and probably in other industrialized societies. From their two national U.S. sample surveys, Veroff, Douvan, and Kulka (1981) later documented that, over the 19-year time span between 1957 and 1976, Americans showed a marked rise in their needs for self-fulfillment and personal freedom (with a questioning of traditional status and authority) and a parallel rise in their desires for intimacy. I return to discuss such macrotrends after first discussing advances on the microfront.

## MICROIMAGES OF PAIR RELATIONSHIPS

### The 1970s

*An "Intersection" Model of Pair Relatedness.* For me, the 1970s began in the summer of 1969, when I started meeting with Snoek to discuss our data on similarity and attraction in established pairings. Snoek and I had each tried to predict the fate of pair relationships over time, but neither of us had found indices of similarity or complementarity associated with two partners' closeness. In contrast, my courtship data showed that relationship progress over a 6-month interval was predicted by the two partners' mutual involvement at Time 1 and the extent of their Time 1 joint activity (Levinger et al., 1970). What, we asked, was going on? Something was happening in these relationships that was not well explained by then-existing conceptions of interpersonal attraction.

Our discussions led us to a more differentiated view of attraction, in which we distinguished among varying degrees of relatedness (i.e., unilateral impression formation, bilateral early encounters between strangers, and a continuum of deeper mutuality). We concluded that mutual relatedness goes beyond the restricted impressions and encounters that then constituted the bulk of the attraction literature, and thus we conceived our "intersection" model of social relatedness where Person's and Other's life spaces overlap increasingly as they become closer (see Lewin, 1940/1948). In Fig. 1.2, the intersection between P and O suggests that, in the mutual relationship, Person and Other have developed an interdependence, whereby they markedly influence each other's "actions, views, and experiences" (Levinger & Snoek, 1972, p. 5). We proposed that, as relationships move from surface contact toward increasing emotional investment, various important changes occur:

1. *communication* shifts from superficial to highly personal disclosures;
2. *shared knowledge* expands from the public to the private selves;
3. *interaction* moves from stereotypic role-taking to the mutually expected;
4. *pair maintenance* changes from passive to active mutual concern;

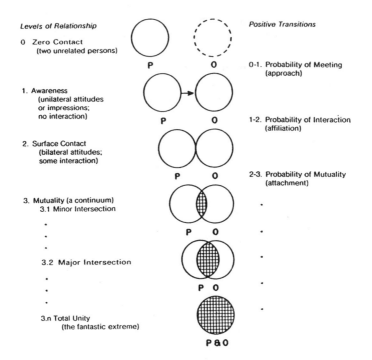

Levels of Relationship

0  Zero Contact
   (two unrelated persons)

1. Awareness
   (unilateral attitudes
   or impressions;
   no interaction)

2. Surface Contact
   (bilateral attitudes;
   some interaction)

3. Mutuality (a continuum)
   3.1 Minor Intersection

   3.2 Major Intersection

   3.n Total Unity
       (the fantastic extreme)

Positive Transitions

0-1. Probability of Meeting
     (approach)

1-2. Probability of Interaction
     (affiliation)

2-3. Probability of Mutuality
     (attachment)

FIG. 1.2.   An intersection model of pair relatedness (Levinger & Snoek, 1972).

5. *evaluation of partners' outcomes* is transformed from using self-centered to using relationship-centered criteria. (Levinger & Snoek, 1972, p. 8)

Those were among the dimensions we used to describe changes from surface to depth. Since then, of course, there have been more systematic formulations of relationship properties and changes (e.g., Berscheid et al., 1989; Borden & Levinger, 1991; Kelley et al., 1983).

Meanwhile, others were studying relationships on both sides of the Atlantic. In England, there were Argyle's (1972) research on interpersonal behavior, Duck's (1973) work on friendship, and Hinde's (1976, 1979) ethology inspired writings on relationships. In the United States, there were Altman's and Taylor's (1973) social penetration theory, which also was influenced by Lewin's images of intersubjectivity; Murstein's (1970) and Lewis's (1973) work on mate selection; Rubin, Peplau, and Hill's Boston Couples Study (e.g., Hill, Rubin, & Peplau, 1976); Raush, Barry, Hertel, and Swain's (1974), Gottman's (1979), and the Gottman et al. (1976) studies of marital interaction; as well as growing sophistication in methodology. Nonetheless, when Huston and I (1978) wrote a comprehensive review on attraction and relationships from 1972 to 1976, we found few citable empirical studies that clearly illuminated the mutual relationship.

## The 1980s

The 1980s revealed a totally different story. There was significant progress in many substantive areas, including attribution, communication, conflict, emotion, gender differences, interdependence, loneliness, love, power, and trust. There also were notable methodological advances, ranging from new indices for behavioral observation and self-report, to measures of affective interchange, to new statistical models. Such work has been reviewed in a number of places (e.g., Clark & Reis, 1988; Duck, 1988; Hendrick & Hendrick, 1992).

Here I discuss only three examples of sophisticated microanalysis, each of which focuses on a limited interactive pair situation: (a) Reis and Shaver's (1988) model of the intimacy process, (b) Levenson and Gottman's (1983, 1985) research on affect linkages in interaction, and (c) Holmes (1991) and Holmes and Rempel's (1989) studies of trust.

*A Model of the Intimacy Process.*    Reis and Shaver's (1988) model (see Fig. 1.3) describes the interaction between two persons and shows the feedback between their feelings, thoughts, and behaviors for a single episode. The process toward or away from greater intimacy can be entered at any of several points, but in Fig. 1.3 it begins with P's motives and needs, which impel him or her to make some sort of disclosure to O. P's act is passed through O's interpretive filter, which, together with O's own motives and goals, determines O's response. This response is in turn interpreted by P, before leading to P's affective and cognitive reaction and a new action. For example, P might tell O, "Today, work was really upsetting," and O might respond in any of many

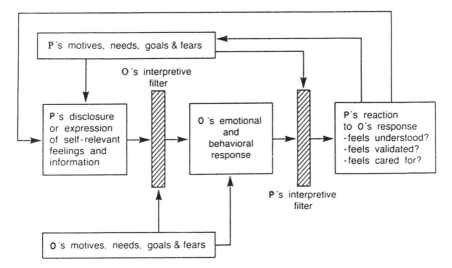

FIG. 1.3.   A model of the intimacy process (Reis & Shaver, 1988).

ways—from being warmly concerned and supportive to giving P a cold stare or a countercomplaint—and this reaction would, of course, affect P's next response and subsequent disclosures. Thus, any given interchange either adds to, subtracts from, or has no effect at all on a pair's aggregate intimacy.

I rearrange Reis and Shaver's (1988) model in Table 1.1 below.

Notice several points. First, both partners' behaviors, feelings, and interpretations are products of their immediate pair interplay and of the external context—their pair's history, their social network, and their wider social environment. Second, the long-term cumulation of P-O exchanges affects both persons' expectations about each other and their relationship. Third, although this model spotlights the single episode, the partners' interpretations (or information processing), feelings (or motivational orientations), and behaviors (or action tendencies) are all culturally derived: They only make sense if we understand the society that these two actors inhabit. The following two examples of recent research on couple interaction both involve such an interplay among partners' interpretations, feelings, and behaviors.

***Studies of Affect Linkage.*** One of the most striking microanalytic findings of the past decade came from Levenson and Gottman's (1983, 1985) research on "physiological linkage and affective exchange" in married couples, which followed Gottman's (1979; Gottman et al., 1976) earlier observation of the patterning of behavior and self-reported affect in satisfied and distressed marriages. Their initial findings, which still require considerable replication and clarification, gave empirical support to the adage that two people can "rub each other the wrong way."

When Levenson and Gottman (1983) compared the interaction of satisfied and dissatisfied couples in their laboratory, they found that, under high-conflict conditions, the physiological arousal of dissatisfied spouses was far more highly correlated than that of satisfied spouses. This physiological linkage between two spouses' concurrent affect explained an extraordinary 60% of couples' dissatisfaction with their marriages—about four times as much as parallel measures of self-reported affect. Levenson and Gottman concluded that spouses in unhappy marriages felt "locked into [a destructive] interaction and were unable to step back [from it]" (p. 596). When such dissatisfied spouses were en-

TABLE 1.1
Rearrangement of Reis and Shaver's (1988) Intimacy Process Model

| (I) Interpretations | (F) Feelings | (B) Behaviors |
|---|---|---|
| Schemas | Motives | Disclosure of self-relevant |
| Expectations | Needs | feelings, information. |
| Attributions | Goals | Reactions to other's responses |
|  | Fears |  |

couraged to vent their feelings about a high-conflict issue, both spouses became simultaneously agitated, angry, or aroused, and they stayed that way throughout that particular interaction episode. In contrast, members of satisfied couples were much less physiologically linked: If one spouse in a happy couple was concerned about a serious difficulty, the other tended to sit back and respond calmly, (a) not getting emotionally caught, and (b) probably helping to reduce the first partner's own arousal.

From outside this microanalytic perspective, however, one can raise questions that demand supplemental data. For example, it is not likely that Levenson and Gottman's low and high satisfied pairs differed not only in their physiological arousal or its linkage, but also in the length and severity of their marital problems? How locked into oppressive external life conditions were these differing couples? Is it not likely that the lives of the unhappy spouses were far more troubling than those of the happy ones, and that the distressed pairs had, prior to the research lab opportunity, avoided full discussion of their mutual problems? And how did these couples differ in their cultural norms about the expression of emotion? Until such issues are addressed, these findings raise more questions than they now answer.

***Studies of Trust and Appraisal.***    Holmes and his co-workers (e.g., Holmes, 1991; Holmes & Rempel, 1989) have done important research on the development and maintenance of trust in married couples. In one study, they asked spouses to watch a video replay of their discussion of a serious issue and compared their reactions with those of neutral judges. Ambivalent spouses (whom Holmes called "medium-trust" spouses) rated their partner's behavior more negatively than did the neutral observers and were generally more sensitive to their partner's immediate behavior than were high-trust spouses, who tended to give "every benefit of the doubt" to their partner's behavior and motives (Holmes, 1988, p. 1). These more trusting and less trusting couples also showed marked differences in their overt interactions.

The cumulative effects are as follows: High-trust spouses display a solid faith in their partner's predictability and dependability and, through this self-assurance, support each other's positive definition of their relationship. In contrast, both low- and medium-trust spouses feel uncertain about the other's dependability or good intentions.

However, what are not yet understood from these studies are the antecedents of trust or mistrust: Why is it that some couples develop and maintain trustful interpretations, feelings, and behaviors? How is trust linked to the partners' histories of past attachments? How much are those histories affected by the wider social context?

Attachment theory (e.g., Bowlby, 1969; Shaver, Hazan, & Bradshaw, 1988) claims that the roots of security and insecurity go back to early childhood. But, one might ask, what leads some families and children to construct a secure environment, and what leads others to harbor insecurity? How much is this a function of individuals, couples, families, and other networks, and how much does it depend on larger social forces? How can one probe the links between those different levels? I consider such questions near the end of this chapter, but first I examine the macroscopic forces that emanate from the social structure in which pair relationships are conducted.

## MACROPERSPECTIVES

The irony of the advances in microanalysis is that, although there is much to be learned, the helpfulness of this knowledge for improving people's actual relationships may be outweighed by broad social forces beyond the psychological purview. I discuss three interlinked sets of such broad forces in the macrosocial environment: (a) the effects of industrialization, technology, and commerce; (b) the pressures toward female equality and the feminization of intimacy; and (c) the barriers against exit from and entrance into close relationships.[2]

### Industrialization and Economic Change

Historians and sociologists have noted that people in Western societies have become increasingly concerned with autonomy and personal control (e.g., Bellah, Madsen, Sullivan, Swidler, & Tipton, 1984; Dizard & Gadlin, 1990; Popenoe, 1988). In America, as early as in the 17th century, people began detaching themselves from the web of kin relationships in traditional family systems; and worldwide, family structures have tended to move "from kin embeddedness to the conjugal form" (e.g., Popenoe, 1988, p. 33). There has been a corresponding growth in the emphasis on romantic love as the basis for marriage and a shift away from parental control of mate selection.

Dizard and Gadlin (1990) argued that the rise of personal autonomy is traceable to both economic and family changes. On the one hand, the spread of commerce and industry has depended on arousing people's desires for autonomy. Earlier injunctions to be thrifty to amass capital are replaced by the stimulation of consumer need, which requires personal independence and one's ability to make choices in the marketplace. On the other hand, this individualistic market orientation helps erode people's dependence on kin and family members. Both parents and children become more conflicted about their interdependencies. For example, wishing to minimize emotional dependency, elders try not to be burdens on their adult children; parents put a greater emphasis on their own work and leisure needs and attend less to their children's support

---

[2]One could also focus on many other forces, such as the world's increasing population growth, its urbanization, or the changes in the natural environment, but these three topics suffice here.

needs; and spouses develop careers independently of one another. Although members of Western societies show a wide range of adaptations to these changes, with some people trying to recreate rigid traditional forms, and others trying to avoid any sort of permanent commitment, almost everyone has become more preoccupied with the conduct of their relationships.

There are now even economic theories of marriage and other relationships (e.g., Becker, 1973; McCrate, 1987; Pollak, 1985) and debates as to which economic theory best applies, but all of these debates consider close relationships in terms of market forces. In one of the most recent of such expositions, McCrate (1987) rejected the metaphor of marriage as a "trade" or "merger" between equals. She argued that the proper metaphor is one of "employment," because traditionally, and still today, men have dominated women both inside and outside the home. She interpreted the rise in the proportion of unmarried American women, a 150% rise from 1957 to 1984 in unmarried U.S. women aged 20–54, as a sign of women's increasing independence and resourcefulness outside the marital institution. Incidentally, McCrate's interpretation was supported by evidence of one of my own studies, which found that female divorce applicants' decisions to finalize their divorces were directly correlated to the women's incomes relative to their husbands' (Levinger, 1979).

That, of course, is a highly individualistic perspective. Comparing a wide range of cultures, Triandis, Bontempo, Villareal, Asai, and Lucca (1988) noted that individualism is highly correlated with a society's gross national product (GNP) as well as with stress. Other authors have reported that members of collectivist societies, which place a low value on a market economy, are far more altruistic and supportive toward one another (e.g., Fiske, 1991), but care far less about love or pair intimacy.

As a number of personality psychologists (e.g., Bakan, 1966; McAdams, 1984) have argued, all humans crave some form of community or communion. If they can get it in a simple tribal existence, the group suffices as the source of communion. However, if the tribe breaks up and people move to the anonymity of urban areas, then people seek new sources of emotional support. Nevertheless, as Durkheim (1897/1951), Slater (1963), and others have contended, the resulting pressures toward pair intimacy and dyadic withdrawal may lead to further family and communal fragmentation, as well as individual feelings of isolation.

## Female Equality and the Feminization of Intimacy

Another macrotrend is the changing status of women. Throughout history, women have had much influence, but more inside the home than outside it (see Guttentag & Secord, 1983). In the legal, political, and economic realms, women have had little power or independence.

However, associated with the economic changes, husband–wife—and, more generally, male–female—relations have become less and less "owner-property" relations (Scanzoni, 1979). The family that emerged during the 19th century became increasingly egalitarian and increasingly marked by love and respect between husband and wife (Degler, 1980)—and even between parents and children. As men increasingly needed intimate pair relationships to add meaning to their lives, and found they could best get such support from a female partner, they gradually ceded power, until today the very definition of *intimacy* implies equality. For instance, in a cross-generational study over a 50-year time period that compared 20-year-old and 70-year-old respondents of either gender, Rands and Levinger (1979) found major increases in the desire for expression and sharing in close relationships. Men have begun to realize that the proper pursuit of intimacy—whether with women, with their children, or even with other men—requires changes in them too. Thus, not only have women become economically and politically more assertive and independent, but men (at least *some* men) have begun to value sensitivity, gentleness, and personal disclosure—qualities formerly out of bounds for them.[3]

Nonetheless, complete gender equality is far short of realization. Not only are there physical differences that enable men to dominate women by size alone, and there continues to be a shocking amount of male–female violence, but persisting economic and political differences maintain gender differences in "structural power" (Guttentag & Secord, 1983). Furthermore, strong normative gender differences remain in even the most egalitarian countries (e.g., although Sweden recently relabeled paid "maternity leave" to be "parental leave" and made it available to fathers as much as mothers, in 1987 Swedish fathers used only 5% of all available leave time, allowing mothers to take the other 95% of the time; see Popenoe, 1988, pp. 143–152).

Also, there are paradoxical psychological effects. Although power differences are much less today than yesterday, women often see them as even more salient than previously. Brehm (1985) pointed out that "when there are huge power differences, most people accept them because [they] have no choice. . . . But as the balance of power shifts, [people's] vision of what they deserve expands, [and despite their greater freedom today, many women] are more aware of being oppressed" (p. 397). In other words, when gender equality appears attainable, it is likely to lead to a greater monitoring of the existing arrangement. But such a careful surveillance of what goes on between two partners is more a sign of a low-trust exchange relationship (Clark & Mills, 1979, chapter 2, this volume; Holmes, 1981) than of a high-trust communal relationship. Indeed, it has been shown empirically that the practice of monitoring another

---

[3]The growth in men's sensitivity and personal disclosure is attested to only by anecdotal evidence. A search of the literature on men's relationships or communication patterns failed to uncover any strong research evidence (J. D. Snoek, personal communication, January 11, 1993).

in itself promotes lack of trust (Strickland, 1958). It is not surprising, then, that wives in traditional marriages, who accept the marital status quo ante, tend to express more trust and marital satisfaction than do wives in more modern partnerships (Peplau & Hill, 1990).

This brings me to my final example of a macrotrend—the reduction of social barriers against getting out of and into a close relationship—where the continued monitoring of one's relationship provides a link between macro- and microconditions.

## Barrier Reduction and its Correlates

It is easier to show how macrochanges have significant microeffects than to show how microlevel actions have repercussions at the macrolevel. However, Berscheid and Campbell's (1981) analysis of the causal links between barrier reduction and close relationship breakup was a valuable approach to the mutual influence between the macro and micro. I here summarize their argument and extend it to unmarried cohabitation.

*Barrier Reduction and Relationship Breakup.*   Berscheid and Campbell (1981) proposed that the historical reduction in legal, economic, religious, and social barriers against the ending of marriages has had both direct and indirect effects on the durability of close relationships. They considered couples' decisions to end their relationships not only as a dependent variable, but also as an independent causal factor in two kinds of feedback loops—a direct loop and an indirect loop.

First, the "reduction of external barriers" leads to direct psychological effects on people's decisions to terminate their close relationships, which in turn lead to further reduction in social barriers. In other words, the more our friends get separated or divorced and the easier it seems, the less will be our own inhibitions against contemplating breakup and the more fragile we will perceive the remaining constraints. In this manner, individual actions and resulting perceptions have cumulative societal effects; the break in one connection puts pressure on other connections, not only in marriages, but in the wider social networks.

Second, there are indirect psychological effects and feedbacks. One indirect effect of barrier reduction is the increasing importance of the "sweetness" of a relationship's contents. The more we perceive exit as a possibility, the more actively we will compare the attractiveness of what we now have with whatever we might have elsewhere. To paraphrase Berscheid and Campbell's (1981) words, when the burden of justifying the sweetness of a relationship is placed on its internal contents, the contents change so that the probability of their becoming sour is increased. This leads partners to carefully monitor their present satisfaction, because having a perpetual choice means one must choose not once but continually, thus expending time and energy in reevaluating the wisdom of one's original choice. Partners in this position will feel unsure about the permanence of their pairing and will desire continued evidence of its goodness.

With people's increased ambivalence about the internal contents of their relationships, they also experience an expanded variety of alternatives. Feeling less dependent on their marriage than heretofore, spouses feel better able to take active strategies to cope with its difficulty. Formerly, an all-accepting loyalty to one's spouse was considered a primary virtue. Today, more active responses of either confrontation or separation are recommended as alternatives.

Furthermore, barriers against exit from and entry into intimate relationships have always been stronger for women than for men, who could desert their families and move elsewhere far more easily than women. Thus, barrier reduction is both an effect of, and an impetus toward, trends toward female equality. As women establish independent roles outside the home, barriers come down and women can leave. But their reduction also affects the entry process and the alternatives to marriage that women *and* men can viably consider (Glenn & Weaver, 1988; Veroff et al., 1981). Alternatives include staying single, entering a same-gender romantic relationship, and unmarried cohabitation. With the expansion of such options, marriage now often seems like a more momentous step than heretofore.

***Unmarried Cohabitation.*** If the barriers against exit from intimate relationships have declined, so also have the formal restraints against entrance. A generation ago in the United States, it was unacceptable for an unmarried couple to live together, and it was hardly an askable category in survey research. (As late as 1967, a Columbia College male and a Barnard College female were denied graduation when they disclosed their unmarried cohabitation.) Today, even public school teachers can cohabit openly without rejection by their community. In America, in particular, this has been an example of extraordinarily rapid social change.

Such rapid change must have its repercussions, however, and at least two questions arise: How does this lack of a formal entry process affect the cohabiting relationship? If marriage does occur, how does premarital cohabitation affect the marriage? So far, there are few solid data and many cultural differences, and change continues at a rapid rate. Nonetheless, I hazard a few answers.

Regarding the immediate quality of the relationship, some social scientists in some societies (such as Sweden or Holland) have claimed that there is no substantial difference between unmarried and married cohabitation (e.g., Trost, 1979), but others have pointed out that, even in Sweden, unmarried unions dissolve more frequently than married ones (Popenoe, 1988). In the United

States, it seems that many young couples drift into cohabiting relationships without clear decision making, often attending more to current convenience than to long-term commitment (e.g., Ridley, Peterman, & Avery, 1978). Comparing a sample of unmarried heterosexual cohabitants with samples of married couples and gay and lesbian couples, Kurdek and Schmitt (1986) recently found their cohabitants had the lowest love and the highest alternative attraction scores, along with the lowest barriers. Another recent study found that cohabitating couples had greater difficulty dealing with their conflicts constructively: Comparing marriage applicants who had previously lived together with applicants who had not, Leonard, Senchak, Nottingham, and McLaughlin (1989) found that the cohabitants reported themselves as "less intimate" and "more likely to withdraw and/or use verbal aggression in response to conflict" than did the noncohabitants.

Regarding postmarital success, most studies have shown either no advantage or significantly less stability (e.g., Jacques & Chason, 1979) and more unresolved conflict among married pairs who previously cohabited (e.g., Stambul, 1976). Most recently, Sweet and Bumpass (1992) concluded from their analysis of Current Population Surveys that, in the United States, the marital disruption rate has been at least 49% higher for premarital cohabitants than for couples who never cohabited.

These findings are explainable in various ways, especially the less conventional norms of nonmarital cohabitants. My own guess, however, is that the causes parallel those discussed by Berscheid and Campbell (1981), in that both presently and previously unmarried cohabitants are more likely to continually monitor their present happiness as well as alternative possibilities, thereby undercutting their current accommodation process.

Although there surely is no simple correspondence between barrier strength and relationship stability, and many pairs survive well despite weak barriers, the reduction of social constraints on either exit or entrance poses serious difficulties for the current and future conduct of securely attached personal relationships.

## HOW DO MACRO- AND MICROVARIABLES INFLUENCE ONE ANOTHER?

"A sudden decline in the world's frog population has scientists not only baffled but alarmed. Why are historically hardy frog species going extinct? And what does their mysterious disappearance signal about the entire ecosystem?" (Yoffe, 1992, p. 36). The puzzling disappearance of frogs from widely separate ecological habitats across the globe was recently uncovered at an international meeting of herpetologists working independently in different countries. Because local conditions at particular sites cannot account for this worldwide reduction in differing species, its causes are now being sought in the macroenvironment (i.e., in increases in ultraviolet radiation or the acidity of water habitats, the effects of pesticides, or the changes in average temperatures). To solve this puzzle, one must look beyond the breeding patterns of particular frog communities—a microissue—to far more general external influences.

Are there analogous mysteries in the realm of personal relationships between humans? I think the answer is partly "yes" and partly "no." Yes, because dramatic changes in some forms of interpersonal behavior (e.g., in interpersonal violence or the breakup of marriages) sometimes can be traced to changes in underlying social conditions (e.g., a growing imagery of violence in general, or a reduced public emphasis on keeping marriages together). No, because interpersonal epidemics may appear more readily explainable, and what is a serious problem for some people is not so for many others. Because people are self-aware and use complex language, they often have their own personal interpretations of changes; thus, it may be harder to obtain wide agreement about what may be mysterious.

Let me return to the interpersonal relations mystery alluded to earlier in this chapter: Why did college students' mean scores on Schutz's (1958) test of "Fundamental Interpersonal Relations Orientations" change so significantly within less than 10 years of the test's publication? This puzzle attracted little attention when it was discovered, and even its discoverers failed to pursue its implications empirically. Looking back years later, however, one can plausibly explain this change in test scores as reflecting dramatic changes in Americans' needs for intimacy and personal control that occurred in the 1960s. In turn, the origin of those changes must have wider causes.

However, a major difficulty is finding ways to make systematic connections among differing levels of analysis. If one wishes to understand phenomena that occur in personal relationships, how can one develop adequate models that represent the interplay among different levels of determinants? To do so, one must recognize more than two levels of analysis. In addition to the micro- and macrolevels, it seems useful also to recognize the individual and the social network levels, as is done next.

## A Kaleidoscopic Digression

A kaleidoscope is a viewing tube that, when rotated, produces a large variety of designs by means of mirrors that reflect the constantly changing patterns made by whatever is visible at the far end of the tube. Most kaleidoscopes contain a finite number of bits of colored glass or other figures at the closed end of the tube, but some newer versions (also called teleidoscopes) are open to the outside world; their images derive from rotating one or more differently colored lenses through which one can look at the outside world.

The teleidoscope offers an analogy to the present problem: Depending on which lens one places between oneself and the phenomena, one will receive different images about what influences a personal relationship. Imagine four contrasting lens, each of which focuses primarily at one of the following levels: (a) the individual level, (b) the pair or interpersonal level, (c) the social network level, and (d) the societal or sociocultural level. Any two or more of these lenses can be combined to reveal the interaction of variegated patterns.

First is a lens that focuses at the individual level, which can also be called the ontogenetic level. Viewed through this rotating lens, each individual's personal interpretations, feelings, and behaviors in a relationship—central to Reis and Shaver's (1988) already mentioned model—spin around his or her core, influencing those of the other pair member. At this level, one would concentrate primarily on the two individuals' unique developmental histories and current personality characteristics that affect their interpretive filters, feelings and goals, or habituated behaviors.

A second lens would feature the pair unit. Here the interpretations, feelings, and behaviors no longer refer to individual properties, but describe the pair relationship's atmosphere (e.g., a couple's degree of trust, its harmony, or its problem-solving skill). Returning to Fig. 3 from Reis and Shaver (1988), this lens refers to the results from a cumulation of a pair's interactions as they can be summarized after a long period of time. Thus, one might characterize a given couple as high in mutual trust, or low in harmony, or inexperienced in solving joint problems. This is the level of the microsystem, which can be indexed by measures of couple communication, pair conflict, or mutual adjustment.

A third lens would spotlight both pair members' social networks, which include family, friends, and occupational context. Here the individual becomes less salient, whereas interpretations, feelings, and behaviors signify group properties such as a group's beliefs, values, or ideology; its emotional supportiveness; or its economic sustenance. This third level, sometimes referred to as the exosystem, contains the immediate life conditions that impinge on one's coping with everyday eventualities. Viewed conceptually, it mediates between understanding a particular personal relationship and viewing the wider society-wide conditions that affect it.

A fourth and final lens would concentrate on the broad sociocultural and physical environment in which individuals live (i.e., the macrosystem). In this chapter, I chose to focus on three aspects of macrosocial change: industrialization and economic change, female equality and the feminization of intimacy, and barrier reduction. The macrosystem is the foundation of all social networks and interpersonal transactions.

One's images of personal relationships depend on how one interrelates these four lenses. As one rotates the teleidoscope, which lens shall one use for creating one's images, and how does one combine them with one another? For example, if one wants to predict the fate of a particular set of long-term relationships (e.g., marriages), how can one interrelate broad social-structural forces with those that operate primarily at the level of the individual or the pair, or even the partners' immediate social context?

## Exploring a Nested Ecological Approach

There seem to be few satisfying answers to these difficult questions. However, I am impressed by Dutton's (1988) approach to analyzing the dynamics of "the domestic assault of women." To diagnose the causes of men's violence against their close female partners, Dutton employed a "nested ecological theory" proposed by Bronfenbrenner (1977) and Belsky (1980). He argued that an individual's behavior is influenced by the interaction of factors at four different levels: the macrosystem, the exosystem, the microsystem, and the ontogenetic or individual level.

Regarding the macrosystem, a man's physical abuse of a woman may be sanctioned by broad culturally mediated beliefs that women should be kept subordinate and in fear of men, and that violence is a proper means to keep them in line. Such beliefs or values exist in the background of a relationship.

The exosystem operates from nearer at hand. It refers to the structures or groups (e.g., friendship or work groups) that influence a person's immediate social settings. Thus "[w]ork stress or the presence or absence of social support might increase or decrease the likelihood of wife assault" (Dutton, 1988, p. 24).

In the case of wife assault, the microsystem level would usually refer to the family unit. Here the lens would focus on the "interaction pattern of the couple, the conflict issues that were salient to them, and the antecedents and consequences of assault (how the man felt, how the woman acted after it was over)" (Dutton, 1988, p. 24).

Finally, the ontogenetic level refers to individual development; it examines what individuals bring to the social interaction from their personalities. At this level, an analyst of domestic assault could attend to men's reactions to a given social situation on the basis of their different learning histories (e.g., differing past exposures to violent role models, differing experiences of dealing with conflict, and differing emotional reactions to male–female disagreement). To investigate men's individual tendencies toward engaging in violence toward their partners, Dutton (1988) suggested an assessment of their communication skills and ability to express affect verbally, their emotional responses to depictions of male–female conflict, and their past exposures to violence in their families of origin.

Nonetheless, there is an irony here. Despite their contrasting emphases, these four different levels are highly interconnected. For example, an individual male's ontogeny is strongly influenced by his surrounding cultural demands and experiences; if his society provides many instances of and excuses for the perpetration of brutality, his early experiences are likely to accustom him to such behavior. Nor can microsystem or exosystem forces be sharply separated from their macrosystem foundations; individual development is strongly affected by changes in the macrosystem.

## Implications for Personal Relationship Research

How shall one apply such interactive ecological thinking to current research problems in personal relationships? Although there are many possible applications, I consider only two topics in this concluding section: (a) attachment phenomena and (b) interdependence phenomena, each the foci of the currently most fertile theories.

*Attachment Phenomena.*    Attachment theory argues that *how* an individual relates to adult intimate partners is strongly influenced by the relationships he or she experienced with his or her parents. In studies performed during the 1980s, Hazan and Shaver (1987) and others found that nearly 60% of their research participants reported themselves as having "secure" interaction styles. Since then, other researchers have found that secure individuals tend to have longer lasting, more stable intimate relationships than individuals with insecure styles, and that the least stable relationships occur when two insecure persons are joined with each other (Kirkpatrick & Davis, in press). Furthermore, there is ample reason to believe that insecure life conditions tend to promote insecurity, both in parental relationships and, consequently, in children.

Now consider that several of the macrosocial conditions examined earlier tend to place stresses on the stable conduct of intimate relationships in contemporary society. A question that relationship researchers should address, in my opinion, is how will such trends affect the close relationships of the future? To what extent can the pessimistic scenarios painted by some current analysts (e.g., Dizard & Gadlin, 1990; Popenoe, 1988) be offset by countervailing forces? What might be the strengths of contemporary partnerships? How can such trends be tracked empirically?

*Interdependence Phenomena.*    Interdependence has generally been examined at the microlevel, the level of pair interactions and events (e.g., Kelley, 1979; Kelley et al., 1983). One has generally been concerned with how the anticipated outcomes of one or both pair members affect their individual and joint behavior. Presumably, the greater the mutual dependence, the greater the influence that partners can exert on each other. When dependence on a relationship is unequal, the less involved member is assumed to have a greater ability to influence it than the more involved one.

Although interdependence theories should apply to relationships in any culture and at any point in history, interdependence phenomena will vary widely. For instance, I noted earlier that today's intimate partners tend to value equality highly, often considering it a necessary property of closeness. Yet this belief is a fairly recent one. Only a century or two ago, male–female relations in marriages and families could better be described as either "owner-property" or as "head-complement" relations (Scanzoni, 1979).

How, then, will current and future macrosocial trends affect the nature of the desired and actual forms of couple interdependence? If greater gender equality should indeed become the rule, how will this affect the future cohesion of close couples? On the one hand, it could facilitate mutual communication and disclosure, because equals usually can speak more frankly to each other than unequals. On the other hand, it could conceivably interfere with such communication, to the extent that one or both partners might prize their independence so much as to drift apart from each other.

## CONCLUSION

This chapter has attempted more to raise questions than to answer them. It has contrasted the social psychologist's usual emphasis on limited microsystem phenomena with a recognition of the powerful influence that macrosystem forces exert on the conduct of relationships. How such forces actually affect particular sets of relationships remains to be determined. But personal relationship researchers can profitably give them greater attention.

## REFERENCES

Altman, I., & Taylor, D. M. (1973). *Social penetration: The development of interpersonal relationships.* New York: Holt, Rinehart & Winston.

Argyle, M. (1972). *The psychology of interpersonal behaviour* (2nd ed.). Hammondsworth: Penguin.

Bakan, D. (1966). *The duality of human existence: Isolation and communion in Western man.* Boston: Beacon.

Bales, R. F., & Borgatta, E. F. (1955). Size of group as a factor in the interaction profile. In A. P. Hare, E. F. Borgatta, & R. F. Bales (Eds.), *Small groups* (pp. 396–413). New York: Knopf.

Becker, G. S. (1973). A theory of marriage: Part I. *Journal of Political Economy, 81,* 813–846.

Bellah, R., Madsen, R., Sullivan, W. M., Swidler, A., & Tipton, S. M. (1984). *Habits of the heart.* Berkeley, CA: University of California Press.

Belsky, J. (1980). Child maltreatment: An ecological integration. *American Psychologist, 35,* 320–335.

Bennis, W. G., Schein, E. H., Steele, F. I., & Berlew, D. C. (1968). *Interpersonal dynamics* (rev. ed.). Homewood, IL: Dorsey.

Berscheid, E., & Campbell, B. (1981). The changing longevity of heterosexual close relationships. In M. J. Lerner & S. C. Lerner (Eds.), *The justice motive in social behavior* (pp. 209–234). New York: Plenum.

Berscheid, E., Snyder, M., & Omoto, A. M. (1989). The Relationship Closeness Inventory: Assessing the closeness of interpersonal relationships. *Journal of Personality and Social Psychology, 57,* 792–807.

Berscheid, E., & Walster, E. (1969). *Interpersonal attraction*. Reading, MA: Addison-Wesley.

Blood, R. O., Jr., & Wolfe, D. M. (1960). *Husbands and wives: The dynamics of married living*. New York: The Free Press.

Bogardus, E. S. (1925). Measuring social distance. *Journal of Applied Sociology, 9*, 299–308.

Borden, V. M. H., & Levinger, G. (1991). Interpersonal transformations in intimate relationships. In W. H. Jones & D. Perlman (Eds.), *Advances in personal relationships* (Vol. 2, pp. 35–56). London: J. Kingsley.

Bowlby, J. (1969). *Attachment and loss: Vol. 1. Attachment*. New York: Basic Books.

Brehm, S. S. (1985). *Intimate relationships*. New York: Random House.

Bronfenbrenner, U. (1977). Toward an experimental ecology of human development. *American Psychologist, 32*, 513–531.

Burgess, E. W., & Locke, H. J. (1945). *The family: From institution to companionship*. New York: American Book.

Burgess, E. W., & Wallin, P. (1953). *Engagement and marriage*. Philadelphia: Lippincott.

Byrne, D. (1969). Attitudes and attraction. In L. Berkowitz (Ed.), *Advances in experimental social psychology* (Vol. 4, pp. 35–89). New York: Academic Press.

Cartwright, D. (Ed.). (1959). *Studies in social power*. Ann Arbor, MI: Institute for Social Research.

Cartwright, D. (1968). The nature of group cohesiveness. In D. Cartwright & A. Zander (Eds.), *Group dynamics* (3rd ed., pp. 91–109). New York: Harper & Row.

Clark, M. S., & Mills, J. (1979). Interpersonal attraction in exchange and communal relationships. *Journal of Personality and Social Psychology, 37*, 12–24.

Clark, M. S., & Reis, H. T. (1988). Interpersonal processes in close relationships. *Annual Review of Psychology, 39*, 609–672.

Degler, C. N. (1980). *At odds: Women and the family in America from the revolution to the present*. Oxford: Oxford University Press.

Dizard, J., & Gadlin, H. (1990). *The minimal family*. Amherst: University of Massachusetts Press.

Duck, S. W. (1973). *Personal relationships and personal constructs: A study of friendship formation*. London: Wiley.

Duck, S. (Ed.). (1988). *Handbook of personal relationships: Theory, research, and interventions*. Chichester, England: Wiley.

Durkheim, E. (1951). *Suicide: A study in sociology*. New York: The Free Press. (Original work published 1897)

Dutton, D. G. (1988). *The domestic assault of women: Psychological and criminal justice perspectives*. Boston: Allyn & Bacon.

Festinger, L. (1954). A theory of social comparison processes. *Human Relations, 7*, 117–140.

Festinger, L. (1957). *A theory of cognitive dissonance*. Stanford, CA: Stanford University Press.

Fiske, A. (1991). The cultural relativity of selfish individualism: Anthropological evidence that humans are inherently sociable. In M. S. Clark (Ed.), *Review of personality and social psychology* (Vol. 12, pp. 176–214). Newbury Park, CA: Sage.

French, J. R. P., Jr., & Raven, B. H. (1959). The bases of social power. In D. Cartwright (Ed.), *Studies in social power* (pp. 150–167). Ann Arbor, MI: Institute for Social Research.

Fromm, E. (1956). *The art of loving*. New York: Harper & Row.

Glenn, N. D., & Weaver, C. N. (1988). The changing relationship of marital status to reported happiness. *Journal of Marriage and the Family, 50*, 317–324.

Goode, W. J. (1956). *After divorce*. New York: The Free Press.

Gottman, J. M. (1979). *Marital interaction: Experimental investigations*. New York: Academic Press.

Gottman, J. M., Notarius, C., Markman, H., Bank, S., Yoppi, B., & Rubin, M. E. (1976). Behavior exchange theory and marital decision making. *Journal of Personality and Social Psychology, 34*, 14–23.

Guttentag, M., & Secord, P. F. (1983). *Too many women? The sex ratio question*. Beverly Hills, CA: Sage.

Hazan, C., & Shaver, P. (1987). Romantic love conceptualized as an attachment process. *Journal of Personality and Social Psychology, 52*, 511–524.

Heider, F. (1946). Attitudes and cognitive organization. *Journal of Psychology, 21*, 107–112.

Hendrick, S. S., & Hendrick, C. (1992). *Liking, loving, and relating* (2nd ed.). Belmont, CA: Brooks/Cole.

Herbst, P. G. (1952). The measurement of family relationships. *Human Relations, 5*, 3–35.

Hill, C. T., Rubin, Z., & Peplau, L. A. (1976). Breakups before marriage: The end of 103 affairs. *Journal of Social Issues, 32*(1), 147–168.

Hill, R. L. (1958). Sociology of marriage and family behavior, 1945–56: A trend report and annotated bibliography. *Current Sociology, 7*(1), 1–8.

Hinde, R. A. (1976). On describing relationships. *Journal of Child Psychology and Psychiatry, 17*, 1–19.

Hinde, R. A. (1979). *Towards understanding relationships*. London: Academic Press.

Hinde, R. A. (1987). *Individuals, relationships, and culture: Links between ethology and the social sciences*. Cambridge: Cambridge University Press.

Hoffman, L. (1981). *Foundations of family therapy*. New York: Basic Books.

Holmes, J. G. (1988). Grant proposal to Canada Research Council.

Holmes, J. G. (1991). Trust and the appraisal process in close relationships. In W. H. Jones & D. Perlman (Eds.), *Advances in personal relationships* (Vol. 2, pp. 57–104). London: J. Kingsley.

Holmes, J. G., & Rempel, J. K. (1989). Trust in close relationships. *Review of Personality and Social Psychology, 10*, 187–220.

Huston, T. L., & Levinger, G. (1978). Interpersonal attraction and relationships. *Annual Review of Psychology, 29*, 115–156.

Jacques, J. M., & Chason, K. J. (1979). Cohabitation: Its impact on marital success. *Family Coordinator, 29*, 35–39.

Jennings, H. H. (1943). *Leadership and isolation*. New York: Longmans, Green.

Kaslow, F. W. (1991). The art and science of family psychology: Retrospective and perspective. *American Psychologist, 46*, 621–626.

Kelley, H. H. (1979). *Personal relationships: Their structures and processes*. Hillsdale, NJ: Lawrence Erlbaum Associates.

Kelley, H. H. (1986). Personal relationships: Their nature and significance. In R. Gilmour & S. Duck (Eds.), *The emerging field of personal relationships* (pp. 3–19). Hillsdale, NJ: Lawrence Erlbaum Associates.

Kelley, H. H., Berscheid, E., Christensen, A., Harvey, J. H., Huston, T. L., Levinger, G., McClintock, E., Peplau, L. A., & Peterson, D. R. (1983). *Close relationships*. New York: W. H. Freeman.

Kenny, D. A. (1988). The analysis of data from two-person relationships. In S. Duck (Ed.), *Handbook of personal relationships* (pp. 57–77). New York: Wiley.

Kerckhoff, A. C., & Davis, K. E. (1962). Value consensus and need complementarity in mate selection. *American Sociological Review, 27*, 295–303.

Kirkpatrick, L. A., & Davis, K. E. (in press). Attachment style, gender, and relationship stability: A longitudinal analysis. *Journal of Personality and Social Psychology*.

Krech, D., & Crutchfield, R. A. (1948). *Theory and problems of social psychology*. New York: McGraw-Hill.

Kurdek, L. A., & Schmitt, J. P. (1986). Relationship quality of partners in heterosexual married, heterosexual cohabiting, and gay and lesbian relationships. *Journal of Personality and Social Psychology, 51*, 711–720.

Leonard, K. E., Senchak, M., Nottingham, C. A., & McLaughlin, I. G. (1989). *Relationship functioning and cohabitation among couples about to be married*. Unpublished manuscript, Research Institute on Alcoholism, Buffalo, NY.

Levenson, R. W., & Gottman, J. M. (1983). Marital interaction: Physiological linkage and affective exchange. *Journal of Personality and Social Psychology, 45*, 587–597.

Levenson, R. W., & Gottman, J. M. (1985). Physiological and affective predictors of change in relationship satisfaction. *Journal of Personality and Social Psychology, 49*, 85–94.

Levinger, G. (1959). The development of perceptions and behavior in newly formed social power relationships. In D. Cartwright (Ed.), *Studies in social power* (pp. 83–98). Ann Arbor, MI: Institute for Social Research.

Levinger, G. (1964a). Task and social behavior in marriage. *Sociometry, 27,* 433–448.

Levinger, G. (1964b). Note on need complementarity in marriage. *Psychological Bulletin, 61,* 153–157.

Levinger, G. (1965). Marital cohesiveness and dissolution: An integrative review. *Journal of Marriage and the Family, 27,* 19–28.

Levinger, G. (1974). A three-level approach to attraction: Toward an understanding of pair relatedness. In T. L. Huston (Ed.), *Foundations of interpersonal attraction* (pp. 99–120). New York: Academic Press.

Levinger, G. (1979). Marital cohesiveness at the brink: The fate of applications for divorce. In G. Levinger & O. C. Moles (Eds.), *Divorce and separation: Context, causes, and consequences* (pp. 137–150). New York: Basic Books.

Levinger, G. (1980). Toward the analysis of close relationships. *Journal of Experimental Social Psychology, 16,* 510–544.

Levinger, G., & Breedlove, J. (1966). Interpersonal attraction and agreement. *Journal of Personality and Social Psychology, 3,* 367–372.

Levinger, G., & Raush, H. L. (1977). *Close relationships: Perspectives on the meaning of intimacy.* Amherst: University of Massachusetts Press.

Levinger, G., Senn, D. J., & Jorgensen, B. W. (1970). Progress toward permanence in courtship: A test of the Kerckhoff-Davis hypotheses. *Sociometry, 33,* 427–443.

Levinger, G., & Snoek, J. D. (1972). *Attraction in relationship: A new look at interpersonal attraction.* Morristown, NJ: General Learning Press.

Lewin, K. (1948). The background of conflict in marriage. In G. Lewin (Ed.), *Resolving social conflicts* (pp. 84–102). New York: Harper. (Original work published 1940)

Lewin, K. (1951). Psychological ecology. In K. Lewin (Ed.), *Field theory in social science* (pp. 170–187). New York: Harper. (Original work published 1943)

Lewis, R. A. (1973). A longitudinal test of a developmental framework for premarital dyadic formation. *Journal of Marriage and the Family, 32,* 16–25.

Lott, A. J., & Lott, B. E. (1965). Group cohesiveness as interpersonal attraction: A review of relationships with antecedent and consequent variables. *Psychological Bulletin, 64,* 259–305.

Marlowe, D., & Gergen, K. J. (1968). Personality and social interaction. In G. Lindzey & E. Aronson (Eds.), *Handbook of social psychology* (Vol. 3, pp. 590–665). New York: Addison-Wesley.

McAdams, D. P. (1984). Human motives and personal relationships. In V. Derlega (Ed.), *Communication, intimacy, and relationships* (pp. 41–70). New York: Academic Press.

McCrate, E. (1987). Trade, merger, and employment: Economic theory on marriage. *Review of Radical Political Economics, 19,* 73–89.

Minuchin, S. (1974). *Families and family therapy.* Cambridge, MA: Harvard University Press.

Moreno, J. L. (1934). *Who shall survive?* Washington, DC: Nervous and Mental Diseases Publishing Co.

Murstein, B. M. (1970). Stimulus-value-role: A theory of marital choice. *Journal of Marriage and the Family, 32,* 465–481.

Newcomb, T. M. (1953). An approach to the study of communicative acts. *Psychological Review, 60,* 393–404.

Newcomb, T. M. (1961). *The acquaintance process.* New York: Holt, Rinehart & Winston.

Parsons, T., & Bales, R. F. (1955). *Family, socialization and interaction process.* New York: The Free Press.

Peplau, L. A., & Hill, C. T. (1990, July). *Sex-role attitudes and dating relationships: A 15-year follow-up of the Boston Couples.* Paper presented at the conference of the International Society for the Study of Personal Relationships, Oxford University, England.

Pollak, R. A. (1985). A transaction cost approach to families and households. *Journal of Economic Literature, 23,* 581–608.

Popenoe, D. (1988). *Disturbing the nest: Family change and decline in modern societies*. New York: Aldine de Gruyter.

Rands, M., & Levinger, G. (1979). Implicit theories of relationship: An intergenerational study. *Journal of Personality and Social Psychology, 37*, 645–661.

Raush, H. L. (1977). Orientations to the close relationship. In G. Levinger & H. L. Raush (Eds.), *Close relationships: Perspectives on the meaning of intimacy* (pp. 163–188). Amherst: University of Massachusetts Press.

Raush, H. L., Barry, W. A., Hertel, R. K., & Swain, M. A. (1974). *Communication, conflict, and marriage*. San Francisco, CA: Jossey-Bass.

Reis, H. T., & Shaver, P. (1988). Intimacy as an interpersonal process. In S. Duck (Ed.), *Handbook of personal relationships* (pp. 367–389). New York: Wiley.

Ridley, C., Peterman, D. J., & Avery, A. W. (1978). Cohabitation: Does it make for a better marriage? *Family Coordinator, 27*, 129–136.

Rubin, Z. (1970). Measurement of romantic love. *Journal of Personality and Social Psychology, 16*, 265–273.

Scanzoni, J. (1979). A historical perspective on husband-wife bargaining power and marital dissolution. In G. Levinger & O. C. Moles (Eds.), *Divorce and separation: Context, causes, and consequences* (pp. 20–36). New York: Basic Books.

Schutz, W. C. (1958). *FIRO-B: A three-dimensional theory of interpersonal behavior*. New York: Holt, Rinehart & Winston.

Secord, P. F., & Backman, C. B. (1964). *Social psychology*. New York: McGraw-Hill.

Shaver, P., Hazan, C., & Bradshaw, D. (1988). Love as attachment. In R. S. Sternberg & M. L. Barnes (Eds.), *The psychology of love* (pp. 68–99). New Haven, CT: Yale University Press.

Simmel, G. (1950). Quantitative aspects of the group. In K. H. Wolff (Ed.), *The sociology of George Simmel* (pp. 87–180). New York: The Free Press. (Original work published 1908)

Slater, P. E. (1963). On social regression. *American Sociological Review, 28*, 339–358.

Stambul, H. B. (1976). *Stages of courtship: The development of premarital relationships*. Unpublished doctoral dissertation, University of California, Los Angeles.

Sternberg, R. S., & Barnes, M. L. (1988). *The psychology of love*. New Haven, CT: Yale University Press.

Strickland, L. H. (1958). Surveillance and trust. *Journal of Personality, 26*, 200–215.

Sweet, J. A., & Bumpass, L. L. (1992). Disruption of marital and cohabitation relationships: A social-demographic perspective. In T. L. Orbuch (Ed.), *Close relationship loss: Theoretical approaches* (pp. 67–89). New York: Springer-Verlag.

Thibaut, J. W., & Kelley, H. H. (1959). *The social psychology of groups*. New York: Wiley.

Triandis, H. C., Bontempo, R., Villareal, M. J., Asai, M., & Lucca, N. (1988). Individualism and collectivism: Cross-cultural perspectives on self-ingroup relationships. *Journal of Personality and Social Psychology, 54*, 323–338.

Trost, J. (1979). *Unmarried cohabitation*. Vasteras, Sweden: International Library.

Veroff, J., Douvan, E., & Kulka, R. A. (1981). *The inner American: A self-portrait from 1957 to 1976*. New York: Basic Books.

Winch, R. F. (1958). *Mate selection: A study of complementary needs*. New York: Harper.

Yoffe, E. (1992, December 13). Silence of the frogs. *New York Times Magazine*, pp. 36–76.

# Chapter 2

# Communal and Exchange Relationships: Controversies and Research

Judson Mills
*University of Maryland*

Margaret S. Clark
*Carnegie Mellon University*

In this chapter, we review a theoretical distinction between communal and exchange relationships and our work supporting the distinction, describing some of our more recent studies in some detail. In addition, we use the chapter as an opportunity to explicitly state and address some concerns that we have often heard over the years in response to our articles and talks.

In a paper published in 1979 (Clark & Mills, 1979), we first distinguished communal relationships, in which members benefit one another on the basis of concern for the other's welfare, from exchange relationships, in which members benefit one another in response to specific benefits received in the past or expected in the future. Exchange relationships follow the dictionary definition of *exchange* as giving or taking one thing in return for another. Benefits are given with the expectation of receiving benefits of comparable value in return. The receipt of a benefit incurs a debt or an obligation to return a comparable benefit.

In communal relationships, the rules governing when benefits are given and received are different. Benefits are given in response to the other's needs or simply to please the other. This may create a pattern of giving and receiving benefits that appears to an observer to follow exchange norms. However, communal norms are distinct from exchange norms. From the perspective of participants in a communal relationship, the benefits given and received are not part of an exchange. In a communal relationship, receipt of a benefit does not create a specific debt or obligation to return a comparable benefit. The general obligation each person has to aid the other when the other has the need is not altered by the receipt of a specific benefit. We believe that friendships, romantic relationships, and family relationships often exemplify communal relationships, whereas relationships between people doing business with one another, acquaintances, and strangers meeting for the first time often exemplify exchange relationships.

The stimulus for our distinction between communal and exchange relationships was a brief comment by the sociologist Irving Goffman (1961) in his book *Asylums*. Goffman made a distinction between what he called social exchange and economic exchange. In our theorizing, we have used the term *exchange relationship* in place of Goffman's term *economic exchange*, because many of the benefits people give and receive do not involve money or things for which a monetary value can be calculated. A benefit is something one member of a relationship chooses to give to the other that is of use or value to the person receiving it. We should mention that benefits are not the same as rewards when the term *rewards* is used to refer to the pleasures, satisfactions, and gratifications the person enjoys, which is the definition of *rewards* given by Thibaut and Kelley (1959). A parent may feel gratified when a sick child becomes well again but this does not constitute a benefit given by the child to the parent.

Because all relationships in which persons give and receive benefits are social, we felt that another term was needed to describe relationships in which each person has a concern for the welfare of the other. The term *communal relationship* seemed most appropriate to us.

We believe that the distinction between communal and exchange relationships is a fundamental one, and that relationships in which there is a concern for the welfare of the other are different in important ways from relationships in which people benefit one another in order to receive specific benefits in return. This is not to say that all communal relationships are the same. There are obviously important differences between relationships between friends, romantic partners, husbands and wives, parents and children, brothers and sisters, and so on.

We have focused on exchange and communal relationships because they are relationships in which people voluntarily provide benefits to one another. Thus, they form the basis for rewarding social interaction. Both kinds of relationships are "just" in the sense that when people conform to the norms of the particular type of relationship, each person's behavior can be considered fair to the other person. This distinguishes these kinds of relationships from other relationships that can be considered exploitative, in which one person takes advantage of another, or relationships in which individuals are competing with one another rather than cooperating.

Most of our research and theorizing has contrasted exchange relationships with mutual communal relationships (i.e., relationships in which each person has a concern for the welfare of the other). By their very nature, exchange relationships are mutual because each person has an obligation to repay benefits given by the other. However, communal relationships can be one-sided relationships, in which one person cares for the other without the other person caring for him or her in return. An example is a parent–child relationship when the child is very young. We believe that caring for infants and young children, which is essential for human survival, is the clearest example of a communal relationship. We speculate that the human tendency to form communal relationships is a biological necessity or, at least, grows out of a biological necessity.

Our past research and theorizing has focused on the qualitative distinction between communal and exchange relationships. We have often looked at factors that have one effect in an exchange relationship and the opposite effect in a communal relationship. For example, we have found that people respond to specific repayments for favors positively when they desire an exchange relationship with the other but negatively when they desire a communal relationship with the other (Clark & Mills, 1979). As we have worked on the distinction between communal and exchange relationships, our ideas have evolved and grown more complex (Clark, 1981; Clark & Mills, 1993; Clark, Ouellette, Powell, & Milberg, 1987; Clark & Waddell, 1985; Mills & Clark, 1982, 1986). The complexities we have faced remind us of a quotation attributed to Albert Einstein: "Everything should be made as simple as possible, but not simpler."

One complexity is that we have found it necessary to consider some quantitative aspects of these qualitatively different relationships. Although exchange relationships do not seem to vary in strength, communal relationships do seem to vary in strength. Some communal relationships are stronger than others. The relationship between cousins is typically not as strong as the relationship between siblings. The relationship between friends is not as strong as the relationship between best friends. Responding to the needs of a person with whom one has a strong communal relationship takes precedence over responding to the needs of someone with whom one has a weaker communal relationship. The stronger the communal relationship, the more costs each person is obligated to incur to benefit the other when the other has a need. Because costs are usually related to the size of the benefits given, people normally meet larger needs in stronger communal relationships.

Another complexity is that it is possible to have both a communal relationship and an exchange relationship with the same other person. For example, one can sell something to a friend or one can marry an employee. In such cases, a separation is typically made between what is appropriate for the business (exchange) relationship and what is appropriate for the family or friendship (communal) relationship. We believe most people have very weak communal relationships with strangers. If a complete stranger has a need that is great, relative to the cost of the benefit that could satisfy that need, most people would feel obligated and willing to benefit the other.

Another quantitative aspect of our qualitative distinction has to do with the certainty about the relationship. This is something that can apply to both exchange and communal relationships. In some communal relationships (e.g., relations between family members), the people involved may be very certain about the nature of their relationships. On the other hand, persons in a new communal relationship, new friends or romantic partners, may be less certain about whether a communal relationship exists. It seems to us that the more certain one is of having a communal relationship with another person, the less careful one has to be about doing something that might be incorrectly interpreted as violating the norms of a communal relationship (e.g., giving money as a gift).

Beginning with the research by Clark and Mills (1979), we have done a number of studies supporting our distinction between communal and exchange relationships, some jointly and others not. We have found that when exchange relationships are desired, people react positively to receiving immediate compensation for favors and positively to requests for repayment of favors they have accepted from others (Clark & Mills, 1979), they keep track of individual inputs into tasks for which there will be a joint reward (Clark, 1984), and they feel exploited when they give help that is not specifically repaid (Clark & Waddell, 1985). In contrast, when subjects are led to desire communal relationships, they react negatively to receiving immediate repayment for favors (Clark & Mills, 1979), they do not appear to keep track of individual inputs into joint tasks (Clark, 1984), and they do not feel exploited when their help is not specifically repaid (Clark & Waddell, 1985). Instead, subjects desiring communal relationships with others are more likely than those desiring exchange relationships to keep track of the others' needs even when they cannot help (Clark, Mills, & Powell, 1986), to help others (Clark et al., 1987), to respond to the others' sadness with increased helping (Clark et al., 1987), to feel good about having provided help to the others relative to not being able to help (Williamson & Clark, 1989, 1992), and to welcome expressions of emotion from the other (Clark & Taraban, 1991).

## FOUR CONTROVERSIAL ISSUES

Despite the foregoing support for the distinction, we have found to our dismay that the distinction is controversial and that a number of objections to our research have been raised. One criticism stemmed from the fact that many of our studies have used a laboratory setting in which people who are strangers to one another are induced by means of an experimental manipulation to desire either an exchange or communal relationships with other people. These studies led to the objection that our research does not say anything about real relationships, relationships that are ongoing. Another objection we have heard often is that the distinction between communal and exchange relationships is not a qualitative one—that people do not follow different norms in these two kinds of relationships, but rather that communal relationships are long-term relationships in which exchange occurs over an extended period of time. A third general criticism of our research is that not everyone behaves according to communal norms in relationships we have said are typically communal ones and that people sometimes behave in communal ways in relationships we have said are typically exchange. In other words, people have argued that there are many instances in which these norms are violated. A fourth common criticism is that our theorizing about communal relationships assumes people are more altruistic than is actually the case.

Before discussing each of these issues in detail, we discuss more extensively some of the more recent research that we have conducted. This research has a bearing on these issues and we believe it is also of interest in its own right.

## FURTHER RESEARCH ON THE DISTINCTION

The first study we review is an experiment on keeping track of inputs into joint tasks by Clark (1984). We start with this research because it forms a background for some of the newer research that we describe, and it is also relevant to some of the controversies to which we return. In the first study in a series of three by Clark (1984), there was an experimental manipulation of desire for a communal or exchange relationship. The dependent measure concerned keeping track of individual inputs into a joint task for which there would be a reward. This was measured by noting which color pen the subjects chose to work with on their part of the task when they knew the color of the pen the other person had already used. It was assumed that subjects who chose a different color pen than the other were interested in keeping track of who had contributed what to the joint task, whereas those who chose the same color pen were not concerned about keeping track of the inputs of each of the persons into the joint task. Choice of a different color pen would make it possible to tell who had done what, whereas choice of the same color pen would obscure who had done what. It was found that people who desired an exchange relationship with the other used a different color pen significantly more often than expected by chance. On the other hand, people desiring a communal relationship with the other used a different color pen significantly less often than expected by chance. In the second and third studies, Clark found that pairs of people who were not acquainted with one another, when placed in the experimental situation, chose a different color pen significantly more often than expected by chance, whereas persons who came to the experiment with a friend tended not to choose a different color pen than their friend had used—a tendency that did not differ from what would be expected by chance.

These results were predicted based on the distinction between exchange and communal relationships. In exchange relationships it is necessary to keep track of contributions or inputs into the relationship to make sure that the benefits from the relationship are allocated fairly. On the other hand, in communal relationships, benefits are given on the basis of needs rather than on the basis of contributions. Therefore, keeping track of contributions to the relationship is not necessary. In the first experiment, subjects desiring a communal relationship actually avoided keeping track of inputs. The best interpretation of this finding is that when people are attempting to form new communal relationships with others, they are concerned with following communal norms and also with avoiding any perception on the others' part that they might prefer an exchange relationship, and thus they take pains to avoid record keeping.

Although keeping track of individual inputs into joint tasks is called for in exchange relationships but not in communal relationships, there is a different type of monitoring that would be expected to occur in communal relationships but not in exchange relationships, namely, keeping track of needs. Communal norms call for members to keep track of one another's needs but exchange norms do not.

Keeping track of needs in communal and exchange relationships was investigated by Clark et al. (1986). They manipulated desire for a communal or exchange relationship as in previous laboratory work (see Clark, 1986). They measured keeping track of the other's needs by how many times the subject checked a box for notes from the other requesting help (Study 1) or how many times the subject turned around to look at lights indicating whether the other person was experiencing difficulty on a task (Study 2). It was found in Study 1 that those desiring a communal relationship were more likely than those desiring an exchange relationship to keep track of the other person's needs if there was no clear opportunity for the other person to reciprocate. In Study 2, a difference in keeping track of needs occurred even when the person was not able to respond to the other's needs, because the task did not permit it.

In a later study, Clark, Mills, and Corcoran (1989) tested both the hypothesis that keeping track of needs would be greater in a communal relationship than in an exchange relationship and the hypothesis that keeping track of inputs into a joint task would be greater in an exchange relationship than in a communal relationship. The dependent measure was the same in all conditions, namely, the number of times that subjects turned around to look at lights that actually never changed. In the needs condition, the subjects were led to believe that a change in the lights meant the other person needed help, which the subjects were not able to provide. In the inputs condition, a change in the lights meant that the other person had made a substantial contribution to a joint task. Rather than experimentally manipulating desire for a communal or an exchange relationship, as in the study by Clark et al. (1986), this study investigated the behavior of members of ongoing communal relationships compared with members of pairs of strangers. Subjects signed up for the experiment with a friend. Some subjects participated with their friend, whereas others participated with someone else's friend.

The results supported the hypothesis that keeping track of the needs of a friend would be greater than keeping track of the needs of a stranger. When a change in the lights meant the other needed help, the number of looks at the lights was significantly greater when the other was a friend than when the other was a stranger. On the other hand, when a change in the lights meant the other had made a substantial contribution to a joint task, the number of looks at the light was greater when the other was a stranger than when the other was a friend. The results of this experiment by Clark, Mills, and Corcoran (1989) provide a conceptual replication of the study on keeping track of inputs by Clark (1984) and also of the study on keeping track of needs by Clark et al. (1986). Later we discuss how these studies on keeping track of inputs and keeping track of needs relate to the controversial issues we outlined earlier. First, we talk about another line of new research concerned with individual differences in relationship orientation that was conducted by Clark and her students.

## RESEARCH ON INDIVIDUAL DIFFERENCES

Clark developed two personality scales—one to assess the extent to which people possess a communal orientation and one to assess the extent to which people possess an exchange orientation toward relationships. The communal scale measures whether people are inclined to watch out for others' welfare as well as whether they expect others to watch out for their welfare. The scale and evidence of its internal consistency, factor structure, and correlations with other scales appeared in a paper by Clark et al. (1987). The 14 communal scale items can be found in Table 2.1. The exchange scale includes items designed to measure whether the person keeps track of inputs into joint tasks, whether he or she makes efforts to specifically repay the other for benefits received, and whether the person expects the other to make efforts to specifically repay the person for benefits given to the other. Evidence of its internal consistency, factor structure, correlations with other scales, and ability to predict theoretically expected behavior are described in a paper by Clark, Taraban, Wesner, and Ho (1989). The nine exchange scale items can be found in Table 2.2. Here we simply mention several studies that provide evidence for the construct validity and usefulness of these scales.

Starting with the communal scale, in one study (Clark et al., 1987, Study 1) this scale was administered early in a semester to an entire subject pool. Later on, without the experimenter knowing their scores, subjects participated in a study in which they had an opportunity to help another person who was sad or not. As expected, it was found that people who had scored high in communal orientation, as determined by a median split, helped significantly more often than did those who scored low in communal orientation. Also,

TABLE 2.1

Items From the Communal Orientation Scale

---

1. It bothers me when other people neglect my needs.
2. When making a decision, I take other people's needs and feelings into account.
3. I'm not especially sensitive to other people's feelings.*
4. I don't consider myself to be a particularly helpful person.*
5. I believe people should go out of their way to be helpful.
6. I don't especially enjoy giving others aid.*
7. I expect people I know to be responsive to my needs and feelings.
8. I often go out of my way to help another person.
9. I believe it's best not to get involved taking care of other people's personal needs.*
10. I'm not the sort of person who often comes to the aid of others.*
11. When I have a need, I turn to others I know for help.
12. When people get emotionally upset, I tend to avoid them.*
13. People should keep their troubles to themselves.*
14. When I have a need that others ignore, I'm hurt.

---

*Note.* Respondents rate each item on a 5-point scale from *extremely uncharacteristic of them* (1) to *extremely characteristic of them* (5). Scores for items followed by an asterisk are reversed prior to calculating a sum indicating the respondent's communal orientation score.

as expected, those high in communal orientation responded to the other's sadness with increased helping, whereas those low in communal orientation did not.

Turning to the exchange scale, several relevant studies have been conducted. For all of them, the exchange scale was administered early in the semester and subjects were recruited and run prior to looking at their status on the scale. One study done by Clark, Taraban et al. (1989) was a replication of the earlier record keeping in joint tasks study. The results were parallel to the earlier ones. When subjects were high in exchange orientation, they kept track of individual inputs into a joint task to a greater extent than one would expect by

TABLE 2.2

Items From the Exchange Orientation Scale

---

1. When I give something to another person, I generally expect something in return.
2. When someone buys me a gift, I try to buy that person as comparable a gift as possible.
3. I don't think people should feel obligated to repay others for favors.*
4. I wouldn't feel exploited if someone failed to repay me for a favor.*
5. I don't bother to keep track of benefits I have given others.*
6. When people receive benefits from others, they ought to repay those others right away.
7. It's best to make sure things are always kept "even" between two people in a relationship.
8. I usually give gifts only to people who have given me gifts in the past.
9. When someone I know helps me out on a project, I don't feel I have to pay them back.*

---

*Note.* Respondents rate each item on a 5-point scale from *extremely uncharacteristic of them* (1) to *extremely characteristic of them* (5). Scores for items followed by an asterisk are reversed prior to calculating a sum indicating the respondent's exchange orientation score.

chance. In contrast, those low in exchange orientation showed no particular tendency to keep track of inputs.

In a second study done by Clark, Taraban et al. (1989), people were simply led to believe they would be participating in a joint task for which there would be a reward and were asked to rate, ahead of time, how they would like to divide up the resultant reward—according to who did what, according to need, or evenly. The first method was considered to be exchange in nature and the second two methods to be communal in nature. (If needs are perceived to be equal, rewards would be divided equally.) Subjects' ratings of the second two methods were simply subtracted from their ratings of the first method, so that higher scores indicated greater preference for dividing rewards in an exchange manner. Subjects high in exchange orientation showed a greater preference for dividing the reward according to who did what (relative to the other two rules) than did those subjects low in exchange orientation.

Finally, in a third study done by Clark, Taraban et al. (1989) people's reactions to receiving help that they were not able to repay were examined. It was expected that people high in exchange orientation would react negatively to this because they would not wish to feel indebted to the other. In contrast, those low in exchange orientation were expected to be happy to receive such help. The design of the study was simple. Subjects were asked to perform a task and they either did or did not receive help that they could not repay from the other. Then, under the guise of preparations for a second, joint task, they rated their first impressions of the other. It was found that if subjects were high in exchange orientation, they appeared to prefer not getting help to getting help. This was evidenced by the fact that their attraction for the other was higher if they did not get help than if they did get help. However, if subjects were low in exchange orientation, just the opposite occurred. That is, they appeared to prefer getting help to not getting help; their attraction for the other was higher if they had received help than if they had not. Changes in mood from before to after the task showed the same pattern of results. However, in the case of moods, the expected differences did not reach significance.

## DISCUSSION OF THE CONTROVERSIES

Having reviewed some recent research on the distinction between communal and exchange relationships, we return to the controversies outlined earlier that have come up in connection with some of our prior work. The criticism of our earlier work as being based only on behavior of strangers in laboratory situations, and thus of having dubious applicability to ongoing relationships, is clearly not relevant to some of the research just described. Beginning with the Clark (1984) studies on keeping track of inputs, behavior of people in ongoing friendships has been contrasted with the behavior of people not previously acquainted, and the results have provided evidence that members of ongoing friendships follow the norms of communal relationships. The study by Clark, Mills, and Corcoran (1989), which investigated keeping track of needs and inputs of friends and strangers, provided additional evidence that our distinction applies to ongoing communal relationships.

Although we have done work on ongoing relationships, we have not lost interest or confidence in laboratory studies in which communal versus exchange relationships are experimentally manipulated. We firmly believe in the value of such experimental work, and have found it to be a great stimulus to the development of our thinking about communal and exchange relationships. We believe the work we have done on ongoing relationships probably would never have developed if we had not done the initial work in the laboratory with experimentally manipulated relationships.

Turning to the controversy about whether the distinction we have drawn is genuinely qualitative or whether communal relationships are just long-term exchange relationships, we feel the weight of the evidence from the studies we have done argues strongly that communal relationships are not just long-term exchange relationships. Beginning with Clark and Mills (1979), a number of studies have shown that a factor that has one effect in our exchange conditions has the opposite effect or no effect in our communal conditions. The study by Clark, Mills, and Corcoran (1989) on keeping track of needs and inputs of friends and strangers is an example of this kind of result. In that study, the number of looks at the light was greater in the needs condition when the other was a friend than a stranger, and it was greater in the inputs condition when the other was a stranger than a friend.

The idea that exchange is really expected in what we have called communal relationships, but that it occurs over an extended period of time, is difficult to reconcile with the findings by Clark, Mills, and Corcoran (1989) and Clark (1984, Studies 2 & 3) that people did not keep track of the inputs of their friends to the same extent as those of strangers. It is also difficult to reconcile with Study 1 reported by Clark (1984), which showed that people induced to desire a communal relationship actually avoided keeping track of inputs, whereas people induced to desire an exchange relationship clearly made efforts to keep track. It is difficult to see how debts, if that is what they are, could be repaid over a long period of time when attention is not paid to keeping track of the debts. Of course, from our point of view, failure to keep track of specific benefits from the other person in a communal relationship is quite understandable because reciprocation of specific benefits is not expected. Rather what is expected is reciprocation of concern and a motivation to meet one's needs if and when they arise.

Another aspect of the results of Clark, Mills, and Corcoran (1989) and Clark et al. (1986) that is difficult to reconcile with the idea that communal relationships are just long-term exchange relationships is the finding that persons in or desiring communal relationships were interested in keeping track of the other person's needs even when they could not respond to those needs. Granting that communal subjects probably expected a longer relationship with the other, it is not reasonable to assume that they kept track of the other's needs to receive a later repayment when they were not even able to help the other. Under those circumstances, keeping track of the other's needs could have nothing to do with creating an obligation for repayment from the other later.

Although we assume communal relationships involve an expectation of a long-term relationship and exchange relationships need not be long term, we regard the variables of communal versus exchange relationship and expected length of the relationship as conceptually independent. It is possible that exchange relationships may occur over a long period. An example is the relationship between a store owner and a long-term customer.

The third persisting criticism of our work is that there are exceptions to communal norms. People often say things like, "In my family people didn't care about each other's needs"; or, alternatively, "I *do* care a great deal about my employees' personal needs." When considering the issue of violations of norms in communal relationships, we should keep in mind that the norms for exchange are also sometimes violated. For instance, people can feel exploited in an exchange relationship by failure on the part of another person to pay the debts that he or she owes. It is important to remember that the fact that violations of norms occur does not disprove the existence of the norms. Norms guide behavior by specifying the kinds of responses that are expected and acceptable in particular situations, but to have any meaning norms must be defined separately from the behavior that actually occurs. Otherwise the norms could not be distinguished from the behavior.

Part of the common definition of a norm involves the application of negative sanctions for violation of the norm. Without the possibility of violation, the concept of negative sanctions would be meaningless. One way to establish that a norm exists is to observe what happens when the norm is violated. One thing that happens is that there are complaints and criticisms about the lack of adherence to the norm. In the case of failure to follow communal norms in communal relationships, the complaints take the form of comments such as, "That's no way to treat your own brother"; or "Some friend you are!"; or the perennial complaint that, "With a friend like you, who needs enemies!" In the case of following communal norms in relationships usually considered to be exchange relationships (e.g., giving an employee paid time off to take care of personal needs), you might hear a complaint of, "That's no way to run a business."

The norms of communal and exchange relationships are not simply accepted by the parties in the relationship but are shared more generally by other persons. Violations can be responded to negatively by those who have an interest in the relationship but are not members of it. For example, the failure on the part of one family member to fulfill his or her obligations to be concerned about the welfare of another family member can be met by negative sanctions from other members of the family. Failure to follow communal norms in a friendship can be greeted with scorn by persons who are merely observers to the relationship. A person who fails to follow communal norms that they have internalized will experience feelings of guilt and self-criticism.

Of course, not all violations of norms are met with sanctions. In some cases, people freely violate the norms because they do not accept or internalize them and do not see them as relevant to the particular social interaction. Here is where the recent work by Clark on individual differences is especially pertinent. Her scales to measure individual differences in communal orientation and exchange orientation have the potential for usefulness in specifying empirically when communal and exchange norms will be followed.

The fourth controversy that we discuss usually takes the form of a criticism that our distinction between communal and exchange relationships assumes people are more altruistic than is really the case—that behavior in communal relationships seems to assume that people are more selfless than is warranted. If we use the dictionary definition of *altruism* as unselfish regard for or devotion to the welfare of others, communal relationships do seem to involve more altruism than exchange relationships. But it is not necessary to assume that behavior in communal relationships is completely unselfish. Behavior in communal relationships can be selfish in the sense that people may follow the norms in a communal relationship to achieve some other goal. In involuntary communal relationships, such as membership in the same family by virtue of birth, the motivation to follow communal norms with respect to another family member may stem from a desire to do one's duty, to be a good family member, or to avoid criticism by other members of the family that one has not behaved properly.

When we consider communal relationships that are voluntary or chosen, it seems that what could be considered selfish motivations can come into play. Normally a strong communal relationship, which may involve considerable cost on the person's part to benefit the other, will not be voluntarily entered into unless it is perceived as mutual (i.e., unless the other person is seen as willing to have the same kind of strong communal relationship with the person as the person has with him or her). The motivation to enter into such a communal relationship may be based on a desire for reciprocation on the other's part, on wanting the other to follow communal norms concerning meeting one's needs. One may respond to the other person's needs when they arise but one also expects the other to respond to one's needs if and when they arise. The motivation to follow communal norms by benefiting the other when the other has a need can be considered as a means to the goal of establishing a mutual, caring relationship in which one's own needs will be satisfied, and thus can be thought of, in a sense, as selfishly motivated.

Probably the most unselfish motivation involved in a communal relationship occurs in a one-sided communal relationship, such as the relationship between a parent and an infant or small child. But here again the motivation may be based on a goal other than simply bringing satisfaction to the child. For example, it may be based on the parent's desire to achieve the goal of considering him or herself a good parent or being considered a good parent by others.

We should also note two interesting aspects of the individual difference work that have implications for the issue of whether following communal norms is unselfish. First, as can be seen from an examination of the communal scale items in Table 2.1, there are two different types of items. One type has to do with a willingness to respond to the other person's needs. For example, "When making a decision, I take other people's needs and feelings into account." A second type indicates that the person expects the other to respond to his or her needs. For example, "It bothers me when other people neglect my needs." These two types of items are highly correlated. In other words, people who say they enjoy responding to others' needs also say they want others to respond to their needs. The same people who seem to be high on a nurturance motivation (i.e., they are willing to provide aid and comfort to others) also have a desire to be nurtured.

The second interesting and relevant aspect of the individual difference work is that the two scales, the communal orientation scale and the exchange orientation scale, are not correlated. It might be thought that there would be a negative correlation with people who are high on communal orientation being low on exchange orientation and vice versa. However, that does not seem to be the case. It may be that people who are really selfish, who are out to get all they can for themselves without any regard for the outcomes of others, are neither communal nor exchange oriented. Rather, they take every opportunity to exploit the other person without any sense of obligation either to meet the needs of others or to repay benefits received from the other. Both communal and exchange relationships assume a willingness to meet one's obligations to the other person. Taking advantage of others, exploiting them by failing to meet one's obligations, is truly selfish behavior.

Finally, it seems appropriate to comment briefly on how our work on communal and exchange relationships relates to other chapters in this volume as well as to other work that is going on in the relationships field as a whole. What one sees if one examines the chapters in this book and the field more generally is a great deal of work concerning close relationships—work on friendship, marriage and divorce, romance and love, attachment, parent–child relationships, intimacy, and so on. It is clear to us that most of the topics in which relationship researchers are currently interested concern what we have called communal relationships. We believe this makes it especially important to distinguish the communal norms governing the giving and receiving of benefits in such relationships from the heretofore much more intensively studied exchange norms.

## ACKNOWLEDGMENTS

Preparation of this chapter was supported in part by National Science Foundation grant BNS 8807894. This chapter was based on an invited address presented at the biannual meeting of the International Society for the Study of Personal Relationships, Vancouver, Canada, July 1988.

## REFERENCES

Clark, M. S. (1981). Noncomparability of benefits given and received: A cue to the existence of friendship. *Social Psychology Quarterly, 44*, 375–381.

Clark, M. S. (1984). Record keeping in two types of relationships. *Journal of Personality and Social Psychology, 47*, 549–557.

Clark, M. S. (1986). Evidence for the effectiveness of manipulations of communal and exchange relationships. *Personality and Social Psychology Bulletin, 12*, 414–425.

Clark, M. S., & Mills, J. (1979). Interpersonal attraction in exchange and communal relationships. *Journal of Personality and Social Psychology, 37*, 12–24.

Clark, M. S., & Mills, J. (1993). The difference between communal and exchange relationships: What it is and is not. *Personality and Social Psychology Bulletin, 19*, 684–691.

Clark, M. S., Mills, J., & Corcoran, D. (1989). Keeping track of needs and inputs of friends and strangers. *Personality and Social Psychology Bulletin, 15*, 533–542.

Clark, M. S., Mills, J., & Powell, M. C. (1986). Keeping track of needs in communal and exchange relationships. *Journal of Personality and Social Psychology, 51*, 333–338.

Clark, M. S., Ouellette, R., Powell, M. C., & Milberg, S. (1987). Recipient's mood, relationship type, and helping. *Journal of Personality and Social Psychology, 53*, 94–103.

Clark, M. S., & Taraban, C. B. (1991). Reactions to and willingness to express emotions in communal and exchange relationships. *Journal of Experimental Social Psychology, 27*, 324–336.

Clark, M. S., Taraban, C. B., Wesner, K., & Ho, J. (1989). *A measure of exchange orientation and its relation to keeping track of inputs, reactions to receiving help, and styles of dividing rewards.* Unpublished manuscript, Carnegie Mellon University, Pittsburgh, PA.

Clark, M. S., & Waddell, B. (1985). Perception of exploitation in communal and exchange relationships. *Journal of Social and Personal Relationships, 2*, 403–413.

Goffman, E. (1961). *Asylums: Essays on the social situation of mental patients and other inmates.* Garden City, NY: Anchor Books.

Mills, J., & Clark, M. S. (1982). Communal and exchange relationships. In L. Wheeler (Ed.), *Review of personality and social psychology* (pp. 121–144). Beverly Hills, CA: Sage.

Mills, J., & Clark, M. S. (1986). Communications that should lead to perceived exploitation in communal and exchange relationships. *Journal of Social and Clinical Psychology, 4*, 225–234.

Thibaut, J. W., & Kelley, H. H. (1959). *The social psychology of groups.* New York: Wiley.

Williamson, G. M., & Clark, M. S. (1989). Providing help and desired relationship type as determinants of changes in mood and self-evaluations. *Journal of Personality and Social Psychology, 56*, 722–734.

Williamson, G. M., & Clark, M. S. (1992). Impact of desired relationship type on affective reactions to choosing and being required to help. *Personality and Social Psychology Bulletin, 18*, 10–18.

# Chapter 3

# Courtship Antecedents of Marital Satisfaction and Love

Ted L. Huston
*University of Texas at Austin*

Most young adults are inexorably drawn toward marriage like, depending on their level of optimism, moths to fire or plants to the light. "It's like [the idea of marriage] was something that was born in my head," said a participant in a study of courtship (Greenblatt & Cottle, 1980, p. 10). Men and women are older today on their wedding days compared with a generation ago, but there has been only a slight decline in the percentage of the population that marries (U.S. Bureau of the Census, 1989; see Surra, 1990, for a review). American society, like most other industrial nations, is replete with strings that first pull individuals into the marketplace of marriage and, eventually, draw them into marriage. The cultural forces at work during mate selection and marriage were eloquently described by Erikson (1976), who, in writing about life in an Appalachian community in West Virginia, suggested:

> No act in life seems more private, more intimate, than the decision by two people to get married. . . . People "select" their mates now, whatever that may mean. But there are . . . spoken and unspoken encouragements that pass among families and friends beforehand, as well as a million other hints and suggestions that become a part of the marriage scene afterward. While we do not know much about those subtle chemistries, it is clear enough that marriage . . . is something of a community affair. It is validated by the community, commemorated by the community, and every married couple in the world knows something about the pressures exerted on that union by interests outside of it. (p. 281)

Nonetheless, mate selection in most Western cultures is seen by its participants as a voluntary transition, a choice mutually undertaken. Individuals become acquainted most usually in prosaic ways (Whyte, 1990), unlike in the movies where enormous ingenuity is used to invent unusual ways for potential mates to first meet (Wolfenstein & Leites, 1970). They then transform their relationship through a series of commitments and ultimately become married. Once married, they create a lifestyle, first as a couple and then, for those who have children, as a family unit. The course of love and commitment undoubtedly is affected by the larger community, as Erikson (1976) noted. But the extent to which a particular relationship is embedded within its larger social context is negotiated over time, both between the partners and among the partners, their kin, and their friends.

This chapter examines the connection between courtship experiences and the early years of marriage. My fundamental interest is to seek to identify the ways in which the lifestyle, satisfactoriness, and stability of a marriage 2 years after the couple is wed can be forecast from data gathered about the spouses' premarital experiences, and how they interacted with each other as newlyweds. Are couples who fall in love quickly and deeply more likely to stay in love after they are wed? Does premarital conflict presage a decline in satisfaction after couples become married?

These questions have a temporal dimension. They seek to connect what happens at one time to another. How does one bridge this chasm of time to identify causal connections between what happens at one time and what happens later? Issues of causality have proved difficult, in part, because social scientists rarely have the resources needed to trace events in detail over extended periods of time. They often cannot separate the typical from the atypical, the enduring from the transitory, and the directional and systematic from those that are cyclical. Moreover, process accounts of relationships bring forth the image that relationships are continuously changing. Such an image is difficult to reconcile with social science because social scientists must capture events in real time. It is my contention, without getting into the larger philosophical issues, that the temporal can be apprehended by examining events at several moments, or periods, of time.

The problems faced by moviemakers are comparable in many ways to those faced by social scientists. Moviemakers create the illusion of movement and change by combining a series of images (Burch, 1973; Eisenstein, 1957; Pudovkin, 1970). Lumet (1965) peppers *The Pawnbroker* with flashbacks, almost subliminal in length, to suggest the impact of past traumas on the principal character's tormented life. The character's anguish is further heightened when, upon the fatal shooting of his assistant, the camera cuts to his impassive face and then crosscuts to his hand as he plunges it through the metal prong on the spindle he used for receipts; the movie ends as he walks the streets alone. Creating and assembling a movie involves linking one scene to another, being careful to set up action so that it seems natural and plausible, given what has come before. Fellini (1964), speaking of his *Juliet of the Spirits*, said, "People always think I improvise my films—that something—some scene, some moment, some idea just flies into my head, and then I put it in. The fact is it's all intentional'' (quoted in Gessner, 1968, p. 44).

Connections are shown in film between events and patterns in a relationship separated in time by days, months, or even years (Gessner, 1968). Johan and Marianne's marriage, in Bergman's (1974) *Scenes from a Marriage*, unravels through a series of conversations recorded close-up by the camera as it cuts back and forth between the spouses as they talk. The scenes in Bergman's film have a thematic, cumulative character, building toward a climax as Marianne and Johan transform their views of each other and their marriage. Jones' (1983) *Betrayal* starts with the end of a love affair and takes the viewer in backward chronological order through a series of scenes to its first hopeful moments, creating a sense of pathos and loss.

Social scientists also have an interest in reaching backward, sometimes across large expanses of time, to show how the goals, attitudes, and psychological dispositions of dating and married partners come into play in contemporary relationships (cf. Bentler & Newcomb, 1978). Life history information and personality measures are used as proxies for previous experience, the hope being to determine, at least indirectly, how the past affects the present. Sometimes researchers, blessed with time and resources, are able to follow people and couples longitudinally and establish connections more directly between the past and the present (e.g., Berg & McQuinn, 1986; Gottman & Krokoff, 1989; Kelly & Conley, 1987).

Social scientists explore similar temporal linkages when they examine such questions as whether passionate love is apt to be short lived and redefined as infatuation (Berscheid & Walster, 1974); turning points in courtship (Baxter & Bullis, 1986; Lloyd & Cate, 1985a); whether couples who have trouble getting along before marriage are more likely than others to fall out of love afterward (Kelly, Huston, & Cate, 1985; Markman, 1979, 1981); or whether married couples who work through their conflicts are more likely to maintain a high level of marital satisfaction than those who avoid their differences (Gottman & Krokoff, 1989). Social scientists such as Gottman (1979) film conversations, and then dissect the film, identifying thematic patterns of action and reaction. Sequences and patterns of interaction are placed, at least implicitly, within a larger temporal context when the spouses' level of marital satisfaction is taken as a representation of the history of the couple's life together prior to when the encounter was filmed.

It is common practice for onlookers to speculate about whether a particular couple in the midst of courtship is likely to create and maintain a happy marriage. Scholars studying the linkage between courtship patterns and marriage have identified various premarital events and patterns as likely precursors of marital distress. It has been claimed, for instance, that couples who take a long time to get to know each other before they become heavily committed are apt to choose a mate more wisely (Grover, Russell, Schumm, & Paff-Bergen, 1985; Waller, 1938). Premarital pregnancy, particularly when it becomes known to the partners prior to when they are committed to marriage, has been found to be associated with high levels of conflict during courtship and early marriage (Surra, Chandler, Asmussen, & Wareham, 1987). It has also been suggested that couples who marry even though they have had a difficult time getting along with one another during courtship are apt to experience conflict and become less happily married than those who have a relatively harmonious courtship (Kelly et al., 1985; Markman, 1979, 1981). Although it is generally conceded that the kind of intense, erotic attraction that often characterizes newfound love does not—and probably cannot—last (Berscheid & Walster, 1974; Waller, 1938), laypersons generally believe such experiences early in a relationship are requisite to becoming committed to marriage (Simpson, Campbell, & Berscheid, 1986). Waller (1938), however, contended that people who fall deeply in love are apt to become disillusioned later once they open their minds to each other's shortcomings. Lovers are not unaware of each other's faults, suggested Waller (1938), but they exclude the emotional meaning of the shortcomings from their consciousnesses.

Research seeking to link particular courtship patterns to marriage has frequently produced contradictory results. Length of courtship, cohabitation, premarital sex, and premarital pregnancy have been found in some studies but not in others to correlate with measures of marital success (see Lewis & Spanier, 1979). Such matters have been investigated because they are presumed to be associated with premature commitment, marrying for convenience (rather than out of love), and stress or conflict. Early commitment, based on rapidly developing love and eroticism, may plant the seeds for later declines in satisfaction and love, once the partners get to know each other better. Marriages of convenience may break down under stress. However, little research, particularly of a longitudinal nature, has been done to link the psychological and interpersonal interior of premarital relationships to marriage.

## MATE SELECTION AS A COMMITMENT PROCESS

The movement of a couple toward matrimony is most fundamentally characterized by the partners' developing consensus that marriage is mutually desired. Such agreement can take place very quickly. Frequently, however, individuals in the embryonic stages of their relationship are uncertain whether they might ultimately be interested in becoming married, and possess an even vaguer sense of what their partner might desire. Thus, certainty about marriage can build quickly or slowly, smoothly or unevenly, or in a continuous upward progression through a series of setbacks. Until recently, these processes were more a topic of speculation than of research (cf. Huston, Surra, Fitzgerald, & Cate, 1981).

When colleagues and I began to consider ways to characterize the development of commitment during courtship (Huston et al., 1981), we concluded that newlyweds' memories for the just-completed courtship would be vivid enough so that they could be primed to reconstruct, in general terms, the events and experiences involved in the development of their commitment toward marriage. Newlyweds, we found, were able to report whether they progressed rapidly to a high level of commitment, and whether there were times when their confidence in the solidarity of the relationship was significantly shaken (and, if so, approximately when these times were). We also assumed that newlyweds would be able to locate reasonably accurately the time when they first felt they were in love, the first time they had sexual intercourse, when they met each other's parents, when they began living together (if they did so prior to marriage), and periods of conflict (see Huston et al., 1981; Miell, 1987; Schwartz, 1990; Surra, 1985; for discussions of autobiographical memory).

The rapidity with which couples become mutually committed reflects the relative strength of forces compelling them toward marriage, and those forces that deter them from marriage or bring the relationship to an end. "Falling in love" and becoming erotically involved represent two powerful forces that, when coupled with normatively based considerations, push couples toward commitment. Conflict, negativity, and ambivalence represent key countervailing forces. Events such as premarital pregnancy or cohabitation are apt to take on significance depending on how they relate to love, eroticism, conflict, ambivalence, and commitment.

In this chapter, using data that were drawn from 168 couples married in central Pennsylvania in 1981,[1] I show how forces toward marriage and countervailing forces operate in the course of premarital commitment. Subsequently, I consider how the forces that draw couples together quickly and those that slow couples' commitment account for variance in the satisfactoriness of the marriage relationship after couples have been married for 2 years. More specifically, I look at whether couples who "fall in love" and become sexually involved early in their relationship are more or less likely to stay in love and to report being happily married. At the same time, I consider whether those who have trouble getting along and who are ambivalent about their relationship before marriage are less likely than those who get along well to establish a satisfactory marital union.

Several features of the project on which the present chapter is based are worth noting because they help delineate the significance and generalizability of the findings. First, the sample was drawn from marriage license records maintained in four counties in a largely rural and working-class area in central Pennsylvania. The sample was largely representative of newlyweds married during

---

[1]Complete details of the study can be found in Huston, McHale, and Crouter (1986), and Huston, Robins, Atkinson, and McHale (1987).

the sampling period in the larger geographical area, at least in terms of the spouses' age at marriage and the status of the spouses' parents' occupations. Second, data were gathered about both the courtship and the marriage from both spouses. Having data from both spouses made it possible to study the effects of each spouse's experiences, dispositions, and attitudes on the partner. Third, the study was longitudinal, thus making it possible to assess the changing significance of courtship experiences for marriage relationships as they unfold over the first 2 years.

## Creating Graphs of the Course of Commitment

To study courtship, my colleagues and I (Huston et al., 1981) developed a protocol that has subsequently been refined and used in several studies to gather data concerning the course of premarital commitment (Cate, Huston, & Nesselroade, 1985; Huston et al., 1981; Lloyd & Cate, 1985a, 1985b; Surra, 1985, 1987; Surra, Arizzi, & Asmussen, 1988; Surra & Huston, 1987). The procedure yields graphic representations of the evolution of commitment from first acquaintance to the wedding day. A set of superimposed graphs, taken from data provided by a husband and a wife, illustrates the kind of information contained in these representations.

Interviewers and newly married spouses created these graphs jointly, starting at the time when the couple first paired off and ending with their wedding day. Husbands and wives constructed the graphs separately, with male and female interviewers, respectively. Participants first were told that couples arrive at the decision to marry in many ways, and that our goal was to get a sense of this variety, not to determine whether one pattern is more typical than another. They then were asked to give a brief, informal description of the relationship from first meeting to marriage. After that, the participants were shown a blank sheet of graph paper, marked with the beginning and end dates of the courtship. The horizontal axis represented "time," with each division standing for 1 month; the vertical axis was to be used to indicate the "chance of marriage" as it changed through time. The participants were asked to estimate the chance of marriage by considering both their own feelings and the feelings they thought their partner had at the time.

To facilitate constructing the graph, participants marked significant events in their relationship on the baseline to help them remember what had been going on at a particular time (see Fig. 3.1). Next, they and the interviewers jointly constructed the trajectory. Participants were asked to indicate the chance of marriage (from 0% to 100%) when they first met their partner and this was marked. Then they were asked to think about when they were aware that the probability had changed and to indicate the chance of marriage at this second point. They then showed, with the help of the interviewer, how the two points should be connected (e.g., whether it was a linear, monotonic progression, or

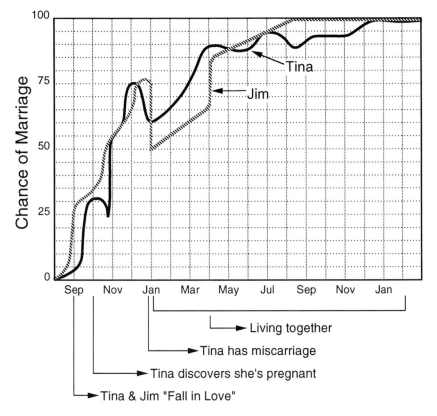

FIG. 3.1.    Courtship of Jim and Tina.

a sudden movement). After connecting the two points, they were asked to explain what led them to believe that the probability of marriage had changed. This same procedure was repeated until the entire trajectory was drawn.

Participants then were asked to examine the graph and to indicate the periods during the premarital relationship when the partners (a) dated each other casually, (b) dated regularly, (c) identified themselves as a couple (but were not committed to marriage), and (d) were committed to marriage. Some couples skipped stages, of course, and others repeated stages after having broken up. Participants were then shown a list of circumstances that often take place during courtship and were asked to indicate if and when these events took place for them. The list included events such as when they first felt they were in love, when they first had sexual intercourse, the months during the relationship in which they lived together, and when the woman became pregnant (if that had occurred).

The interviewers then pointed to the period when the partners were a couple (but were not committed to marriage), asking them to recreate a vivid image of what the relationship was like during this period. They used their memory of this period as the basis for filling out a questionnaire originally developed by Braiker and Kelley (1979) and designed to measure four dimensions of relationships: (a) love, measured in terms of feelings of belonging, closeness, and attachment; (b) ambivalence, conceived as feelings of confusion concerning the partner and anxiety about increasing commitment and about loss of independence; (c) conflict, as reflected in anger and disagreement; and (d) maintenance, assessed in terms of communication designed to increase satisfaction or decrease dissatisfaction. Of these, conflict was inherently a dyadic phenomena, and, as a consequence, we combined the reports into a single index.

The procedure, which generally took between 15 and 45 minutes to complete, depending on the length and complexity of the courtship, was used to create 336 graphs, taken from 168 husband–wife pairs. Figure 3.2 shows some of the variety found in the graphs.

### Characterizing and Distinguishing Courtships

As can be seen from Fig. 3.2, some courtships take a rocky, uneven path toward marriage, whereas others progress extremely rapidly, with the couple marrying within months or even weeks after they first become involved. Still others

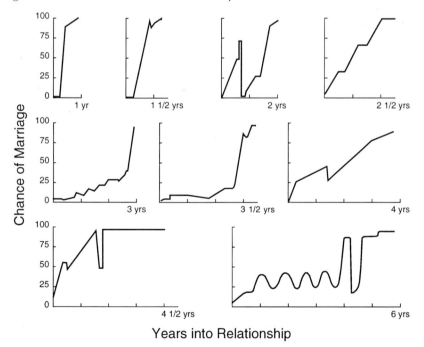

FIG. 3.2.   Illustrations of shapes of courtship graphs.

get off to a quick start, become stalled for a few months or even a year, and then move forward again. The variety found in the growth of commitment can be distinguished, to a large extent, in terms of (a) the overall length of the courtship, (b) the rate at which commitment accelerates (i.e., time in months to move from 25% to 75% chance of marriage), and (c) the number of downturns in the probability of marriage. The top right graph and the middle left graph are similar in length, for example, but they differ considerably in the rate of acceleration and the number of downturns.

Table 3.1 shows that the more quickly partners fall in love and become sexually involved, the shorter their courtship, the more rapidly their commitment escalates, and the fewer the number of downturns. A courtship following such a pattern was described by Laurie, who indicated that the chance of marriage was 70% after her first date with her future husband. She said, "From then on, we were around each other constantly. . . . I had the feeling we would marry soon." Janice, whose courtship with Rob lasted just over 3 years, described the slow growth of their commitment: "[I]t took me a long time before I was sure that I really loved him. . . . It was hard to get to know him at first; he had just broken up with another girl and I think he was reluctant [to get involved]."

Table 3.1 also shows that the more couples reportedly experienced conflict, the longer their courtship lasted, the slower their commitment accelerated, and

TABLE 3.1

Correlations of Attitudes Toward Partner and Interpersonal Events with
Length of Courtship, Rate of Acceleration of Commitment,
and Number of Downturns

| Variables | Length of Courtship | Rate of Acceleration[a] | Number of Downturns |
|---|---|---|---|
| Time (in months) to "fall in love" | | | |
| Male partner | .56* | .52* | .24* |
| Female partner | .46* | .34* | .18* |
| Time (in months) to first sexual intercourse | .48* | .32* | .13 |
| Love | | | |
| Male partner | −.28* | −.27* | −.22* |
| Female partner | −.12 | −.13 | −.14* |
| Ambivalence | | | |
| Male partner | .35* | .36* | .30* |
| Female partner | .09 | .07 | .27* |
| Maintenance | | | |
| Male partner | −.25* | −.27* | −.22* |
| Female partner | −.07 | −.06 | −.02 |
| Conflict | .32* | .39* | .44* |

Note. *$p$ < .01. $N$ = 162.
[a]Higher values equal slower rates.

the more downturns they experienced. Rayleen, a woman involved in a 2-year, turbulent courtship that resulted in a calamitous marriage, seemed to contradict herself in talking about how she and her fiancé dealt with conflict:

> David and I have never really had any conflicts. . . . He barked a lot and I listened and I might get upset and cry a little, but I understood why he was upset. . . . I used to react. Now, I absorb what he has to say because I realize the type of person he is. If I were to say something back it would just make it worse. So, if he's doing something to start a fight . . . like calling me stupid, or something . . . I just wait until he's more calmed down and I'm more calmed down . . . then I'll discuss it with him.

Men's love, ambivalence, and maintenance correlated in expected ways with the length of the courtship, the rate at which commitment accelerated, and the number of downturns. Women's ambivalence, love, and maintenance were not significantly correlated with either the length of the courtship or how rapidly the commitment accelerated. Ambivalence on the part of women, however, did correlate with the number of downturns. Patty, a woman involved in a short, tumultuous courtship, described how her future husband's ambivalence about marriage surfaced once they were engaged, briefly plummeting her hopes for marriage:

> I finally confronted Terry and said: "Why don't you tell me you don't want to see me for a couple of days, that you have other things to do. Why do you leave me waiting." He protested: "Well, I need my space to do what I want and I don't want to be responsible to anyone. I'm just coming out of a serious relationship, so it's just the way I am." And then I got really mad and said: "Well, if that's the way you are, I don't think I can take this anymore, so let's just end it." But then later on [that day] I had a talk with a good friend and I reconsidered. I went to him, and I said: "I think we can try to work with it if this is what your character is at the time."

The impression that the course of commitment in premarital relationships resonates more to men's than to women's predilections can be tested systematically using hierarchical multiple regressions, in which the psychological orientations of each partner are entered separately and in different orders as groups of predictors. By reversing the order of entry of the men's and women's orientations toward the relationship, it was possible to gain a sense of the relative importance of their orientations as correlates of the length of courtship, the rate at which commitment accelerated, and the number of downturns. The initial step involved entering the first person's report of the time it took in months to fall in love, as well as that same person's love, ambivalence, and willingness to engage in relationship enhancing behaviors (maintenance) during the time when they were a couple but not yet committed to marriage. The other spouse's reports about the same matters were subsequently entered. The lines in Table 3.2 labeled "unique $R^2$" show the change in $R^2$ when the men's and women's psychological orientations were entered after the orientations of their partner. Table 3.2 shows that the unique $R^2$ was significant for both men and women for each graph-based variable, suggesting that the commitment trajectory reflected both partners' psychological leanings toward and away from commitment. The amount of variance uniquely associated with husbands' premarital orientations toward the relationship, however, was considerably greater in regard to each graph-based variable, indicating that the course of courtship was more closely aligned with men's than the women's propensities.

The gender differences were particularly evident with regard to the rate at which the couples' commitment to marriage accelerated, with men's proclivities about the relationship uniquely accounting for more than five times as much of the variance as women's (28% compared to 5%). The beta weights shown in Table 3.2 are for the full model, once both spouses' dispositions were entered into the equation. They were generally consistent with the correlations shown in Table 3.1, except that men and women's levels of romantic love, as indexed by the Braiker and Kelley (1979) measure, no longer had any association with the graph-based variables.

The results shown in Table 3.2 do not include the two inherently dyadic variables indicated in Table 3.1—the length of time before the pair first had

TABLE 3.2

Hierarchical Multiple Regressions—Men and Women's Psychological
Orientations Toward the Partner and Relationship and Courtship Length,
Rate of Acceleration, and Number of Downturns as Criterion Variables

| Variables | Length | Rate of Acceleration[a] | Downturns |
|---|---|---|---|
| Male Partners' | | | |
| Time (in months) to fall in love | .43** | .41** | .21** |
| Love | .00 | .05 | .10 |
| Ambivalence | .12 | .18* | .21* |
| Maintenance | −.19* | −.25** | −.24** |
| Unique $R^2$ | .25** | .28** | .14** |
| Female Partners' | | | |
| Time (in months) to fall in love | .28** | .16* | .01 |
| Love | −.09 | −.17+ | −.08 |
| Ambivalence | .01 | .00 | .25** |
| Maintenance | .10 | .16+ | −.13 |
| Unique $R^2$ | .09** | .05* | .08** |
| $R^2$ | .47 | .40 | .23 |
| Multiple $R$ | .68** | .63** | .48** |

*Note.* Beta weights for full model are tabled.
*$p < .05$.  **$p < .01$.  +$p < .10$.  $N = 126$.
[a]Higher values equal slower rates.

intercourse, and the extent to which the couple reportedly experienced conflict during the "couple" stage of their courtship. Hierarchical multiple regressions were carried out in which these dyadic variables were considered together after the other more psychological variables had been entered. The inclusion of the dyadic variables significantly increased $R^2$ ($p < .01$) with regard to all three criterion variables, with the increase in $R^2$ being 11%, 8%, and 8% for length, acceleration, and downturns, respectively. Couples who had sexual intercourse earlier, had shorter ($F = 34.83$, $p < .01$) and more accelerated ($F = 6.93$, $p < .01$) courtships. Couples who had more conflict and negativity had longer courtships ($F = 7.34$, $p < .01$), in which the progression of commitment was slower ($F = 17.87$, $p < .01$) and more fitful (as indexed by downturns; $F = 16.40$, $p < .01$).

To summarize, the results are consistent with popular thinking that "falling in love" and becoming sexually involved both tend to push relationships toward marriage.[2] Men's ambivalence appears to lengthen the courtship, to slow the rate of acceleration, and to create downturns in commitment. The correlations in Table 3.2 pertaining to maintenance suggest that men who are highly invested—as indexed by their willingness to bring their ideas into the relationship, to disclose, and to show a willingness to change in order to improve it—are involved in shorter, more accelerated, and less turbulent courtships. The fact that the men's level of ambivalence and maintenance, but not the women's, is related to patterns of movement toward and away from marriage is consistent with the idea that patriarchal values lie beneath contemporary mate selection patterns, particularly in small cities, towns, and rural areas such as the ones in which the study sample was drawn.

## COURTSHIP PATTERNS AND MARRIAGE

I now consider whether courtship patterns predict marital stability and cohesion. Are people who are less willing to make efforts to improve their relationship, or who are ambivalent about it before marriage, less likely to establish a mutually satisfying union? The theorized connection between courtship experiences and marriage has been conceptualized by social scientists in two distinct ways. Some scholars, such as Waller (1938), believe that once partners begin to court each other they become primed to feel a sense of enchantment and, at the same time, are apt to suppress emotions, such as anger or hurt, that might undermine romantic feelings. Waller (1938) suggested that strong romantic feelings frequently carry into marriage, setting the partners up for

---

[2]It is important to recognize that these observations are based on data gathered from couples who married each other. It is possible that "falling in love" or becoming sexually involved may also quickly end relationships.

disillusionment once they begin to know each other more fully. Accordingly, premarital problems during courtship can be likened to an undetected virus. Unless checked, the virus will surface in the marriage and erode the partners' bond, making the relationship vulnerable. Thus, couples who have trouble getting along before marriage are expected to experience declines in satisfaction and love from the time when they are newlyweds to when they have been married a little bit more than 2 years.

The second model, which I refer to as the "perpetual problem" model to distinguish it from the "disillusionment" model noted earlier, suggests that the psychological states and interpersonal patterns that are identified with commitment during courtship are associated with the spouses' feelings of love and satisfaction during courtship, when the couples are newlyweds, and beyond. This model suggests that problems that surface during courtship weaken the bond between the partners at that time, that such problems typically persist, and that, as a consequence, they foretell later problems. Proponents of this "early determinism" view, such as Burgess and Wallin (1953), have argued that courting couples enter marriage with their eyes open to each other's character strengths and flaws. They pointed out that most people are aware that, in order to marry a real person instead of a fantasized mate, they have to compromise with their ideals.

### Premarital Antecedents of Marital Love and Satisfaction

Table 3.3 summarizes the correlations between features of premarital relationships and spouses' love and marital satisfaction when they are newlyweds and after they have been married just more than 2 years. Love was measured with the Braiker and Kelley (1979) scale described earlier; it taps the extent to which spouses report that they care about their partner, feel attached, and believe their relationship is special. Marital satisfaction was gauged using a scale adapted from Campbell, Converse, and Rodgers (1976) to measure life satisfaction. The scale consists of a single item in which spouses are asked to assess their overall satisfaction with their marriage, and a series of bipolar adjectives such as miserable–enjoyable, rewarding–disappointing, and full–empty. The marital satisfaction scale used in the present research program requires spouses to make a series of judgments about the affect the relationship generates. The more frequently used global assessments of "marital quality" require spouses to assess their "compatibility" and to characterize their relationship in terms of such things as how frequently they have sexual intercourse and how well they get along. These more global measures confound subjective evaluations of the relationship with its antecedents and behavioral correlates (see Fincham & Bradbury, 1987; Huston, McHale, & Crouter, 1986; Huston & Robins, 1982). Reports of love and satisfaction are, of course, highly correlated, with correlations increasing over time and ranging from .55 (for wives as newlyweds) to .76 (for

TABLE 3.3

Correlations Between Courtship Experience and Love and Satisfaction in Marriage

| | Newlyweds | | | | Married 2 Years or More | | | |
| | Husbands | | Wives | | Husbands | | Wives | |
| Courtship Experience | Love | Satisfaction | Love | Satisfaction | Love | Satisfaction | Love | Satisfaction |
|---|---|---|---|---|---|---|---|---|
| Graph-based features | | | | | | | | |
| Length of courtship | -.31** | -.13+ | -.18* | -.16* | -.12+ | -.11 | -.01 | -.01 |
| Rate of acceleration[a] | -.41** | -.22** | -.27** | -.25** | -.21** | -.16* | -.03 | -.00 |
| Downturns | -.26** | -.23** | -.18* | -.19* | -.15* | -.16* | -.12+ | -.08 |
| Husbands' premarital orientation | | | | | | | | |
| Time (in months) to "fall in love" | -.27** | -.10 | -.16* | -.10 | -.09 | -.02 | .02 | .03 |
| Love | .53** | .33** | .11 | .25** | .42** | .18* | .22** | .14* |
| Ambivalence | -.50** | -.39** | -.27** | -.25** | -.11 | -.29** | -.16* | -.20** |
| Maintenance | .41** | .22** | -.04 | .24** | .30** | .00 | .09 | -.04 |
| Wives' premarital orientation | | | | | | | | |
| Time (in months) to "fall in love" | -.06 | -.05 | -.22** | -.19* | -.02 | -.02 | -.12+ | -.11 |
| Love | .13* | .07 | .49** | .14+ | .08 | .29** | .23** | .27** |
| Ambivalence | -.06 | -.06 | -.33** | -.37** | -.13+ | -.22** | -.40** | -.30** |
| Maintenance | .04 | .22** | .18* | .04 | .11 | .15* | .11 | .08 |
| Dyadic events/patterns | | | | | | | | |
| Time (in months) to first intercourse | .00 | .08 | -.03 | .05 | .06 | .06 | .02 | .08 |
| Conflict | -.23** | -.30** | -.28** | -.40** | -.25** | -.21** | -.19* | -.29** |

Note. *p < .05. **p < .01. +p < .10. N = 126.

[a]Higher values equal slower rates.

husbands 2 years into marriage). Despite these relatively high correlations, spouses are able to distinguish between love and satisfaction, as evidenced by one woman in our study who, in summarizing her feelings, said: "I'm very unhappy with my marriage right now—we never see each other [with him working and me with the baby]—but I still love my husband and I'm sure that if you come back and interview us in seven years I'll love him just as much as I do now."

The "perpetual problems" view of the origins of marital distress leads us to expect that premarital problems will be reflected in how spouses feel about each other as newlyweds and, because the problems are apt to persist, after they have been married 2 years. The pattern of significant correlations shown in Table 3.3, based on 126 intact marriages, provides striking support for the idea that courtship experiences forecast love and satisfaction, both when spouses are newlyweds and 2 years later. Of the 168 couples who participated in the study, 126 remained married through the three phases of data collection. Fourteen couples were separated or divorced prior to what would have been their second wedding anniversary. The other 28 couples were split evenly between those who dropped out of the study and those who moved out of the interview area or who were not interviewed because of scheduling problems. In addition to computing the bivariate correlations shown in Table 3.3, a series of multiple regressions was carried out with each set of predictors. The three graph-based features of courtship, for example, were regressed on each of the eight marital criterion variables. Sets of regressions also were done using the three other clusters of variables shown in Table 3.3—husbands' premarital orientations, wives' premarital orientations, and dyadic events and patterns. The results of these regressions show that some variables become less important when considered along side others, and that some clusters of premarital predictors become less predictive of marital satisfaction and love with time.

The forces that push couples toward commitment and the forces that hold them back from commitment are consistently associated in expected ways with spouses' feelings of love and satisfaction, particularly among newlyweds. The longer the courtship, the more slowly commitment accelerates; and the more downturns, the less satisfied and in love spouses are as newlyweds. Couples who "fall in love" more slowly are less in love and less satisfied as newlyweds; the rapidity with which couples fall in love, however, is unrelated to spouses' feelings about each other and their relationship after they have been married for a couple of years. Couples who fell in love relatively slowly did not differ in regard to any of the marital criterion variables when the number of months it took them to fall in love was entered into the regression equation simultaneously with love, ambivalence, and maintenance. Men and women who fell in love relatively slowly reported being less in love and more ambivalent about their relationship when they reached the "couple" stage of their courtship (number of months to "fall in love" and love: $r = -.16$, $p < .05$, for men; and

$r = -.14, p < .05$, for women; number of months to "fall in love" and ambivalence: $r = .25, p < .001$, for men; and $r = .21, p < .01$, for women). The inverse correlation between how quickly people fall in love and their ambivalence, coupled with the relatively strong associations between ambivalence and the marital outcome variables, no doubt accounts for why falling in love slowly does not contribute to explaining variance in the marital outcomes when it is put in a regression with ambivalence.

The correlations between premarital conflict and marital outcomes when couples are newlyweds and after they have been married 2 years, shown in the bottom row of Table 3.3, are consistent with previous research (e.g., Kelly et al., 1985), which found that couples who experienced more conflict premaritally are less in love and less satisfied after they marry. Couples involved in courtships filled with considerable conflict, compared with those that are relatively harmonious, are, as courting couples, less in love (men: $r = -.21, p < .01$; women: $r = -.18, p < .05$) and more ambivalent about their relationship (men: $r = .45, p < .001$; women: $r = .47, p = .001$).

The correlations between husbands' and wives' premarital orientations toward the relationship and their love and satisfaction once they have become married are shown in the middle sections of the table. Look particularly at correlations involving premarital love, ambivalence, and maintenance. These correlations are based on spouses' assessments of their relationship for the period of time when "they were a couple, but not yet committed to marriage." To be considered a "couple," the partners had to be regularly seeing each other and exclusively involved. The correlations in Table 3.3 provide strong evidence supporting the idea that couples' love and ambivalence before marriage consistently predict marital love and satisfaction. The multiple regressions also show strong and consistent associations between premarital ambivalence and husbands' and wives' love and satisfaction in marriage, both when couples are newlyweds and after they are married for 2 years. When premarital love is regressed on the marital outcome variables along with the other variables with which it is grouped in the table, it does not account for a significant amount of the variance in how spouses feel about each other after they are married, except when these spouses' love for each other when they were newlyweds is used as the criterion.

The entire set of regressions, considered together, point to premarital problems—particularly as indexed by ambivalence, conflict, and a slower progression toward commitment—as important elements of the premarital relationship predictive of marital satisfaction and love. The course of early marriage can be traced, in part, to couples' courtship experiences. It appears that Burgess and Wallin (1953) were correct in suggesting that problems that surface during courtship affect partners' feelings toward each other prior to marriage, as newlyweds, and once they have been married for awhile.

The "disillusionment" model of the origins of marital distress suggests that features of the premarital relationship, if they affect the marriage at all, are more apt to influence partners' feelings toward each other after the "psychic honeymoon" is over. Love reaches its apex early in marriage, according to Waller (1938), because people are particularly motivated at that time to disattend to experiences that might undermine their romantic feelings. Later, once they have developed a relatively stable marital lifestyle, the causes of the premarital problems are likely to resurface. These ideas suggest that the premarital variables might become more strongly related to love and marital satisfaction after couples have been married for a time rather than when they are newlyweds. However, the results of the regressions run counter to such a suggestion. The multiple $R$s are invariably higher when premarital variables are used to account for newlyweds' love and satisfaction compared with when spouses have been married for 2 years.[3]

The "disillusionment" hypothesis received support, nonetheless, when we used courtship variables to predict declines in satisfaction and love over the first 2 years of marriage. To do these analyses, it was necessary to control for differences among the husbands and wives in their satisfaction and love when they were newlyweds. Hierarchical multiple regressions were carried out, in which spouses' newlywed scores on the specific marital outcome variable of interest were entered into the regression equation first, followed by the cluster of premarital predictors of interest. This approach to the analysis, in effect, converts the marital outcome variables to "change scores." These change scores can be viewed as decline because, on average, spouses' love and satisfaction decline over the first 2 years of marriage (MacDermid, Huston, & McHale, 1990).

The most striking result derived from these hierarchical regressions pertains to the diagnostic significance of women's premarital ambivalence, which predicts declines in both wives' love ($p < .001$) and husbands' satisfaction ($p < .05$). Wives married to husbands who were less in love when the couple was dating also tend to fall out of love after they become married ($p < .10$). These findings further underline the importance of ambivalence, suggesting that it comes out in different ways in relationships at different points in their history. It will be recalled that premaritally it was when men, rather than women, were ambivalent about the relationship that progress toward marriage was slow and rocky. Ambivalence before marriage, however, predicts both husbands' and wives' love and satisfaction shortly after they are married and a year later. These findings suggest that it is wives' premarital ambivalence,

---

[3]There were 16 pairs of regressions that could be used to compare the premarital variables as predictors of marital love and satisfaction. The multiple $R$ in 14 of the 16 regressions was significant ($p < .05$) either when couples were newlyweds, after they had been married 2 years, or both, and in each of these cases it was higher for the spouses when they were newlyweds compared with when they had been married longer.

rather than husbands', that has a delayed or "sleeper" effect on marriage, an effect that amplifies its effect on the relationship when couples are newlyweds.

## Premarital Antecedents of Early Separation and Divorce

Of the 168 couples who participated in the original study, 14 had separated or divorced within 2 years after they were wed. These couples were compared with the 126 couples who were known to have remained married until shortly beyond their second wedding anniversary. The small number of couples who separated or divorced early in marriage suggests that considerable caution needs to be exercised in drawing conclusions about how such couples differ from those who stayed married. A series of $t$ tests was carried out to determine whether the two groups could be differentiated with regard to the graph-based features of courtship, the men's and women's premarital orientations, or the interpersonal events and patterns. Couples who separated or divorced, compared with those who stayed married, were involved in longer courtships, $t(138) = -2.58$, $p < .03$, courtships in which commitment accelerated more slowly, $t(138) = -1.96$, $p < .05$, and courtships having more downturns in commitment, $t(138) = -1.65$, $p < .10$. Such findings, when considered in the context of those reported earlier concerning premarital antecedents of marital love and satisfaction among the couples who stayed married, would suggest that separated and divorced couples might report more premarital conflict and ambivalence, or less love. However, the two groups of couples were not differentiable in regard to any of these variables. One possible reason for this is that conflict and ambivalence may be more likely to surface in premaritally distressed relationships at times in the relationship other than when the partners think of themselves as a "couple"—the time frame used when the assessments of conflict and ambivalence were made.

Curiosity about the courtships of the separated and divorced couples led me to create profiles of their courtships. I abstracted the courtships of the divorced couples from the narratives provided by the couples. The courtship of Mike and Debbie, described next, provides a sense of the character of courtships that end in divorce shortly after the marriage is consummated.

> Mike and Debbie were both 23-year-old high school graduates when they were married, after a 3-year courtship that on graph paper looks as close to typical as any in the sample. "When I first met her," Mike said, "I just had that feeling she was gonna be the right one. I mean there was just a certain feeling there— there was some kind of pull. Mike reports: "I was very afraid for a long time to actually come out and tell her how I felt. It wasn't long before [we met] that she had broken up from her boyfriend . . . they had been engaged and were gonna get married and she broke it off. . . . I think she was looking for someone

she could depend on, [someone] that she didn't have to take care of. . . . It was very difficult for her to talk to anybody about her problems and she opened up and started talking to me which I'd say gave her a sense of security. . . . Her mother used to get on her back an awful lot, give her a hard time. She would get really upset and then she'd get really mad and then she would finally break down and tell me what was bothering her, which would make her feel a lot better. Anger inside doesn't do no good.''

Debbie's version mirrors Mike's: ''Mother and I just started getting into it all the time . . . he just had the patience and understanding and he sort of helped me through it. I guess it was then that it hit us that we loved each other!'' Later in the interview, she elaborates: ''I was never one to express any feeling at all; I was always quite in a shell, nobody could break through it. I don't know how he did it, but he did.'' Of all the 168 women in the study, Debbie scored lowest on the ''maintenance,'' subscale of the Braiker and Kelley (1979) measure.

The conflicts with her mother continued through the courtship, intensifying at times to physical violence. When she came in late at night one night, her mother came at her with the sweeper hose from the vacuum. She left home for 4 days and by the time she returned she felt ''things were pretty well set.''

It didn't work out that simply, however, and they put off their marriage on several occasions, until Debbie wasn't sure whether Mike would ever be ready to marry. ''He said he wanted to but he was scared. . . . He just made up excuses, first he wanted to buy a house and then he wanted to buy the land and build and I said if we don't get married now, we're never gonna have the money. . . . It's just if you want things you'll get them. . . . I finally got him to make the decision. It's funny but it's the truth. I was at the gynecologist—I've wanted a kid for 2 years, but I couldn't have one without getting married—and I was talking to him about the [physical] problems I've had since I was 13 and he said I'm getting older and that it would be to my advantage [not to wait too long to start a family]. He said 'is there anything else I can do for you today?' and I said 'yeah, call my fiance and tell him to marry me because I want to start my family.' So I went to Mike and I said 'I'm not pressuring you or pushing you into anything but if we are going to get married we better decide soon because the chances [for having a child] are lesser and lesser as I get older and older.' I said 'can we set a date or can't we?' He wanted to set it for June or July, but said April 4th, and that's when we were married.''

It was immediately clear from doing the profiles that most of the couples were young when they began dating each other, and that their courtships had a chaotic quality to them. The observation about the youthfulness of the partners was confirmed statistically, with the separated and divorced spouses being younger, on average, by about 3 years when their relationship was first initiated: [men: $t(138) = 2.58$, $p < .02$; women: $t(138) = 3.24$, $p < .01$].

The chaotic nature of the courtships is more difficult to establish as a systematic finding. It is easy, knowing that a couple separated or divorced, to identify elements in their courtship consistent with that outcome. It is difficult, however, given the multifarious details and the small sample size of separated or divorced couples, to establish specific causal linkages between courtship experiences and marital stability.

## CONCLUSION

In conclusion, I return to the motion picture metaphor to make some final observations concerning variations in how couples cross the bridge from courtship into the early years of marriage. In the film *The Best Years of Our Lives* (Wilder, 1946), the hero, who had lost a limb during World War II, returns home to his prewar sweetheart. She very much wants to marry him, but he, confusing her affection for pity, continuously rejects her overtures. In the end, he comes to appreciate her love and they are married. The development of the relationship makes sense to the audience. Critical praise tends to be given to pictures because they, with reasonably faithfulness, portray what the audience will accept as reality. But motion picture scenarios need not be faithful to empirical reality; they only need to mesh with common acceptance of the bounds of such reality.

In the study of courtship and marriage, in contrast to the moviemaking industry, the goal is to determine which of a set of plausible premarital causes most often operate and with what consequences. The causal pathways are complex, and no researcher is in a position to systematically explore them all. Moreover, the significance of particular potential ''causes'' is often difficult to identify. Such causes are frequently embedded in, and hence covary with, other factors that operate, either singly or in concert, to produce particular effects.

With these qualifiers and observations in place, I draw on the findings to identify key elements that might be incorporated into a movie portraying the transition from courtship into early marriage. The movie would be set in a small town or a rural area in the Appalachian mountains in central Pennsylvania. The story line for the movie would show, as a matter of course, that commitment resonates to forces that pull couples into marriage, such as love, and forces that deter commitment, such as conflict. The movie would highlight, however, the particular bearing men's, rather than women's, investment in the relationship has in pushing couples toward commitment. The movie would also portray how men's ambivalence about the relationship (rather than women's) deflects the course of commitment from marriage. The script writer, in focusing on the significance of men's feelings and motivations, nonetheless would also foreshadow the long-term significance of women's ambivalence for the satisfactoriness of the marriage. Perhaps this could be accomplished by showing women's ambivalence as a reaction to problems that surface in the courtship, or as developing out of knowledge of their partners' ambivalence.

The picture would bring out that the quickness with which couples "fall in love," and the extent to which they are romantically in love during the courtship, does not foretell how they will feel about each other after they have been married for awhile. The length of time that partners dated, how slowly they became committed, how much conflict they experienced in their relationship, and how ambivalent they were premaritally would instead be brought into focus to foreshadow how they feel about each other later. The final element that might be included, one that completes the story and brings it full circle, would show how women's premarital ambivalence, although unrelated to the course of premarital commitment, nonetheless is a precursor of decline in wives' marital love and husbands' marital satisfaction.

The story could be rendered to create a sense of pathos, with the audience slowly realizing that when cupid's arrow is poisoned with ambivalence that love weakens with time, leaving the lovers to wonder, as the song goes, where their love has gone. This picture may not win an Academy Award, but its details will correspond to the reality of most Americans, at least to the extent that what happens to them is similar to what occurred with my research sample. It is perhaps not surprising that celebrated movie courtships—such as that of Elaine and Benjamin in *The Graduate* (Nichols, 1967)—rarely yield sequels. Love can conquer all, at least long enough for some couples to marry, but it is difficult to imagine the heroine's ambivalence about Benjamin as having been set aside, never to surface again. We know what happened *When Harry Met Sally* (Reiner, 1989): There was a slow uptake and a lot of missed signals, but eventually their friendship grew into romance and they were married. But what would the sequel show? Would *Harry and Sally II* be a story of calamity, chaos, or contentment?

## ACKNOWLEDGMENTS

This research was supported by National Institute of Mental Health grant MH-33938. The author would like to thank Gilbert Geis and Catherine Surra for providing helpful comments on earlier drafts of this manuscript.

## REFERENCES

Baxter, L., & Bullis, C. (1986). Turning points in developing romantic relationships. *Human Communication Research, 12*, 469–493.

Bentler, P., & Newcomb, D. (1978). Longitudinal study of marital success and failure. *Journal of Consulting and Clinical Psychology, 46*, 1053–1970.

Berg, J., & McQuinn, R. D. (1986). Attraction and exchange in continuing and noncontinuing dating relationships. *Journal of Personality and Social Personality, 50*, 942–952.

Bergman, I. (Director). (1974). *Scenes from a marriage* [Film]. Stockholm, Sweden: Cinematograph AB.

Berscheid, E., & Walster, E. (1974). A little bit about love. In T. Huston (Eds.), *Foundations of interpersonal attraction* (pp. 355–381). New York: Academic Press.

Braiker, H., & Kelley, H. H. (1979). Conflict in the development of close relationships. In R. L. Burgess & T. L. Huston (Eds.), *Social exchange in developing relationships* (pp. 135–168). New York: Academic Press.

Burch, N. (1973). *Theory of film practice.* New York: Praeger.

Burgess, E., & Wallin, P. (1953). *Engagement and marriage.* Chicago: Lippincott.

Campbell, A., Converse, P., & Rodgers, W. (1976). *Quality of American life: Perception, evaluation, and satisfaction.* New York: Russell Sage.

Cate, R., Huston, T. L., & Nesselroade, J. (1985). Premarital relationships: Toward the identification of alternative pathways to marriage. *Journal of Social and Clinical Psychology, 4*, 3–22.

Eisenstein, S. (1957). *Film form.* Cleveland, OH: World.

Erikson, K. (1976). *Everything in its path: Destruction of community in the Buffalo Creek Flood.* New York: Simon & Schuster.

Fincham, F., & Bradbury, T. (1987). The assessment of marital quality: A reevaluation. *Journal of Marriage and the Family, 49*, 797–809.

Gessner, R. (1968). *The moving image: A guide to cinematic literacy.* New York: Dutton.

Gottman, J. (1979). *Marital interaction: Experimental investigations.* New York: Academic Press.

Gottman, J., & Krokoff, L. (1989). Marital interaction and satisfaction: A longitudinal view. *Journal of Consulting and Clinical Psychology, 57*, 47–53.

Greenblatt, C., & Cottle, T. (1980). *Getting married: A new look at an old tradition.* New York: McGraw-Hill.

Grover, K. J., Russell, C. S., Schumm, W. R., & Paff-Bergen, L. A. (1985). Mate selection processes and marital satisfaction. *Family Relations, 34*, 383–386.

Huston, T. L., McHale, S., & Crouter, A. (1986). When the honeymoon's over: Changes in the marriage relationship over the first year. In R. Gilmour & S. W. Duck (Eds.), *The emerging field of personal relationships* (pp. 109–132). Hillsdale, NJ: Lawrence Erlbaum Associates.

Huston, T. L., & Robins, E. (1982). Conceptual and methodological issues in studying close relationships. *Journal of Marriage and the Family, 44*, 901–925.

Huston, T. L., Robins, E., Atkinson, J., & McHale, S. (1987). Surveying the landscape of marital behavior: A behavioral self-report approach to studying marriage. In S. Oskamp (Ed.), *Family processes and problems. Applied social psychology annual* (Vol. 7, pp. 45–72). Newbury Park, CA: Sage.

Huston, T. L., Surra, C., Fitzgerald, N., & Cate, R. (1981). From courtship to marriage: Mate selection as an interpersonal process. In S. Duck & R. Gilmour (Eds.), *Personal relationships* (Vol. 2, pp. 53–88). London: Academic Press.

Jones, D. (Director). (1983). *Betrayal* [Film]. Hollywood, CA: 20th Century-Fox.

Kelly, E. L., & Conley, J. J. (1987). Personality and compatibility: A prospective analysis of marital stability and marital satisfaction. *Journal of Personality and Social Psychology, 52*, 27–40.

Kelly, C., Huston, T. L., & Cate, R. (1985). Premarital correlates of the erosion of satisfaction in marriage. *Journal of Social and Personal Relations, 2*, 167–178.

Lewis, R., & Spanier, G. (1979). Theorizing about the quality and stability of marriage. In W. Burr, R. Hill, F. Nye, & I. Reiss (Eds.), *Contemporary theories about the family* (Vol. 1, pp. 268–294). New York: The Free Press.

Lloyd, S., & Cate, R. (1985a). The developmental course of conflict in dissolution of premarital relationships. *Journal of Social and Personal Relationships, 2*, 179–194.

Lloyd, S., & Cate, R. (1985b). Attributes associated with significant turning points in premarital relationship development and dissolution. *Journal of Social and Personal Relationships, 2*, 419–436.

Lumet, S. (Director). (1965). *The pawnbroker* [Film]. Hollywood, CA: Landau/Allied Artists.

MacDermid, S., Huston, T. L., & McHale, S. (1990). Changes in marriage associated with the transition to parenthood: Individual differences as a function of sex role attitudes and changes in the division of household labour. *Journal of Marriage and the Family, 52*, 475–486.

Markman, H. (1979). Application of a behavioral model of marriage in predicting relationship satisfaction of couples planning marriage. *Journal of Consulting and Clinical Psychology, 47*, 743–749.

Markman, H. (1981). Prediction of marital distress: A five-year follow-up. *Journal of Consulting and Clinical Psychology, 49*, 760–762.

Miell, D. (1987). Remembering relationship development: Constructing a content for interaction. In R. Burnett, P. McGhee, & D. D. Clarke (Eds.), *Accounting for relationships: Explanation, representation, and knowledge* (pp. 60–73). London: Methuen.

Nichols, M. (Director). (1967). *The graduate* [Film]. Hollywood, CA: Embassy Pictures.

Pudovkin, V. I. (1970). *Film technique and film acting*. New York: Grove.

Reiner, R. (Director). (1980). *When Harry met Sally* [Film]. Hollywood, CA: Castlerock Productions.

Schwartz, N. (1990). Assessing frequency reports of mundane behaviors: Contributions of cognitive psychology to questionnaire construction. In C. Hendrick & M. S. Clark (Eds.), *Research methods in personality and social psychology* (pp. 98–119). Newbury Park, CA: Sage.

Simpson, J., Campbell, B., & Berscheid, E. (1986). The association between romantic love and marriage: Kephart (1967) twice revisited. *Personality and Social Psychology Bulletin, 12*, 363–372.

Spanier, G. (1976). Measuring dyadic adjustment: New scales for assessing the quality of marriage and similar dyads. *Journal of Marriage and the Family, 38*, 15–28.

Surra, C. A. (1985). Courtship types: Variations in interdependence between partners and social networks. *Journal of Personality and Social Psychology, 49*, 357–375.

Surra, C. A. (1987). Reasons for changes in commitment: Variations by courtship type. *Journal of Social and Personal Relationships, 4*, 17–33.

Surra, C. A. (1990). Research and theory on mate selection and premarital relationships in the 1980s. *Journal of Marriage and the Family, 52*, 844–865.

Surra, C. A., Arizzi, P., & Asmussen, L. (1988). The association between reasons for commitment and the development and outcome of marital relationships. *Journal of Social and Personal Relationships, 5*, 47–63.

Surra, C. A., Chandler, M., Asmussen, L., & Wareham, J. (1987). Effects of premarital pregnancy on the development of interdependence in relationships. *Journal of Social and Clinical Psychology, 5*, 123–139.

Surra, C. A., & Huston, T. L. (1987). Mate selection as a social transition. In D. Perlman & S. Duck (Eds.), *Intimate relationships: Development, dynamics, and deterioration* (pp. 89–120). Beverly Hills, CA: Sage.

U.S. Bureau of the Census. (1989). *Marital status and living arrangements: March 1988. Current population reports, Series P-20, No. 433*. Washington, DC. Government Printing Office.

Waller, W. (1938). *The family: A dynamic interpretation*. New York: Cordon.

Whyte, M. K. (1990). *Dating, mating, and marriage*. New York: Aldine de Gruyter.

Wilder, W. (Director). (1946). *The best years of our lives* [Film]. Hollywood, CA: Goldwyn Productions.

Wolfenstein, M., & Leites, N. (1970). *Movies: A psychological study*. New York: Atheneum.

# Chapter 4

# Secret Relationships:
# The Back Alley to Love

Julie D. Lane
Daniel M. Wegner
*University of Virginia*

Vows are exchanged, parents blubber, rice is thrown . . . and the newly wedded couple lives happily ever after. Sigh, this must be love. If we are asked to draw a mental picture of a close relationship, many of us would visualize something along the lines of the traditional public ceremony of marriage. In our culture, this is the essence of togetherness, the front door to a lifelong loving relationship. As much as these images warm our hearts, however, face it—this is an unabashedly idealistic view of how an intimate relationship begins.

In reality, couples may often follow a very different pathway to intimacy, one that is hidden from public view and discussed only in whispers. Romantic partners must sometimes find a back alley to love, one devoid of public commitment, a partnership forged instead through secret meetings and concealed communication. Instead of the solid foundation of a marriage known to all, partners in secret relationships establish their connections without the social support that comes with the consent of their families or friends, without acknowledgment, and without ceremony or ritual. They are strikingly alone in their togetherness, isolated from all the usual accompaniments of conventional romance. However, although the clandestine route they travel is unorthodox, partners in a secret romantic relationship experience emotions and interdependencies that are no less real than those felt by members of a traditional public couple.

Ironically, keeping a close relationship under wraps can even increase the overall intensity of feelings and introduce aspects of obsession to the attraction. Secrecy's power to enhance a relationship derives from the fact that the maintenance of secrecy can become deeply absorbing for the relationship partners.

The main focus of this chapter is detailing just how this back alley—the secret relationship—may work in reaching the goal of intimacy. Like a public ceremony of marriage, secrecy has the power to bond people together in ways that transcend simple togetherness. Partners involved in secret romantic liaisons must use mental control strategies such as suppression of thoughts of the secret and inhibition of relationship-appropriate emotions to prevent themselves from revealing the relationship to outsiders (see Wegner, 1989; Wegner & Schneider, 1989). Even as they are trying to think about their secret on some level to keep track of what must be hidden, they must also try not to think about it, lest these thoughts guide behavior. The drives toward these conflicting mental states can throw the mind of a secret relationship partner into a state of obsessive preoccupation with thoughts of the secret.

To examine how secrecy can intensify a close relationship, it is important to consider the psychology of secrecy in some depth. To begin with, we review the status of secrecy in current psychological theory. Then, we discuss the characteristics that distinguish a secret from a nonsecret relationship. We argue that, due to special constraints of their union, secret relationship partners construct a much different reality than do partners in nonsecret relationships, a reality that is marked by diligent attempts at management of secret thoughts. The chapter then describes the specific cognitive processes that undergird the maintenance of secret relationships, and explores their operation in several studies. Finally, the chapter turns to an examination of the forms of close relationship that secrecy can promote, as distinct from those that arise from more traditional relationship beginnings.

## THE PSYCHOLOGY OF SECRECY

Secrecy has often been recognized as the fundamental factor in the division of the individual from the social group. In essence, once a person finds it necessary to hold something secret from others, the secret detaches the person from others, setting individual thoughts and feelings apart from those that are freely communicated among people. Freud (1913/1953) portrayed this schism between person and society in his writings on social taboos—those behaviors that cannot be performed, and sometimes cannot even be discussed. He argued that taboos reflect societal outrage at the impulses that arise instinctually from individuals, and implied in this that the real or imagined prohibitions that keep a person from telling others about some private thought or deed are the beginning of the person's own individuality.

It is in this sense that secrecy is an important skill required for the healthy mental development of an individual. Prior to the development of a capacity for secrecy, the person is in what Szajnberg (1988) called a symbiotic relationship with the social world, not really separate from others in thought or emotion. Hence, maturation entails the development of an ability to hold information away from the social milieu and to imagine oneself as a repository of information that can be kept from others. Thus, secrecy lets people achieve a sense of their own identity apart from the larger society to which they belong. Tournier (1963/1965) suggested that "to have secrets, to know how to keep them to one's self, to give them up only willingly, constitutes the first action in the formation of the individual" (p. 9), and also proposed that secrets are "indispensable instruments of this emancipation" (p. 8). Secrecy frees people from the confines of total social control and represents the beginning of self-control.

Thus, a secret social relationship is a stepping-off point for many individuals, the beginning of autonomy from family or prior relationships and the path to the development of a new identity. With newfound individuality and isolation from past social connections, however, comes a certain degree of autonomous mental control (Wegner & Erber, 1993). The individual who is capable of secrets from others becomes concerned with controlling his or her thoughts and feelings. Romantic thoughts or emotions that were once uncontrolled and freely expressed become sources of personal concern, aspects of self that must be hidden and dealt with privately. So, although secrecy is critical for creating the beginnings of individuality, it is problematic as well. Secrecy creates the self and at the same time carries the implication that the self is socially undesirable. Things that are secret are often assumed to be disapproved.

Not all secrets are created equally. There are some secrets that are merely interesting and a bit embarrassing. For instance, a friend recently discovered she was related to Vice President Dan Quayle (although quite distantly), and she is very selective about who knows about it. If everyone found out this little tidbit, however, she would not be overly mortified. On the other side of the coin, there are Secrets. This capital S brand includes those that may make others drool upon hearing. The item leading the list of most kept secrets is pretty easy to guess. Yes, it is sex (Hillix, Harari, & Mohr, 1979; Norton, Feldman, & Tafoya, 1974). It is odd that the most common theme of people's secrets is also the subject that most piques others' interest in people's lives. People are mesmerized by the secret sex lives of others. Countless books expound on the subject. Pick a president of the United States, for example—almost any president—and you can probably find some information incriminating him in the improper conduct of his sex life (Giglio, 1991; Morgan, 1976; Ross, 1988).

Even if the secret is not particularly interesting, the very fact that it is secret seems to imbue it with a fascinating and sordid quality. Simmel (1908/1950) explained that, although a secret is neutral and it "has no immediate connection with evil, evil has an immediate connection with secrecy" (p. 331). People assume that whatever is being held from them must be sordid because most of the sordid stories they have heard throughout life have been kept hidden at one time. It is no wonder that there is so much pressure on people who attempt to keep a romantic relationship a secret. They must feel that if they slip and reveal an inkling of their relationship, outsiders will be waiting to pounce to hear all the dirty details.

Everyone knows that people enjoy unraveling other people's secrets, but there are certain benefits that also can befall the secret bearer. Secret keepers can experience considerable excitement and pleasure at maintaining a secret. Ekman (1985) found that when people conceal something from others, as is the case in secrecy, they experience a thrill. He called this feeling "duping delight." He classified three conditions that contribute to the total amount of duping delight experienced: the challenge of the target, the challenge of the lie, and the presence of an appreciative audience. The more that each of these factors is true, the greater will be duping delight.

In instances in which partners decide to keep their relationship with each other a secret, they may unknowingly endow it with an air of mystery and intrigue. Bok (1982) remarked that ". . . secrecy is the carrier of texture and variety. Without it, and without the suspense and wit and unexpectedness it allows, communication would be oppressively dull—lifeless in its own right" (p. 24). Along the same vein, Linquist (1989) explained that for secret adulterous lovers, being discreet becomes a high priority, yet at the same time it increases the excitement. The partners she interviewed who were involved in adulterous liaisons found difficulty in maintaining secrecy, and thus felt intense inner tension even though they appeared calm outwardly.

Why should secrecy in a relationship increase excitement? There is something qualitatively different about secret romantic relationships that distinguishes them from close nonsecret relationships. It is by examining this distinctiveness that the mystery of secrecy's relationship-enhancing effects can be understood.

## THE UNIQUENESS OF SECRET RELATIONSHIPS

There are some fundamental differences in structure between secret and nonsecret relationships. Reality for secret relationship partners is different in many ways. Tefft (1980) observed that the very nature of a relationship and its members are affected by secrecy. Simmel (1950) explained that secrecy expands people's horizons, allowing them to construct two or more realities at any given time. Both partners in secret relationships are responsible for socially constructing and maintaining this aura of secrecy.

The unique reality that partners in secret relationships form creates a psychological boundary between themselves and others (Bok, 1982). The "us" and "them" constructs of secret relationships are distinct from those of nonsecret relationships. In nonsecret relationships, the "us" and "them" groups have full knowledge of each other's existence, or theoretically could without resistance, whereas in secret relationships the awareness among the two groups is inequitable; the "them" group is left unaware of the very essence of the "us." Extra effort must be expended inside the relationship to maintain the "us" in this circumstance.

The conscious separation of "us" and "them" through secrecy implies that if the "them" group knew what the "us" group was hiding, a resulting tension or clash would ensue (Bok, 1982). Thus, secrecy results in a dynamic process between insiders and outsiders (Tefft, 1980). Warren and Laslett (1980) explained that secrecy is distinguished from privacy in that the imposition of the former occurs when it is believed that those excluded from the secret would find the hidden behaviors or thoughts to be insulting or damaging. Partners in covert relationships keep their union a secret to avoid negative repercussions from others. In turn, the valence of a secret actually increases by virtue of the secret keeper disallowing outsiders to glimpse this hidden reality (Richardson, 1988; Simmel, 1908/1950; Tournier, 1963/1965). Just as the value of the secret increases as it is hidden, so does the closeness of the emotional bond between two people who keep a secret from outsiders (Tefft, 1980; Tournier, 1963/1965).

Another distinctive characteristic of secret liaisons is their effortful, nonautomatic nature. Compared with nonsecret relationships, secret relationships require the exertion of additional cognitive energy to control relationship- and partner-related thoughts and actions. This conclusion follows from Gilbert's (1993) observation that it takes work to depart from the truth. He noted that understanding something and believing it are the same thing, and that effortful thought and conscious cognitive adjustment are needed if people are to attach a value of "false" to those propositions they wish to deny or falsify. The things people understand to be true will normally come to mind automatically and effortlessly when situations call them forth. People must then apply extra work to adjust these truths toward whatever social impression they wish them to make. Secret information that people wish to keep from others does not come to mind readily in its denied form (Wegner, Wenzlaff, Kerker, & Beattie, 1981), and wells up instead in forms that must be translated or simply suppressed for social consumption. The same rule can be applied to relationships. People's automatic thoughts about a secret romantic relationship are the uncensored truth, so added work is required each time they think them on the way toward speaking or acting.

This additional exertion required of secret liaison partners is particularly evident whenever the partners are in each others' presence with people from whom they are hiding their relationship. Partners in a hidden relationship sometimes become acutely aware of their shared secret and their separateness from others as a result of the social presence of the clandestine partner (Wegner & Erber, 1993). While the partner is near, the mind goes into overdrive, and concentration on anything else but the partner or the relationship becomes almost impossible. The attempt to control information sometimes takes on a life of its own and gets out of hand. The security measures that the partners establish to prevent their relationship from being discovered become obsessive (Tefft, 1980). This situation definitely contrasts with what occurs when partners in a nonsecret relationship come into contact with each other in a social setting. Nonsecret partners simply see each other approach and then they greet. They do not experience this presence as an intrusive triggering event that suddenly requires massive calculation and subterfuge.

For example, imagine the maneuverings in which two co-workers have to engage to see each other when intracompany dating is strictly forbidden. It is hard enough for the lovers outside of work, always having to look over their shoulders to make sure they do not recognize anyone from the office, but it is the workplace that offers the toughest challenge. When they interact in the presence of others, it takes everything in their willpower to appear calm and collected. Beads of perspiration may form on their brows, their cheeks blaze red, and all the while countless thoughts spin in their minds: "Am I standing too close? . . . Be sure not to smile too broadly. . . . Don't look now. . . . Include others in the conversation. . . . Don't say anything about last night's dinner. . . . Just act normal and try to think of something else."

All this turmoil suggests that the end of a secret relationship could be a relief. If the relationship becomes nonsecret and continues in the public sphere, the need for calculated management of thoughts and emotions would come to an end, and the obsessive preoccupation with the partner and the relationship should wane. Because secrecy is no longer, its cognitive consequences should not endure. Attention can be shifted instead to concentrating on, or at least not avoiding, thoughts of the relationship and this shift results in a reduced level of obsessive preoccupation. A much different scenario can be imagined when secrecy is removed from a relationship because the relationship comes to an end. Partners who have exited secret relationships but maintain continuing secrecy run the risk of being bombarded with thoughts of their old flame for a long, uncomfortable time.

Thus, secrecy is more than a simple social circumstance. It is a complicated endeavor whose dangers introduce lasting intrigues and contingencies. It requires intensive thought, and therefore should be understood as a circumstance that creates a special state of mind. We turn now to the psychological characteristics of this unusual state.

## COGNITIVE EFFECTS OF SECRECY

If people had complete control over their minds, they could have a secret and that would be that. They would have no fear whatsoever of leaking it. However, such perfection remains far from people's grasp. It is not clear whether the mind can operate to keep a secret indefinitely. People cannot keep secrets, including secret relationships, without experiencing some cognitive consequences of that secrecy.

The problem with secrecy is that people try to control their secret-relevant behavior by directing their minds. When the behavior to be controlled is keeping a secret, people attempt to accomplish this by engaging in a mental control strategy, namely thought suppression. Thought suppression is used to keep the ideas of the secret out of mind so that its keeper will not accidentally reveal it. This strategy is enlisted as an aid to inhibiting states of mind that are incompatible with the unwanted behavior (Wegner, 1992). At the same time, however, the secret keeper must retain the secret in mind at some level to make sure that it is not revealed. The maintenance of a secret relationship requires both concentration on appropriate thoughts and suppression of inappropriate ones.

This set of strategies is often used to smooth people's daily interactions with others. One line of evidence for the claim that people use thought suppression in this way when trying to keep a secret comes from a study by Carr and Axsom (1992). Subjects in this study talked with a disabled person who was seated in a wheelchair. Some subjects were instructed specifically not to think of the handicap when they interacted with the disabled person, another group was instructed to allow themselves to think about the handicap during the interaction, and another group was not given a mental control strategy to use.

Those people given the suppression instructions looked much like the no-instruction control group on the dependent measures, in that both groups appeared quite comfortable with the interaction. In contrast, the group asked to think about the handicap showed signs of significant discomfort during the interaction and reported afterward that it was not pleasant. This suggests that the no-instruction control group was naturally using a strategy much like thought suppression to cope with the potentially uncomfortable social encounter. On a postinteraction questionnaire, these two experimental groups compared with the think-about-it group also reported a higher ratio of positive thoughts regarding the disability to total thoughts. Apparently, most people would be quite troubled if they were not allowed to use thought suppression to keep unwanted secret thoughts at bay during an interaction.

Although keeping a secret can sometimes provide temporary relief, as evidenced from the previous study, it is not at all apparent that this inclination works to people's benefit in the long run. People who can truly keep secrets (those people who keep secrets well because they have no one to tell do not count) are a dying breed, almost literally. When people manage to keep a secret from others successfully, they often find resulting, harmful complications such as psychological burnout (Larson, 1985). In Pennebaker and Chew's (1985) research, subjects who tried not to tell a secret also displayed high physiological arousal as indexed by skin conductance level (SCL), which may have serious health consequences over an extended period of time. Letting go of secrets, especially in cases where the secrets are of a traumatic nature, can benefit a person's health outcomes (Pennebaker, Barger, & Tiebout, 1989; Pennebaker & Susman, 1988). This information should help lessen any guilt someone may have about ruining a surprise party or prematurely revealing any gift contents. The next time you slip and tell something you aren't supposed to tell, you now have a justification on health grounds.

It is easy to understand why people who keep secrets experience so much stress. Simmel (1908/1950) aptly described this constant pressure to tell: "The secret puts a barrier between men but, at the same time, it creates the tempting challenge to break through it, by gossip or confession—and this challenge accompanies its psychology like a constant overtone" (p. 334). DePaulo's (1992) work indicated in this vein that keeping secrets places a heavy mental load on a person. She found that it is extremely difficult for people to suppress the nonverbal behavior associated with a particular emotion they are feeling. The secret bearer must concentrate on keeping these nonverbal communication channels from leaking.

Besides controlling nonverbal behavior, secret keepers are faced with the added burden of keeping a tight rein on their mental processes. When the secret bearers are in the presence of those people from whom they want to keep the secret, two simultaneous cognitive maneuvers are at work. The secret keepers must vigilantly hold the secret idea at the back of their minds, and at the same time they try not to think of the secret so they do not act in such a way or say things that will expose the outsider to the secret. Additionally, when a person keeps a secret, much mental baggage becomes attached (Wegner, 1989). A secret bearer has to remember who does and who does not know the secret, as well as what cover story has been simulated for this particular person to hide the secret. As long as secret keepers are in the presence of someone from whom they are intent on keeping the secret, their minds will try to push the secret thought and all related thoughts from consciousness.

Think back to the previously mentioned wheelchair study, in which subjects who were not supplied any strategy to use for interacting with a disabled person and those who suppressed the handicap showed less discomforting thoughts during and after the interactions than subjects who thought about the disability (Carr & Axsom, 1992). However well the suppression strategy worked at decreasing uncomfortable feelings about the handicap during and after the interaction, subjects using this strategy paid for it, in a sense, later. In a subsequent period, they became preoccupied with the thought of that person's disability. Although the suppression and control groups indicated more predominantly positive thoughts compared with those of the nonsuppression group, they indicated a significantly higher level of overall preoccupation with the handicap following the interaction: They could not stop thinking about it.

This study is a choice example that the effects of keeping secrets do not end with thought suppression. There is an interesting phenomenon known as thought rebound that accompanies trying not to think of something (Wegner, Schneider, Carter, & White, 1987). The harder a person tries to suppress thoughts of something, the more these suppressed thoughts may return to consciousness when suppression is subsequently terminated and the thought is invited to mind. A vicious cycle created by thought rebound may perpetuate itself and can eventually create an obsession-like pattern of thoughts. The person tries not to think of the unwanted thought and, later on relaxing the suppression, finds the thought returns to mind. However, it does so intrusively, and therefore engenders yet another attempt at suppression.

This obsessive preoccupation with unwanted thoughts may be a key factor responsible for the difficulty in keeping a secret. As mentioned earlier, secret keepers (in this instance, relationship partners) attempt to suppress thoughts of the secret item so that their behavior does not betray them by inadvertently revealing the secret. Simultaneously, they must actively think about the secret so they know what they should not let slip. People are virtually unable to carry on these dual processes. They find the secret thought returns repeatedly, sometimes in the most inopportune circumstances, and they must put it out of mind again. Over time, they find the thought is recurring at a nightmarish pace, and they must suppress it over and over. They end up deeply preoccupied with thoughts of each other and with the relationship, and they wonder how they have become so obsessed.

This reasoning suggests that people holding a secret will show many of the same cognitive symptoms as people suppressing a thought. For example, both groups should show high levels of cognitive accessibility of the unwanted or secret thought. When these people are placed under some cognitive load, the thought should still be so automatically accessible that it is easily brought to mind. Wegner and Erber (1992) showed this in the case of suppression. In their first study, these researchers had subjects either suppress thoughts of a target word (e.g., *car*) or concentrate on that word. Subjects under these instructions were then asked to make word associates to a series of different word prompts. Subjects under high cognitive load (time pressure to respond) who suppressed the target word responded more often with the target word when supplied with target-related prompts (e.g., *wheel*) than did subjects who concentrated on the target word.

In a second study, Wegner and Erber (1992) had subjects either think or not think about a target word for 5 minutes, and then asked them to perform a computerized Stroop-type color-naming task. Subjects saw words appearing on the screen and were asked to respond with key presses to indicate the color in which the words were printed. During this task, the subjects were asked either to suppress or think about the target word, all the while rehearsing a two-digit number (low load) or a nine-digit number (high load). The study found that subjects who attempted to suppress thoughts under high load as compared with those under low load or those who consciously concentrated on the thought showed slower reaction times on the color-naming task when confronted with the target. Apparently, suppressing a thought increased the likelihood that the cognitive access to the thought interfered with color naming. In sum, suppressing a thought under a cognitive load increases the accessibility of this unwanted thought to consciousness.

These studies were used as a basis for a study by Wegner and Lane (1993), which looked at the extent to which secrecy instigates similar cognitive effects. If people actively suppress thoughts of the secrets when keeping secrets, similar results to the previous hyperaccessibility study should be found. Secret keepers under high cognitive load should show an increased access to and preoccupation with the secret thoughts. Subjects in this study read instructions indicating that the experimenter either knew or did not know their target word (e.g., *mountain*). Subjects who thought the experimenter did not know the target word were instructed to keep it secret from her during the entire experiment. They were told that during the computer task the experimenter would be standing over their shoulder and watching their reactions to guess their target word. Subjects in the secret condition were also told that following the computer task the experimenter would ask them questions to guess the target word. Nonsecret subjects were simply told that the experimenter would be standing over their shoulder during the computer task, and that afterward she would be asking the subject questions about the target word.

Subjects were then given either a two-digit number (low cognitive load) or a nine-digit number (high cognitive load) to rehearse during the computer task. All subjects performed a two-color Stroop reaction time (RT) task on the computer. For each of a series of words appearing on a computer monitor, subjects pressed either a red key or a blue key corresponding to the color in which the word was printed. The words included administrations of the target word, nontarget words, and target-related words. In accord with the prediction, subjects who kept a word secret from the experimenter under high cognitive load showed higher color-naming reaction times for the target word and target-related words than subjects in the other conditions (see Fig. 4.1). Apparently, keeping a secret works to make the secret thought highly accessible to consciousness. The finding that suppression and secrecy both have this effect suggests that secrecy may produce this result by prompting people to suppress the secret thoughts.

The cognitive accessibility of secret thoughts is also likely to influence emotional reactions to the thoughts. For example, Wegner, Shortt, Blake, and Page (1990) discovered that suppressing exciting thoughts resulted in increased sympathetic arousal. Subjects who suppressed the thought of sex compared with thoughts of more neutral topics showed increased SCL. Although this effect waned after a few minutes, for suppression subjects SCL continued to surge whenever subjects reported that the exciting thought intruded on their consciousness. It would seem that keeping a relationship secret, which involves

**COLOR-NAMING REACTION TIME (MS)**

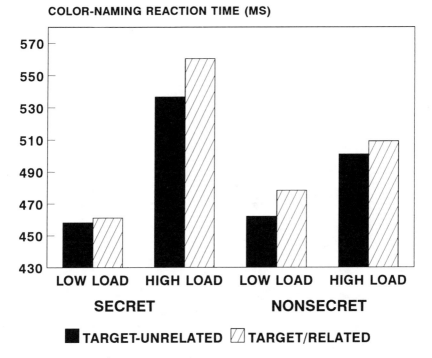

FIG. 4.1. Mean color-naming reaction times. Subjects who were either keeping a target word secret or not made keypress responses to name the colors of target-unrelated versus target words and target-related words under high or low cognitive load. Based on data from Wegner and Lane (1992).

suppression of a potentially very exciting thought, might result in sustained emotional responses to thoughts of the partners.

Research by Wegner and Gold (1993) was also pertinent to this conclusion, because it examined the physiological reactions people experience when trying to suppress thoughts of an old romantic flame. Subjects were instructed to think about a past romantic partner who either was still desired or not, and then they either suppressed thoughts of this old flame or of the Statue of Liberty. Following this period, they were asked to think about the old flame again. It was found that subjects who suppressed thoughts of the still-desired partner showed higher SCL in this final thought period than subjects who suppressed thoughts of the Statue of Liberty or of the undesired old flame. Subjects who suppressed thoughts of an undesired flame talked more about that person in the final period than subjects in the other two conditions, and yet their SCL did not increase to the levels of subjects who suppressed their still-desired relationship. Contrary to common advice to not think about problems, these findings suggest that suppressing an emotional unwanted thought sensitizes people to its recurrence. When these thoughts return after being suppressed for so long, they "shock the system" and create an exaggerated physiological response.

These research findings lead to the general conclusion that secrecy influences the state of mind of the secret keeper. Secret knowledge becomes highly accessible to consciousness, apparently as a result of attempts to suppress it. If the secret is about an emotional topic, the suppression process may introduce the further complication of a chronic emotional reaction to the information. Secrets are the foci of strong cognitive and emotional activity.

## JOINING SECRECY AND ATTRACTION

So far the cognitive and physiological consequences of secrecy have been discussed, but there remains a missing link in the chain leading from secrecy to attraction. We suspect that obsessive preoccupation is the central factor in this relationship. Thoughts of the secret are suppressed and then rebound until partners become preoccupied with the secret relationship and with their secret partner. Tesser's (1978) work tied together these mental processes to partner attraction. He found that thought preoccupation with a particular topic can create an intensification of emotion toward that object. Hence, increased thinking about an originally positive stimulus should result in even higher levels of liking for that stimulus. In fact, Tesser and Paulhus (1978) discovered that partners in romantic relationships reported more love toward each other the more they thought about each other. Applying this research to the secrecy/attraction issue at hand, when partners in a secret relationship experience the components of obsessive preoccupation—cyclical suppression and thought intrusions—with their relationship or partner, this should result in attitude polarization or, in other words, increased attraction.

There are several examples of such effects in the prior research literature. For instance, if secrecy leads to increased attraction between romantic relationship partners, this result should be found in relationships with a simpler format (Wegner, 1989). When a person keeps his or her relationship to the other and his or her feelings secret from that person, as in the case of crushes and fantasies, obsession and attraction should result. Olson, Barefoot, and Strickland (1976) sought to determine if introducing secrecy to a one-sided relationship could increase attraction to the unknowing partner. Subjects who covertly followed around a confederate indicated increased pleasurable excitement and more favorable impressions of the confederate than did subjects who kept surveillance openly, and than did subjects who just watched a videotape of the confederate.

A related effect was observed by Driscoll, Davis, and Lipetz (1972) in their analysis of the influence of psychological reactance (Brehm, 1966) on attraction. From questionnaire measures gathered from couples, they discovered that more parental interference in a love relationship increased the feelings of love between relationship partners. In accord with reactance theory, when partners in a relationship feel that they are being forced to hide their relationship and experience negative pressure toward this relationship from the outside, they will act in such a way to restore their freedom. The more that outside forces attempt to quell the relationship, the more positive feelings and attitudes toward the relationship will become. This "Romeo and Juliet" effect would only seem to be relevant to the secrecy-to-attraction connection in cases in which the forbidden couple uses secrecy to deal with opposing external forces. We suspect that instead of partners' reactance to relationship-opposing forces, it is the secrecy they must use—and its cognitive consequences—that create the heightening of attraction.

Yet another instance of secrecy yielding attraction appeared in research by Baumeister, Wotman, and Stillwell (1993) on the phenomenon of one-sided or unrequited love. In this study, when people looked back on the crush situation, rejecters were more negative in their accounts than were would-be lovers. Although this finding is partially explained in terms of the rejecters being confronted with a no-win situation, there could be more at work. It is also possible that the would-be lovers kept their infatuation somewhat secret, whereas rejecters had no motivation to do this. This secrecy could have led to increased preoccupation with and attraction to the object of their affection.

Past unrequited crushes as well as past relationships were examined more directly in two survey studies by Wegner, Lane, and Dimitri (in press). Subjects answered questions about actual past relationships that they thought about most and least and about unfulfilled past crushes they thought about most and least. They then indicated the degree to which each of these relationships had been secret at the time. Predictions were that the past relationships and crushes still thought about most often would be the ones that had been secret while they were ongoing. In fact, subjects indicated that past relationships and crushes they currently thought about were more likely to have been secret than those past love interests on which they no longer ruminated. This finding supports the notion that secrecy promotes romantic preoccupations or obsessions. The second study (Wegner et al., in press) examined how much individuals' reports of the secrecy of past relationships covaried with their reports of current preoccupation with those relationships. Results showed that current obsessive preoccupation did indeed significantly help predict which relationships had been secret.

Although these studies lend credence to the argument that secrecy leads to thought preoccupation of relationship partners, no firm causal connection can be established. To test experimentally the idea that secrecy of a relationship causes partners to become preoccupied with each other and the relationship, which then leads to their further attraction toward each other, a touching study was conducted.

## THE FOOTSIE STUDY

The essence of the dynamic interplay between secrecy and attraction is best displayed in a surreptitious game of footsie under the table. Many a flame has been sparked in such a sneaky (or sneakerless) manner. Footsie-playing partners who are at a table with other people are in close proximity and must be careful not to reveal their secret touchings. Maintaining this covert relationship requires every move and word to be guarded. Everyone who plays footsie, ticklish and nonticklish alike, must face the challenge of devising a strategy to keep their secret relationship from becoming public during interactions with others. It is possible that keeping this involvement a secret can lead the partners to grow preoccupied with thoughts of each other, thereby increasing their attraction.

The purpose of our footsie study (Wegner et al., in press, Study 3) was to examine whether mixed-gender laboratory pairs who kept their physical foot contact a secret had increased thought preoccupation with and attraction toward each other. Predictions were that subjects who kept covert foot contact would indicate greater attraction to their partners, due to obsessive preoccupation with partner and relationship-related thoughts, than subjects who did not keep foot contact secret or who did not make foot contact at all.

Unacquainted subjects were assembled in groups of four, with same-gender subjects sitting diagonally from each other. They were then told that they were going to be teammates in a card game called the "Communication Game" with the person across from them, thus forming two mixed-gender pairs. Team members then received identical instructions from the experimenter. Subjects in the contact condition read that their job was to play the game using a method of natural nonverbal communication: They were to keep their feet in contact with their partner's feet the entire time. The contact pairs in the secret condition were also told that they were not to inform the other team of their foot contact. Contact subjects in the nonsecret condition read that it was acceptable for them to let the other team know what they were doing. Noncontact teams read instructions saying that the other team would be communicating nonverbally and that all they needed to do was to play the game. After showing everyone how to play the card game, the experimenter left the room and allowed the teams to play the game for 10 minutes. When she returned, she split up the males and females into different rooms and had them complete two questionnaires assessing their attraction for their partner versus the opposite-gender member of the other team and the degree to which they were preoccupied with thoughts about their partner versus the other.

Analyses on a composite measure of attraction revealed that subjects who kept their foot contact secret reported greater attraction toward their partner than subjects who did not play footsie. In line with our expectations on the power of secrecy, subjects who played footsie secretly also indicated more attraction to their partners than subjects who played footsie in the open. Quite a different pattern of results was found for subjects who did not make foot contact. Among these no-contact bystander couples, subjects who were aware of the other team's nonsecret touching reported greater attraction than did those noncontact subjects who did not know the other team was touching.

A behavioroid measure that asked the subjects how much they wanted to be in a future study with their partner versus the opposite-gender member of the other team was also examined as a potential indicator of attraction. Analyses from this measure were consistent with those from the attraction measure. Subjects who kept their physical relationship a secret had higher average scores on this measure than subjects who had no foot contact or than those who had contact but did not keep it secret.

The mechanism underlying the secrecy-to-attraction process is hypothesized to be the obsessive preoccupation with thoughts of the relationship or partner. As a measure of this, thought preoccupation was assessed by a single questionnaire item asking how much thoughts of the partner kept popping to mind. In the secret condition, teams that made foot contact reported higher preoccupation with their partner than teams that did not. There was a trend in the data for teams that made foot contact secretly to indicate greater preoccupation than those teams that did so openly, although this was not significant. When thought preoccupation was covaried out of the analyses on attraction and behavioroid measures, there was no significant interaction of secrecy and foot contact for the attraction or behavioroid measures. Thus, obsessive preoccupation seemed to be a key element for the influence of secret contact on attraction. These results support the idea that secret relationships are indeed a back alley to love.

Mood and misattribution of arousal were tested as possible mediators of secrecy's influence on partner attraction. Subjects' self-reports of good mood, bad mood, and nervousness did not show patterned increases or decreases in the secret contact condition. From these findings, mood and misattribution of arousal alternatives were not given any support. It seems that of all explanations of the secrecy/attraction connection proffered as of yet, obsessive preoccupation stands out as the most likely mechanism.

Although the thrust of this chapter has been on the positive emotions that secrecy can bring to partners in secret relationships, there is another side to secrecy's effects, one that may bring forward some of the more unseemly behaviors in relationships. Compared with the ceremony of marriage, the ordeal of secrecy can have some unexpected influences on the form the relationship may take. In the next section, we describe how imposing secrecy on a relationship can pave the way for deviant behaviors and thought processes to take shape in these relationships.

## SECRECY'S EMPOWERMENT OF DEVIANCE

There are two effects of secrecy that abet the creation of abnormal patterns of behavior and thinking in close relationships: Secrecy isolates relationship partners from external others, and it promotes obsessive thinking about the relationship. In nature, when a particular species of animal or plant is isolated from others of its kind, the wheels of evolution can turn to concoct eventually quite a different form of what originally was. Isolation can work in a similar manner with relationships. Secrecy allows aberrant behaviors or thoughts in relationships to occur unbridled and untouched by outsiders. Secret relationships give the appearance that their partners are wrapped up in a warm, dry cocoon, safely secluded from the realities of the outside world. In this unchecked hideaway, a strange new relationship can evolve, one in which any oddity that arises can mushroom into full-fledged deviance.

It maintains a sense of rightness with the world to think that those people engaged in relationships characterized by kinky and perverse behavior belong to subcultures far removed from the more respectable society. However, secrecy enables these deviant patterns of behavior in close relationships to develop, due to isolation from disapproving others, in the home or the office right next to yours. For example, in many seemingly happy and "normal" families, incestuous relations are maintained and perpetuated by a conspiracy of silence (Christiansen & Blake, 1990). Partners in physically and mentally abusive relationships also hide themselves behind the shield of secrecy (Meares & Orlay, 1988). Even the abused party keeps this unhealthy relationship secret from outsiders due to reasons such as fear of the abuser, embarrassment, and so on. By keeping this relationship secret, the abusing and the abused partners are not allowing external forces to intervene and discredit the structure of the relationship (Ferraro & Johnson, 1989).

Sheltered as they are from the scrutiny of the outside world, roles and interaction routines within the relationship can be constructed without regard to socially normal conventions. Quirks in the relationship can be nurtured in the hothouse atmosphere of secrecy and grow into bizarre patterns. Like the minor oddities or socially disapproved activities that may be kept secret by an individual, and that therefore can develop privately into serious obsessions and perversions, activities of the secret couple that begin on caprice can develop into truly eccentric interaction practices. For example, in her interview study of single women involved in secret affairs with married men, Richardson (1988) discovered that secret relationship partners form their own realities by creating unique rituals and symbolic objects.

The predilection toward obsessive thought is the other effect of secrecy that empowers development of deviance in close relationships. Many lovers are obsessed with partners during the relationship, but for secret lovers the thought preoccupation has a tendency to be that much more intense. Thus, obsessive thinking about the partner and the relationship might continue for a long time. Secrecy in these cases may be imposed on the aspects of the relationship relating to the abusive or socially disapproved behavior, rather than the relationship. The victim may be ashamed and keep the abuse from others, and the abuser may insist on secrecy as a way to maintain the inequitable relationship. But both victim and abuser may find themselves cognitively preoccupied with the relationship because of the secrecy that has been imposed on this aspect of it. Even if their thoughts about each other have little resemblance to love or attachment in the usual senses, their thoughts may become so intrusive and uncontrollable that they invite the self-perception of obsession. Victim, abuser, or both may be caught up in a remarkably persistent fascination with their destructive relationship for the very reason that they have kept it from public view.

Perhaps secrecy magnifies the qualities of whatever relationship it touches. If it is used to hide a healthy relationship, it may enhance it by adding more zing. But if it is used to hide an unhealthy relationship, its secluding effect and the tendency toward obsessive thought that it produces can form a strange new creature or, in the worst case, a monster.


## CONCLUSION

On the topic of romance, 17th-century English writer Behn (1686) held that "Love ceases to be a pleasure when it ceases to be a secret." Our analysis of the role of secrecy in close relationships concurs with this observation—at least in the general suggestion that keeping a relationship secret can promote partners' psychological attachment. We do not really know that secrecy is a key ingredient for love. For that matter, it is not clear at all that secrecy enhances partners' interdependence, that it yields greater compatibility, or that it promotes greater satisfaction or ease of interaction. In other words, we are not in a position to argue that secrecy influences relationship quality, structure, or degree of satisfaction.

Rather, secrecy has personal effects on the psychology of each partner. It increases each partner's tendency to try at times to suppress thoughts of the other and the relationship, it increases the degree to which partners experience thoughts of the relationship in an intrusive manner, and it intensifies the emotions that the partner feels about the relationship. When there is reason for love, all this concentration may make love bloom. But in this sense, it may be that secrecy forms a false attachment, a connection that is forged in each person's mental turmoil rather than in the crucible of relationship development. When the secret is revealed and the confusion following a "coming out" subsides, there may be little that remains on which a successful partnership can be built. This fate is not inevitable, of course, because the intense attention and emotion focused on the relationship during its secret phase could also lead to the discovery of lasting interaction patterns and valued partner traits that could form the foundation for a new life in the open. Whether people enter a relationship from the back alley or the front door, it may make no difference once they are inside.

# REFERENCES

Baumeister, R. F., Wotman, S. R., & Stillwell, A. M. (1993). Unrequited love: On heartbreak, anger, guilt, scriptlessness, and humiliation. *Journal of Personality and Social Psychology, 64*, 377–394.

Behn, A. (1686). *The lover's watch*. London: Vinecourt.

Bok, S. (1982). *Secrets: On the ethics of concealment and revelation*. New York: Pantheon.

Brehm, J. W. (1966). *A theory of psychological reactance*. New York: Academic Press.

Carr, K., & Axsom, D. (1992, August). *Thought suppression during interactions with victims*. Paper presented at the meeting of the American Psychological Association, Washington, DC.

Christiansen, J. R., & Blake, R. H. (1990). The grooming process in father–daughter incest. In A. L. Horton, R. L. Johnson, L. M. Roundy, & D. Williams (Eds.), *The incest-perpetrator: A family member no one wants to treat* (pp. 88–98). Newbury Park, CA: Sage.

DePaulo, B. M. (1992). Nonverbal behavior and self-presentation. *Psychological Bulletin, 111*, 203–243.

Driscoll, R., Davis, K. E., & Lipetz, M. E. (1972). Parental interference and romantic love: The Romeo and Juliet effect. *Journal of Personality and Social Psychology, 24*, 1–10.

Ekman, P. (1985). *Telling lies: Clues to deceit in the marketplace, politics, and marriage*. New York: W. W. Norton.

Ferraro, K. J., & Johnson, J. M. (1989). How women experience battering: The process of victimization. In D. H. Kelly (Ed.), *Deviant behavior* (3rd ed., pp. 247–264). New York: St. Martin's.

Freud, S. (1953). Totem and taboo. In J. Strachey (Ed.), *The standard edition of the complete psychological works of Sigmund Freud* (Vol. 13, pp. 1–162). London: Hogarth. (Original work published 1913)

Giglio, J. N. (1991). *The presidency of John F. Kennedy*. Lawrence, KS: University Press of Kansas.

Gilbert, D. T. (1993). Assent of man: Mental representation and the control of belief. In D. M. Wegner & J. W. Pennebaker (Eds.), *Handbook of mental control* (pp. 57–87). Englewood Cliffs, NJ: Prentice-Hall.

Hillix, W. A., Harari, H., & Mohr, D. A. (1979). Secrets. *Psychology Today, 13*, 71–76.

Larson, D. G. (1985). Helper secrets: Invisible stressors in hospice work. *American Journal of Hospice Care, 2*, 35–40.

Linquist, L. (1989). *Secret lovers*. Lexington, MA: Lexington Books.

Meares, R., & Orlay, W. (1988). On self-boundary: A study of the development of the concept of secrecy. *British Journal of Medical Psychology, 61*, 305–316.

Morgan, K. S. (1976). *Past forgetting: My love affair with Dwight D. Eisenhower*. New York: Simon & Schuster.

Norton, R., Feldman, C., & Tafoya, D. (1974). Risk parameters across types of secrets. *Journal of Consulting Psychology, 21*, 450–454.

Olson, J. M., Barefoot, J. C., & Strickland, L. H. (1976). What the shadow knows: Person perception in a surveillance situation. *Journal of Personality and Social Psychology, 34*, 583–589.

Pennebaker, J. W., Barger, S. D., & Tiebout, J. (1989). Disclosures of traumas and health among Holocaust survivors. *Psychosomatic Medicine, 51*, 577–589.

Pennebaker, J. W., & Chew, C. H. (1985). Behavioral inhibition and electrodermal activity during deception. *Journal of Personality and Social Psychology, 49*, 1427–1433.

Pennebaker, J. W., & Susman, J. R. (1988). Disclosures of traumas and psychosomatic processes. *Social Science Medicine, 26*, 327–332.

Richardson, L. (1988). Secrecy and status: The social construction of forbidden relationships. *American Sociological Review, 53*, 209–219.

Ross, S. (1988). *Fall from grace: Sex, scandal, and corruption in American politics from 1702 to the present*. New York: Ballantine Books.

Simmel, G. (1950). *The sociology of Georg Simmel* (Kurt H. Wolff, Trans.). Glencoe, IL: The Free Press. (Original work published 1908)

Szajnberg, N. (1988). The developmental continuum from secrecy to privacy in a psychodynamic milieu. *Residential Treatment for Children & Youth, 6*, 9–28.

Tefft, S. K. (1980). Secrecy, disclosure, and social theory. In S. K. Tefft (Ed.), *Secrecy, a cross-cultural perspective* (pp. 35-74). New York: Human Sciences Press.

Tesser, A. (1978). Self-generated attitude change. In L. Berkowitz (Ed.), *Advances in experimental social psychology* (Vol. 11, pp. 289-338). New York: Academic Press.

Tesser, A., & Paulhus, D. (1978). Toward a causal model of love. *Journal of Personality and Social Psychology, 34,* 1095-1105.

Tournier, P. (1965). *Secrets* (J. Embry, Trans.). Richmond, VA: John Knox Press. (Original work published 1963)

Warren, C., & Laslett, B. (1980). Privacy and secrecy: A conceptual comparison. In S. K. Tefft (Ed.), *Secrecy: A cross-cultural perspective* (pp. 25-34). New York: Human Sciences Press.

Wegner, D. M. (1989). *White bears and other unwanted thoughts: Suppression, obsession, and the psychology of mental control.* New York: Viking.

Wegner, D. M. (1992). You can't always think what you want: Problems in the suppression of unwanted thoughts. In M. Zanna (Ed.), *Advances in experimental social psychology* (Vol. 25, pp. 193-225). San Diego, CA: Academic Press.

Wegner, D. M., & Erber, R. (1992). The hyperaccessibility of suppressed thoughts. *Journal of Personality and Social Psychology, 63,* 903-912.

Wegner, D. M., & Erber, R. (1993). Social foundations of mental control. In D. M. Wegner & J. W. Pennebaker (Eds.), *Handbook of mental control* (pp. 36-56). Englewood Cliffs, NJ: Prentice-Hall.

Wegner, D. M., & Gold, D. B. (1993). *Fanning old flames: Arousing romantic obsession through thought suppression.* Manuscript submitted for publication.

Wegner, D. M., & Lane, J. D. (1993). *The cognitive consequences of secrecy.* Unpublished manuscript.

Wegner, D. M., & Lane, J. D., & Dimitri, S. (in press). The allure of secret relationships. *Journal of Personality and Social Psychology.*

Wegner, D. M., & Schneider, D. J. (1989). Mental control: The war of the ghosts in the machine. In J. S. Uleman & J. A. Bargh (Eds.), *Unintended thought* (pp. 287-305). New York: Guilford.

Wegner, D. M., Schneider, D. J., Carter, S. R., III, & White, T. L. (1987). Paradoxical effects of thought suppression. *Journal of Personality and Social Psychology, 53,* 5-13.

Wegner, D. M., Shortt, J. W., Blake, A. W., & Page, M. S. (1990). The suppression of exciting thoughts. *Journal of Personality and Social Psychology, 58,* 409-418.

Wegner, D. M., Wenzlaff, R., Kerker, R. M., & Beattie, A. E. (1981). Incrimination through innuendo: Can media questions become public answers? *Journal of Personality and Social Psychology, 40,* 822-832.

# Chapter 5

# Domains of Experience: Investigating Relationship Processes From Three Perspectives

Harry T. Reis
*University of Rochester*

*God is in the details.*
—attributed to Ludwig Mies van der Rohe

It is perhaps trite to note that the fabric of a relationship is contained in the social events that involve its members. Far from being a simple clarion call to an event-based research program, this assertion points to a set of concerns and assumptions that demonstrate how difficult it may be to study relationships from the perspective of interaction events. The theoretically sophisticated researcher, well read in communication theory, social psychology, and sociology, knows that interaction is strongly influenced by contextual variables. From personality theory and developmental psychology, we have learned that individuals have meaningfully unique ways of construing their experience, and that these construals may be what matters most. From personal experience, we know that the thoughts, feelings, and content of social interaction do not stand apart from day-to-day activities and goals; rather, they are intrinsically woven into the ebb and flow of everyday life.

These considerations suggest that a full understanding of the importance of relationships in human endeavors requires an appreciation of the events that transpire in ongoing, daily socializing. Yet we did not always have conceptual models or methodological options for disentangling these levels of analysis from one another. Heretofore, researchers were faced, in the most general sense, with the choice between two paradigms: experiments and self-generated summaries. (This latter category, described later, includes most questionnaires and many structured interviews.) To be sure, there were options within these categories. Experiments could be true experiments or quasi-experiments, and they could be conducted in laboratories or in field settings. But experimental research is limited to studying a single setting, making it difficult to examine more than a small set of contextual variations. Self-generated summary methods are even more diverse. Questionnaires and interviews can be highly structured or open ended, and they can be administered anonymously or face to face. But they usually involve recall and retrospection, as well as an awareness of details and variations to which most people are generally oblivious.

In the decision tree of research strategies, these two approaches traditionally provided the first branches between which an irrevocable choice had to be made. Although this choice was often, and appropriately, based on the well-known pros and cons of each method (Montgomery & Duck, 1991), the decision to pursue one or the other strategy necessarily entailed various disciplinary traditions, method effects, alternative explanations, and potential threats to internal or external validity. These factors have often made it difficult for researchers to find ways to study everyday, spontaneous social interaction in its natural context.

In this chapter, I describe an alternative to these two approaches—one that exemplifies a growing family of methods for examining daily activity in some detail. Many variations on this theme are being developed, some of which are not entirely new. What is most novel about these methods is that they focus attention on a class of events different from those that relationship researchers traditionally study. These events are the individual events that comprise everyday social life (i.e., the feelings, thoughts, and activities that occur in people's daily encounters with others). The study of everyday life events, and especially of the processes that underlie them, has the potential to add new dimensions to our understanding of personal relationships.

The choice among research methods, as described earlier, is often thought to be largely methodological. Although this is of course true, focusing on methodology obscures a more important conceptual distinction: the phenomenal domain to which research applies. The nature of these domains is described shortly. Experiments, self-generated summaries, and diary methods each address relationships from a different perspective. As such, each method is best used to ask somewhat different questions about the same general processes or behaviors. Therefore, findings from these distinct perspectives should not be expected to map onto one another perfectly. Indeed, discrepancies may be a valuable source of insight into the impact of methodological, contextual, and individual difference factors. Moreover, as a set, these three approaches can be used to triangulate around a given phenomenon or theoretical account, not only to ensure that findings are not method bound, but also to demonstrate that a given principle applies across domains. The primary advantage of diary measures, relative to self-generated summaries and experiments, is their ability to demonstrate the relevance and operation of interaction and relationship processes in spontaneous, natural social activity.

## THE CONCEPTUAL RATIONALE:
## THREE DOMAINS OF INQUIRY

Social scientists have recently become interested in the nature and impact of daily experience (DeVries, 1992; Tennen, Suls, & Affleck, 1991). The justification for this focus represents a subtle, but nevertheless significant, paradigm shift. In the past, much attention has been directed at major life events and landmark occurrences (e.g., marriage and divorce; coping with serious illness, injury, or death; and work or family transitions). The daily experience approach, in contrast, is concerned with the multitude of "small events" that comprise everyday activity and thought. This is not to suggest that major life events do not matter—of course they do. But the daily experience approach contends that the recurrent "mundane, little experiences" of everyday life also matter. The phrase "mundane, little experiences" refers to the many and varied thoughts, feelings, and actions that fill most of people's waking time and occupy the vast majority of conscious attention.

Daily event research is predicated on two general assumptions. First, although a given event may be inconsequential, the cumulative impact of many of these events over time is likely to be considerable. The second assumption is that the study of daily experience provides unique and novel insights into an understanding of human behavior (Larson & Csikszentmihalyi, 1983). This is primarily because these phenomena, embedded as they are in the ebb and flow of spontaneous, ongoing activity, are the substantive content of human thought and action. Illustrations of this point are provided later in this chapter.

The daily experience approach did not originate in relationship research. Some of the earliest studies were conducted in clinical or industrial settings (cf. Wheeler & Reis, 1991). Later, Csikszentmihalyi, Larson, and Prescott (1977) developed the Experience Sampling Method (ESM) for examining the nature and distribution of thoughts, feelings, and behaviors in everyday life. This approach may be especially valuable in relationship research. As Duck (1988) and Hinde (1987), among others, have noted, relationships emerge from interactions. Although this process is not well understood, it seems reasonable to presume that certain characteristics of interactions, as they are interpreted and assimilated by the participants, give rise to general perceptions about a relationship. These features are likely to arise repeatedly in the ebb and flow of contact between two persons. But there are several reasons why systematic patterns may only be evident across multiple interactions.

First, social contacts between two partners usually vary widely in nature and function: Some interactions are intimate and emotionally engaging; others involve companionship or routine maintenance tasks; and still others are trivial and uninteresting. A second reason is the likelihood that relationship patterns may only emerge from contingency analyses of interactions: For example, the type of interactions that follow a particularly distressing conversation; how one partner responds to particular life circumstances of the other; or how they share different roles and responsibilities. Third, the significance of social interactions often depends on the manner in which individuals interpret them. For example, an intimate self-disclosure may be seen as an attempt to create intimacy, seek advice, or manipulate the other. To document how individual interaction events and characteristics come to produce the sense of a relationship, a central task for relationship researchers, it is necessary to track these processes across the stream of ongoing interaction.

I noted earlier that the various approaches to studying relationships were each associated with a particular phenomenal domain. I now describe these three domains. They are entitled reconstructed experience, exemplary experience, and ongoing experience. Because ongoing experience is least familiar, I contrast it with the other two approaches. In doing so, my aim is not to imply that one or another strategy is generally preferable, but that these three approaches should be viewed as complementary. Each offers a somewhat different perspective on interaction and relationships; their synthesis within a single research program with a unified conceptual aim is likely to be particularly fruitful.

## The Domain of Reconstructed Experience

Social science research, and relationship research in particular, commonly relies on self-report questionnaires to describe past experience. Herein, subjects may be asked to evaluate and summarize their past experiences with a particular class of events (e.g., "How often have you socialized with your close friends during the past month?"). Alternately, some questionnaires ask subjects to characterize their feelings about some facet of their lives (e.g., "How do you feel when you do poorly on a test?" and "How do you react when faced with a difficult challenge?"). Earlier, I referred to such methods as self-generated summaries because they require that subjects consider all past experiences in the area of interest, and then produce a summary assessment of that experience. These summaries may be collected in writing or in an oral interview. In either case, the defining feature is that subjects provide some sort of aggregated evaluation of prior activities.

Self-generated summaries are an important source of data about personal impressions, but researchers miss the mark when these reports are interpreted as objective information (i.e., as an unbiased or otherwise accurate summary of the past) or even as consensually agreeable evaluations. That is because these reports are the product of an extensive and complex set of cognitive and motivational processes by which experiences are encoded, stored, retrieved, and given personal meaning (Erdelyi, 1974; Fiske & Taylor, 1991; Ross, 1989). Thus, a critical caveat is in order whenever self-generated summaries are used: They represent the individual's reconstruction of past experience and not an objective account of that experience. Of course, in many instances such impressions are properly the focus of research interest, and in these cases self-generated summaries are the appropriate tool.

There are two broad reasons for this caution, one methodological and the other conceptual. The methodological reason is that people's accuracy in recalling and summarizing past events, even over relatively short time spans, is limited. This refers not only to the ability to remember those events, with or without experimenter-provided cues, but also to the capacity to recapture thoughts and feelings at a later time and then describe them accurately. Some of the factors that constrain recall stem from the cognitive limitations of human information processing, whereas others are more motivational. They include the following.

***Recall.*** All other things being equal, the greater the number of events to be described, the less salient each event in memory. Also, the longer the time interval between occurrence and assessment, the more likely it is that people will have difficulty recalling an event. Transitory factors like mood can significantly alter the impressions that subjects "remember." For example, mood at the time of report may influence the recall and evaluation of social action (Erber, 1991; Forgas, Bower, & Krantz, 1984).

***Selection.*** When people are asked to describe past activities within a given area (e.g., marital interaction or emotional expression) it is unclear how they choose which particular events to report. After all, people typically have multiple and diverse experiences within such categories. Researchers often assume that the events being described are representative of the more general class, or perhaps randomly selected. But studies of cognitive heuristics have repeatedly shown that the most accessible instances (i.e., cases that come readily to mind) are more likely to be chosen than more mundane instances. Undoubtedly, certain social interactions are more memorable, and hence accessible, than others (e.g., traumatic arguments, deeply passionate encounters, betrayed trusts, and shared secrets). Furthermore, recency biases may make yesterday's lunchtime conversation more accessible. (In fact, there is a need for systematic research to determine what features make different social encounters more or less available. Affective content, recency, and frequency are three reasonable candidates; Gilligan & Bower, 1984; Schwarz, 1990; Wyer & Srull, 1986.)

***Aggregation.*** Even if people could remember all relevant instances, it is not clear how they would conduct the mental arithmetic needed to produce a summary judgment. Suppose Gail and Phil have socialized 15 times during the past 2 weeks. Suppose further that 3 of those interactions were great fun, 2 were mildly amusing, 2 were annoying, 1 was outright hostile, and the remaining 7 were decidedly mundane. When asked how enjoyable her interaction with Phil was, how will Gail combine these 15 events to a single estimate? Several heuristics might be useful: the simple arithmetic mean; means weighted by duration, intimacy, or emotional intensity (Anderson, 1981); attention to the most recent, the most unusual, the most available, or the most representative interaction (Tversky & Kahneman, 1982); or choice of that instance that presents herself in the most positive light. Questionnaire research typically assumes that aggregation is accomplished in some straightforward fashion, or at least that aggregation processes operate equivalently across subjects. These assumptions seem questionable, however. Hedges, Jansdorf, and Stone (1985) showed that subjects' reports of their overall mood for a given day were more likely to resemble extreme momentary moods than true averages of ongoing states.

*Motivated Distortion.*    Self-serving motives may substantially influence people's impressions and recollections (Deaux, 1992; Fiske & Taylor, 1991). In their reports, people sometimes strive to create certain impressions (e.g., Baumeister, 1982; Jones & Pittman, 1982), either consciously or without awareness. Research and practice in the psychodynamic tradition has established that defense mechanisms, such as repression, denial, and projection, may alter memories of the past (Westen, 1992). In current theorizing, the self is conceptualized as a system for organizing information about ourselves, and for regulating interaction with the social environment in a manner that fulfills individual needs. People are better able to remember events that are consistent with their self-conceptions than events that diverge (Higgins & Bargh, 1987; Swann & Read, 1981). Ambiguous events are often interpreted in a manner than enhances their consistency with existing self-conceptions (Swann, 1990). As elaborated later, when past events are inconsistent with people's self-concepts or important needs, people often reinterpret the past, not randomly, but in a way that maximizes the validation, coherence, or adaptiveness of their memories for the self (Ross, 1989; Sanitioso, Kunda, & Fong, 1990; Steele, 1988). This position is of course similar to that of functional theories (Smith, Bruner, & White, 1956), which hold that expressed attitudes must be functional, or useful, to the self in some manner.

The notion that motivated distortion is psychologically useful for the self implies that the issues involved in autobiographical reconstruction are not just methodological problems to be circumvented. If retrospective impressions deviated from contemporaneous accounts solely by virtue of the limitations of human memory and cognition, then researchers would only need to follow subjects on their daily rounds with a lightweight, unobtrusive camcorder. With suitable coding, judges would be able to extract thorough and highly accurate assessments of a subject's social experiences from these records. Such data would undoubtedly be valuable, but they would omit a crucial ingredient: the subject's personal, idiosyncratic interpretation of those experiences. As argued previously, these interpretations are likely to shed the most revealing light on the processes by which objective events and interactions acquire psychological meaning.

This process is nicely illustrated by two research programs. Ross (1989) proposed that recollections of personal history are guided more by implicit theories of the self than by the actual content of prior events. In one representative study (McFarland, Ross, & DeCourville, 1989), for 4 to 6 weeks, women kept daily records of the degree to which they had experienced various menstrual symptoms on that day. They also completed questionnaires describing their personal beliefs about menstrual symptoms. Two weeks later, subjects were asked to recall the symptoms they had previously described. These ratings resembled their beliefs about menstrual symptoms better than they resembled their actual symptoms, as had been previously recorded. Similarly, McFarland and Ross (1987) had university students evaluate their dating partners a few months apart. When asked at the second rating to recall their earlier impressions, subjects' responses were more similar to their current feelings than to their actual prior ratings. This was especially true for traits that are generally believed to be stable over time. These studies indicate that when people try to recall past feelings, they are likely to rely on present states and personal understandings of the qualities under scrutiny to "decide" how they must have felt, rather than directly accessing reliable mental images of those events.

A recent set of studies by Sanitioso et al. (1990) further exemplified this principle. They hypothesized and found that when people are motivated to believe that they possess a given trait, they may bolster their desired self-conceptions by selectively searching autobiographical memory for relevant supporting evidence. Of course, this process is constrained by the limits of available memories. But most people have had diverse experiences during their lives, making it relatively easy to locate in memory exemplars of many different traits. For example, most people can easily recall a time when they were exceptionally supportive to a friend in need; they can also remember times when they were aloof and unhelpful. This process is similar to the hypothesis-confirmatory bias that has been shown in studies of judgments about others (Snyder & Swann, 1978). People appear to use a "satisficing" rather than an optimizing strategy in scanning their personal histories—ceasing information search once a feasible answer has been found (cf. Shaklee & Fischhoff, 1982).

It therefore seems reasonable to conclude that self-generated assessments about the past may substantially reflect the self-conceptions that people are motivated to believe they possess. Once again, this need not be considered a methodological liability; it simply indicates that such measures must be interpreted in this rarified light. Developmental psychologists who study retrospections about childhood have learned to live with this limitation, and even thrive on it. Similarly, relationship researchers can extract important principles about the ways in which people understand their present and past relationships from this perspective (e.g., Harvey, Weber, & Orbuch, 1990; Metts, Sprecher, & Cupach, 1991).

The importance of the self in giving meaning to reports of relationship events also has been illustrated by research in the adult attachment tradition. As Bowlby (1969) first proposed, and subsequent research has supported, adults possess mental models about close relationships (Main, Kaplan, & Cassidy, 1985; see Hazan & Shaver, in press, for a review). Presumably, these models, sometimes referred to as inner working models, arise from prior experiences in significant childhood and, perhaps to a lesser extent, adult relationships. Once established, these mental models serve as prototypes or standards against which the behavior of current or potential interaction partners is evaluated and interpreted. Thus, consider how the three standard attachment types might each describe a 2-week period following the move to a new city, in which they had not yet made new acquaintances. An avoidant person might say that slight social contacts are typical of his or her life because "isolation is the human condition." On the other hand, an anxious, ambivalent individual might feel distressed and panicky, believing that his or her social inadequacies were keeping others away. A secure person might be expected to conclude that it was hard to make friends in a new place. For present purposes, the key point is that these three very different conclusions may derive from the same social circumstances; the differing interpretations shed light on the person and on the operation of attachment processes in adult relationships.

To sum up, self-generated impressions and retrospections are best used to shed light on the processes by which people interpret their experiences. In making a similar point about how people retell their relationship histories, Duck (1988; Duck & Sants, 1983) cleverly applied the metaphor of "digestion." In his view, retrospective accounts of relational events depend on the manner in which people chew on, swallow, and extract substance from those events. The product is clearly transformed in both outward appearance and internal structure, but its final form nevertheless derives from the original ingestion. By comparing input events and output impressions, valuable insights into the psychologically interesting processes that govern self-understanding may be gained.

## The Domain of Exemplary Experience

This category encompasses those situations in which behavior is observed in a specific, controlled, or otherwise special setting. Included are observational studies conducted in uniform, intrinsically interesting settings, such as playgrounds, offices, and living rooms, as well as most laboratory experiments, in which the impact of one or more experimentally induced variables is assessed in a standardized, tightly controlled setting. *Exemplary* has two definitions in standard English (*American Heritage Dictionary*, 1976). One definition is "commendable; worthy of being imitated." Especially when subjects are aware of being observed or monitored (but not *only* then), their behavior may represent optimal rather than typical performance (Ickes & Tooke, 1988). Such well-known tendencies as impression management, self-justification, social desirability, desire to be helpful, and politeness rules all impel behavior that might look different away from the scrutiny of researchers. Thus, for example, shy people participating in a study of conversational behavior might try to be assertive to avoid being perceived as bashful. Compliant subjects have been known to try to help experimenters (who are often fellow students) by inferring their hypothesis and acting accordingly.

Note that awareness of being observed is not the only reason why particular settings may induce exemplary behavior. Many contexts, notably including research laboratories, are replete with cues that elicit formal, polite, generous, or introspective behaviors that may differ from the behaviors that people display in everyday life. For example, a therapy office may evoke considerably more self-reflection than one's office or dining room. Similarly, a hospital setting may suggest caring and sympathy, whereas a child-care center may induce nurturance or playfulness. The situational demands of standard research laboratories have not been studied extensively. Nevertheless, its seems clear that they invoke characteristic expectations, moods, goals, and action scripts that may substantially alter thoughts and behavior, intentionally or unintentionally (Altman, 1975). Clark and Reis (1988) speculated that, for these and other reasons, relationship partners may interact differently in the laboratory than in their natural, freely chosen settings.

The other definition of *exemplary* is "serving as an illustration; typical." In most experiments, researchers assume that subjects' reactions are typical, or representative, of their natural responses to the conditions that have been created. This premise, inherent in the concept of external validity, provides the background context against which the power of experimental designs for validating causal models can be exploited. But the self-same conditions that provide experimental designs with this power (namely, highly controlled settings) also constrain the breadth of situations to which findings may be confidently applied. That is, as seasoned experimentalists know, slight changes in settings or procedures may sometimes engender large changes in behavior. Researchers seldom pay as much attention to defining the boundary conditions of a phenomenon as they do to identifying and characterizing the process. An irony here is that boundary conditions are nothing more than moderator variables. What looks like a moderating boundary condition to one researcher is often the primary interest of another researcher.

As a theoretician, John Bowlby was known as one of the master generalists of our time; but all the same, in 1978 he noted that the wise researcher will

. . . concentrate attention on a limited aspect of a limited problem. If in making his selection he proves sagacious, or simply lucky, he may not only elucidate the problem selected but also develop ideas applicable to a broader range. If his selection proves unwise or unlucky he may merely end up knowing more and more about less and less. (Bowlby, 1988, pp. 40–41)

To paraphrase Bowlby, wisdom and luck are determined not so much by the validity of one's findings, but more so by the breadth of circumstances to which those findings apply. In other words, it is important to identify just what situations and processes the observed behaviors are exemplary of, in the sense of typical. This is analogous to answering a series of general questions about a given phenomenon: How often does it occur? When does it occur, and how much impact does it have? What contextual or background conditions are necessary for this process to operate? How generalizable is the phenomenon to other, conceptually similar situations? What conditions enhance or diminish the effect? The answer to these and related questions go a long way toward identifying the precise location of a particular finding in the catalog of relationship phenomena.

In summary, the study of exemplary behavior, in both senses of this word, is a proper and essential task for relationship researchers. Our understanding of relationship processes will be advanced by carefully controlled studies that permit causal inference and inform researchers about how people react under particular well-specified conditions. At the same time, however, this knowledge will be most viable when complemented by a broader accounting of the processes being exemplified. The next section of this chapter proposes that studies of everyday social experience are ideal for establishing this larger perspective.

## The Domain of Ongoing Experience

This category of experience includes studies that focus on the nature of spontaneous, everyday experience. The relevant data are usually detailed descriptions and evaluations that are contemporaneous with the actual events. Verifying the causal antecedents of a given behavior with the greatest internal validity is generally not the overriding concern, as it is in most experimental studies. Rather, these methods are designed to examine specific processes or behaviors within the stream of ongoing, spontaneous, and voluntary social activity. With suitable analysis, they permit identification and specification of the contexts in which these behaviors naturally occur; they offer opportunities to examine the consequences of those behaviors as they are embedded in the ebb and flow of action; and they can provide accurate, detailed summaries of the prevalence of particular phenomena in everyday life.

What comes under the heading of ongoing experience? This research is generally concerned with the feelings, thoughts, and actions that occur spontaneously in everyday life. For example, several researchers examined the structure and impact of natural variations in mood (e.g., Clark & Watson, 1988; Larsen, 1987). Csikszentmihalyi and Larson (1984) and Delespaul and deVries (1987) described the cognitive activity of high school students and psychiatric patients, considering, among many variables, the nature of intrinsic motivation, boredom, and alertness and their effects on mental health, academic performance, and social functioning. Several research groups have studied the impact of daily hassles and other stressors on individual well-being, mental health, and marital relations (Bolger, DeLongis, Kessler, & Schilling, 1989; Stone & Neale, 1984). Hoyle (1990) investigated the influence of self-focused attention on momentary fluctuations in self-esteem. Hormuth (1990) and Campbell, Chew, and Scratchley (1991) examined stability and change in the self-concept. Robinson (1987) was interested in how people distributed their time across many activities in a typical day. Duck, Rutt, Hurst, and Strejc (1991) described the features of ordinary social conversations. Finally, my colleagues and I have been concerned with the antecedents and consequences of several dimensions of social participation, including intimacy, physical attractiveness, loneliness, and the distribution of socializing across different partners and genders (summarized in Reis & Wheeler, 1991).

These studies share an interest in the small, often mundane moments and occurrences of everyday life. They focus on the vast and diverse array of ideas, images, feelings, and episodes that fill people's waking time and occupy most of their conscious thoughts and attention. Daily life events have a structure and rhythm of their own. Sometimes they are variable and ephemeral, and at other times they are stable and continuous; sometimes they are vivid and arousing, and at other times they are humdrum and inconsequential. The assumption behind the daily life approach is that these experiences are important in their own right, and that together they can provide valuable insights about human behavior.

Focusing on ongoing activity has particular merit for relationship researchers. It is often assumed that the substance of a relationship is most likely to be revealed in its most compelling events: an exceptionally intimate moment, an intense conflict, or a milestone occasion. But ongoing relationships are composed of a small number of such episodes surrounded by many more moments of lesser salience: washing dishes together, watching television, shopping for groceries, playing games, and having idle or task-oriented conversations. This point has been substantiated in several studies. For example, Hays (1984) and Duck et al. (1991) found that even in intimate relationships, most interactions were relatively low in intimacy and not distinguishable from casual acquaintanceships. Similarly, unpublished analyses from our own data repeatedly have shown that even in people's most intimate friendships, the majority of interactions are not experienced as highly intimate. The regularities and patterns inherent in daily interactions can provide important clues about the functioning of social relationships.

Daily experience studies may also be useful for building a descriptive database, an important goal in the early stages of research (Hinde, 1979). The potential value of these methods is not limited to description, however, as some have assumed. Daily life data are readily amenable for testing process-oriented hypotheses of the sort traditionally examined in theory-testing research. For example, daily ratings of stress and social activity have been used to test theories about the impact of stress on spousal interaction (Bolger et al., 1989), and to evaluate Reis and Shaver's (1988) intimacy model (Lin, 1992). Daily diary data offer a particularly valuable opportunity for testing theories about the role of affect and cognition in social interaction. In everyday life, people interact with others repeatedly and variably, usually with mixed motives, hidden agendas, incomplete or contradictory information, divided attention, interfering contextual cues, and little interest in going beyond simple, snap judgments. In such settings, reactions to others may differ in interesting and important ways from the affects and judgments that are experienced when attention is focused and people are trying to be reasonable. Therefore, these data may provide useful counterpoints to data collected with more traditional methods.

One point merits reiteration by way of concluding this section. Although each of the three domains described previously relies on a distinct methodology, the primary implication of this distinction is conceptual. Studies of reconstructed experience tell how people understand their lives and past activities. Studies of exemplary experience are informative about people's behavior in particular, well-specified circumstances. Studies of daily experience provide information about the thoughts, feelings, and activities that occur in everyday life. The fullest understanding of relationships is likely to result from research that incorporates all three perspectives.

## METHODS FOR STUDYING DAILY LIFE EXPERIENCE

Because daily life measures are not as well known as self-generated summary measures and experiments, the next section of this chapter presents a brief overview of existing procedures. Tennen et al. (1991) and Duck (1991) offered a more comprehensive introduction. A historical account was provided by Wheeler and Reis (1991).

The first measures of this sort were developed by behaviorally oriented clinical psychologists who were interested in tracking the frequency of various behaviors in everyday life (Lindsley, 1968). The obvious impracticality of following people around in their daily lives led to the development of contemporaneous, semi-objective recording procedures. In these applications, devices such as portable wrist counters and paper-and-pencil logs were used to keep track of the frequency of various events, both positively valued (such as smiling) and negatively valued (such as smoking and alcohol consumption). The purpose of these records was to provide an objective and compelling account of the prevalence of the target events, so that behavior modification techniques might be used to alter them.

Self-recording of daily events became a more popular research tool in the 1970s, when two technological advances made more sophisticated protocols possible. The first was the development of digital technology, which allowed researchers to repeatedly signal subjects without requiring face-to-face presence. The second was the computer, which permitted rapid tabulation and analysis of far more data than had been manageable previously. These two developments led Csikszentmihalyi and his colleagues to develop the ESM, the most widely used method for studying daily events (Csikszentmihalyi et al., 1977). Many variations on the event sampling theme have subsequently been developed, each designed to address somewhat different questions or situations. The taxonomy that follows, proposed by Wheeler and Reis (1991), illustrates the range of these procedures.

## 1. Interval-Contingent Recording

With this method, participants report on their experiences at regular, predetermined intervals. Typically, these intervals are chosen to demark theoretically or logically meaningful units of time or activity (e.g., at the end of each day or after every meal). This is the oldest and most widely used method for reporting ongoing experiences. Examples include daily accounts of stressful experiences (Bolger et al., 1989), descriptions of mood four times each day (Hedges et al., 1985), and daily reports of headaches (Blanchard et al., 1990).

## 2. Signal-Contingent Recording

Herein, subjects are instructed to describe their activities whenever signaled by the researcher, usually via beepers, pagers, or telephone calls. Signal intervals can be fixed, random, or a combination of both (in which case signals are randomly generated within fixed blocks of time). The ESM is a prototypical signal-contingent method. Subjects carry pagers or portable, preprogrammed beepers, and are signaled at several randomly selected instances (typically between 7 and 10 times per day). When cued, they complete a brief questionnaire describing their current activities, thoughts, and impressions. Signal-contingent recording has been used to study adolescent experience (Csikszentmihalyi & Larson, 1984), stability and change in the self-concept (Hormuth, 1990), the daily life of ambulatory chronic mental patients

(Delespaul & deVries, 1987), and intimacy motivation (McAdams & Constantian, 1983).

## 3. Event-Contingent Sampling

This method requires a report from participants every time an event meeting some predetermined definition has occurred. The frequency of the relevant events, and hence subjects' reports, usually varies from subject to subject and from one time period to another. An unambiguous definition of events requiring a report is key, so that all such events are described. Timeliness in completing the records is also important. The Rochester Interaction Record (RIR; Reis & Wheeler, 1991) is an event-sampling method, in that it requires subjects to complete a record whenever social interactions lasting 10 minutes or longer have occurred. Event-sampling has also been used to study conversations (Duck et al., 1991), lies (DePaulo, Kirkendol, Epstein, Wyer, & Hairfield, 1990), social comparison (Wheeler & Miyake, 1992), and fluctuations in self-esteem (Hoyle, 1990).

### Comparison of the Three Protocols for Relationship Research

It may be useful to describe the relative advantages and disadvantages of these three procedures for relationship research. Interval-contingent methods are most appropriate when researchers need to characterize ongoing experience across fixed and regular time periods (e.g., hourly, daily). The longer the interval and the more malleable the behavior in question, the greater the possibility that retrospection biases will influence the data. Because diary methods are intended to minimize such distortion, interval-contingent methods should be used only when the time between the event and its description is short, when the phenomenon itself is easily remembered, or when short-term aggregated impressions are desired. For example, marital researchers might be interested in daily summaries of affect and conflict, because days are a time unit with intrinsic functional meaning. A major advantage of interval-contingent recording is its simplicity. Subjects need only complete the instrument at the appointed time (which experimenters might even control, as by telephoning subjects once a day). Also, especially when time intervals are equal, interval-contingent methods lend themselves to time-series analysis.

Signal- and event-contingent recording reduce the likelihood of forgetting or reappraising by requiring reports that are close in time to the event. Signal-contingent methods are most useful for assessing the prevalence of certain events or feelings in daily life. For example, if one wanted to know how often people are alone or with others, one would only need to compute the percentage of responses during which subjects report social contact. Similarly, the relative predominance of positive or negative affect in daily life might be tabulated in this fashion. Especially when signaling is random, signal-contingent methods have the considerable advantage of avoiding systematic biases introduced by fixed-time assessments. For example, people may always feel lethargic after dinner, or they may usually feel annoyed after having put their children to sleep.

On the other hand, the rarer the event in question, the less useful signal-contingent methods are, because the number of instances in which the signal and event coincide would be diminished. Therefore, signal-contingent recording renders infeasible the study of variation within a class of even moderately scarce events. For example, if one wanted to compare the intimacy levels of interactions with same-gender best friends and romantic partners, it is unlikely that more than a few relevant episodes would be obtained in a week of random signals. Data would have to be collected for a prohibitively long time before an acceptably large database was acquired. With even rarer events (e.g., feelings and practices regarding sexual activity or family conflict), the necessity of focusing directly on the events of interest with event-contingent recording becomes clear. Event-contingent recording also has the benefit of including all criterion events, minimizing the possibility that self-selection or signaling happenstance will omit significant episodes.

The choice between signal-contingent and event-contingent sampling should depend on the researcher's goals. Event-contingent sampling is generally preferable when: (a) researchers are interested in a limited domain of events, such as conversations, social interactions, or deception; (b) those events can be defined clearly for subjects; and (c) variation with a category of behavior is to be studied, requiring a large number of events. On the other hand, signal-contingent sampling should be chosen when: (a) researchers are interested in the relative distribution of thoughts, feelings, or behaviors across time or context; or (b) comparison of experiences in different settings is of primary interest.

A recent study by Reis, Delespaul, and deVries (1993) demonstrated that in those situations in which both methods were appropriate, similar results were produced by event- and signal-contingent methods. In their study, 42 Dutch university students kept both the RIR and ESM for 1 week. Correlations among RIR variables and the ESM scores taken from only those signals in which subjects were socializing ranged from .28 to .79. Thus, both methods seem capable of providing useful data about everyday social activity.

## TWO EXAMPLES: INTEGRATING RESEARCH
## FROM DIVERGING PERSPECTIVES

The central premise of this chapter is that knowledge and insights that integrate all three perspectives described earlier are likely to provide the most fully rounded picture of the processes that affect relationship behavior. From self-generated summaries, we learn about how people make sense of their experiences in relationships. From studies of exemplary behavior, we acquire information about the impact of particular conditions on relationship behavior, which may allow for specification of causal mechanisms. From studies of everyday experience, we can examine these processes as they operate in the ebb and flow of spontaneous and natural social activity.

It may be helpful to illustrate the benefits of complementary perspectives with two concrete examples. The first example is based on existing studies of loneliness. The second example, concerning adult attachment theory, is hypothetical to show how these varying perspectives may also be useful in theory development and research planning.

## Loneliness

Relationship researchers became interested in studying loneliness during the mid-1970s. To encompass this research, Perlman and Peplau (1981) offered a discrepancy model, which proposed that loneliness resulted from a self-perceived discrepancy between desired and actual levels of social activity. This model did not specify what sorts of discrepancies might be more or less influential, but simply that people had to feel that existing circumstances did not satisfy their ideals. Research into the nature and correlates of loneliness was greatly facilitated by the development of several self-report inventories, notably the revised UCLA (Russell, Peplau, & Cutrona, 1980) and NYU (Rubenstein & Shaver, 1982) Loneliness scales. With these and other similar scales, a total loneliness score is derived from answers to a set of standard questions. This score then can be related to whatever antecedents and consequences are of conceptual interest. These measures have led to an extensive and robust literature, which has greatly enhanced researchers' understanding of this important human concern (Peplau & Goldston, 1984).

Self-report questionnaires such as the UCLA and NYU scales fall into the domain of self-generated summaries, as described earlier, because they require subjects to select, aggregate, and evaluate their prior experiences. Most of the existing literature has used this approach. How have these studies been complemented by the exemplary experience and everyday activity perspectives? Looking first at the former, laboratory studies of loneliness have provided important clues about the precise nature of loneliness. For example, Jones and colleagues showed that lonely people are more negative in their evaluations of new acquaintances, and that they communicate with others in a more self-focused, less responsive fashion (summarized in Jones, 1982). Other laboratory studies have also implicated the role of deficient communication skills in loneliness (Solano, Batten, & Parrish, 1982; Spitzberg & Canary, 1985). These studies complement self-report questionnaire research in two ways. First, they identify with greater specificity the nature of the social skills deficits that characterize lonely persons. Second, by providing independent accounts of observed behavior, it can be ascertained that the reported problems of lonely persons are characteristic of their actual behaviors, rather than biased views of their own interactions.

Diary studies have complemented questionnaire research on loneliness in a different manner. Early studies (e.g., Russell, 1982) suggested that lonely people's social interactions were broadly deficient (i.e., that lonely people felt that their social lives were deficient in a wide variety of respects). Wheeler, Reis, and Nezlek (1983) had subjects keep the RIR for 2 weeks. Subsequently, subjects completed the UCLA Loneliness scale so that the daily interaction profile of lonely persons could be distinguished from that of nonlonely college students. Their data showed that two factors were closely linked to loneliness: a relatively smaller proportion of interactions with females (regardless of the subject's own gender) and a relative absence of intimacy. Because interactions with females were generally more intimate than interactions with males (cf. Reis, in press), both of these results point to the absence of intimacy, rather than other specific factors (e.g., physical isolation, lack of group involvement, lesser enjoyment), as the primary gap in lonely persons' social lives.

These findings illustrate how the three approaches to studying loneliness may complement one another. Self-generated summary studies of loneliness indicate that people who feel lonely also feel that their social lives are broadly deficient. The exemplary approach experiments suggest that certain communication skill deficits may contribute to their sense of isolation. The diary studies reveal that lack of intimacy may be the main absence in their daily lives. Together these studies provide a fuller portrayal of what loneliness entails than any one approach could do alone.

## Adult Attachment Theory

Recently, relationship researchers have begun to apply attachment theory to the study of adult close relationships. The enthusiasm for this application grew from Hazan and Shaver's (1987) seminal studies, which demonstrated that attachment theory, although posited and first tested in the context of early childhood, could generate fruitful hypotheses about adult relationships. The essence of attachment theory is that humans have an evolutionarily based need for proximity to caregivers, and that this need is evident in a variety of affective, behavioral, and cognitive reactions to the presence and absence of close relationships (Bowlby, 1969). According to the theory, early experiences in attachment relationships are likely to engender adult attachment styles that resemble one of three general patterns. Securely attached individuals are able to maintain satisfying close relationships, and generally have positive mental models about themselves and their relations with others. Insecure attachment may take either of two forms. Avoidant persons typically eschew close relationships with others, finding it uncomfortable to depend on others while believing that "true love never lasts." Anxious, ambivalent individuals, on the other hand, tend to fall in love quickly, desire high levels of closeness and union, and feel that their love and caring is never fully reciprocated. Shaver and Hazan (in press) provided a comprehensive summary of this research.

Following Hazan and Shaver's (1987) lead, most adult attachment research is of the self-generated summary variety. Subjects are classified into one of the three attachment styles, either by their choice of one category from description of the three basic types or by virtue of their response to questionnaire items. Thus, categorizations are based on the manner in which individuals recall and evaluate past relationship experiences. Studies using this method have yielded a rich bounty of empirical findings. For example, self-generated attachment styles have been related to attitudes and affect about romantic love and same-gender friendships; sexual behavior and alcohol use; self-disclosure; patterns of interpersonal problems; and feelings about work and death.

Despite the value of these findings, however, a common criticism is that they stem from self-reported attachment styles. That is, because many of the outcomes being studied are also assessed by self-report, it is possible that the observed relationships reflect general processes of attitude or self-concept consistency, rather than attachment processes in particular. Studies from the exemplary and everyday experience domains may be useful in addressing this criticism. To date, such research is in an incipient stage. However, to illustrate the value of integrating divergent perspectives within a single conceptual focus, it may be useful to outline these possibilities.

One of Bowlby's (1969) central propositions was that attachment behaviors should be most evident when the attachment system is activated (i.e., when some threat is perceived to the security of the person, or when the availability of the attachment figure is imperiled). Kobak and Hazan (1991) and Simpson, Rholes, and Nelligan (1992) developed exemplary experience analogs for doing so by engaging subjects in discussions of personal disappointments and loss, or by having them anticipate an experimental procedure that arouses "considerable fear and distress in most people." Similarly, a technique developed by Murray and Holmes (1992) might also be adapted for this purpose. They activated relationship-relevant defenses by having subjects read a passage that vividly describes relationship conflict and losses. By activating the attachment system, these procedures should allow researchers to directly observe behavioral, affective, and cognitive reactions in certain contexts. How do people respond to their partners' distress, for example, and how does this response affect the relationship subsequently? Does a supportive response facilitate development of more positive working models of others?

Studies of everyday social experience might also shed light on the operation of attachment processes. For example, one might examine the ongoing social experience of securely and insecurely attached individuals. To the extent that their everyday social activities differ, irrespective of the degree of attachment threat and felt insecurity, the impact of attachment processes would appear to be considerably more pervasive than originally proposed. For example, do insecurely attached individuals generally experience heightened negative affect when socializing, or is this a more contextually limited experience? On the other hand, it has been suggested that attachment processes are most likely to be evident in close relationships, in which the potential for threat exists. This hypothesis might be evaluated by comparing patterns of daily social interaction with close partners and with others (e.g., acquaintances, co-workers). When used in this fashion, the diary approach has two primary advantages. First, it provides contemporaneous accounts about ongoing social activity in its natural, spontaneous context. Second, because diary reports are collected event by event, rather than in aggregate, distortions of the sort discussed earlier are likely to be minimized (cf. Ritter & Langlois, 1988). Diary data do not rule out bias in interpreting and reporting a given event, of course. However, because they are rooted in a single concrete event, because responses are obtained virtually contemporaneously with the event in question, and because they do not require summarization or recall of multiple events, diary reports minimize many of the problems that make self-reports difficult to interpret.

## CAVEAT AND CONCLUSIONS

The general point of this chapter has been to argue that three different methodological approaches that have evolved in the study of relationships actually represent something broader: three distinct conceptual perspectives on relationship phenomena. When represented in this manner, it becomes apparent that a full understanding of the nature and role of relationships in human life is most likely to be obtained from simultaneous use of all three viewpoints. Thus, the daily event approach should not be considered as a substitute for self-generated summary questionnaires or laboratory experimentation. The former are appropriate for determining how people understand events and relationships in their lives, and the latter are of course best for testing causal hypotheses or examining behavior under carefully controlled conditions. Many questions are best addressed with these two approaches, and it would not be desirable to adopt life event methods in their stead. But the accuracy of self-generated summary data have been questioned, and diary data can shed valuable light on the processes inherent in retrospection and reconstruction. Similarly, the generalizability and external validity of laboratory-based findings have been questioned, and it is important for the field to begin testing hypotheses about the nature and prevalence of its favored constructs in everyday, spontaneous life.

Self-recording of daily events is often touted as an alternative to traditional self-report methods, primarily because it is less susceptible to memory loss and other sources of inaccuracy. For example, Costa and McCrae (1987) asserted that standard checklists of somatic complaints are likely to produce biased estimates of healthfulness, in part because neuroticism affects retrospective interpretations of past symptoms. They suggested that daily reports are less likely to be so affected, and they recommended that such diaries be used when objective medical information is not available. Such usage of these methods is entirely consistent with the logic of diary methods. But if this were the only way that daily event methods were used, researchers would be overlooking a potentially more generative role, and that is in complementing the two traditional domains of inquiry discussed earlier.

If most questionnaires and interviews deal with reconstructions and other personal impressions of past experience, then daily event-based methods provide a unique window into the all-important processes by which these reconstructions are generated. Comparison of contemporaneous reports of daily-life experience with retrospective summaries and accounts of those same experiences can illuminate the cognitive and motivational processes by which new information is integrated into a stable view of oneself in relation to others. If laboratory experiments provide valuable insights about behavior in controlled settings, then daily event studies offer the valuable counterpart of investigating the same processes in their natural context. From the standpoint of developing theoretical principles about relationships, and applying them in intervention settings, identifying the role of contextual factors is no less important than establishing the precise causal mechanisms that govern the process (Holmes & Boon, 1990).

Thus, no single perspective or research strategy is inherently preferable. Triangulation in the form of multiple perspectives is desirable. Each approach has its own advantages and disadvantages; much more importantly, each is capable of providing unique insights. Wider adoption of a more diverse set of paradigms, especially within the focus of a single conceptual issue, has the potential to add significantly to the bank of empirical data and theoretical constructs. This can only enrich our understanding of human interaction and relationships.

## REFERENCES

Altman, I. (1975). *The environment and social behavior.* Monterey, CA: Brooks/Cole.

*American Heritage Dictionary.* (1976). Boston: Houghton-Mifflin.

Anderson, N. H. (1981). *Foundations of information integration theory.* New York: Academic Press.

Baumeister, R. (1982). A self-presentational view of social phenomena. *Psychological Bulletin, 91,* 3–26.

Blanchard, E. B., Appelbaum, K. A., Radnitz, C. L., Michultka, D., Morrill, B., Kirsch, C., Hillhouse, J., Evans, D. D., Guarnieri, P., Attanasio, V., Andrasik, F., Jaccard, J., & Dentinger, M. P. (1990). A controlled evaluation of thermal biofeedback and thermal biofeedback combined with cognitive therapy in the treatment of vascular headache. *Journal of Consulting and Clinical Psychology, 58,* 216–224.

Bolger, N., DeLongis, A., Kessler, R. C., & Schilling, E. A. (1989). Effects of daily stress on negative mood. *Journal of Personality and Social Psychology, 57*, 808–818.

Bowlby, J. (1969). *Attachment.* New York: Basic.

Bowlby, J. (1988). *A secure base: Parent-child attachment and healthy human development.* New York: Basic Books.

Campbell, J. D., Chew, B., & Scratchley, L. S. (1991). Cognitive and emotional reactions to daily events: The effects of self-esteem and self-complexity. *Journal of Personality, 59*, 473–505.

Clark, M. S., & Reis, H. T. (1988). Interpersonal processes in close relationships. *Annual Review of Psychology, 39*, 609–672.

Clark, L. A., & Watson, D. (1988). Mood and the mundane: Relations between daily life events and self-reported mood. *Journal of Personality and Social Psychology, 54*, 296–308.

Costa, P. T., & McCrae, R. R. (1987). Neuroticism, somatic complaints, and disease: Is the bark worse than the bite? *Journal of Personality, 55*, 299–316.

Csikszentmihalyi, M., & Larson, R. (1984). *Being adolescent.* New York: Basic Books.

Csikszentmihalyi, M., Larson, R., & Prescott, S. (1977). The ecology of adolescent activity and experience. *Journal of Youth and Adolescence, 6*, 281–294.

Deaux, K. (1992). Focusing on the self: Challenges to self-definition and their consequences for mental health. In D. N. Ruble, P. R. Costanzo, & M. E. Oliveri (Eds.), *The social psychology of mental health: Basic mechanisms and applications* (pp. 301–327). New York: Guilford.

Delespaul, P. A. E. G., & deVries, M. W. (1987). The daily life of ambulatory chronic mental patients. *The Journal of Nervous and Mental Disease, 175*, 537–544.

DePaulo, B. M., Kirkendol, S. E., Epstein, J. E., Wyer, M., & Hairfield, J. (1990). *Everyday lies.* Unpublished manuscript, University of Virginia, Charlottesville.

DeVries, M. W. (1992). *The experience of psychopathology.* New York: Cambridge University Press.

Duck, S. (1988). *Relating to others.* Chicago: Dorsey Press.

Duck, S. (1991). Diaries and logs. In B. Montgomery & S. Duck (Eds.), *Studying interpersonal interaction* (pp. 141–161). New York: Guilford.

Duck, S., Rutt, D. J., Hurst, M. H., & Strejc, H. (1991). Some evident truths about conversations in everyday relationships: All communications are not created equal. *Human Communication Research, 18*, 228–267.

Duck, S., & Sants, H. (1983). On the origin of the specious: Are personal relationships really interpersonal states? *Journal of Social and Clinical Psychology, 1*, 27–41.

Erber, R. (1991). Affective and semantic priming: Effects of mood on category accessibility and inference. *Journal of Experimental Social Psychology, 27*, 480–498.

Erdelyi, M. H. (1974). A new look at the New Look: Perceptual defense and vigilance. *Psychological Review, 81*, 1–25.

Fiske, S. T., & Taylor, S. E. (1991). *Social cognition* (2nd ed.). New York: McGraw-Hill.

Forgas, J. P., Bower, G. H., & Krantz, S. E. (1984). The influence of mood on perceptions of social interactions. *Journal of Experimental Social Psychology, 20*, 497–513.

Gilligan, S. G., & Bower, G. H. (1984). Cognitive consequences of emotional arousal. In C. E. Izard, J. Kagan, & R. B. Zajonc (Eds.), *Emotions, cognition, and behavior* (pp. 547–588). Hillsdale, NJ: Lawrence Erlbaum Associates.

Harvey, J. H., Weber, A. L., & Orbuch, T. L. (1990). *Interpersonal accounts: A social psychology perspective.* Cambridge, MA: Blackwell.

Hays, R. B. (1984). The development and maintenance of friendship. *Journal of Social and Personal Relationships, 1*, 75–98.

Hazan, C., & Shaver, P. (1987). Romantic love conceptualized as an attachment process. *Journal of Personality and Social Psychology, 52*, 511–524.

Hazan, C., & Shaver, P. R. (in press). Attachment as an organizational framework for research on close relationships. *Psychological Inquiry.*

Hedges, S. M., Jansdorf, L., & Stone, A. A. (1985). Meaning of daily mood assessments. *Journal of Personality and Social Psychology, 48*, 428–434.

Higgins, E. T., & Bargh, J. A. (1987). Social cognition and social perception. *Annual Review of Psychology, 38*, 369–425.

Hinde, R. A. (1979). *Towards understanding relationships.* New York: Academic Press.

Hinde, R. A. (1987). *Individuals, relationships and culture: Links between ethology and the social sciences.* New York: Cambridge University Press.

Holmes, J. G., & Boon, S. D. (1990). Developments in the field of close relationships: Creating foundations for intervention strategies. *Personality and Social Psychology Bulletin, 16*, 23–41.

Hormuth, S. E. (1990). *The ecology of the self: Relocation and self-concept change.* New York: Cambridge University Press.

Hoyle, R. H. (1990). *Social interaction and the focus of self-attention.* Unpublished manuscript, University of Kentucky, Lexington.

Ickes, W., & Tooke, W. (1988). The observational method: Studying the interaction of minds and bodies. In S. Duck (Ed.), *Handbook of personal relationships: Theory, research and interventions* (pp. 79–97). New York: Wiley.

Jones, E. E., & Pittman, T. S. (1982). Toward a general theory of strategic self-presentation. In J. Suls (Ed.), *Psychological perspectives on the self* (pp. 231–262). Hillsdale, NJ: Lawrence Erlbaum Associates.

Jones, W. H. (1982). Loneliness and social behavior. In L. A. Peplau & D. Perlman (Eds.), *Loneliness: A sourcebook of current theory, research and therapy* (pp. 238–252). New York: Wiley.

Kobak, R. R., & Hazan, C. (1991). Attachment in marriage: Effect of security and accuracy of working models. *Journal of Personality and Social Psychology, 60*, 861–869.

Larsen, R. J. (1987). The stability of mood variability: A spectral analytic approach to daily mood assessments. *Journal of Personality and Social Psychology, 52*, 1195–1204.

Larson, R. W., & Csikszentmihalyi, M. (1983). The experience sampling method. In H. Reis (Ed.), *Naturalistic methods to studying social interaction in the behavioral sciences* (pp. 41–56). San Francisco, CA: Jossey-Bass.

Lin, Y. C. (1992). *The construction of the sense of intimacy from everyday social interaction.* Unpublished doctoral dissertation, University of Rochester, New York.

Lindsley, O. (1968). A reliable wrist counter for recording behavioral rates. *Journal of Applied Behavior Analysis, 1*, 77–78.

Main, M., Kaplan, N., & Cassidy, J. (1985). Security in infancy, childhood, and adulthood: A move to the level of representation. *Monographs of the Society for Research in Child Development, 50*(1–2, Serial No. 209), 66–104.

McAdams, D. P., & Constantian, C. A. (1983). Intimacy and affiliation motives in daily living: An experience sampling analysis. *Journal of Personality and Social Psychology, 45*, 851–861.

McFarland, C., & Ross, M. (1987). The relation between current impressions and memories of self and dating partners. *Personality and Social Psychology Bulletin, 13*, 228–238.

McFarland, C., Ross, M., & DeCourville, N. (1989). Women's theories of menstruation and biases in recall of menstrual symptoms. *Journal of Personality and Social Psychology, 57*, 522–531.

Metts, S., Sprecher, S., & Cupach, W. R. (1991). Retrospective self-reports. In B. M. Montgomery & S. Duck (Eds.), *Studying interpersonal interaction* (pp. 162–178). New York: Guilford.

Montgomery, B. M., & Duck, S. (Eds.). (1991). *Studying interpersonal interaction.* New York: Guilford.

Murray, S. L., & Holmes, J. G. (1992). *Seeing virtues in faults: Negativity and the transformation of interpersonal narratives in close relationships.* Unpublished manuscript, University of Waterloo, Ontario, Canada.

Peplau, L. A., & Goldston, S. E. (1984). *Preventing the harmful consequences of severe and persistent loneliness.* Rockville, MD: National Institute of Mental Health.

Perlman, D., & Peplau, L. A. (1981). Toward a social psychology of loneliness. In S. Duck & R. Gilmore (Eds.), *Personal relationships: 3. Personal relationship in disorder.* London: Academic Press.

Reis, H. T. (in press). The interpersonal context of emotions: Gender differences in intimacy and related behaviors. In V. E. O'Leary & J. Sprock (Eds.), *Gendered emotions.* Newbury Park, CA: Sage.

Reis, H. T., Delespaul, P., & deVries, M. (1993). *A comparison of two methods of experience sampling.* Unpublished manuscript, University of Rochester, New York.

Reis, H. T., & Shaver, P. (1988). Intimacy as an interpersonal process. In S. Duck (Ed.), *Handbook of personal relationships* (pp. 367–389). Chichester, England: Wiley.

Reis, H. T., & Wheeler, L. (1991). Studying social interaction with the Rochester Interaction Record. In M. P. Zanna (Ed.), *Advances in experimental social psychology* (Vol. 24, pp. 270–318). San Diego: Academic Press.

Ritter, J. M., & Langlois, J. H. (1988). The role of physical attractiveness in the observation of adult-child interactions: Eye of the beholder or behavioral reality? *Developmental Psychology, 24*, 254–263.

Robinson, J. P. (1987). Microbehavioral approaches to monitoring human experience. *The Journal of Nervous and Mental Disease, 175*, 514–518.

Ross, M. (1989). Relation of implicit theories to the construction of personal histories. *Psychological Review, 96*, 341–357.

Rubenstein, C. M., & Shaver, P. (1982). The experience of loneliness. In L. A. Peplau & D. Perlman (Eds.), *Loneliness: A sourcebook of current theory, research and therapy* (pp. 206–223). New York: Wiley.

Russell, D. (1982). The measurement of loneliness. In L. A. Peplau & D. Perlman (Eds.), *Loneliness: A sourcebook of current theory, research and therapy* (pp. 81–104). New York: Wiley.

Russell, D., Peplau, L. A., & Cutrona, C. E. (1980). The revised UCLA loneliness scale: Concurrent and discriminant validity evidence. *Journal of Personality and Social Psychology, 39*, 472–480.

Sanitioso, R., Kunda, Z., & Fong, G. T. (1990). Motivated recruitment of autobiographical memories. *Journal of Personality and Social Psychology, 59*, 229–241.

Schwarz, N. (1990). Assessing frequency reports of mundane behaviors: Contributions of cognitive psychology to questionnaire construction. In C. Hendrick & M. S. Clark (Eds.), *Research methods in personality and social psychology* (pp. 98–119). Newbury Park, CA: Sage.

Shaklee, H., & Fischhoff, B. (1982). Strategies of information search in causal analysis. *Memory and Cognition, 10*, 520–530.

Shaver, P. R., & Hazan, C. (in press). Adult romantic attachment: Theory and evidence. In D. Perlman & W. Jones (Eds.), *Advances in personal relationships* (Vol. 4). London: Jessica Kingsley Publishers.

Simpson, J. A., Rholes, W. S., & Nelligan, J. S. (1992). Support seeking and support giving within couples in an anxiety-provoking situation: The role of attachment styles. *Journal of Personality and Social Psychology, 62*, 434–446.

Smith, M. B., Bruner, J. S., & White, R. W. (1956). *Opinions and personality.* New York: Wiley.

Snyder, M., & Swann, W. B. (1978). Hypothesis-testing processes in social interaction. *Journal of Personality and Social Psychology, 36*, 1202–1212.

Solano, C. H., Batten, P. G., & Parrish, E. A. (1982). Loneliness and patterns of self-disclosure. *Journal of Personality and Social Psychology, 43*, 524–531.

Spitzberg, B. H., & Canary, D. J. (1985). Loneliness and relationally competent communication. *Journal of Social and Personal Relationships, 2*, 387–402.

Steele, C. M. (1988). The psychology of self-affirmation: Sustaining the integrity of the self. In L. Berkowitz (Ed.), *Advances in experimental social psychology* (Vol. 21, pp. 261–302). San Diego, CA: Academic Press.

Stone, A., & Neale, J. (1984). A new measure of daily coping: Development and preliminary results. *Journal of Personality and Social Psychology, 46*, 892–906.

Swann, W. B., Jr. (1990). To be adored or to be known: The interplay of self-enhancement and self-verification. In R. M. Sorrentino & E. T. Higgins (Eds.), *Foundations of social behavior* (Vol. 2, pp. 408–448). New York: Guilford.

Swann, W. B., Jr., & Read, S. J. (1981). Acquiring self-knowledge: The search for feedback that fits. *Journal of Personality and Social Psychology, 41*, 1119–1128.

Tennen, H., Suls, J., & Affleck, G. (1991). Special issue on studying small events. *Journal of Personality, 59*(3).

Tversky, A., & Kahneman, D. (1982). Judgment under uncertainty: Heuristics and biases. In D. Kahneman, P. Slovic, & A. Tversky (Eds.), *Judgment under uncertainty* (pp. 3–20). New York: Cambridge University Press.

Westen, D. (1992). The cognitive self and the psychoanalytic self: Can we put our selves together? *Psychological Inquiry, 3*, 1–13.

Wheeler, L., & Miyake, K. (1992). Social comparison in everyday life. *Journal of Personality and Social Psychology, 62*, 760–773.

Wheeler, L., & Reis, H. T. (1991). Self-recording of events in everyday life. *Journal of Personality, 59*, 339–354.

Wheeler, L., Reis, H., & Nezlek, J. (1983). Loneliness, social interaction, and sex roles. *Journal of Personality and Social Psychology, 45*, 943–953.

Wyer, R. S., & Srull, T. K. (1986). Human cognition in its social context. *Psychological Review, 93*, 322–359.

# Chapter 6

# Using the Social Relations Model to Understand Relationships

David A. Kenny
*University of Connecticut*

Relationships are important to everyone. They provide people with the most rewarding and exasperating moments in life. They can drive people to ecstasy as well as to despair. Despite, or perhaps because of, their importance, very little is known about them. In this chapter, a new approach to the study of relationships, called the Social Relations Model (Kenny & La Voie, 1984; Malloy & Kenny, 1986), is described. This approach is beginning to provide a number of new insights into relationships (Clark & Reis, 1988). Although the model is highly mathematical, it is relatively simple to understand. Also, although it is a methodology, it does have embedded within it a theoretical orientation to social relationships that is developed in this chapter.

What follows is a nontechnical account of what is rather complicated. Complicated explanations are avoided here because such detail has been presented in other papers (Kenny, 1981, 1990a, 1990b; Kenny & La Voie, 1984; Warner, Kenny, & Stoto, 1979). The reader should be forewarned that what follows is an outline of an approach and not the full approach. Thus, reading this chapter explains the usefulness of the model but it does not provide sufficient information to implement the model.

Although the Social Relations Model is a very important tool in the understanding of relationships, it is just one tool of many. Moreover, for certain areas of research, it may not be the most appropriate framework within which to study relationships. My years of working in the area of methodology have taught me an important lesson: Pick the area of interest and that will then drive the methodology. All too often researchers let the method determine the question.

In looking at relationships, one can consider three different domains. First, there is the affective domain: How do people feel about each other? Second, there is the cognitive domain: What thoughts do people think about each other? Finally, there is the behavioral domain: How do people treat each other? In this chapter, all three domains are examined. However, research using the Social Relations Model on relationships has concentrated on the cognitive and affective components. Behavioral data present various difficulties. First, one can only observe behavior for a short period of time, and this short period of time gives rise to a mass of data that requires hours of coding. In addition, ordinarily one must observe behavior outside its usual context, therefore the people realize that they are being observed. Despite these difficulties, future work with the model must include behavioral measures.

The organization of this chapter is as follows. The first section explains the Social Relations Model. Its components are introduced and there are illustrations of how the model has been used. The next section attempts to provide the conceptual and methodological interpretation of the meaning of *relationship* within the Social Relations Model. Then affect or liking is discussed, and it is demonstrated that affect is largely relational. The next section considers interpersonal perception. The last section discusses how the Social Relations Model can be used to study the ways in which special relationships differ from ordinary relationships.

## THE SOCIAL RELATIONS MODEL

### Components

Consider two co-workers Jack and Jill who, after working together for a few months, know each other casually. Jack and Jill have formed impressions of each other. Each can be asked whether they think that the other is intelligent, friendly, lazy, and anxious. For instance, take Jack's impression of Jill's intelligence. Assume that Jack believes that Jill is a very intelligent person. The following question can be asked: Does Jack think that all people are intelligent? For instance, Jack may be somewhat dim-witted, and so everybody, compared with him, seems rather bright. To the extent that some people think individuals are intelligent and other people think that individuals are not intelligent, there exists what is called an actor effect.

Jack may think that Jill is smart and so may everybody else. This effect is called a partner effect. Just because everybody thinks that Jill is smart does not mean that she is in fact smart. At issue is how others tend to see the person.

The terms *actor effect* and *partner effect* are generic terms that are used in the Social Relations Model. Within specific applications, different terms might be used. For instance, with social perception data, the actor effect might be called a perceiver effect and the partner effect a target effect. For affective data, the partner effect measures how popular or likeable a person is. For behavioral data, the actor effect measures how frequently the person engages in the behavior, and the partner effect measures how much of the behavior the person elicits from others.

Both actor and partner are individual-level effects in that both refer to a person. Neither of them is relational. The last component, called the relationship effect, is a dyadic effect, which here measures how Jack uniquely feels about Jill. Say that Jack is in love with Jill and is infatuated with her. He may see her as a very intelligent woman, despite that others do not see her as intelligent and despite that he does not see others as intelligent. Relationship effects are effects that emerge after the individual-level effects are removed. That is, the relationship effect measures how intelligent Jack sees Jill after removing how much Jack thinks that others are intelligent and how much others think that Jill is intelligent.

So far, the relationship component has been defined as the unique response that Jack makes to Jill. However, if Jack responds randomly to all his interaction partners, he will uniquely respond to Jill but it would not be said that Jack has a relationship with Jill. As the relationship effect has been defined so far, it contains both relationship and error (Ingraham & Wright, 1986). Relationship effects need to be separated from error. This can be accomplished by observing Jack with Jill at two or more times or with two or more measures. If he is relating to Jill, then he will respond somewhat consistently to the same question across the two occasions or measures. If he is responding randomly, then he will behave differently at each time. By observing Jack with Jill with two or more measures, relationship can be separated from error.

## Design Considerations

To study relationships using the Social Relations Model, each person must be observed with multiple partners. If one is to understand how Jack sees Jill, one must compare that perception to how Jack sees Helen, Jane, and Betty; and one must compare it to how Frank, Tom, and Peter see Jill. No relationship can be studied in isolation.

In the Social Relations Model, there are two basic designs: round robin and block. In a round robin design, each person interacts with or rates everyone in the group. If the research participants were members of a sorority, in a round robin design each member would be paired with every other member. In a block design, the group is broken up into two subgroups, and each person rates or interacts with everyone in the other subgroup.

## Illustration of Variance Partitioning

One of the major uses of the Social Relations Model is the partitioning of variance. Researchers observe social interaction and then determine the proportion of variance that is attributable to actor, partner, and relationship. Table 6.1 presents the variance partitioning for three variables. Presented are a behavior, a perception, and an affect. For illustration purposes, very striking examples are considered. Data from most studies are not so clear-cut.

The first variable is filled pause, which comes from the Duncan and Fiske (1977) study. Filled pause is a pause during a speaker's turn that contains a semantically meaningless vocalization, such as "uh." The subjects of this study were students at professional schools at the University of Chicago. There were 88 subjects and 176 interactions. The coded interactions were the last 5 minutes of a 7-minute interaction between strangers. The study used a block design with two members in one subgroup and two in the other. There were then four people in each block with 22 blocks in total.

Duncan and Fiske (1977) did not use the Social Relations Model, however their data were re-analyzed by Kenny and Malloy (1988). The largest amount of variance in filled pause, well over half, was at the level of the actor. Some people used more filled pause than others. Of the 28 nonverbal behaviors analyzed by Kenny and Malloy, filled pause showed the largest amount of actor variance. Because there was only a small amount of partner variance, there was not much evidence that some people elicited more filled pause from their partners. Relationship variance was large, but because there was only a single measure of filled pause, it was not known if the relationship variance reflected chance or relational aspects.

The second example is taken from an unpublished study by Hallmark and Kenny (1990). Groups of strangers, five to six in number, were formed. People sat in a circle, and an experimenter asked them three different questions about what they would do in various situations. For instance, they were asked what they would do if they saw another person cheating on an examination. After the questions were completed, the subjects rated each other on a series of traits. The two traits that are discussed here are outgoing–reserved and talkative–silent. These two measures are treated as indicators of an extroversion construct. The results in Table 6.1 clearly show that the largest variance

TABLE 6.1
Proportion of Variance for Three Variables

| Variable | Actor | Partner | Relationship | Error |
|----------|-------|---------|--------------|-------|
| Filled pause | .63 | .03 | .34 | — |
| Extroversion | .06 | .39 | .27 | .28 |
| Liking | .19 | .07 | .50 | .24 |

component was partner. Some people were rated as very extroverted, and others were rated as very introverted. There was also a fair amount of variance at the relationship level.

The last example examines affect. Levine and Snyder (1980) gathered data from two classes of children aged 5 to 6 years old. There were 25 children in each class. Each child rated how much he or she wanted to sit with, work with, and share with the others in his or her class. These three measures can be treated as replications, therefore a separation of relationship and error can be made. As shown in Table 6.1, the largest portion of variance was at the relationship level. There were rather weak popularity effects in that the partner variance was only 7% of the variance. There was a tendency for some people to like people and for others to dislike people in that nearly 20% of the variance was actor variance.

## Reciprocity

One of the most useful purposes of the Social Relations Model is that it allows researchers to measure reciprocity in a new and interesting way. Returning to Jack and Jill, if Jack thinks that Jill is intelligent, does Jill think that Jack is intelligent? Are their perceptions mirror images of one another? Sometimes perceptions are complementary: Jack thinks that Jill is intelligent, but Jill thinks that Jack is stupid.

Within the Social Relations Model, there are two types of reciprocity. First, there is reciprocity at the dyadic level. Jack's relationship effect with Jill in the Social Relations Model is correlated with Jill's relationship effect with Jack. This correlation is referred to as dyadic reciprocity. It is also possible to correlate Jack's actor effect with his partner effect. So it can be asked whether a person who tends to see others as intelligent tends to be seen by others as intelligent. This correlation is usually referred to as the actor–partner correlation, and it examines reciprocity at the individual level of analysis.

## MEANING OF RELATIONSHIP EFFECTS

What is the meaning of the relationship effect within the Social Relations Model? There are two fundamentally different ways to interpret the relationship effect: individual difference based and interaction based. Consider the variable of trust. To what extent does Jack trust Jill? The first explanation, individual difference based, is that the relationship effect is explainable in terms of the individual differences in the two people. For instance, Jack does not trust Jill because Jill is a female and Jack does not trust females. So in principle Jack's lack of trust could have been predicted before the two ever met. The second explanation, interaction based, is that Jack's lack of trust emerges out of the interaction. What happened between the two people resulted in the level of trust that Jack has for Jill. For this explanation, the level of trust could not be predicted before the interaction began. The relationship history must be scrutinized carefully to understand the relational outcome. In sum, relationship variance may indicate the statistical interaction between dispositional variables of the two participants, or it may indicate truly interactional aspects.

Relationships variance may be overestimated if the combination of actor and partner effects do not operate in a simple linear fashion. There are two particular types of nonlinearity that are worrisome: multiplicative functional form and bilinear interactions.

In a multiplicative functional form, actor and partner effects do not add together as they are assumed to do in the Social Relations Model, but rather they multiply together. For instance, consider a measure of social acuity: How accurately does actor A judge partner B? It is probably more reasonable in this context to argue that actor and partner effects do not add but rather multiply. That is, if the actor has no ability or the partner does not provide sufficient information, the actor must necessarily be inaccurate. Accuracy is the product of actor ability and partner expressivity. The simple solution to this problem of nonadditivity is a logarithm transformation. If the model is multiplicative, then a logarithmic transformation turns the model into an additive model.

A second type of nonlinear effect is a bilinear interaction. Imagine the case in which people judge other people's intelligence. It may be that some actors are better judges than others. For instance, actor A may be quite sensitive, B less so, and C has no sensitivity. In some sense, the amount of partner variance differs from actor to actor. The standard Social Relations Model assumes that all judges are equally sensitive. The presence of bilinear interactions would inflate the estimate of relationship variance in that differences in sensitivity would be mistakenly treated as relationship variance. Work is currently underway to estimate the differential sensitivity of actors within the Social Relations Model.

## AFFECT

Affect or liking is the quintessential relational variable. However, researchers not using the Social Relations Model have assumed that affect is relational but they have not demonstrated it. Affect need not necessarily be relational; it might be that affect is determined largely by the properties of the target (e.g., physical attractiveness).

There are two ways in which the Social Relations Model can show that affect is truly a relational variable. The first way is to show that most of the meaningful variance in affect lies at the level of relationship. So affect is relational if its variance lies at the dyadic level. The second way to show that affect is relational is to show that the variance in affect is reciprocal, especially when the interactants have known each other for a long period of time. These two questions are examined in the next two sections.

## Variance

Table 6.2 presents the variance partitioning from a number of studies that have examined affect. To be included, a study must both measure affect and have multiple measures so that relationship and error can be separated. Also, only studies involving adults are included in the table. The studies have been divided into three types. The first two types involve the initial interactions between two people. In the first type the interactions are one on one or dyadic, and in the second type the interactions take place in a group. The final type of study is one in which the people have known each other for a long period of time. For the over-time studies with single measures of liking, the last two time points were treated as replications. The Dabbs and Ruback (1987) data are the averages across three studies using the same measures.

Table 6.2 clearly shows that generally the dominant variance component is relationship. The median proportion of relationship variance across the 10 studies is .40. Quite clearly, relationship plays a very important role in determining affect. The partner variance, which measures the tendency for some people to be liked and others not to be liked, was not very large in any of the studies except Newcomb (1961). The median partner variance is only .12, and the median actor variance is only .17. Clearly affect is relational. Whom a

TABLE 6.2
Proportion of Variance for Attraction Measures

| Study | Actor | Partner | Relationship | Error |
|---|---|---|---|---|
| First encounters: One-on-one | | | | |
| Burleson (1982) | .20 | .18 | .32 | .30 |
| Kenny and Bernstein (1982) | .00 | .05 | .55 | .40 |
| First encounters: Groups | | | | |
| Kashy (1988) | .32 | .06 | .44 | .18 |
| Dabbs and Ruback (1987) | .30 | .13 | .37 | .19 |
| Park and Flink (1989) | .36 | .11 | .38 | .16 |
| Long-term acquaintance | | | | |
| Curry and Emerson (1970) | .15 | .12 | .41 | .32 |
| Burleson (1982) | .17 | .18 | .30 | .35 |
| Newcomb (1961) | — | .41 | .50 | .10 |
| Wright et al. (1985) | .05 | .16 | .30 | .48 |
| Malloy and Albright (1990) | .10 | .00 | .50 | .40 |

*Note.* For the Newcomb study, there is no actor variance because the data are ranks.

person likes depends more on the relationship than on who the partner is or who is doing the liking.

Although relationship is the dominant component in ratings of liking, there are two additional points that should be raised in examining the results in Table 6.2. First, in the group studies there is a substantial amount of variance for actor. This result probably indicates that, within groups, some people like being in the group and others do not, a result discussed by Kenny, Hallmark, Sullivan, and Kashy (1993). Second, the Newcomb (1961) study indicated very high levels of agreement about who is liked in the group and who is not. This group was a residential group of older men returning to college. This group evidently developed a common set of norms with which to evaluate each other.

## Reciprocity

The second issue is whether attraction is reciprocal. If Jack likes Jill, does Jill like Jack? Conversely, if Jack hates Jill, does Jill hate Jack? Even though everyone has been on the losing end of unrequited love, if someone spurns someone else, the latter quickly learn to not love the former (unless you are Glenn Close in the film *Fatal Attraction*). Reciprocity of attraction is so obvious that it hardly needs an empirical demonstration. But when Kenny and Nasby (1980) set out to look for empirical confirmation of reciprocity of attraction, we could not find it. Moreover, the then dean of researchers in the field of acquaintance and attraction, Theodore Newcomb, titled his 1979 article "Reciprocity of Attraction: A Nonconfirmation of a Plausible Hypothesis."

Reciprocity of attraction does exist, but to demonstrate that it does actor and partner effects must be removed. Returning to Jack and Jill, consider how much Jack likes Jill. Jack's actor effect would measure the extent to which Jack tends to like others in general. Jill's partner effect would measure the extent to which Jill is liked by others. The relationship effect would measure how Jack feels about Jill after removing Jack's actor effect and Jill's partner effect. To measure reciprocity, Jack's relationship effect is correlated with Jill's relationship with Jack (Kenny & La Voie, 1982, 1984; Kenny & Nasby, 1980).

Table 6.3 presents the dyadic reciprocity correlations from the 10 studies in Table 6.2. All the correlations in the table are at the level of the relationship. For each study, attraction was measured either at two times or by two different measures, therefore error can be removed from true relationship. The results clearly show that there is little reciprocity of attraction in first encounters, averaging only .22. But in long-term interactions, reciprocity of attraction averages to .61. Reciprocity of attraction then emerges in long-term relationships, which is further evidence of attraction's relational nature.

TABLE 6.3
Reciprocity Correlations

| Study | Dyadic Reciprocity |
|---|---|
| First encounters: One-on-one | |
| Burleson (1982) | .26 |
| Kenny and Bernstein (1982) | .29 |
| First encounters: Groups | |
| Kashy (1988) | .26 |
| Dabbs and Ruback (1987) | .13 |
| Park and Flink (1989) | .18 |
| Long-term acquaintance | |
| Curry and Emerson (1970) | .48 |
| Burleson (1982) | .49 |
| Newcomb (1961) | .58 |
| Wright et al. (1985) | .74 |
| Malloy and Albright (1990) | .75 |

## Self-Disclosure

If a variable operates in the same way as affect (i.e., it has large amounts of relationship variance and high levels of reciprocity), that variable is likely to be highly tied to affect. One such variable appears to be reported self-disclosure. Three studies have examined the variable of self-disclosure within a Social Relations Model framework. Miller and Kenny (1986) asked members of a sorority whether they were willing to disclose to the other women on high and low intimacy topics. Reno and Kenny (1992) had strangers dyadically interact and get to know each other, and people then rated how private their partners' disclosures were. Montgomery's (1984) study was similar to Reno and Kenny's, but in her study interactions took place over a longer period of time and were in a group. She had class members rate each other's openness at three time points during the semester.

Table 6.4 presents the key results from these studies. Consider first the variance partitioning. As is evidenced by the weak partner variance, except for the Montgomery (1984) study, there is little agreement about who is disclosing and who is not. The likely reason for the high agreement about who is disclosing in the Montgomery study is that interactions were in a group and the students were instructed to be disclosing to each other. Thus, disclosure was not to a single person but to a group. Thus, there is a tendency for some people to disclose to all of their interaction partners and others to not disclose at all.

Because relationship effects are confounded with error, it cannot be unequivocally claimed that relationship is the dominant component in self-disclosure. However, from Miller and Kenny (1986) it is known that there is

TABLE 6.4
Self-Disclosure Variance Partitioning and Correlation with Liking

| Study | Actor | Partner | Relation | Dyadic Reciprocity | Correlation with Liking |
|---|---|---|---|---|---|
| Reno and Kenny (1992) | .34 | .00 | .65 | .21 | .16 |
| Miller and Kenny (1986) | | | | | |
|   High intimacy | .13 | .00 | .87 | .67 | .41 |
|   Low intimacy | .38 | .01 | .61 | .63 | .41 |
| Montgomery (1984) | | | | | |
|   Time 1 | .44 | .18 | .38 | − .07 | .48 |
|   Time 2 | .20 | .24 | .56 | .11 | .47 |
|   Time 3 | .19 | .27 | .54 | .26 | .58 |

a substantial correlation of .86 between willingness to disclose high intimacy topics and willingness to disclose low intimacy topics at the relationship level. Thus, for long-term acquaintance, it is likely that the bulk of the variance in relationship variance (confounded with error) is true relationship variance.

Also presented in Table 6.4 are the dyadic reciprocities for disclosure. They are generally positive, and they are higher with increased acquaintance. Only in the study by Miller and Kenny (1986) were there long-term relationships, and that study showed the highest level of reciprocity.

For the studies that correlated liking with disclosure, one sees that the correlations are positive, and the correlations appear to increase with greater acquaintance. There is very good evidence that reported self-disclosure is a relational variable.

## INTERPERSONAL PERCEPTION

The bulk of my effort in the application of the Social Relations Model has been in the area of interpersonal perception. The topic of interpersonal perception, although not entirely ignored in the close relationships area (Sillars & Scott, 1983), has not been a major one. Given that these efforts in this area were extensively detailed in Kenny (1988) and Malloy and Albright (1990), only a brief presentation is given here.

Table 6.5 lists nine fundamental questions in interpersonal perception. Consider three women, Alice, Betty, and Carol, who are referred to here as A(lice), B(etty), and C(arol). In Table 6.5, the symbol A(B) represents Person A's perception of B on a given trait. The symbol A(A) represents self-perception, and the symbol A(B(A)) represents meta-perception: how A thinks that B sees A. So if the trait is anxious, then A(B) represents how anxious Alice thinks that Betty is, A(A) represents how anxious Alice sees herself, and A(B(A)) represents how anxious Alice thinks that Betty thinks that Alice is. Finally, the symbol B represents Betty's actual standing on the trait.

TABLE 6.5
Fundamental Questions in Interpersonal Perception

| Question | Symbols |
|---|---|
| Assimilation | $A(B) = A(C)$ |
| Consensus | $A(C) = B(C)$ |
| Uniqueness | $A(B) <> A(C)$ |
| | $A(C) <> B(C)$ |
| Reciprocity | $A(B) = B(A)$ |
| Target accuracy | $A(B) = B$ |
| Meta-accuracy | $A(B) = B(A(B))$ |
| Assumed reciprocity | $A(B) = A(B(A))$ |
| Assumed similarity | $A(B) = A(A)$ |
| Self–other agreement | $B(A) = A(A)$ |

*Note.* A, B, C are persons and parentheses are perceptions. Double parentheses are meta-perceptions.

The first question in Table 6.5 is assimilation. Do people see others in the same way? Assimilation can be assessed by an examination of the amount of actor variance. The greater the actor variance, the greater the assimilation.

The second question is consensus: Do two raters of a common target agree with one another? Consensus can be assessed by the amount of partner variance in trait ratings. If people exactly agree with each other about the standing of targets on a trait, then all of the variance in the measure is partner variance.

The third question concerns uniqueness: Does an actor view a partner in a way that is different from how he or she views others and different from how the partner is viewed by others? Uniqueness is indexed by the level of relationship variance.

Reciprocity concerns the extent to which two people have mirror images of each other. As was explained in the previous sections, there are two types of reciprocity: one at the individual level and the other at the dyadic level.

Target accuracy concerns the correctness of a perception. If Betty thinks that Alice is lazy, is Alice in fact lazy? An obvious difficult issue in measuring target accuracy is ascertaining a person's actual standing on a trait.

The next two questions concern meta-perception. The first, meta-accuracy, asks whether people know what others think of them. The second, assumed reciprocity, asks whether people think that others see them as those people see others.

The last two questions concern the relationship between self- and other perception. The first question, assumed similarity, concerns whether people see themselves the way that they see others. The second question, self–other agreement, concerns whether others see a person the way that he or she sees him or herself.

The bulk of the research effort has been focused on the second question of consensus (Albright, Kenny, & Malloy, 1988; Kenny, 1991; Kenny, Albright, Malloy, & Kashy, 1993; Kenny & Malloy, 1988). Consensus is an important question for a variety of reasons. First, it has important theoretical significance in a number of areas for social scientists. Social psychologists have studied consensus to determine if person perception reflects more the "eye of the beholder" than the target being perceived. Personality psychologists have been interested in consensus because the presence of consensus validates the notion of individual differences. Methodologists have studied consensus because observation is often the method of data collection, and consensus then serves as a measure of reliability.

The second general reason why consensus is an important question is that it is a necessary condition to address three other questions. To measure self–other agreement and target accuracy and meta-accuracy at the individual level, it must first be established that there is consensus. For instance, if there were no consensus, it would make no sense to ask whether a person sees him or herself as others do, because how can self agree with others if others are not in agreement.

Kenny et al. (1993) extensively studied the relationship between consensus and acquaintance. For extroversion, people seem to pick up information very quickly, without even needing to interact with the person.

Kenny (1991) identified two obvious but neglected factors that need further study in this area. The first concerns the extent to which the information that two judges have overlaps. If the two judges are together when they see the target, then they are more likely to agree than when they see target separately. The second neglected factor concerns the extent to which the judges have the same meaning systems. If they label or interpret the same behavior differently, they do not agree.

The second question on which we focused is the accuracy question (Kenny & Albright, 1987). Most of the effort has been in the area of meta-accuracy. Do people know what others think of them? Meta-accuracy seems pivotal to the smooth functioning of relationships. That is, if people are able to know what is going on in their partners' heads, then their relationships would be more harmonious.

There are two types of meta-accuracy. The first is individual meta-accuracy: Do people know how others see them in general? The second is dyadic meta-accuracy: Do people know who in particular sees them as especially high on the trait and who sees them as particularly low on the trait? In my work with DePaulo (DePaulo, Kenny, Hoover, Webb, & Oliver, 1987; Kenny & DePaulo, 1993), we showed that meta-accuracy can be high at the individual level but is rarely very high at the dyadic level. Thus, people seem to know how they generally come across, but they do not really know how they are differentially seen by others.

## SPECIAL DYADS

Some relationships appear to be qualitatively different from others. The time that people spend with their lovers, best friends, and therapists seems to be very different from the time they spend with acquaintances. Some of people's interaction partners are special, and others are ordinary partners.

It must be established empirically as well as theoretically how interactions with special others differ from those with ordinary others. That is, most theorists assume but never really demonstrate that special relationships are in fact different from ordinary relationships. How can this be done? First, an analysis of ordinary dyads is performed (Kenny, 1990b). Then the data from special dyads are forced to fit into the ordinary dyad mold. It can then be seen where there is a lack of fit, and that will establish the differences between the two types of relationships.

Consider part of the results from Kenny and Kashy (1993). We re-analyzed data collected by Miller, Campbell, Twedt, and O'Connell (1966). We studied 294 people who were members of 16 different living groups. Each person nominated their five closest friends in the group. We then matched as many people as we could with a close friend, mutual choice. With a beginning total of 294 people, we created 119 friendship pairs, and most were mutual first choices.

The data used by Miller et al. (1966) were taken from a study by Campbell, Miller, Lubetsky, and O'Connell (1964), which was a study of projection: Do people with certain personalities see the world differently from those with other personalities? Because the focus was on comparing different theories of projection, most of the 27 traits were very negative (e.g., suspicious, hostile, and prying). A factor analysis of the 27 traits indicated four factors. The first factor, which we called obnoxious, contained most of the negative traits. The second factor, which we called competent, contained all the positive traits as well as the trait strict, which evidently was positively valued during the early 1960s in the United States. The third factor contained the negative traits of suspicious, touchy, and secretive, therefore we labeled this factor paranoid. The final factor contained the traits dependent, anxious, and gullible, and we called it naive.

Two sets of results are presented. The first question concerns consensus: Do two friends agree more in rating a target than two acquaintances agree? As can be seen in Table 6.6, when friends rated a common target they agreed more than nonfriends. So if Andrew and Charles are friends and they rate George, they agree more than they would if they were not friends.

There are at least three explanations for this effect. First is the communication explanation. That is, Andrew and Charles agree because they have discussed George and have shared with each other their points of view concerning George. This discussion has led each to be influenced by the other. The second explanation is the common stimulus effect. Presumably friends spend more

TABLE 6.6
Correlations of Perceptions Between Friends and Acquaintances

| | Factor | | | |
|---|---|---|---|---|
| Question | Obnoxious | Competent | Paranoid | Naive |
| Consensus | | | | |
| Acquaintances | .26 | .36 | .14 | .14 |
| Friends | .36 | .44 | .23 | .22 |
| Assimilation | | | | |
| Acquaintances | .33 | .21 | .41 | .29 |
| Friends | .47 | .36 | .48 | .35 |

time together than do nonfriends. If this is so, it is likely that when Andrew is observing George, Charles is often present. That is, when judging George, Andrew and Charles are using overlapping information. The third explanation is that when two friends observe the same behavior, they interpret or label that behavior in the same way. Friends may share more similar meaning systems than acquaintances.

The communication explanation is bolstered by the fact that the female friends exhibited this effect much more so than the male friends. If it is true that women more often discuss with each other their feelings about other people in the group than do men, then the communication effect may be the reason for heightened consensus between female friends.

The second result found was that friends were seen as more similar to each other than they actually were. This effect is called assimilation, and the results are presented in Table 6.6. When George judged the friends Andrew and Charles, he saw their personalities as more similar than he saw the personalities of two people who were mere acquaintances. It is possible that friends were in fact more similar in their personalities than acquaintances. According to analyses in Kenny and Kashy (1993), about half of the increase in assimilation in the perception of friends versus acquaintances is due to similar personalities. The other half is due to a tendency to see friends as more similar than they really are.

## CONCLUSION

My previous work using the Social Relations Model may have led to the mistaken impression of my point of view. In a number of papers, I have focused on the actor and partner effects, and I have treated relationship effects as little more than error. I do not believe that individual processes are a crucial aspect of relationships. Rather, I believe that individual-level processes cloud the truly relational aspects of interpersonal behavior. Researchers need to strip away these individual-level effects to see what is really going on in relationships. A major theoretical impetus behind the Social Relations Model is that social life is relational, but the actor and partner effects must be removed to reveal it.

What has been done is to provide a statistical definition of a relationship. Although a relationship cannot be captured fully in a statistical analysis, statistics can help. The statistics give some insight into what is meant by a relationship. If a person behaves in exactly the same way with all of his or her interaction partners, it does not seem justifiable to speak of him or her as relating to his or her partners. The Social Relations Model captures the unique aspect of relationships.

One might even argue that, to demonstrate that people are relating to one another, one must show that there is relationship variance (Ross & Lollis, 1989). This might be particularly appropriate for developmental psychology, where the question of at what age do children learn to relate uniquely to their partners is a critical one. Certainly the Social Relations Model can be one tool in determining at what age and with whom children develop relationships. Moreover, it should prove useful in determining when and how adults form relationships, and how close relationships differ from ordinary relationships.

Too much of my work, and that of others, has examined equal-status, positive relationships. Using the four dimensions found by Wish, Deutsch, and Kaplan (1976), which characterize dyadic relationships, researchers have concentrated too much on cooperative, equal-status, socioemotional, and intense relationships, and have seriously neglected unequal-status relationships.

Relationship researchers have only just begun to exploit the usefulness of the Social Relations Model to study relationships. Thus, it is premature to forecast the directions for future research. Hopefully, the model will embolden researchers to ask the questions that they are really interested in so that they can probe more deeply into the fascinating area of relationships.

## ACKNOWLEDGMENTS

This work was supported in part by a grant from the National Institute of Mental Health RO1-MH4029501 and by the National Science Foundation grants BNS-8807462 and BNS-908077. I would like to thank Kathryn Dindia, Bryan Hallmark, Loring Ingraham, and Deborah Kashy for commenting on an earlier version of this chapter.

## REFERENCES

Albright, L., Kenny, D. A., & Malloy, T. E. (1988). Consensus in personality judgments at zero acquaintance. *Journal of Personality and Social Psychology, 55*, 387–395.

Burleson, J. A. (1982). *Reciprocity of interpersonal attraction within acquainted versus unacquainted small groups*. Unpublished doctoral dissertation, University of Texas, Austin.

Campbell, D. T., Miller, N., Lubetsky, J., & O'Connell, E. J. (1964). Varieties of projection in trait attribution. *Psychological Monographs, 78* (15, Whole No. 592).

Clark, M. S., & Reis, H. T. (1988). Interpersonal processes in close relationships. In M. R. Rosenzweig & L. W. Porter (Eds.), *Annual review of psychology* (Vol. 39, pp. 609–672). Palo Alto, CA: Annual Reviews.

Curry, T. J., & Emerson, R. M. (1970). Balance theory: A theory of interpersonal attraction? *Sociometry, 33,* 216–238.

Dabbs, J. M., Jr., & Ruback, R. B. (1987). Dimensions of group process: Amount and structure of vocal interaction. In L. Berkowitz (Ed.), *Advances in experimental social psychology* (Vol. 20, pp. 123–169). Orlando, FL: Academic Press.

DePaulo, B., Kenny, D. A., Hoover, C., Webb, W., & Oliver, P. V. (1987). Accuracy of person perception: Do people know what kind of impressions they convey? *Journal of Personality and Social Psychology, 52,* 303–315.

Duncan, S., & Fiske, D. W. (1977). *Face to face interaction: Research, methods, and theory.* Hillsdale, NJ: Lawrence Erlbaum Associates.

Hallmark, B., & Kenny, D. A. (1990). *The effect of rating a person at a time or a trait at a time on the variance components of the social relations model.* Unpublished manuscript, University of Connecticut, Storrs.

Ingraham, L. J., & Wright, T. L. (1986). A cautionary note on the interpretation of relationship effects in the Social Relations Model. *Social Psychology Quarterly, 49,* 93–97.

Kashy, D. A. (1988). *Intergroup processes: A social relations perspective.* Unpublished masters thesis, University of Connecticut, Storrs.

Kenny, D. A. (1981). Interpersonal perception: A multivariate round robin analysis. In M. B. Brewer & B. Collins (Eds.), *Scientific inquiry and the social sciences: A volume in honor of Donald T. Campbell* (pp. 288–309). San Francisco, CA: Jossey-Bass.

Kenny, D. A. (1988). Interpersonal perception: A social relations analysis. *Journal of Social and Personal Relationships, 5,* 247–261.

Kenny, D. A. (1990a). Design and analysis issues in dyadic research. In C. Hendrick & M. S. Clark (Eds.), *Review of personality and social psychology* (Vol. 11, pp. 164–184). Newbury Park, CA: Sage.

Kenny, D. A. (1990b). What makes a relationship special? In T. Draper & A. C. Marcos (Eds.), *Family variables: Conceptualization, measurement, and use* (pp. 161–178). Newbury Park, CA: Sage.

Kenny, D. A. (1991). A general model of consensus and accuracy in interpersonal perception. *Psychological Review, 98,* 155–163.

Kenny, D. A., & Albright, L. (1987). Accuracy in interpersonal perception: A social relations analysis. *Psychological Bulletin, 102,* 390–402.

Kenny, D. A., Albright, L., Malloy, T. E., & Kashy, D. A. (1993). *Consensus in interpersonal perception: Acquaintance and the big five.* Unpublished manuscript, University of Connecticut, Storrs.

Kenny, D. A., & Bernstein, N. (1982). *Interactions between opposite-sex strangers.* Unpublished data set, University of Connecticut, Storrs.

Kenny, D. A., & DePaulo, B. M. (1993). Do people know how others view them?: An empirical and theoretical account. *Psychological Bulletin, 114,* 145–161.

Kenny, D. A., Hallmark, B. W., Sullivan, P., & Kashy, D. A. (1993). The analysis of designs in which individuals are in more than one group. *British Journal of Social Psychology, 32,* 173–190.

Kenny, D. A., & Kashy, D. A. (1993). *Enhanced coorientation in the perception of friends: A social relations analysis.* Unpublished manuscript, University of Connecticut, Storrs.

Kenny, D. A., & La Voie, L. (1982). Reciprocity of attraction: A confirmed hypothesis. *Social Psychology Quarterly, 45,* 54–58.

Kenny, D. A., & La Voie, L. (1984). The social relations model. In L. Berkowitz (Ed.), *Advances in experimental social psychology* (Vol. 18, pp. 142–182). Orlando, FL: Academic Press.

Kenny, D. A., & Malloy, T. E. (1988). Partner effects in social interaction. *Journal of Nonverbal Behavior, 12,* 34–57.

Kenny, D. A., & Nasby, W. (1980). Splitting the reciprocity correlation. *Journal of Personality and Social Psychology, 38,* 249–256.

Levine, J., & Snyder, H. (1980). *Social perception among five and six years old.* Unpublished data set, University of Pittsburgh.

Malloy, T. E., & Albright, L. (1990). Interpersonal perception in a social context. *Journal of Personality and Social Psychology, 58,* 419–428.

Malloy, T. E., & Kenny, D. A. (1986). The social relations model: An integrative methodology for personality research. *Journal of Personality, 54,* 101–127.

Miller, L. C., & Kenny, D. A. (1986). Reciprocity of self-disclosure at the individual and dyadic levels: A social relations analysis. *Journal of Personality and Social Psychology, 50,* 713–719.

Miller, N., Campbell, D. T., Twedt, H., & O'Connell, E. J. (1966). Similarity, contrast, and complementarity in friendship choice. *Journal of Personality and Social Psychology, 3,* 3–12.

Montgomery, B. (1984). Individual differences and relational interdependences in social interaction. *Human Communication Research, 11,* 33–60.

Newcomb, T. M. (1961). *The acquaintance process.* New York: Holt, Rinehart & Winston.

Newcomb, T. M. (1979). Reciprocity of attraction: A nonconfirmation of a plausible hypothesis. *Social Psychology Quarterly, 42,* 299–306.

Park, B., & Flink, C. (1989). A social relations analysis of agreement in liking judgments. *Journal of Personality and Social Psychology, 56,* 506–518.

Reno, R. R., & Kenny, D. A. (1992). Effects of self-consciousness and social anxiety on self-disclosure among unacquainted individuals: An application of the social relations model. *Journal of Personality, 60,* 79–94.

Ross, H. S., & Lollis, S. P. (1989). A social relations analysis of toddler peer relationships. *Child Development, 60,* 1082–1091.

Sillars, A. L., & Scott, M. D. (1983). Interpersonal perception between intimates: An integrative review. *Human Communication Research, 10,* 153–176.

Warner, R., Kenny, D. A., & Stoto, M. (1979). Round robin analysis of variance for social interaction data. *Journal of Personality and Social Psychology, 37,* 1742–1757.

Wish, M., Deutsch, M., & Kaplan, S. J. (1976). Perceived dimensions of interpersonal relations. *Journal of Personality and Social Psychology, 33,* 409–420.

Wright, T. L., Ingraham, L. J., & Blackmer, D. R. (1985). Simultaneous study of individual differences and relationship effects in attraction. *Journal of Personality and Social Psychology, 47,* 1059–1062.

# Chapter 7

# A Developmental Model of the Relations Between Mother–Child Attachment and Friendship

Kathryn A. Kerns
*Kent State University*

As individuals progress through life, they meet new people, have new experiences, and forge new relationships. Yet, they are not starting afresh in every new situation or relationship; rather, they bring their organization of cognitions, feelings, and behavior with them. That is, people have personalities. Personality theorists (e.g., Block, 1977) have been interested in identifying the coherence in an individual's development. The notion of coherence is that an individual's behavior is predictable across time and situations. There is more continuity in an individual's behavior across situations (Epstein, 1981) than was once suspected (Mischel, 1968). Recent longitudinal work (Caspi, Elder, & Bem, 1987, 1988; Huesman, Eron, Lefkowitz, & Walder, 1984) has suggested that there is a great deal of coherence in personality from childhood to adulthood.

Researchers interested in studying personal relationships have begun to ask similar questions. They have examined whether there is coherence over time in the qualities of an individual's relationships. They also have addressed the question of whether there is a detectable coherence across an individual's many relationships. The latter involves identifying key dimensions of different personal relationships (e.g., parent–child, peer) and examining how the different relationships relate to one another.

*Personality* refers to an individual's characteristic pattern of behavior (Wiggins, 1973). By contrast, *relationship* is a dyadic construct that refers to the affect, cognition, and behavior of two people (Hinde, 1979; Park & Waters, 1988). According to Hinde, two individuals are said to have a relationship if they have had a series of interactions occurring over a period of time. Because relationships include the patterning of interactions between two people, they are more than descriptions of either individual's behavior (Hinde, 1979).

Naturally, there is an interplay between personality and relationships. Individuals bring skills, attitudes, and affects to each relationship. The two individuals then establish patterns of interaction. In addition, relationships shape personality development. These themes reemerge throughout this chapter.

Wiggins (1973) suggested that traits are summaries, rather than causes, of behavior. To say that someone is aggressive means that the person has acted aggressively in the past, is unlikely to treat others gently, and is likely to act aggressively in the future. The term *trait* thus summarizes consistency in an individual's behavior.

Similarly, relationships are summaries, rather than causes, of behavior (Park & Waters, 1988). Descriptions of relationships refer to consistencies in the affect, cognition, and behavior of a particular dyad. The question of coherence across relationships becomes one of identifying coherence in the behavior of different relationship dyads in which an individual participates. For example, some investigators have examined links between parent–child and peer relationships, and found that parental warmth and control predict peer competence (Baumrind, 1973; Parke et al., 1989; Sroufe, 1988).

This chapter presents a framework for thinking about links between a child's relationship with his or her mother and best friend. It addresses the question of how and why there might be links between parent–child and peer relationships. The theoretical perspective for examining parent–child relationships is Bowlby's (1973, 1982) and Ainsworth's (1972, 1982) theory of social development. Because parent–child attachment has its most profound implications for other close relationships (Sroufe & Fleeson, 1986), this chapter focuses on associations between attachment and friendship. No single theoretical perspective is adopted to examine friendship. Rather, the ideas of a number of different theorists are integrated. Children's friendships are discussed by identifying the salient issue for friendship at different developmental periods. Finally, this chapter presents a developmental model of the predicted relations between parent–child attachment and friendship. The proposed model is developmental, in that different dimensions of friendship are predicted to correlate highest with security of attachment at different ages.

The model makes predictions at two levels. At the level of the individual, it identifies the relationship skills that facilitate the development of friendship in a given developmental period. At the relationship level, it identifies salient qualities of friendship for each developmental period. The model suggests how quality of mother–child attachment might influence both relationship skills and qualities of friendship.

The chapter is organized into four sections. The first section provides a brief review of Bowlby's (1973, 1982) theory of mother–child attachment. The second section provides a summary of theories of friendship. In the third section,

I discuss a model that predicts relations between attachment security to caregivers and qualities of a child's friendships. Mechanisms to account for continuity are also discussed. In addition, this section provides a discussion of the model's limitations and suggests directions for future research. The final section discusses how a dyadic perspective contributes to an understanding of cross-relationship continuities.

## OVERVIEW OF ATTACHMENT THEORY

Bowlby (1973, 1982) and Ainsworth (1972, 1982) have proposed a theory of social development that highlights the importance of the mother-child bond. The theory was proposed to explain the origin and implications of individual differences in the quality of mother-child relationships. Although children form attachments to both mothers and fathers, the theory has focused on mother-child relationships because mothers are more often the primary caregivers.

According to the theory, all children become attached to their primary caregiver(s). However, patterns of caregiving over the first year of life produce differences in the security of parent-child attachments. Security of attachment reflects the degree to which a child can use a parent as a secure base from which to explore, and as a source of comfort in times of distress (Ainsworth, Blehar, Walters, & Wall, 1978; Bowlby, 1982). The child seeks a balance between exploration and proximity seeking (Bowlby, 1982). The infant is likely to explore in a safe environment, but is expected to seek out the mother for comfort in times of distress. Thus, it looks as if the baby's behavior is organized with the set goal of "felt security" (Sroufe & Waters, 1977). The development of a secure attachment relationship is expected to place the child on a more optimal developmental pathway (Bowlby, 1988; Sroufe, 1988).

One line of research has focused on identifying patterns of caregiving that influence the development of a secure attachment (see Ainsworth et al., 1978; Sroufe, 1988, for reviews). Children who experience responsive, sensitive caregiving tend to become securely attached to their mothers. Children who experience unresponsive caregiving, or who have a psychologically unavailable mother, tend to form insecure or anxious attachment relationships with their mothers. It is said that these children are anxiously attached because they are uncertain about whether their mothers will be responsive, available, and a source of comfort in times of distress.

A challenge for attachment theorists has been how to define and measure quality of mother-child attachment. Ainsworth, Bell, and Stayton (1971) and Ainsworth et al. (1978) developed a laboratory test to assess an infant's secure base pattern of behavior. The test has been validated by examining the home behaviors of mothers and infants (Ainsworth et al., 1978; Bosso, 1985; Grossman, Grossman, Spangler, Suess, & Unzer, 1985; Vaughn & Waters, 1990).

The test, called the Strange Situation, examines the baby's ability to use the mother as a secure base. The procedure involves a sequence of separations and reunions between the infant and mother. In the original study (Ainsworth et al., 1971), three patterns of reunion responses were identified. Children who received responsive, sensitive caregiving greeted their mothers on reunion, tended to seek proximity or interaction and, if distressed, could be calmed by their mothers. These children, approximately two thirds of the sample, were identified as securely attached. Children who received insensitive caregiving combined with maternal rejection avoided their mothers on reunion; this pattern of attachment was labeled anxious-avoidant. Children who received insensitive caregiving but were not rejected by their mothers showed a mixture of proximity seeking and anger toward their mothers on reunion. In addition, many of these infants were difficult to soothe. This pattern of attachment was labeled anxious-ambivalent. These three patterns of attachment have been identified reliably with the Strange Situation in numerous other studies.

The Strange Situation is widely used because it is an economical way to assess an infant's caregiving history. In addition, the Strange Situation has a wide range of external correlates. For example, longitudinal studies have found that securely attached toddlers and preschoolers are better able to use their mothers as a resource when working on a difficult task, show fewer conduct problems, are more socially competent around peers, and have higher self-esteem (see Bretherton, 1985; Greenberg & Speltz, 1988; Sroufe, 1983).

One limitation of the Strange Situation is that it is currently validated as a measure of attachment security only for 12- to 18-month-olds, although efforts are underway to develop a method of scoring Strange Situation reunions in 3-year-olds (Cassidy, Marvin, & the Attachment Group of the MacArthur Network, 1987). Main and colleagues (Main, Kaplan, & Cassidy, 1985; Main & Cassidy, 1988) developed a separation–reunion procedure for assessing security of attachment in 6-year-olds. One study showed that 6-year-old attachment classifications are correlated with home behavior (Solomon, George, & Ivins, 1987). This system is harder to score than the 1-year-old system (Main & Cassidy, 1988), however, and has yet to be adopted widely.

An alternative approach to measuring attachment security is to focus on describing home behaviors of children and infants. Waters and Deane (1985) recently developed an Attachment Q-set for describing home behavior that can be used to assess security of attachment in 1- to 4-year-old children. With this measure, children receive a score on a continuum of attachment security, rather than being classified as securely or insecurely attached to their mothers. Recent data demonstrate convergence between Strange Situation classifications and Attachment Q-set assessments with infants and toddlers (Bosso, 1985; Vaughn & Waters, 1990). Security scores derived from mothers' or observers' q-sort descriptions are also correlated with observers' ratings of maternal sensitivity and responsiveness (Pederson et al., 1990; Teti, Nakagawa, Das, &

Wirth, 1991), behavior with friends (Park & Waters, 1989) and siblings (Teti & Ablard, 1989), and self-esteem (Park, 1989).

Bowlby (1982) suggested that there are changes in the nature of parent–child relationships in the preschool years as a result of the child becoming a more competent and skilled social partner. The mother–child relationship becomes what Bowlby termed a *goal-corrected partnership*. At this time, the child as well as the mother can act to regulate the dyad's interactions. As a result, parent–child communication becomes a central component of the relationship (Bretherton, 1987). Securely attached children and their mothers are expected to engage in more negotiation (Greenberg & Speltz, 1988) and to have a more open and calm communication style (Bretherton, 1987), compared to anxiously attached children and their mothers. Thus, communication style as well as patterns of secure base behavior may be signs of attachment security in the preschool years.

Methods of assessing attachment security in young children are focused on the interactions of mother and child. In middle childhood, however, the frequency and intensity of specific attachment behaviors wanes (Bowlby, 1982). Main (Main et al., 1985; Main & Cassidy, 1988) suggested that the assessment of attachment beyond the preschool years must move to the level of representation. That is, attachment can be assessed at older ages by assessing a child's cognitions about the attachment relationship. A few cognitive measures of attachment have already been developed (Cassidy, 1988; Main et al., 1985), and measures to assess security of attachment in middle childhood are currently being constructed (Park & Hazan, 1989). However the lack of methods for assessing attachment security beyond early childhood has limited the study of parent–child attachment.

Bowlby (1982) suggested that in adulthood the partner in a close, intimate relationship becomes an individual's attachment figure. That is, the role of attachment figure is transferred from parent to peer. Recently it has been suggested that adult love relationships can be understood by conceptualizing adult bonds as attachments (Collins & Read, 1990; Hazan & Shaver, 1987; Shaver & Hazan 1988). In these approaches, secure and anxious attachment are thought of as love styles, rather than as descriptors of a particular relationship. Thus, the hypothesis is that by adulthood individuals have attachment styles that are incorporated into an individual's personality. If attachment style is a component of personality rather than a description of a particular relationship, individuals would be expected to have the same patterns of attachment with different partners. To date, however, no studies have examined whether adults have the same or different attachment styles in different love relationships.

The results of many studies provide convergent validity for the attachment construct. Sroufe (1988) recently suggested that evidence of discriminant as well as convergent validity is needed to define the limits of the attachment

construct. Security of attachment is expected to correlate with social relationships and social interaction, but is not expected to be highly correlated with
measures of IQ or physical development (Sroufe, 1988). In the preschool years,
security of attachment is uncorrelated with IQ (Waters, Wippman, & Sroufe,
1979). In addition, security of attachment to mother correlates with maternal
ratings of conduct and peer acceptance, but is uncorrelated with maternal ratings of physical and cognitive competence (Park, 1988). Further research on
the noncorrelates of security will help to define the boundaries of the attachment construct.

## SUMMARY

Attachment is viewed as a close tie or bond between two individuals. Early
patterns of mother–child and father–child attachment develop based on a child's
caregiving history with a particular parent. Children learn a variety of skills
within the context of parent–child relationships.

The study of attachment has been limited by a lack of methods to assess
security of attachment beyond early childhood. What are needed are developmentally appropriate assessments of attachment security for older children so
that links between attachment and friendship can be examined concurrently.
Some behaviors, such as seeking out the attachment figure in times of distress,
may be important markers of security throughout life. By contrast, other behaviors, such as communication style or clinging to the attachment figure, may
serve as markers of secure attachment in some developmental periods but not
others.

Finally, taking a developmental perspective to the study of attachment raises
the issue of whether attachment security is best conceived of as a measure of
a particular relationship or a core component of personality. Current methods
of assessing adult attachment style may be measures of relationships, or they
may be measures of personality. It could be that relationships in childhood
and adolescence contribute to the development of a stable style or orientation
toward close relationships, which emerges in adolescence or adulthood.

## THE NATURE OF FRIENDSHIP

Children typically have a variety of playmates, but only a few are labeled as
friends. There are many ways to define friendship. Mannarino (1980) suggested
that the key component of friendship is reciprocity of liking and esteem. Unlike family relationships, peer relationships are voluntary. As a result, reciprocity of liking is crucial to maintain friendship. The high degree of liking and
esteem friends hold for each other distinguishes friendships from other peer

relationships. Thus, friends are important people because they like you and hold you in high regard.

Friendship can be distinguished from peer acceptance. The construct of peer acceptance refers to the degree to which a child is accepted by the peer group. The most popular children are typically very socially competent (Hartup, 1983). By contrast, trust, loyalty, and companionship, rather than competence, are issues in friendship (Hartup, 1983; Mannarino, 1980). The importance of distinguishing between peer acceptance and friendship was illustrated in a recent study of aggressive and nonaggressive children (Cairns, Cairns, Neckerman, Gest, & Gariepy, 1988). Although aggressive boys were significantly less popular, they did not have fewer friends than their nonaggressive classmates.

This section provides a review of theories about friendship and relevant research findings. The purpose of the review is to outline changes in friendship by identifying the key friendship issue at different developmental periods. This review is intended to be selective and illustrative rather than exhaustive. For each developmental period, I identify: the goal of friendship, the individual skills necessary to attain the goal, and the desired friendship quality (see Table 7.1). Note that the skills refer to the behavior of the individual in the relationship, whereas friendship quality is a property of the friend dyad.

### Friendship in Early Childhood

Gottman (1983; Gottman & Mettetal, 1986) delineated a set of social processes that contribute to friendship in early childhood. First, for young children to establish friendships, they must be able to resolve conflicts and maintain a climate of agreement. Next, children need to be responsive to and commu-

TABLE 7.1
Overview of Developmental Changes in Friendship

| Goal of Friendship | Necessary Skills | Salient Friendship Quality |
|---|---|---|
| Early childhood | | |
| Establish coordinated interaction | Conflict resolution strategies | Harmony |
| | Responsiveness | Responsiveness |
| | | Coordinated interaction |
| Middle childhood | | |
| Develop chumship/alliance with peer | Sensitivity to another | Companionship |
| | Gossip | Stability |
| Adolescence | | |
| Address emotional needs | Trust | Intimacy |
| | Self-disclosure | Self-exploration |
| Adulthood | | |
| Meet affiliative needs | Build social networks | Social support |
| | Ability to rely on others | Satisfaction |

nicate clearly with one another. Finally, children must be able to work together to achieve coordinated and elaborated interaction, such as sustained fantasy play. Coordinated play is viewed as the most important and central process for peer interaction in early childhood (Gottman & Mettetal, 1986).

Data on friendship formation and the behavior of friend pairs support the model. Gottman (1983) found that resolving conflicts, engaging in coordinated play, and communication clarity discriminated pairs of newly acquainted children who "hit it off" from pairs of acquainted children who did not. In addition, children engaged in more fantasy play and self-disclosure, display more positive affect, and use more mutually satisfying conflict resolution strategies when playing with friends than when playing with nonfriends (Foot, Chapman, & Smith, 1977; Gottman, 1983; Hartup, Laursen, Stewart, & Eastenson, 1988; Vespo, 1985).

In summary, play is a central component of peer interaction at this age. Skills that facilitate coordinated interaction, such as effective conflict resolution and responsiveness, are important for friendships. If relationship partners have the requisite social skills, then the friendship should be characterized by harmony, responsiveness, and coordinated interaction.

## Friendship in Middle Childhood

Sullivan (1953) suggested that in middle childhood children begin to form "chumships" (i.e., a close alliance with one other child). Chumships are stable peer relationships that provide children with companionship. Failure to develop a chumship is expected to lead to loneliness (Sullivan, 1953). Sullivan suggested two other benefits of chumship. First, children have opportunities to learn sensitivity to another and to try and understand another's perspective. The learning of interpersonal sensitivity is viewed as an important precursor to altruism. Second, chums provide validation of children's self-worth.

Several studies have examined friendship in middle childhood. Mannarino (1980) compared 10- and 11-year-old boys who did or did not have chums. The criteria for defining chumship were threefold: high scores on a chumship checklist (Mannarino, 1980), stable friendship choice over a 2-week period, and preference for the friend rather than playing with other friends. The two groups were matched on IQ and peer acceptance. Boys with chums reported higher self-worth and were more altruistic.

Other studies have found that school-aged children behave differently toward friends and acquaintances. When with friends, children are more affective, interactive, cooperative, and mutually directed (for a review, see Hartup, 1983). These studies suggest that collaboration with a peer is an important achievement at this age.

A similar view was offered by Gottman and Mettetal (1986), who suggested that friends are trying to build solidarity at this age. They suggested that children share gossip as a way to promote cohesion and closeness. Gottman and Mettetal found that unacquainted older children and adolescents who "hit it off" engaged in a greater amount of negative-evaluation gossip. These results suggest that exchanging gossip facilitates peer relationships in middle childhood by increasing the liking and cohesion in peer dyads.

In summary, participation in friendship at this age involves collaborating with a peer. Being sensitive to another's wishes and sharing gossip with a peer are important skills for establishing and maintaining friendships.

### Friendship in Adolescence

Adolescence is a time when children are trying to balance needs for autonomy with needs for intimacy and understanding (Bryant, 1989). One hallmark of adolescence is that peers, and not just parents, become an important source of emotional support. In this way, children can begin to experience autonomy from parents, yet still have their emotional needs met. A major change in friendship in adolescence is that it becomes an important source of intimacy (see Berndt, 1982). In addition, Gottman and Mettetal (1986) suggested that friendships in adolescence support self-exploration. It is in the context of a close, supportive relationship with a peer that an adolescent feels free enough to reveal and critically discuss aspects of the self.

When asked about what makes a person a friend, adolescents cite intimacy, understanding, and loyalty more often than preadolescents (Hartup, 1983). These findings are typically stronger for girls than for boys (Buhrmester & Furman, 1987). In addition, girls self-disclose more intimate information with friends than with acquaintances (Gottman & Mettetal, 1986). Fewer studies have included boys. Because boys tend to disclose intimate information less often than girls (Berndt, 1982), intimacy in boys' friendships may have to be measured in other ways.

There has been very little research on adolescent friendships. In part, this may be because of the emergence of peer groups. The role of friendship may change, so that friends meet needs not fulfilled by groups. A growing literature on peer groups (see Brown, 1989) has suggested that groups meet adolescents' needs for identity and belongingness. Because they are dyadic, friendships may provide the context for intimacy and self-exploration.

In general, adolescence is a time when friendships become a source of intimacy and provide a context for self-exploration. Trust and self-disclosure skills are expected to facilitate the development of intimate friendships.

### Friendship in Adulthood

Prior to late adolescence or adulthood, individuals rely primarily on same-gender friends and parents for companionship and intimacy. In adulthood, individuals begin to form close attachment bonds usually with members of the other gender. Particularly for men (Reis, Senchak, & Solomon, 1985), intimate relationships with a partner becomes the primary source of intimacy and social support.

Adult friendships still play an important role. Weiss (1982) suggested that attachments (love relationships) and friendships serve different functions in adulthood. Attachments meet a person's emotional needs. If a person is not involved in an attachment relationship, he or she may experience loneliness. Adult friendships meet an individual's social or affiliative needs. That is, having a circle of friends makes a person feel as if he or she is part of a community. Weiss presented data to support this distinction. Married couples who had recently moved to a new city were not lonely, but felt they were not integrated into a larger community. Single people (who had not recently moved) sometimes felt lonely, but did not feel like they were isolated from the larger community. Thus, although attachment may be the primary relationship in adulthood, friendships serve other needs. In particular, friendships are a source of intimacy and mutual support (Hays, 1988).

Two types of individual skills are necessary for achieving social support from friends. First, individuals must be able to identify potential friends and build social networks. Second, they must be able to rely on others. Relying on others may be more difficult for some people in adulthood, because self-reliance is part of the adult role. Nevertheless, if individuals cannot rely on others, they will not be able to receive social support.

The functions of friendship in adulthood may change as individuals face life tasks and adult responsibilities, such as raising children (Dickens & Perlman, 1981). The amount of interaction among friends declines from early to middle adulthood, although intimacy in adult friendships remains constant (Dickens & Perlman, 1981; Hays, 1988). The functions of friendship may also depend on the availability of kin. If no kin live nearby, friends may be relied on more for help and support in times of crises.

In summary, adulthood is a time that marks a transition in social relationships. Most adults develop a love relationship, which becomes the primary peer relationship. Adult friendships augment attachment bonds. Building social networks and being able to rely on others are important prerequisites for attaining social support.

## A DEVELOPMENTAL MODEL OF ATTACHMENT AND FRIENDSHIP

In this section, I propose a model that predicts associations between a child's relationships with his or her mother and best friend. The model proposes continuity across relationships. The model tries to answer two questions. First, it addresses the question of why one would expect links between a child's relationships with mother and friends. The section on mechanisms primarily elaborates how a person's expectations produce continuity in behavior across social partners.

Second, the model delineates the ways in which security of attachment and friendship are likely to be linked. The model is designed to integrate predictions derived from attachment theory and friendship theories. This model is a shift from earlier work examining links between parent–child and peer relationships in that developmental changes in friendship are explicitly considered. Thus, the model attempts to move beyond the hypothesis that good relationships in one domain will correlate with good relationships in another by specifying which friendship qualities will correlate highly with attachment security at different ages.

### Mechanisms of Continuity

The model incorporates two types of mechanisms to account for continuity. First, children learn certain skills within the mother–child relationship that generalize to other relationships (Putallaz, 1987; Putallaz & Heflin, 1990). These skills are acquired either through modeling or reinforcement/punishment contingencies. Learning mechanisms have been discussed at length elsewhere and are not elaborated on here.

Second, individuals develop a set of expectations about social partners and relationships. These expectations, or working models (Bowlby, 1973; Young, 1986), subsequently guide behavior, producing substantial continuity across relationships. Most psychologists agree that expectations guide behavior. But in the domain of relationships, what do people have expectations about? The concept of working models and their content are elaborated next by suggesting ways that the expectations of securely and insecurely attached children may differ.

In the context of attachment theory, Bowlby (1973) proposed a mechanism to account for continuity across an individual's relationships. By age 3, children have developed a set of expectations about what others are like. In Bowlby's terms, children have rudimentary *working models*. Working models have been conceptualized as schemes or scripts that summarize children's past relationship experiences (Bretherton, 1985). Alternatively, working models may be thought of as internalized rules for relationships (Main et al., 1985). Sroufe and Fleeson (1986) suggested that children not only develop views of others, but come to internalize the nature of early attachment relationships so that they carry forward an understanding of how to relate to others based on earlier experiences in attachment relationships. A child's experiences in the mother–child relationship form the foundation of a child's working model. Working models also incorporate other relationship experiences, such as those with other family members. Bowlby (1973) termed them *working* models because new or divergent experiences can modify an individual's expectations. An individual's working model of others and relationships is built up throughout infancy, childhood, and adolescence (Bowlby, 1979; Sroufe & Fleeson, 1986).

Bowlby (1973, 1982) proposed that working models are the mechanism linking early relationship experiences to later behavior. Thus, it is the expectations that are carried forward from early to later relationships (Bowlby, 1973; Sroufe & Fleeson, 1986). Expectations guide an individual's behavior in two different ways. First, working models are the filters through which an individual interprets experiences (Bretherton, 1985; Sroufe & Fleeson, 1986). Consequently, individuals interpret any experience or event in a way consistent with their working model. For example, a person who considers others untrustworthy may interpret a partner's request to spend more time alone to mean the partner is seeing other people.

Second, working models may lead individuals to recreate past patterns of interaction by seeking out relationships that confirm their expectations (Sroufe & Fleeson, 1986). Thus, a child who feels rejected by a parent may come to expect other partners to be rejecting as well. In a study with preschool play pairs (Troy & Sroufe, 1987), some pairs of children were observed to engage in a pattern of behavior termed *victimization*. In all pairs where victimization occurred, at least one child had an anxious-avoidant attachment to mother. Troy and Sroufe (1987) suggested that these children had learned the victim-victimizer role and were recreating these roles in new relationships.

Young (1986) presented a similar perspective to explain why some adults have problems in friendships. According to Young, individuals have three schemas: one for self, one for others, and one for relationships. In addition, individuals have schemas for close (family) relationships and social (peer) relationships. Experiences in close relationships lay the foundations for an individual's relationship schemas. Cognitive consistency is achieved when individuals seek out and interpret experiences in ways that are consistent with their schemas. Sometimes social and close relationship schemas differ, but consistency across the two is the norm (Young, 1986). Like Bowlby (1973) and Sroufe and Fleeson (1986), Young argued that friendship dysfunctions are a result of schemas containing negative information about self, others, and relationships.

Working models contain information about several key relationship issues (Bowlby, 1979; Bretherton, 1985; Main et al., 1985; see also Young, 1986). First, children may have expectations about how responsive and available social partners are likely to be (Bowlby, 1973). A child who has a responsive, available mother may expect other partners to be responsive and available as well. Bowlby (1979) suggested that individuals differ in the degree to which they think other people are willing to serve as a secure base or source of support. Sroufe (1988) provided anecdotal evidence that insecurely attached children may expect to be rebuffed, and thus are easily discouraged from seeking out others in social interactions. In sum, expectations that others will be unresponsive and unavailable may prevent children from engaging in interaction and receiving support from others.

Second, children develop views about whether the world is an interesting, fun, and exciting place to explore. Securely attached children, who are confident in the availability of their mothers, may be more confident about exploring their world. Securely attached children are more enthusiastic when working on tasks (Matas, Arend, & Sroufe, 1978). They are also more willing to engage strangers (Main & Weston, 1981), form friendships more readily (Elicker, Englund, & Sroufe, 1992), and are more affectively positive around classmates (Waters et al., 1979). In addition, securely attached children are less dependent around adults as preschoolers and preadolescents (Elicker et al., 1992; Sroufe, Fox, & Pancake, 1983). The data suggest that securely attached children may be more eager or willing to explore their environments.

Third, children's attributions about another's behavior are likely to depend on how they have been treated in the past. For example, a child who feels he or she has been treated unfairly may also be more likely to make negative attributions about others' motives. Dodge's (1980) work on the attributions of aggressive boys is relevant. When another person causes harm and it is unclear if he or she acted purposefully, aggressive boys are more likely to think the person meant to cause harm than are nonaggressive boys. That is, their working model leads them to believe that people harm you intentionally. It could be that securely and insecurely attached children, who have had different caretaking experiences, differ in the extent to which they have a positive or negative bias when inferring another's intentions, particularly when the situation and the motives for another's actions are ambiguous. Support for this hypothesis comes from a study showing that avoidantly attached preschoolers are more likely than securely attached preschoolers to make negative attributions about another's behavior (Suess, Grossman, & Sroufe, 1992).

Fourth, working models may include information about how conflicts are resolved. From the preschool years on, parents and children are capable of engaging in joint planning of events and solutions. Children's perceptions about the use of power and control in relationships will likely be influenced by the degree to which their parents use power-assertive techniques rather than negotiation strategies to settle parent–child conflicts. Because of the influence of modeling, children of power-assertive parents are more likely to view confrontational strategies as legitimate and to adopt them as a means for resolving disputes when resolving conflicts with others, including peers.

Fifth, children may form views about how to cope with negative emotions. Greenberg and Speltz (1988) suggested that mothers of insecurely attached children try to restrain rather than cope with their children's displays of negative affect. As a result, insecurely attached children do not have the opportunity to learn strategies for modulating their emotions. In particular, it has been suggested that insecurely attached children are uncomfortable talking about their emotions and feelings in relationships (Bretherton, 1987; Main et al., 1985). In addition, insecurely attached children may not learn how to respond empathically to others (Kestenbaum, Farber, & Sroufe, 1989).

Finally, children develop expectations about the degree to which others can be trusted. Bowlby (1979) suggested that some individuals have difficulty initiating relationships because they view potential partners as untrustworthy. Judgments about trust, in turn, are likely to affect how much children rely on others and are willing to self-disclose. Thus, trust, obtaining support, and intimacy are interdependent.

No doubt, people's expectations in these different areas are correlated. For example, it is unlikely that a person would engage in intimate self-disclosure with a social partner viewed as unresponsive and unavailable. Still, it is useful to think about these issues separately because they may be more or less important for friendship, depending on the individual's developmental level. In addition, different expectations may be most important at different points in the course of a relationship. For example, seeing the world as an interesting place may impact on relationship initiation, whereas trust and intimacy may be more important for maintaining attachment bonds.

Evidence is accumulating that expectations or behavior patterns developed within the mother–child relationship may guide a child's behavior in social interaction. When playing with peers, securely attached children are more affectively positive, interactive, and socially competent (Erickson, Sroufe, & Egeland, 1985; Lieberman, 1977; Pastor, 1981; Sroufe, 1983; Waters et al., 1979). The results suggest there may be qualitative differences in the social skills and peer relationships of securely and insecurely attached children.

## Links Between Attachment and Friendship

Both theory and previous research suggest there are links between parent–child and peer relationships. This section explores those links, drawing on attachment theory as well as theories of friendship.

To date, attachment theorists have made general predictions about how security of attachment and friendship might be related. For example, Sroufe and Fleeson (1986) suggested that securely attached children will develop closer and deeper friendships. But will this be as true of 3-year-old friends as 15-year-old friends? Because the nature of friendship changes as children get older, I propose that security of attachment will be most strongly related to different dimensions of friendship at different ages. In part, my model is proposed to make past predictions about the implications of attachment more precise. Thus, the model recasts past theorizing in a developmental framework. The model is also based on available data linking attachment and friendship.

In presenting the model, I describe how I think security of attachment to mother affects a child's ability to address the major friendship issue in a given developmental period. Of course, relationships with other family members will also have an impact on a child's ability to relate to others. But for now, I focus on what Bowlby considered the first and most important relationship—a child's tie to his or her mother.

For simplicity, the life span is divided into four developmental periods: early childhood (ages 3–7), middle childhood (ages 8–12), adolescence (ages 13–18), and early adulthood (ages 18–24). The ages given for each developmental period should be taken as approximations. Infancy and the toddler period are excluded because it is not clear that peer relationships in these periods meet the definition of friendship (Vandell & Mueller, 1980). Middle and late adulthood are not considered because romantic partners, rather than parents, are an individual's primary attachment figure.

The model is outlined in Fig. 7.1. Relationship experiences are assumed to build on one another, so that there is continuity over time in the quality of a child's friendships. Individuals who have friendship difficulties at one age may have more difficulties in the next developmental period. Conversely, individuals who possess good relationship skills are presumed more likely to negotiate friendship at the next level.

Because relationship skills are expected to show continuity over time, old patterns of interaction are likely to persist. As a result, later relationship difficulties are in addition to, not in place of, earlier difficulties. For example, anxiously attached adolescents may still have problems resolving disagreements, but negotiating intimacy and trust may be a more important or salient issue.

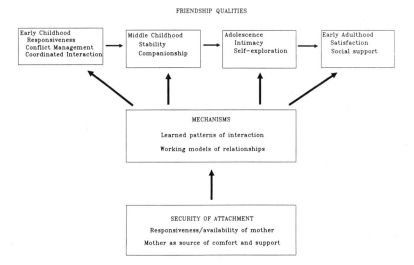

FIG. 7.1.   Relations between security of attachment and friendship qualities.

Of course, it is not just early relationships but the quality of current attachments that is important. Parent–child attachments may undergo change over time (Erickson et al., 1985). If people begin to accumulate relationship experiences that conflict with the original tenets of their model, change in expectations can occur. The proposed model predicts concurrent (as opposed to predictive) associations between attachment security and friendship.

The model makes predictions at the level of the relationship. The relationship quality will depend in part on the interactive skills of both partners. If the level of analysis was the individual rather than the relationship, I predict that security of attachment would correlate with the developmentally appropriate friendship skills (see Table 7.1). Differences in the friendships of securely and insecurely attached children reflect differences in the children's relationship skills and expectations.

## Early Childhood

In early childhood, the goal in friendship is to establish coordinated interaction (Gottman & Mettetal, 1986). Conflict resolution and interactive skills are necessary to achieve this goal.

Hartup (1986) suggested that securely attached children's friendships will function more smoothly. This would occur if securely attached children are more socially skilled at interacting with peers. Several studies have found that securely attached preschoolers are more socially competent with peers (for reviews, see Park & Waters, 1988; Sroufe & Fleeson, 1986), and consequently they may be better at resolving conflicts. Securely attached children also engage in less negative behavior, and as a result the flow of play may be disrupted less often. It may be easier for securely attached children to maintain coordinated interaction.

Sroufe and Fleeson (1986) suggested that patterns of interaction established in the parent–child relationship become internalized and subsequently generalized to other relationships. One hypothesis is that securely attached children who have received responsive caregiving are likely to be more responsive to other people later. Securely attached children are more responsive and better at sustaining interaction with an unfamiliar peer (Lieberman, 1977), suggesting that styles of interaction occurring in the mother–child relationship may carry over into other relationships.

To date, only one study has examined the relations between attachment security and friendship quality (Park & Waters, 1989). Relations between attachment and friendship were examined by comparing the play interactions of two groups of friend dyads. In one group, both dyad members were securely attached to mother; in the other group, one member was securely attached and the other member was insecurely attached to mother. The secure-secure dyads were more harmonious, responsive, and less controlling than secure–insecure dyads. However, there were no differences between the groups on a measure of coordinated interaction. The pattern of results provides partial support for the proposed model.

In summary, securely attached preschoolers, by virtue of being responsive social partners and better able to resolve conflicts, may have less difficulty establishing responsive and harmonious friendships and achieving coordinated play in early childhood.

## Middle Childhood

In middle childhood, the goal is to establish a chumship or one-on-one alliance with a peer (Sullivan, 1953). This requires the ability to be sensitive to and collaborate with another.

Several studies have found that mothers of securely attached children are more sensitive to their children than mothers of insecurely attached children (see Pianta, Sroufe, & Egeland, 1989). Children who receive sensitive and responsive caregiving from their mothers may subsequently be more sensitive and responsive to others. Securely attached preschoolers are more empathic toward peers' distress than are insecurely attached preschoolers (Kestenbaum et al., 1989). In middle childhood, when children become even better at understanding others' perspectives and feelings (Harter, 1983), there may be differences in how sensitive securely and insecurely attached children are toward their friends.

In addition, if securely attached children continue to be better at resolving disagreements, they may have less difficulty establishing and maintaining chumships. Hartup (1986) suggested that securely attached children will develop more stable friendships. This difference may not emerge until middle childhood. This is because when children enter primary school, their potential peer group widens. Thus, children have more choice about who they want as a friend—and may find it easier to terminate undesirable friendships—once they begin school.

The hypothesis is that securely attached children's friendships, compared with those of insecurely attached children, will be more stable and provide companionship. Only one study has examined attachment and friendship in middle childhood (Elicker et al., 1992). The subjects were 11-year-old children enrolled in the longitudinal Minnesota Mother–Child Project. Data on attachment in infancy, assessed with the Strange Situation, was available for all participants. The children were enrolled in a summer camp and given opportunities to meet and become friends with other children at the camp. Interviews with children and direct observation were used to assess the children's peer relationships. Children with secure attachment histories spent more time with peers, suggesting that they were able to meet needs for companionship in their peer relationships. In addition, children with secure attachment histories were more likely to form friendships. Children also completed a measure of interpersonal sensitivity, and children with avoidant histories scored lower than all other children.

In summary, in middle childhood securely attached children are more sensitive to others and spend more time with peers. These findings suggest that securely attached children may be more successful at maintaining chumships and, consequently, may be less lonely in middle childhood.

## Adolescence

The goal of friendship in adolescence is to meet needs for intimacy and support. The development of a close friendship provides a context for self-exploration.

Sroufe and Fleeson (1986) suggested that securely attached children's relationships will be closer and deeper, compared with the relationships of anxiously attached children. I predict that attachment-related differences in intimacy will be strongest in adolescence, when intimate self-disclosure becomes more important for friendship. As some individuals begin to self-disclose more, and thus there is more variability in the degree to which people self-disclose, individual differences in self-disclosure may emerge.

Main et al. (1985) also suggested that securely attached children engage in more open communication when discussing their relationships with their parents. This open style may make it easier for a securely attached adolescent to engage in intimacy and self-exploration with a best friend. These hypotheses about attachment and friendship have not yet been tested.

In summary, adolescents develop feelings about trust based on experiences with their primary caregivers. Views about trust may be modified in the context of other close relationships. Feelings of trust may translate into open and easier communication about intimate topics with friends. As adolescents participate in intimate relationships outside the family, they may develop general relationship styles or orientations.

## Adulthood

In late adolescence and adulthood, individuals face the task of developing close relationships with peers of the opposite gender. Bowlby (1973, 1982) argued that parent–child attachment has its most profound effects on later attachment relationships. Thus, secure attachment in childhood may have a bigger influence on the quality of an individual's adult love relationships than on friendships.

Friendships are an important source of social support in adulthood (Hays,

1988). Individuals must build social networks and have the capacity to rely on others to obtain social support. Friendships also meet adults' needs for affiliation and belongingness (Weiss, 1982).

Bowlby (1979) suggested that securely attached adults are able to identify potential sources of support and can rely on others for help. It could be that secure individuals, who have come to expect that social partners will be available and responsive in times of stress (Bretherton, 1985), use their social networks more readily and thus feel lonely less often. The ability to develop social networks and rely on others is especially important in adulthood when individuals leave the family.

In adulthood, attachment has been reconceptualized as a general relationship style, rather than as a description of a particular relationship. New methodologies have been introduced for studying adult attachment style (Hazan & Shaver, 1987; Main et al., 1985). Recent data indicate that secure adults are less lonely and more satisfied with friendships and romantic relationships (Hazan & Shaver, 1987; Kobak & Sceery, 1988). These results suggest that secure adults may be better able to develop and utilize social networks. As a result, their friendships are more satisfying.

## Summary and Limitations of Model

In this chapter, I offered a model to explain links between a child's relationship with mother and best friend. It is assumed that individuals develop working models of relationships, which summarize their past relationship experiences. Like Freud (1949), Bowlby (1982) suggested that the mother–child relationship is the first and most important relationship in a young child's life, and the relationship that will have the greatest impact on a child's expectations for other relationships. Expectations and relationship skills developed within the mother–child relationship are expected to generalize to other relationships. As a consequence, there is some continuity expected across an individual's many relationships.

The proposed model predicts associations between security of mother–child attachment and qualities of children's friendships. The literature on children's friendships suggests that there are developmental changes in friendship. The model examines how a secure attachment to mother would affect a child's ability to address the major goal of friendship in a particular period.

At this point, the model is based more on theoretical writings than on the results of empirical research. Many of the hypotheses remain to be tested or are in need of replication. The model is offered as a guide for future research.

There are certain boundaries or limits to the model. The model is not intended to be deterministic. That is, the establishment of a poor relationship with one's mother may make later relationships more difficult to negotiate, but it will not invariably cause later problems. In this section, I discuss reasons why there may be discontinuity from mother–child to peer relationships.

First, the model does not address how environmental factors could influence the quality of the mother–child relationship. Continuity in the parent–child relationship rests on continuity in caretaking and child rearing (Lamb, 1988; Sroufe, 1988). Studies with stable, middle-class families have demonstrated an impressive degree of continuity in mother–child relationships within infancy (Waters, 1978) and from infancy to early childhood (Main et al., 1985). Factors that account for changes in security of mother–child attachment have rarely been examined. Two studies (Thompson, Lamb, & Estes, 1982; Vaughn, Egeland, Sroufe, & Waters, 1979) have suggested that stress in the home environment can lead to changes in the quality of parent–child attachment. Presumably, stress on parents diminishes their ability to provide optimal caregiving for their children. Therefore, early relationship patterns do not invariably predict later relationships because experience may intervene (Sroufe, 1988). An important topic for future research will be to assess the degree of continuity in mother–child relationships across time.

Second, a parent may be more or less successful in providing comfort and support and setting reasonable socialization goals in different developmental periods (Erickson et al., 1985). For example, a mother who has provided good care to an infant may or may not be able to provide appropriate help and aid to a preschooler. Thus, a mother's ability to adapt to her child's developmental level will affect continuity in the quality of the mother–child relationship (Erickson et al., 1985).

Third, other relationships besides the mother–child tie have an impact on a child's working model of relationships. Father–child and sibling relationships may serve to modify a child's expectations for relationships. Main and Weston (1981) found that infants insecurely attached to mother but securely attached to father outperformed infants insecurely attached to both mother and father on several measures of social interaction. In addition, insecurely attached children who later develop good relationships with peers may modify their expectations about relationships. In fact, this is why Bowlby used the term *working* models—the term *working* refers to the fact that they are subject to revision. Although expectations for relationships tend to persist, in part because people tend to behave in ways that confirm their expectations, change can occur if an individual has powerful relationship experiences that conflict with his or her relationship expectations. Main et al. (1985) suggested that individuals may be able to rework their models in adolescence and adulthood after attaining formal operations, particularly if they have different experiences in adult love relationships.

Fourth, the impact of the mother–child relationship depends on whether working models are relationship specific or summaries of all relationship experiences. If individuals compartmentalize their working models, they may have different expectations for different relationship partners. An individual's working models are likely to be more differentiated and relationship specific if the person has had different experiences with different partners.

Finally, a note about interpreting effects of one relationship on another: I do not mean to reify relationships. *Relationships* are not causal mechanisms; rather, I am using the term to summarize the affect, cognition, and behavior of a particular dyad (Park & Waters, 1988). To say that the mother–child relationship influences later relationships means that past experiences may affect how an individual approaches new relationship partners. Relationship skills and expectations developed in the context of the mother–child relationship influence a child's interactions—and thus relationships—with others.

## A DYADIC PERSPECTIVE

The discussion so far has assumed that individuals create relationships by themselves. That is, I have ignored potential partner effects. However, all relationships involve two people. Therefore, the characteristics of one partner will only partially determine the tone of the relationship. That is, the interactions between two people define the relationship. For example, for an insecurely attached child it may be important whether a potential relationship partner is securely or insecurely attached. For this reason, Hinde (1979), Levinger (1977), and Maccoby (1984) suggested that the dyad is the appropriate level of analysis in studying relationships.

Two studies suggested the dyadic approach is useful when examining how patterns of attachment influence the qualities of peer relationships. In one study (Troy & Sroufe, 1987) mentioned earlier, three types of dyads were compared: dyads containing two securely attached children, two insecurely attached children, or one securely and one insecurely attached child. The dyads played together for several sessions. A pattern of behavior termed *victimization* was identified. This pattern was never seen if at least one child in the dyad was securely attached. In every case where this pattern was identified, at least one child in the dyad had an anxious-avoidant attachment to mother. In a second study of best friend pairs (Park & Waters, 1989), secure–insecure dyads were more controlling and less harmonious and responsive than secure-secure dyads. There was at least one securely attached child in all the dyads, suggesting that it is the combination of social partners that is important. Thus, to gain a clearer perspective on relationships, it is necessary to take into account the relationship histories of both partners.

Ideally, then, testing a model of links between mother–child attachment and friendship would involve studying three types of friend dyads: dyads in which both children are securely attached, dyads in which both children are insecurely attached, and dyads in which one child is securely attached and the other child insecurely attached. The model presented in this chapter predicts differences in the friendships of securely and insecurely attached children. The assumption is that securely attached children are more competent in relationships. The differences outlined here should be found when comparing secure-secure and insecure-insecure friend dyads. But what about the secure–insecure dyads? What will their friendship be like?

This raises the question of how individual competencies combine to influence the quality of social interaction and relationships. In the case of secure–insecure dyads, the members differ in their relationship competence. Waters (personal communication, 1987) and I proposed three competing models that make different predictions about the overall competence of dyads containing one competent and one less competent member.

**Facilitative Performance Model**

The performance of the mixed competence dyads is equivalent to the performance of the competent dyads. The model assumes that the behavior of the less competent member is facilitated by the more competent member, and the result is that the dyad exhibits socially competent behavior. For example, the more competent child might direct the dyad toward more advanced play.

**Average Performance Model**

The performance of the mixed competence dyads is greater than the incompetent dyads but inferior to the competent dyads. This model assumes that the more competent behavior of one member is balanced out by the less competent behavior of the other member, so that the dyad's behavior is neither extremely competent nor extremely incompetent but average.

**Decrement Performance Model**

The performance of the mixed competence dyads is equal to the performance of the incompetent dyads. The assumption is that the inappropriate behavior of the less competent member has a negative effect on the more competent member. For example, one naughty child might convince another child to act out.

There have been no studies designed to examine how competent, incompetent, and mixed competence dyads differ. Studies of mixed-age interaction partially address the question of how individual competencies relate to dyadic functioning in social situations because older children should be more socially skilled than younger children. In one study (Loughee, Grueneich, & Hartup, 1977), three types of dyads were constructed: same-age younger (SAY), same-age older (SAO), and mixed-age (MA). They found that the mixed-age dyads scored intermediate on measures of social interaction and verbal communication (SAO > MA > SAY). In general, this suggests that there is an averaging effect occurring in mixed-competence dyads.

In summary, relationships are always dyadic. In any relationship, some combination of the skills of the partners will contribute to relationship quality. These three models could be applied to the study of how differences in individuals' social skills affect dyadic interaction and qualities of relationships.

## CONCLUSIONS

The study of personal relationships has grown rapidly since the 1970s. One recent focus in the study of relationships is identifying links across an individual's relationships. This chapter has proposed links between the two worlds of childhood (Hartup, 1979): families and peers. With Bowlby's (1973, 1982) and Ainsworth's (1972, 1982) theory of social development serving as the guiding framework, a model was proposed that predicts links between a child's security of attachment to mother and qualities of the child's friendships. The model attempts to integrate attachment theory, friendship theories, and available data.

The model proposed is a carry-over model, in that positive relationship qualities in family relationships are predicted to correlate with positive relationship qualities in peer relationships. Although there are plenty of data to support a carry-over model, few investigators have explicitly attempted to test a compensatory model. Sullivan (1953) suggested that peer relationships, or what he termed *chumships*, can serve a therapeutic function. According to Sullivan, good experiences within peer relationships can undo some of the damage caused by poor early experiences in family relationships. One direction for future research would be exploring the conditions that promote compensatory effects.

Taking into account a child's developmental level will make predictions between parent and peer relationship more precise. Marked developmental changes occur in friendships in part because friendships serve different functions at different ages (Buhrmester & Furman, 1987). This chapter has focused on one dimension of parent–child relationships that is important throughout childhood: security. Other dimensions of parent–child relationships may be more or less important, depending on a child's developmental level. A developmental analysis could be applied to the study of parent–child relationships to identify the critical dimensions of parent–child relationships at different developmental periods.

In addition, there are other links in a child's network that could be explored. Father–child relationships are rarely examined (for an exception, see Parke et al., 1989). There has also been very little observational research on the interactions of siblings. Because different relationships serve different functions, exploring links between different types of relationships will aid in understanding how relationships influence development.

Finally, when links are shown across relationships, mechanisms need to be proposed to account for the continuity. One mechanism could be working models (Bowlby, 1973) or relationship schemas (Young, 1986), which presumably summarize an individual's expectations about relationships and guide an individual's behavior in relationships. Although cognitive psychologists have developed many methods for assessing schemas, almost no research has been conducted on people's cognitions about relationships. Second, learning mechanisms such as reinforcement or modeling may also account for continuity in an individual's behavior across social partners (Putallaz, 1987). Third, the model assumes that the relationship skills of individuals contribute to the quality of a relationship. Another area of research might focus on identifying the skills needed in different types of personal relationships. A broad empirical base on the links between relationships can serve as a guide in the search for mechanisms to account for continuity.

## ACKNOWLEDGMENTS

Parts of this chapter were written while the author was funded on an NIMH postdoctoral training grant (No. MH15780) awarded to the University of Denver. Thanks are extended to Elizabeth Wehner, Gary Levy, Robin Gilmour, Ralph Erber, and L. Alan Sroufe for their helpful comments on an earlier draft of this chapter.

## REFERENCES

Ainsworth, M. D. S. (1972). Attachment and dependency: A comparison. In J. L. Gewirtz (Ed.), *Attachment and dependency* (pp. 97–137). Washington, DC: Winston.

Ainsworth, M. D. S. (1982). Attachment: Retrospect and prospect. In C. M. Parkes & J. Stevenson-Hinde (Eds.), *The place of attachment in human behavior* (pp. 3–30). New York: Basic Books.

Ainsworth, M. D. S., Bell, S. M., & Stayton, D. J. (1971). Individual differences in Strange Situation behavior in one-year-olds. In H. R. Schaffer (Ed.), *The origins of human social relations* (pp. 17–57). London: Academic Press.

Ainsworth, M. D. S., Blehar, M. C., Waters, E., & Wall, S. (1978). *Pattern of attachment: A psychological study of the Strange Situation.* Hillsdale, NJ: Lawrence Erlbaum Associates.

Baumrind, D. (1973). The development of instrumental competence through socialization. In A. D. Pick (Ed.), *Minnesota symposia and on child psychology* (Vol. 7, pp. 3–46). Minneapolis: University of Minnesota Press.

Berndt, T. J. (1982). The features and effects of friendship in early adolescence. *Child Development, 53,* 1447–1460.

Block, J. (1977). Advancing the psychology of personality: Paradigmatic shift or improving the quality of research. In D. Magnusson & N. S. Endler (Eds.), *Personality at the crossroads.* Hillsdale, NJ: Lawrence Erlbaum Associates.

Bosso, O. R. (1985). *Attachment quality and sibling relations*. Unpublished doctoral dissertation, University of Toronto, Canada.

Bowlby, J. (1973). *Attachment and loss: Vol. 2. Separation: Anxiety and anger*. New York: Basic Books.

Bowlby, J. (1979). *The making and breaking of affectional bonds*. New York: Tavistock.

Bowlby, J. (1982). *Attachment and loss: Vol. 1. Attachment*. New York: Basic Books.

Bowlby, J. (1988). Developmental psychiatry comes of age. *American Journal of Psychiatry, 145*, 1–10.

Bretherton, I. (Ed.). (1985). Attachment theory: Retrospect and prospect. *Monographs of the SRCD, 50* (Serial No. 209).

Bretherton, I. (1987). New perspectives on attachment relations: Security, communication, and internal working models. In J. D. Osofsky (Ed.), *Handbook of infant development* (2nd ed., pp. 1061–1100). New York: Wiley.

Brown, B. B. (1989). The role of peer groups in adolescents' adjustment to secondary school. In T. J. Berndt & G. W. Ladd (Eds.), *Peer relationships in child development* (pp. 188–215). New York: Wiley.

Bryant, B. K. (1989). The need for support in relation to the need for autonomy. In D. Belle (Ed.), *Children's social networks and social supports* (pp. 332–351). New York: Wiley.

Buhrmester, D., & Furman, W. (1987). The development of companionship and intimacy. *Child Development, 58*, 1101–1113.

Cairns, R. B., Cairns, B. D., Neckerman, H. J., Gest, S. D., & Gariepy, J. L. (1988). Social networks and aggressive behavior: Peer support or peer rejection? *Developmental Psychology, 24*, 815–823.

Caspi, A., Elder, G. H., Jr., & Bem, D. J. (1987). Moving against the world: Patterns of explosive children. *Developmental Psychology, 23*, 308–313.

Caspi, A., Elder, G. H., Jr., & Bem, D. J. (1988). Moving away from the world: Life-course patterns of shy children. *Developmental Psychology, 24*, 824–831.

Cassidy, J. (1988). Child-mother attachment and the self in six-year-olds. *Child Development, 59*, 121–134.

Cassidy, J., Marvin, R. S., & The Attachment Group of the John D. and Catherine T. MacArthur Network on the Transition From Infancy to Early Childhood. (1987). *Attachment organization in 3- and 4-year-olds: A classification system*. Unpublished scoring manual.

Collins, N. L., & Read, S. J. (1990). Adult attachment, working models, and relationship quality in dating couples. *Journal of Personality and Social Psychology, 58*, 644–663.

Dickens, W. J., & Perlman, D. (1981). Friendship over the life-cycle. In S. Duck & R. Gilmour (Eds.), *Personal relationships: 2. Developing personal relationships*. New York: Academic Press.

Dodge, K. A. (1980). Social cognition and children's aggressive behavior. *Child Development, 51*, 162–170.

Elicker, J., Englund, M., & Sroufe, L. A. (1992). Predicting peer competence and peer relationships in childhood from early parent-child relationships. In R. Parke & G. Ladd (Eds.), *Family-peer relationships: Modes of linkage*. Hillsdale, NJ: Lawrence Erlbaum Associates.

Epstein, E. (1981). The stability of behavior: On predicting most of the people most of the time. *Journal of Personality and Social Psychology, 37*, 1097–1126.

Erickson, M. F., Sroufe, L. A., & Egeland, B. (1985). The relationship between quality of attachment and behavior problems in a high-risk sample. *SRCD Monographs, 50* (Serial No. 209).

Foot, H. C., Chapman, A. J., & Smith, J. R. (1977). Friendship and social responsiveness in boys and girls. *Journal of Personality and Social Psychology, 35*, 401–411.

Freud, S. (1949). *An outline of psychoanalysis*. New York: Norton.

Gottman, J. M. (1983). How children become friends. *Monographs of the SRCD, 48* (Serial No. 201).

Gottman, J. M., & Mettetal, G. (1986). Speculations about social and affective development: Friendship and acquaintanceship through adolescence. In J. M. Gottman & J. G. Parker (Eds.), *Conversations of friends* (pp. 192–237). New York: Cambridge University Press.

Greenberg, M. T., & Speltz, M. L. (1988). Attachment and the ontogeny of conduct problems. In J. Belsky & T. Nezworski (Eds.), *Clinical implications of attachment* (pp. 177–218). Hillsdale, NJ: Lawrence Erlbaum Associates.

Grossman, K., Grossman, K. E., Spangler, G., Suess, G., & Unzer, L. (1985). Maternal sensitivity and newborns' orientation responses as related to quality of attachment in Northern Germany. *Monographs of the SRCD, 50* (Serial No. 209).

Harter, S. (1983). Developmental perspectives on the self-system. In P. H. Mussen (Ed.), *Handbook of child psychology* (4th ed., pp. 275-385). New York: Wiley.

Hartup, W. W. (1979). The social worlds of childhood. *American Psychologist, 34*, 944-950.

Hartup, W. W. (1983). Peer relations. In P. H. Mussen (Ed.), *Handbook of child psychology* (4th
ed., pp. 103-196). New York: Wiley.

Hartup, W. W. (1986). On relationships and development. In W. W. Hartup & Z. Rubin (Eds.),
*Relationships and development* (pp. 1-26). Hillsdale, NJ: Lawrence Erlbaum Associates.

Hartup, W. W. Laursen, B., Stewart, M. I., & Eastenson, A. (1988). Conflict and the friendship
relations of young children. *Child Development, 59*, 1590-1600.

Hays, R. B. (1988). Friendship. In S. Duck (Ed.), *Handbook of personal relationships* (pp. 391-408).
New York: Wiley.

Hazan, C., & Shaver, P. (1987). Romantic love conceptualized as an attachment process. *Journal
of Personality and Social Psychology, 52*, 511-524.

Hinde, R. A. (1979). *Towards understanding relationships*. London: Academic Press.

Huesman, L. R., Eron, L. D., Lefkowitz, M. M., & Walder, L. O. (1984). Stability of aggression over time and generations. *Developmental Psychology, 20*, 1120-1134.

Kestenbaum, R., Farber, E. A., & Sroufe, L. A. (1989). Individual differences in empathy among
preschoolers: Relation to attachment history. *New Directions for Child Development, 44*, 51-64.

Kobak, R. R., & Sceery, A. (1988). Attachment in late adolescence: Working models, affect regulation, and representations of self and other. *Child Development, 59*, 135-146.

Lamb, M. E. (1988). Predictive implications of individual differences in attachment. *Journal of
Consulting and Clinical Psychology, 54*, 817-824.

Levinger, G. (1977). Re-viewing the close relationship. In G. Levinger & H. L. Rausch (Eds.),
*Close relationships.* Amherst: University of Massachusetts Press.

Lieberman, A. F. (1977). Preschoolers' competence with a peer: Relations with attachment and
peer experience. *Child Development, 48*, 1277-1287.

Loughee, M. D., Grueneich, R., & Hartup, W. W. (1977). Social interaction in same- and mixed-
age dyads of preschool children. *Child Development, 48*, 1353-1361.

Maccoby, E. E. (1984). Commentary: Organization and relationships in development. In W. Collins
(Ed.), *Minnesota symposia on child psychology* (Vol. 15, pp. 155-161). Hillsdale, NJ: Lawrence
Erlbaum Associates.

Main, M., & Cassidy, J. (1988). Categories of response to reunion with the parent at age 6: Predictable from infant attachment classifications and stable over a 1-month period. *Developmental
Psychology, 24*, 415-426.

Main, M., Kaplan, N., & Cassidy, J. (1985). Security in infancy, childhood, and adulthood: A
move to the level of representation. *Monographs of the SRCD, 50* (Serial No. 209).

Main, M., & Weston, D. R. (1981). The quality of the toddler's relationship to mother and to
father: Related to conflict behavior and the readiness to establish new relationships. *Child Development, 52*, 932-940.

Mannarino, A. P. (1980). The development of children's friendships. In H. C. Foot, A. J. Chapman, & J. R. Smith (Eds.), *Friendship and social relations in children* (pp. 45-63). Chichester, England: Wiley.

Matas, L., Arend, R. A., & Sroufe, L. A. (1978). Continuity of adaptation in the second year:
The relationship between quality of attachment and later competence. *Child Development, 49*,
547-556.

Mischel, W. (1968). *Personality and assessment.* New York: Wiley.

Park, K. A. (1988). Unpublished raw data.

Park, K. A. (1989, April). *Self-esteem: One mediator of the relation between security of attachment and behavioral conduct.* Paper presented at the biennial meetings of SRCD, Kansas City, MO.

Park, K. A., & Hazan, C. (1989). *Measure of security of attachment for preadolescents.* Unpublished measure, University of Denver, CO.

Park, K. A., & Waters, E. (1988). Traits and relationships in developmental perspective. In S. Duck (Ed.), *Handbook of personal relationships* (pp. 161–176). Chichester, England: Wiley.

Park, K. A., & Waters, E. (1989). Security of attachment and preschool friendships. *Child Development, 60,* 1076–1081.

Parke, R. D., MacDonald, K. B., Burks, V. M., Carson, J., Bhavnagri, N., Barth, J. M., & Beitel, A. (1989). In K. Kreppner & R. M. Lerner (Eds.), *Family systems of life span development* (pp. 65–92). Hillsdale, NJ: Lawrence Erlbaum Associates.

Pastor, D. L. (1981). The quality of mother-infant attachment and its relationship to toddler initial sociability with peers. *Developmental Psychology, 17,* 323–335.

Pederson, D. R., Moran, G., Sitko, C., Campbell, K., Gesquire, K., & Acton, H. (1990). Maternal sensitivity and the security of infant-mother attachment: A Q-sort study. *Child Development, 61,* 1974–1983.

Pianta, R. C., Sroufe, L. A., & Egeland, B. (1989). Continuity and discontinuity in maternal sensitivity at 6, 24, and 42 months in a high-risk sample. *Child Development, 60,* 481–487.

Putallaz, M. (1987). Maternal behavior and children's sociometric status. *Child Development, 58,* 324–340.

Putallaz, M., & Heflin, A. H. (1990). Parent-child interaction. In S. R. Asher & J. D. Coie (Eds.), *Peer rejection in childhood* (pp. 189–216). New York: Cambridge University Press.

Reis, H. T., Senchak, M., & Solomon, B. (1985). Sex differences in the intimacy of social interaction: Further examination of potential explanations. *Journal of Personality and Social Psychology, 48,* 1204–1217.

Shaver, P. R., & Hazan, C. (1988). A biased overview of the study of love. *Journal of Social and Personal Relationships, 5,* 473–501.

Solomon, J., George, C., & Ivins, B. (1987, April). *Mother-child interaction in the home and security of attachment at age six.* Paper presented at the biennial meetings of the Society for Research in Child Development, Baltimore, MD.

Sroufe, L. A. (1983). Infant-caregiver attachment and patterns of adaptation in preschool: The roots of maladaptation and competence. In M. Perlmutter (Ed.), *Minnesota symposium in child psychology* (Vol. 16, pp. 41–81). Hillsdale, NJ: Lawrence Erlbaum Associates.

Sroufe, L. A. (1988). The role of infant-caregiver attachment in development. In J. Belsky & T. Nezworski (Eds.), *Clinical implications of attachment* (pp. 18–38). Hillsdale, NJ: Lawrence Erlbaum Associates.

Sroufe, L. A., & Fleeson, J. (1986). Attachment and the construction of relationships. In W. W. Hartup & Z. Rubin (Eds.), *Relationships and development* (pp. 57–71). Hillsdale, NJ: Lawrence Erlbaum Associates.

Sroufe, L. A., Fox, N. E., & Pancake, V. R. (1983). Attachment and dependency in developmental perspective. *Child Development, 54,* 1615–1627.

Sroufe, L. A., & Waters, E. (1977). Attachment as an organizational construct. *Child Development, 48,* 1184–1199.

Suess, G. J., Grossman, K. E., & Sroufe, L. A. (1992). Effects of infant attachment to mother and father on quality of adaptation in preschool: From dyadic to individual organisation of self. *International Journal of Behavioral Development, 15,* 43–65.

Sullivan, H. S. (1953). *The interpersonal theory of psychiatry.* New York: Norton.

Teti, D. M., & Ablard, K. E. (1989). Security of attachment and infant-sibling relationships: A laboratory study. *Child Development, 60,* 1519–1528.

Teti, D. M., Nakagawa, M., Das, R., & Wirth, O. (1991). Security of attachment between preschoolers and their mothers: Relations among social interaction, parenting stress, and mothers' sorts of the Attachment Q-set. *Developmental Psychology, 27,* 440–447.

Thompson, R. A., Lamb, M. E., & Estes, D. (1982). Stability of mother-infant attachment and its relationship to changing life circumstances in an unselected middle-class sample. *Child Development, 53,* 144–148.

Troy, M., & Sroufe, L. A. (1987). Victimization among preschoolers: Role of attachment history. *American Academy of Child and Adolescent Psychiatry, 26*, 166–172.

Vandell, D. L., & Mueller, E. C. (1980). Peer play and friendships during the first two years. In H. C. Foot, A. J. Chapman, & J. R. Smith (Eds.), *Friendship and social relations in children* (pp. 181–208). New York: Wiley.

Vaughn, B. E., Egeland, B., Sroufe, L. A., & Waters, E. (1979). Individual differences in mother-infant attachment at twelve and eighteen months: Stability and change in families under stress. *Child Development, 50*, 971–975.

Vaughn, B. E., & Waters, E. (1990). Attachment behavior at home and in the laboratory: Q-sort observations and Strange Situation classifications of one-year-olds. *Child Development, 61*, 1965–1973.

Vespo, J. E. (1985). *Children's relationships with friends and acquaintances in preschool classes.* Unpublished doctoral dissertation, State University of New York at Stony Brook.

Waters, E. (1978). The reliability and stability of individual differences in infant-mother attachment. *Child Development, 49*, 483–494.

Waters, E., & Deane, K. E. (1985). Defining and assessing individual differences in attachment relationships: Q-methodology and the organization of behavior in infancy and early childhood. *SRCD Monographs, 50* (Serial No. 209).

Waters, E., Wippman, J., & Sroufe, L. A. (1979). Attachment, positive affect, and competence in the peer group: Two studies in construct validation. *Child Development, 50*, 821–829.

Weiss, R. S. (1982). Attachment in adult life. In C. M. Parkes & J. Stevenson-Hinde (Eds.), *The place of attachment in human behavior* (pp. 171–184). New York: Basic Books.

Wiggins, J. S. (1973). *In defense of traits.* Unpublished manuscript, University of British Columbia, Canada.

Young, J. E. (1986). A cognitive-behavioral approach to friendship disorders. In V. J. Derlaga & B. A. Winstead (Eds.), *Friendship and social interaction* (pp. 247–276). New York: Springer-Verlag.

# Chapter 8

# Continuities in the Development of Intimate Friendships: Object Relations, Interpersonal, and Attachment Perspectives

Ruth Sharabany
*University of Haifa*

The goal of this chapter is to describe the place of intimacy within the context of life-span development (infancy, childhood, adolescence, and young adulthood). One is struck by the existence of three different, uncoordinated perspectives related to the life-span development of close relationships, particularly the development of intimate friendships. One perspective is the developmental sequence of the significant people during one's life span: first parents; then friends of the same gender; and then friends of the opposite gender, spouses, and children. A second perspective is the developmental sequence of various functions and processes, such as attachment, friendship, and love. A third perspective is the different theories. Each theory has a different focus on a particular developmental phase and on a particular process. Theories of object relations, based on clinical work with adults, focused on early relations with a significant other in infancy. The attachment theory began with a focus on infancy. It is with this theory that the significance of early relationships with caregiver begins. Interpersonal relationship theories additionally emphasize the friendship phase. Social psychologists emphasize close relationships in adulthood and love. For example, one area of study is the components of love: intimacy, commitment, and passion.

Intimate friendship was considered a specific phase lasting from early childhood through early adolescence. However, it seems that an intimacy component is present in all significant close relationships from infancy through adulthood. Thus, the terms *intimate friendship* and *intimacy* are used here interchangeably. Within this context, there are several important transitions. There is the transition from infancy, in which attachment to the parents is the most prominent feature, into middle childhood, when intimate friendships are developed with peers. Then, there is the transition made from middle childhood into adolescence and adulthood, when intimacy in relations with opposite-gender friends, lovers, and spouses are the central characteristics.

The present chapter attempts to relate three theoretical frameworks: object relations, interpersonal, and attachment. An attempt to compare or integrate systematically these three perspectives is beyond the scope of the present chapter. Rather, I draw attention to the transitions noted earlier where different perspectives arise by each approach. I argue that an integrative view of these three theories is acceptable, and I proceed to define the area of intimate friendship as a core concept of the present chapter. It is my view that none of these three paradigms is simple. It is often a temptation for the sake of prediction to translate them into simple linear models, which often results in reductionism. However, neither the reality nor the theories are so simple. An example of this phenomenon are the three categories of attachment that carry the promise for simple classification and simple long-term prediction, yet once they have been researched the picture emerges as more complicated yielding division into more categories, and subcategories.

It seems that the state of the art in the area of close relationships is one of a pendulum or a broadening spiral that keeps spinning. I believe that many concepts appear in a germinal way in the beginning of the examination of an issue (e.g., close relationships) as well as the examination of specific aspects of the area (e.g., issues of continuity vs. discontinuity). However, each development in this field involves the process of thesis, antithesis, and synthesis, and the latter becomes the new thesis prone to new antithesis. This view does not see antithesis as excluding the thesis, but as sharpening, challenging, and becoming part of it in a modified way. Perhaps this is one reason that apparently contradictory assumptions do not create a problem that calls for an immediate remedy. Although these do deserve attention and are considered unfinished business, they are part of an ongoing process. Piaget noted that what often seems in the empirical sciences as antithesis turns out to be a differentiation of the previous thesis (Bringuier, 1988). Although in principle this seems to be true, often an area of psychology develops a loyalty to a narrow range of specific concepts and a specific methodology. Several processes may operate to keep different schools separate. These processes include the use of different terms (e.g., *attachment* vs. *dependency*), the use of different levels of analysis (e.g., behavior vs. internal working models), and the focus on different aspects of content (such as friendship vs. attachment vs. intimacy). Additionally, sociological processes influence science, and schools become segregated by their journals and professional clubs for many reasons: limitations of time, continuity of the issue at hand, comparability and replication, limitations of resources, and the need to have professional identity by creating definitions of what is acceptable and what is not acceptable. (For further discussions, see Kuhn, 1970; Suppe, 1984.)

There are exceptional cases when data obtained by one school are usable in other schools. However, data obtained by one school are often disregarded by the other schools (Rakover, 1986), or are rejected and criticized openly. The following is an example of the current degree of segregation within the area of close relationships. In a book that reviews very thoroughly object relation theories, Bowlby's work was mentioned very briefly (Greenberg & Mitchell, 1983). This is systematically so, because full articles are written in the realm of social psychology or developmental psychology relevant to close relationships, which generally exclude the contributions of psychoanalytic writings on the basis of irrelevance. An example of a new and rare exception was Hartup's article (1989) on social development, which noted Freud's contribution to the field. There are several examples of papers that adopt an integrative approach and choose to emphasize the complementarity of various approaches, rather than the apparent contrasts, in the interest of mutual fertilization. One such example is a paper on the complementarity of structural Kohlbergian approach and socialization approach within the area of prosocial and moral development (Gibbs & Schnell, 1985). Another example is a paper on altruism (Sharabany & Bar-Tal, 1982). A final example is the 1987 presidential address of Fred Pine to Division 39 of the American Psychological Association (APA). In this talk, he addressed different psychoanalytic perspectives on psychoanalytic psychotherapy. He integrated Kohutian, object relations, and Freudian perspectives, even though these paradigms evolved as divergent and contrasting to each other and are viewed as separate. According to Pine, all three approaches are useful in clinical work (Pine, 1988, 1990).

Regarding the area of close relationships within psychology, it seems premature to attempt compartmentalization. A reflection of the aspiration to integrate theories, paradigms, and different fields within this area was in the heart of the beginning of the Society for Research in Personal Relationship (Gilmour & Duck, 1986). I take license in this chapter to ignore inherent contradictions among the various approaches, and dwell on the common, the additive elements, and the complementary aspects of these approaches.

## INTIMATE FRIENDSHIP: A WORKING DEFINITION

The entering point for a definition of *intimate friendship* is based on Sharabany (1974, 1980; Sharabany & Rodgers, 1980). The definition of *intimacy* is an inclusive one, such that there are elements that can vary in quality and quantity, but all are components of one concept. This definition includes structure aspects and content aspects. Structural components are described first. An intimate friend is one who is nominated and regarded so by the respondent. The partner returns both the degree of reciprocity of choice (i.e., as best friend, friend, etc.) of the friend, as well as the mutuality (the extent to which behaviors and feelings of one partner in dyadic intimacy are returned). Mutuality may potentially differentiate various balances within relationships and styles of relations. Another structural aspect of intimate friendship is apparent when a person describes both a best friend and another friend. In such a case, one can discover which aspects single out the best friend, and thus which aspects are considered more intimate by that particular person. In other words, there is a degree of personal profile that differentiates for the respondent what he or she considers close. This personal differentiation has not been frequently used.

The content of the intimate relationship includes eight dimensions. The first dimension is frankness and spontaneity, which is a form of self-disclosure. The second is sensitivity and knowing. This is a sense of empathy or understanding that is not necessarily achieved through talking. The third dimension is attachment—the degree of being attached to the friend. The fourth is the degree of exclusiveness and uniqueness of the relationships with the friend. The fifth dimension is the degree of helping the friend and sharing with the friend. The sixth is the degree of being able to take and impose on the friend, which shows some degree of openness and readiness to be vulnerable while being helped. The seventh dimension is common activities—the extent to which one participates in activities with one's best friend. The final dimension is trust and loyalty, the degree to which one can rely on the help and nonbetrayal of the friend.

The definition of *intimate friendship* was proposed some years ago (Bigelow & LaGaipa, 1975; Sharabany, 1973). Since then, many dimensions of intimacy have been researched (reviewed in Sharabany, 1993). The rationale for including them has been well supported using different procedures in different countries (Engelstein, 1987; Jones & Dembo, 1986; Sharabany, Friedman, & Eshel, 1985). The intimacy dimensions have been related to gender roles (Jones & Dembo, 1989) and to identity and loneliness (Wiseman & Lieblich, 1993). This definition is inclusive enough to capture developmental changes (Jones & Dembo, 1989; Sharabany, Gershoni, & Hoffman, 1981), as well as changes by small-group intervention (Shechtman, 1991) and changes in intimacy following treatment intervention with married couples (Beery, 1992). Individual differences have been captured in studying children of divorce (Hertz-Lazarowitz, Rosenberg, & Guttman, 1989), as well as in differences between exceptionally bright children versus normal peers (Mayseless, 1993). This definition of intimacy has been useful in studying differences in socialization settings (kibbutz vs. city, reviewed in Sharabany & Wiseman, 1993), and has been the basis for an intimacy scale (Sharabany, 1993). The concept of intimacy is similar to earlier work on close relationships (Reusch, Block, & Bennett, 1953) as well as to very recent work (i.e., Sternberg, 1986).

In comparing this definition of *intimacy* with Sternberg's components of intimacy in his definition of *love* (Sternberg, 1986), one discovers an appreciable degree of conceptual overlap. Sternberg listed components of intimacy, and claimed that this is a pool of intimacy ingredients from which various elements in different combinations and intensities are drawn. Of Sternberg's three components of love, the passion aspect (which is mostly sexual in nature) is not included in this definition of *intimacy*. Sternberg's commitment aspect is partly represented in some of the present variables such as trust, loyalty, and exclusiveness. Similarly, there is overlap between the present broad definition of intimacy as close relationship with Hazan and Shaver's (1987) operational definition. Other definitions of *intimacy* have specified the central aspect as communication and self-disclosure (i.e., Reis & Shaver, 1988). Although self-disclosure does seem to be the most advanced social skill developmentally and central to the definition, a multidimensional definition is preferred (see Chelune & Waring, 1984; Derlega, 1984; Levinger & Raush, 1977, for excellent reviews; Reis, 1990; Youniss & Smollar, 1985).

The relative importance of the components of such a definition should be a function of intimacy maturation, personal profile, socialization, culture, and gender (see Sharabany, 1980; Sharabany & Rodgers, 1980, on the nature of intimate friendship). Lastly, the current proposed model of intimacy is a model that says that close relationships are a nucleus that is central and feeds other levels of social relations. It is a stable core that is slow to change. Once this core is touched, it is possible that the change would be generalizable and transferable to other relationships. Intimate friendship, and the intimacy component in any close relationship, is analogous to pillars of a building. When there are changes in this area, large changes in other social relationships are expected as well. For this reason, although changes are expected in intimacy, a profound impact is needed to bring about this change. For example, a change in degree of trust or in one's ability to request and use help would need a very meaningful catalyst.

## OBJECT RELATIONS

The perspective of object relations provides several elements for understanding intimate relationships. Object relations is sometimes referred to as the British school within psychoanalytic tradition. It is well known that the psychoanalytic tradition is a very large theoretical umbrella that hosts diverse approaches under its roof. Some of these approaches deserve the title "theory" in and of themselves. The following description is an attempt to see a few trees in this forest. The heterogeneous contributions of Klein, Winnicott, Balint, Fairbairn, and others come to mind. A large group of psychoanalysts adopted a social interactional view of the development of relationships. The old Freudian motivation underscoring instinct gratification (such as food and sex) was replaced explicitly and implicitly in some mixed way with the notion of "object seeking" innate tendency. In the current explanation of close relationships, the weight of social interaction and the shaping of developmental processes has increased greatly. The individual has a tendency to seek connection with others, and, in turn, is shaped by these relations. Individuals are seen as molded within relationships and seeking connection with others. Thus, although the inherent biologism assumed within psychoanalytic thought was not abandoned, it was downplayed. Likewise, instinct gratification lost the eminent position in the formation of a relationship. Relationships are viewed as significant in and of themselves and become a powerful motive. It follows that the emphasis is on a gradual differentiation of the self from the internalized others (internal objects). Internal objects are the representations of actual interactions with others, modified by a specific perspective of the individual (such as his or her stage of development). The internal objects reflect real experiences of real persons from infancy. The degree to which these internal objects are based on real interactions with significant others (e.g., caregiver, mother, father), or are overshadowed by some innate givens and greatly based on fantasy, is a point of difference among the various versions of object relations theorists (e.g., Klein vs. Winnicott). There are two aspects that are agreed on by both approaches, whether they emphasize the reality or fantasized element in the interaction of parent and child: First, these interactions are a basis for generalization and learning in the future, and, second, the child is learning both parts of the interaction. Later, the child may play out either the parental role or his or her own (e.g., either the aggressor or the victim; the loving or the beloved one). Thus, the parent–child interaction establishes a repertoire and options for the child's future close interactions. In some ways the repertoire is limited, and in other ways it is unpredictable. A common thread is the modifiability of these internal objects as a result of later significant relationships and interventions such as psychotherapy (Osofsky, 1982).

An example of current research being conducted in the area of object relations is that of Blatt and his associates. Their work on object representation runs parallel to other research groups investigating similar concepts. According to Blatt (1990), the concept of the object is a complex cluster of templates that develops within the context of need gratifying in significant personal relationships and is then generalized as schemes for all cognitive/affective endeavors. The development of the representation of the object is a function of the interaction between the innate and the developing capacities of the individual and his or her experience in important interpersonal transactions. The work of Blatt and Schichman (1983) integrate the emotional interpersonal perspective with the cognitive abilities perspective, drawing both from psychoanalysts and Piaget. Blatt et al. defined *levels of representation*. Their dimensions included conceptual level (concept vs. abstract), degree of viewing the object (as need fulfilling vs. viewing the object as separate), and relating to external versus internal qualities of the object. These dimensions were validated by independent developmental work of Blatt and associates (Blatt, 1974, 1990; Blatt & Schichman, 1983; Blatt, Wiseman, Prince-Gibson, & Gatt, 1991).

Object relations is a mine for formulations examining the development of close relationships and their changeability through processes such as psychotherapy. An example of this point is offered by one of the pioneering primary papers integrating mainstream developmental psychology with object relations and with attachment theory. Osofsky (1988) compared processes of attachment in babies with processes occurring in psychoanalytic psychotherapy. In the therapeutic relationship, there are elements of parenting and an equality basis in the relationships. These elements are to be found either in the parent–child relationship or later in integrated, mature adult relationships. In object relations theory, relations are developed in dyadic interaction with the person who satisfies basic psychological and psychological needs, assuring the physical as well as the psychological survival of the infant. Once object relations are established between the object and the child, attachment can develop with this love object, as well as with any other human being in the child's environment. Bowlby (1982) defined the object that is likely to elicit this attachment behavior as older or wiser than the infant, thus making the process open for a broad spectrum of attachments, not just the biological mother. According to Bowlby (1969, 1973), attachment behavior is a behavior that results in a person attaining or retaining proximity to some other differentiated and preferred individual. That individual is usually conceived of as a stronger and/or wiser person, and thus becomes a figure of attachment. Within psychoanalytic therapy, the process of transference to the analyst is viewed as a recreation of this intensive early attachment in a repetitive way. It is promoted through the interventions of the treatment, which are assumed to allow the patient to be free and secure enough in the therapeutic relationship to explore and test new thoughts and feelings with less fear, or at least a loosening of the defensive structure. The analyst, like the good parent, needs to be available, consistent, responsive, and ready to intervene judiciously. Osofsky suggested that analytic interpretations could be considered as judicious interventions, not just at times that the more dependent, child-like person may be heading for trouble, but also to open up new ways of thinking about experiences and situations (Osofsky, 1988; Peterson & Moran, 1988).

So far, the previous discussion is an example of the integration of object relations psychoanalytic concepts with attachment concepts. Several additional concepts from object relations theory may be borrowed as potential clarifiers of issues in the development of close relations.

First, each one of the significant relations may contribute a different model. The question of which model would prevail would be answered based on the developmental stage. Second, there are important elements of the unconscious that play an important role in close relationships. A person may be striving in one direction and simultaneously be driven toward another one (e.g., strong need to be distant, driven by fear of being abandoned). Third, there is a concept called "defense mechanism" that attempts to chart different ways in which people cope with internal information that is threatening or incongruent. An example is that it is possible for "insecure" individuals to use a mechanism of "split" in their relations. They relate to others either as "all bad" or as "all good." This contrasting perception may operate with different relations (mother good, father bad) or within the same one (you were great, now you are no good). Finally, having several incongruent integrated internal models may create problems. Certain pathologies may be looked on as having a discrepant picture of self versus other in various ways.

## INTERPERSONAL APPROACH

Within psychoanalytic thought, Sullivan (1952) has contributed a unique perspective on intimate friendship. Sullivan represented the interpersonal perspective (although there are other theorists with the perspective; e.g., Eric Fromm, Fromm-Reichman, Clara Thompson).

Sullivan's most basic premise was an interactional definition of personality. His unit of observation was always the interpersonal field. The interpersonal perspective is one step removed from the object relations perspective. There is an emphasis on continuous development in one's interpersonal relationships. A need for a new mode of relationships emerges in each stage of development. Although great emphasis is placed on the parents as a source for the primary model of close relationships, new interactions carry distinct and powerful potential to produce change. Thus, it is within the interpersonal perspective that there is a developmental continuity between relationships with parents to relationships with peers, particularly chums in the juvenile area. Intimacy and closeness with same-gender peers becomes the springboard for the heterosexual intimacy that follows. Several developmental studies followed Sullivan's theories and tried to chart more specific maps of the evolution of key relationships for each stage of development. One such compelling theoretical paper is by Buhrmester and Furman (1986). They suggested a developmental matrix in which social needs change and are replaced by other needs, and the people and relationships who are expected to provide these needs change in a developmental sequence. For example, although companionship can be provided to children between the ages of 2 and 6 by their parents, at ages 6–9 the experience of being accepted replaces the simpler need for companionship. The providers of this new social need are peers (Buhrmester & Furman, 1986; Youniss & Smollar, 1975).

The work of Sullivan (1952) was central to the area of close relationships from several aspects. First, it was the main, and almost only, work in intimacy within research in psychology up to the beginning of the 1970s. Second, the concepts of friendship and closeness were likewise introduced and survived within the Sullivanian writings. Sullivan devoted a significant place to friendship, and particularly same-gender friendship, in his theory of development of social relationships and personality. He maintained that culture makes a specific contribution in shaping the modes and field of battle (i.e., overoccupation with sex is considered an artifact of our culture, which delays sex and is not considered a significant and central phase).

According to Sullivan (1952), intimate friendship can be a means to facilitate and come to grips with parental relationships. Sullivan claimed that friendship can be a healing relationship that aids the adolescent in correcting the egocentric view of the self within and in addition to the relations with family (i.e., sibling, father, mother). Friendship serves adolescents as a nonjudgmental relationship. The relationship has standards that allow friends to become critics of each other, whereas simultaneously allowing a process of admission of offense and reparation of breach. Youniss and Smollar (1985) demonstrated these Sullivanian principles in their research.

Although the main frame of Sullivan's (1952) theory was psychoanalysis and psychodynamic theory, Sullivan added a special component into the examination of close relationships. Sullivan's orientation was toward components of the here-and-now interaction, in contrast to the object relation school that is rich and loose in speculations about the internal psychic structure. This accentuation of the here-and-now interaction is combined with the personal meaning that a person attaches to his or her behavior.

Sullivan's (1952) understanding of patterns of personal behavior has three components. The first is an emphasis on real and observable behavior as events of interpersonal relations. This emphasis on reality of the relationships is both in the past (the real interaction with parents) and in the present (the real interaction of the person with others). This is unlike the traditional psychoanalysis stress on the transferential aspect.

The second component is a concept of interpersonal field. One cannot understand the personality in isolation. The only meaningful context for grasping the fundamentals of human experience is within the interpersonal field. According to Sullivan (1952), the child is enmeshed in relations with others and discovers him or herself in interaction. Sullivan studied patterns of behavior, interactions, and anxiety transmitted through the caregiver. The infant discovers the object in him or herself in relation to the other objects. There is a process of internalization so that interactions with close and meaningful others become the cumulative basis for future interpersonal encounters. However, one always changes as a result of an interaction. There is continuous and mutual shaping with the here and now. The child shapes, structures, and restores his or her own experience, behavior, and self-perception to maintain the best possible relatedness with parents. The personality of the child shapes itself only in complement with the personality of parents. The third component is that development occurs when new forms of contact and relatedness with others introduce themselves, such as a need for a new mode of relations with playmates like oneself. This results in a more specific intimacy with one other person, and is followed by heterosexual love.

Sullivan (1952) described two groups of needs: needs for security (i.e., being free from anxiety and fear) and needs for satisfactions. Other emotional needs emerge over the course of development. The infant seeks bodily contact and needs contact with adults. The young child seeks participation of adults as an audience in his or her play and efforts. The juvenile seeks competition, cooperation, and compromise with juveniles. A preadolescent seeks an intimate, collaborative, and loving relationship with someone of the same gender— a chum. Interestingly, mainstream Freudians are currently moving in Sullivan's direction. The fundamental motivating force is understood to be the search of, and establishment of, relations with others. This adoption of Sullivanian concepts is not only occurring in an overt and open way. Therapy within psychoanalytic circles, under different terms and concepts, is recognizing that real relationship processes between therapist and client are central in influencing the change in the patient's life. The novel aspect is that this is happening within quite conservative circles.

In sum, examples of concepts that can be borrowed from the interpersonal school of psychoanalysis include the following. Internal working models are shaped continuously by interactions with people. These are real elements in the interactions (as opposed to the meaning of them divorced from the real element). These internal working molds have ways of being modified by, and change as a result of, new interactions based on here and now. Finally, there is a core of intimacy in close relationships throughout the life span (of which intimate friendships is one example).

## THE ATTACHMENT PERSPECTIVE

Bowlby has been the forefather of this perspective, and Ainsworth has been the pillar who provided the Strange Situation paradigm (Ainsworth, Blehar, Waters, & Wall, 1978). Although Bowlby worked on bringing etiological concepts into the description of mother–child attachment relations, it was Ainsworth's experimental paradigm that gave the objective and observable tools that have been part of the mainstream of developmental psychology (Ainsworth, 1985). The attachment paradigm occupies an interesting zone that grew out of the work of psychoanalytically trained psychologists. It gained momentum by providing a specific operationalization, the Strange Situation, as well as a clear classification into secure, ambivalent, and avoidant patterns of attachment. Gradually, the attachment paradigm has divorced itself from its historical psychoanalytic origins by casting the paradigm in ethological terms. The paradigm offered new observable scientific methods and created new terms to be more specific and operationalized (although it was also criticized, e.g., Lamb, Thompson, Bardner, Charnov, & Estes, 1984). Historically, attachment theory was developed on the basis of object relations theory. The theory of attachment is an attempt to explain both attachment behavior with its episodic appearance and disappearance, and also the enduring attachments that children and other individuals make to particular others—attachment bond. There are seeds in attachment theory both for the behavioral and observable elements representing the social behavioral scientific approach, and for the enduring aspects that would later become the basis for research into the presentational realm. Bowlby believed that the biological survival element is most important in attachment. There is an element of insurance in attachment (i.e., that someone either older or wiser will be helpful). Bowlby differentiated attachment from dependency in the following manner: Dependency may be an undifferentiated behavior, whereas attachment is to a specific other. Bowlby distinguished between an attachment bond and attachment behavior. Children show habitual preference in attachment bond and enduring attachment to the mother figure. Depending on circumstances, one can see a hierarchy of preferences so that, in extremity, even a kind stranger may be a target of attachment behavior (Bowlby, 1982). The emphasis on early experiences, which are then central to the process of selection and accumulation of new experiences, is drawn from the psychoanalytic theory. Individuals who grow up in unfavorable circumstances are very likely to reexperience new situations based on their previous frame (Bowlby, 1982).

The child's attachment to the mother is part of an archaic heritage whose function is survival. The mother does not become important because she provides food. She is important from the beginning of life. The power of primary attachment to the mother is betrayed by the true mourning reaction of children to the loss of their mothers. The early attachments are intense and specific. Confidence in the availability of attachment figures underlies the emotional continuities in the development of intimate relationships.

Object relations, interpersonal, and attachment perspectives generally agree with Bowlby in this area. Many of Bowlby's formulations of his theory traced their antithesis position in reference to the most conservative point of view of the psychoanalytic school. Bowlby's position stressed the gap between his theory and traditional psychoanalysis by referring mainly to old Freudian concepts. He chose to downplay the object relations perspective, which was much closer to his own. In contrast to Bowlby's efforts to underscore how his theory differed from the psychoanalytic theory, quite often Bowlby's work was integrated into the object relations group in the psychoanalytic school.

Bowlby introduced the term *working models* to replace the concept of internal object. Originally, the concept of object was derived from feeding and seeing the object as secondary to having a basic biological need satisfied. A good internal object, as specified by object relations theorists, is equivalent to a work-ing model of an attachment figure who is conceived as accessible, trustworthy, and ready to help when called. Working models are based on real experiences, rather than on internal worry and fantasies that transform by interpretation of the experience of reality.

There have been several original contributions to the theory of attachment. One of these contributions was by Main, Kaplan, and Cassidy (1985). They offered deep insight into the understanding of how attachment relations trans-form into representations and working models. Main has studied attachments of adults via interpretation and analysis of subjects' reports of their past rela-tionships with their parents. She categorized and classified the subjects by paying attention to what she terms *structural* aspects of working models. These easily could be termed *defense mechanisms* by the object relations school, rather than aspects of working models. For example, difficulty in remembering childhood experiences or incoherent reports are elements that count in the classification as structural, and they are signs of insecurity. The concept of insight, which is central to the psychoanalytic tradition as a whole, is also reflected in her classification. For example, when the subject reports having a new perspective and a new understanding of early insecurities, and has experienced parental faults but is able to forgive them, the subject is then classified as more secure.

In sum, the attachment group has made several significant contributions to the understanding of continual relationship. Some of the ways to define and observe attachment behavior have been very meaningful, such as the replace-ment of the term *dependency* (which became badly perceived and was contrast-ed with independence) with the term *attachment*. The attachment group has contributed to the assertion that there is a life-long element of bonding that one does not need to overcome later in life. The introduction of an internal working model, as opposed to internalized objects, made room for multiplici-ty, for change, and for internal structure that is one step removed from the specific people. New developments connect the present description of relations between adults and their parents with current internal working models of close relationships.

## LIFE-SPAN'S MODELS: TRANSITIONS FROM ONE CLOSE RELATIONSHIP TO THE OTHER

When one examines different models of changes during the life span, from one close relationship to the next, the relevance of the three different theories be-comes clearer. Close, mature relations are the culmination of various building blocks collected throughout the various stages of development. The attachment element is from infancy and the intimacy element is from childhood. Still, this does not mean that changes do not occur. It has been well documented in longitudinal studies of personality that there are patterns of continuity that are observable, as well as patterns that seemingly lack continuity, or a complex model of continuity (Block, 1991). There are different styles and patterns of close relationships for each of these building blocks. One is aware of several styles of love (Levy & Davis, 1988), several styles of forming couples (in marriage) and close relationships (Fitzpatrick, 1988), and several styles of attachment (Ainsworth, 1989).

The attachment theory creates an illusion that there is a direct continuity between the early attachments (to mother, father, caregiver, etc.) and the romantic relationships later as adults. For example, Ainsworth (1982) quoted Freud as claiming that the relationship between an infant and his or her mother is not only the most important object relation, but also the prototype of all subsequent love relations. There have been findings by Hazan and Shaver (1987) that support the notion that there is coherency between the concurrent relationship to parents and the relationship to romantic partners. However, in their work on attachment of adults and romantic love, they did not avoid an implication of direct continuity from infancy and early childhood to adulthood and romantic relationship (Shaver, Hazan, & Bradshaw, 1988).

An allusion to the prototype model is found in Weiss (1982):

> Adults establish a bond to other adults that is in essential aspects identical to the attachments that children make to their primary caretakers. . . . This bond is not to be found in some degree in every emotionally significant relationship adults maintain, but rather just as is the case with attachment in children, it appears only in relationships of central emotional importance. (p. 175)

Namely, elements of caregiving, bonding, and uniqueness seem to be characteristic of attachments to parents and later to spouses (or their equivalent). They seem to have the intensity of within-family relations whether original parents' family or a new one with a spouse. Several studies have casted doubt on the validity of this leap from early attachment to love as attachment in adulthood. Some studies have had difficulties finding concurrent correlation and match between attachment to mother and attachment to father as early as infancy (Lamb, 1977; Main & Weston, 1981; Oppenheim, Sagi, & Lamb, 1988). These studies showed that the infant or child may have several patterns of attachment to different adults concurrently. Thus, the continuity from infancy to adulthood involves qualities of the relations, rather than a similar prototype. This was explained by Marris (1982):

> Children learn first through their experience of attachment that there is a class of attachmentships. . . . They can recognize a unique bond between themselves and each other person of this class. Perhaps the easiest way to see uniqueness as a generalizable quality is in intimate friendships. We evolve with each of our closest friends an idiosyncratic relationship of mutual loyalty; each is irreplaceable and its loss would grieve us, yet we can sustain, if we are lucky, a good intimate friendship. All these unique relationships share the same qualities. They are nurturing, can claim priority, and are more or less exclusive. (pp. 198–199)

Although attachments in infancy can be a basis for later close relationships, the initial complexity of attachments, as well as additional experiences of intimacy with peers, need to be taken into account.

A developmental model that does not assume a prototype is the model suggested by Park (1988). She assumed attachment to parents to be a basis for later development. In her model, she carefully suggested that in each stage of development securely attached children are more likely to form more positive relationships and friendships. She also claimed that securely attached children have less difficulties forming and maintaining friendships in early childhood. In middle childhood, securely attached children develop more stable relationships. In adolescence, securely attached adolescents are more intimate. In late adolescence and adulthood, the more secure these individuals are, the more satisfying are their love and romantic relationships. Thus, qualities of early attachment are continuous but not a prototype. The continuity from one stage of development to the next is based on the accomplishment of secure attachment in infancy. Having secure attachment will lead children to positive development in subsequent stages.

A different model of life-span transition from close relationships in one phase to close relationships in the following phase is the model suggested by Hassan and Bar-Yam (1987). They stressed that a variety of interpersonal experiences in the preceding stages contribute in important ways to subsequent relationships, including early attachment, the negotiation of oedipal romance in the preschool age, the juvenile's experience of idealizing hero worship, and the young adolescent's experiences in dyadic chumship as well as in their later crushes and infatuations with the opposite gender.

The model suggested by Hassan and Bar-Yam (1987) is similar to the Sullivanian model and to Buhrmester and Furman's (1986) model. In a very thoughtful outline, Buhrmester and Furman charted a model in which each stage of development is fed by the previous one, which then leads and feeds the next stage. Also, in each stage of development, there is a unique function that either emerges or fully develops in that stage. In other words, intimate friendship has the potential to occupy a much more significant role in the development of close intimate relations, as well as later in romantic relationships. This core intimacy mediates between early stages of attachment and later stages of romantic relationships or love relationships.

## FROM PARENTS TO PEERS, FROM ATTACHMENT
## TO INTIMATE FRIENDSHIP

Attachment theory was conceived as a general theory of personality development by Bowlby. However, to date, attachment research has focused primarily on infancy and early childhood and, as Kobak and Sceery (1988) claimed, primarily on relationships with parents.

Social developmental psychology has focused on peer interactions and on popularity, and only recently has started to concentrate on close relationships, friendships, and intimate friendships (Hartup, 1989). According to both attachment theory and object relations theory, early relationships set the stage for social and emotional development. For example, children with secure relationships in infancy often turn out to be more popular in nursery school than insecurely attached ones (Struff & Gleason, 1986; quoted in Hartup, 1989).

A more Sullivanian point of view would emphasize the plasticity and potential for change, despite the continuity from attachment to intimate friendships. There are several examples in the literature that show that when the balance between the degree of attachment, exposure, and contact to the parents is tipped toward exposure and contact with peers, there are some alternative patterns. These patterns do not show quite the same linearity of greater attachment to the parents and greater attachment to the peers. An example is the old studies of the Harlows, which showed that there are different functions of parents and peers. Thus, to show mature relationships to peers in adulthood, it is necessary to have had contact and exposure to both normal parents and normal peers.

In some studies on the Kibbutz, we found that, in cases where children sleep in the children's houses as opposed to sleeping in the parents' house, there are some reservations in the strength of attachments and degree of exclusivity with the peers. There appeared to be two main factors: both the reduced exposure to the parents and the increased contact with peers. This configuration produces different patterns of close relationships with the peers (Sharabany, Arnon, & Kav-Venaki, 1981).

Likewise, young delinquents who report greater severity of punishment from their fathers simultaneously show more intimate contact with their friends, compared with the same socioeconomical class children who were not delinquents (Hodish, Sharabany, & Hertz-Lazarowitz, 1989; Sharabany, Hertz-Lazarowitz, & Hodish, 1993). An integration of theories and hypotheses in moral development was suggested by Gibbs and Shnell (1985). Such an integration in social development was suggested by Hartup (1989):

> Although many investigators find it necessary to assert strong views about these questions, it is entirely possible that everyone is right: that is, relationships may be founded, to some extent, on early temperamental differences, and these, together with relationships, residues (e.g., working models), account for continui-

ties in developmental outcomes from intimate friendship to mature adult love.
(p. 124)

## INTIMACY IN CONCURRENT RELATIONSHIPS
## IN ADULTHOOD

The lay conception of love is characterized more by affectionate qualities than
passionate qualities (Clark & Reis, 1988). Sternberg (1986) listed three elements of love: passion (sexual), commitment, and intimacy. The following
points stress the centrality of the intimacy element in love in general.

Sternberg and Grajek (1984) examined the love scale of Rubin (1973) and
the interpersonal scale of Levinger, Rands, and Talaber (1977) and noted that
these scales focus primarily on the intimacy components of close relationships.
An interesting, and to some extent surprising, finding was that the structure
of intimacy in love does not appear to differ consequentially from one loving
relationship to another. This finding suggests that the intimacy component of
love forms a common core in loving relationships.

The continuity that seems to exist between intimate friendship and love,
and particularly the intimacy aspect of love, is found in the existence of common elements such as mutual communication and understanding, mutual giving
and receiving of help, and emotional support in counting on the loved one.
All these are elements listed by Sternberg (1986), and many of them overlap
the list of intimacy components in intimate friendship described in Sharabany
(1974), Sharabany et al. (1981), Bigelow (1977), and Bigelow and LaGaipa
(1975).

According to Sternberg (1986), the degree of love one experiences for one
member of one's nuclear family (mother, father, sibling close in age) tends
to be predictable from the love one feels for another member of that nuclear
family. However, intensity of love experienced toward members of one's nuclear
family does not predict amounts of love one experiences for individuals outside the nuclear family (Sternberg, 1986).

Adults aged 18–70 (mean age 32) report that the love one experiences for
one's lover is not predictable from the love one experiences for one's best friend
of the same gender. In other words, it seems that the romantic or the passionate element, when added to heterosexual relations, changes the picture somewhat and makes the transition in relationships from family to same gender to
other gender complicated and not very clear (Sternberg, 1986; Sternberg &
Grajek, 1984).

*Adult love* was defined by Bowlby (1980, 1988a, 1988b) as an integration
of three behavioral systems: attachment, sexuality, and caregiving. Similarly,
it was defined by Sternberg (1986) as composed of three elements: intimacy,
commitment, and passion. These three elements of adult love may operate

differently in various relationships, in various phases of relationships, and, of course, in various developmental phases. Both object relations theory and attachment theory have bypassed intimate friendship on their way from attachment with parents to adult love.

An example is an article that has the inspiration of a breakthrough in terms of the marriage of concepts and theory (Shaver et al., 1988). In their interest in adult love as an attachment, they leapt from early attachments to parents to later romantic love, and only mentioned infatuation in kindergarten as a continuous stepping stone to adult love. With the exception of Sullivan, this approach seems to be justified from several points of view. Rubin, author of several books on friendship, discussed the lack of biological basis for intimate friendships of the same gender. Therefore, she did not see any basis to look for overlaps between intimate friendships and adult romantic relationships (L. Rubin, personal communication, 1988).

Recent empirical evidence (Sternberg, 1986) also has shown that intimacy with a same-gender friend is not correlated with intimacy with a lover or an opposite-gender friend. A study of mothers who were asked to describe their intimate friendships with their husbands and their intimacy with a close friend of the same gender also showed no correlation (Mayseless, Sharabany, & Sagi, 1992). Nevertheless, remembering Sullivanian theory, there may be a correlation and direct transitions from same-gender intimacies to opposite-gender intimacies with lovers if one compares across developmental levels, rather than comparing simultaneous relationships. An example is the study by Lev-Ran and Sharabany (1981), in which we followed the same children longitudinally from 5th grade to 12th grade. We found that there were correlations between the children's descriptions of intimate friendships at 5th grade and their intimate friendships with the opposite gender at the 12th grade. Continuity can be conceptualized in several ways. A prototype model, which implies a direct copy from one phase to the other, does not withstand the test. A model that underscores continuity with the same qualities from one stage to a later one also is not supported by the studies on love by Sternberg and Grajek (1984). We suggest that a promising model is one that charts continuity from one function to another function in the following stage (e.g., trust with mother predicts openness with spouse). Additionally, the concurrent similarity of intimate relationships between spouse and parent may be quite diminished, because elements of intimacy that were grown and nurtured in relations with parents are transferred to the spouse and taken away in this form from the parents (Sharabany, Mayseless, Tzur, & Treinin, 1992). One should further remember that the well-documented gender differences in intimate friendships (cf. Reis, Senchak, & Solomon, 1985; Wheeler, Reis, & Nezlek, 1983) must play some role in masking the continuities that exist between intimacy of the same-gender friend and the intimacy with opposite-gender lovers.

Although attachment and object relations theories assume continuity in their early working models, their modifiability throughout the life span is also recognized. Therefore, it seems unwise to assume that only the early components of attachment to parents have long-lasting effects, and that effects of profound intimate friendships would not affect the style of the personal relationships at the adult phase.

Perhaps one may examine the transitions through the life cycle as the reorganization of intimacy in relationships that occurs as a result of (a) the addition of sexuality and (b) the addition of commitment. In our studies, it seemed that the intimacy component of close relationships shifted from same-gender friends to opposite-gender friends when sexuality arose, and to spouses and partners when commitment was made. The term *shift* emphasized the zero-sum element: less intimacy with same-gender friends and more intimacy with spouse (Sharabany, Friedman, & Eshel, 1985, 1986). Having recognized intimacy as consisting of several components, we suggest similar continuities rather than identical phases. Rather than the transition being in phases and figures, there is continuity from one aspect to another (e.g., trust with mother leading to openness with spouse, both being components of intimacy; Sharabany et al., 1992).

## SUMMARY

In this chapter, I tried to relate three different theories: object relations, attachment, and interpersonal relationships. I tried to see how all three theories considered the various close relationships to different figures formed through the phases of the life span. I specifically examined two transitional points within intimate relationships: (a) transition from attachment to parents to intimate relationships with peers; and (b) transition from intimate friendships of same gender to opposite-gender relationships, which are often called love. These two transitional points seem to call for a convergence of the three different points of view and for an integration of theories, which on the surface seem to be different. However, these intersections of transition, from early attachment to intimate relationships and from intimate friendships to adult love, appear to warrant the consideration of all three perspectives.

## ACKNOWLEDGMENTS

Part of this article was written while the author was a visiting scholar at the Block Project, Department of Psychology, University of California, Berkeley; and at the Department of Social Sciences, Maquarie University, Sydney, Australia. The study was supported by the National Institute of Mental Health grant HM 16080 to Jack and Jean H. Block. An early version of this chapter was presented as keynote address at the International Conference on Personal

Relationships at the University of British Columbia, Vancouver, Canada, July 1988. Thanks are due to Brian J. Bigelow, Jack Block, Jacqueline Goodnow, Mary Main, Suzanne Manton, Ofra Mayseles, Melissa Quilter, Melinda Travis, Mary True, and Sigal Tzur for academic and personal support.

## REFERENCES

Ainsworth, M. D. S. (1982). Attachment: Retrospect and prospect. In C. M. Parkes & J. Stevenson-Hinde (Eds.), *The place of attachment in human behavior* (pp. 3–30). New York: Basic Books.

Ainsworth, M. D. S. (1985). Attachaments across the life span. *Bulletin of the New York Academy of Medicine, 61,* 792–811.

Ainsworth, M. D. S. (1989). Attachments beyond infancy. *American Psychologist, 44*(4), 709–716.

Ainsworth, M. D. S., Blehar, M. C., Waters, E. C., & Wall, S. (1978). *Patterns of attachment: A psychological study of the strange situation.* Hillsdale, NJ: Lawrence Erlbaum Associates.

Beery, A. (1992). *Program of marriage enrichment: An evaluation study.* Unpublished master's thesis, School of Social Work, Tel Aviv University, Israel.

Bigelow, B. J. (1977). Children's friendship expectations: A cognitive developmental study. *Child Development, 48,* 246–253.

Bigelow, B. J., & LaGaipa, J. J. (1975). Children's written descriptions of friendship: A multidimensional analysis. *Developmental Psychology, 11,* 857–858.

Blatt, S. J. (1974). Levels of object representation in anaclitic and introjective depression. *The Psychoanalytic Study of the Child, 24,* 107–157.

Blatt, S. (1990). Interpersonal relatedness and self-definition: Two personality configurations and their implications for psychopathology and psychotherapy. In J. Signer (Ed.), *Repression and dissociation: Defense mechanism and personality styles.* Chicago: University of Chicago Press.

Blatt, S. J., & Schichman, S. (1983). Object representation of dependent people. *Psychoanalysis and Contemporary Thought, 6,* 187–254.

Blatt, S. J., Wiseman, H., Prince-Gibson, E., & Gatt, C. (1991). Object representations and change in clinical functioning. *Psychotherapy, 28*(2), 273–283.

Block, J. (1991, August). *Studying personality the long way.* Paper presented at the annual meeting of the American Psychological Association, San Francisco.

Bowlby, J. (1969). *Attachment and loss: Vol. 1. Attachment.* New York: Basic Books.

Bowlby, J. (1973). *Attachment and loss: Vol. 2. Separation: Anxiety and anger.* New York: Basic Books.

Bowlby, J. (1980). *Attachment and loss: Vol. 3. Loss.* New York: Basic Books.

Bowlby, J. (1982). Attachment and loss: Retrospect and prospect. *American Journal of Orthopsychiatry, 52*(4), 664–678.

Bowlby, J. (1988a). Developmental psychiatry comes of age. *American Journal of Psychiatry, 145*(1), 1–10.

Bowlby, J. (1988b). *A secure base: Clinical application of attachment theory.* London: Routledge.

Bringuier, J. C. (1988). *Halemidah Haemushit: Sichot im Piaget* [Human learning: Conversations with Piaget]. Jerusalem: Keter.

Buhrmester, D., & Furman, W. (1986). The changing functions of friends in childhood: A neo-Sullivanian perspective. In V. J. Devlega & B. A. Winstead (Eds.), *Friendship and social interaction* (pp. 41–62). New York: Springer-Verlag.

Chelune, G. J., & Waring, E. M. (1984). Nature and assessment of intimacy. In P. McReynolds & G. E. Chelune (Eds.), *Advances in psychological assessment* (Vol. 6). San Francisco, CA: Jossey-Bass.

Clark, M. S., & Reis, H. T. (1988). Interpersonal processes in close relationships. *Annual Review of Psychology, 39,* 609–672.

Derlega, V. J. (1984). *Communications, intimacy and close relationships.* Orlando, FL: Academic Press.

Engelstein, N. (1987). *The relationship between intimacy and best friend and identity formation in adolescence and early adulthood.* Unpublished doctoral dissertation, School of Education, George Washington University, Washington, DC.

Fitzpatrick, M. A. (1988). *Between husbands and wives.* London: Sage.

Gibbs, J. C., & Schnell, S. V. (1985). Moral development "versus" socialization—A critique. *American Psychologist, 40*(1), 1071–1080.

Gilmore, R., & Duck, S. (Eds.). (1986). *The emerging field of personal relationships.* Hillsdale, NJ: Lawrence Erlbaum Associates.

Greenberg, J. R., & Mitchell, S. A. (1983). *Object relations in psychoanalytic theory.* Cambridge, MA: Harvard University Press.

Hartup, W. W. (1989). Social relationships and their developmental significance. *American Psychologist, 44*(2), 120–126.

Hassan, A. B., & Bar-Yam, M. (1987). Interpersonal development across the life span: Communion and its interaction with agency in psychosocial development. *Contemporary Human Development, 18,* 102–128.

Hazan, C., & Shaver, P. (1987). Romantic love conceptualized as attachment process. *Journal of Personality and Social Psychology, 52*(3), 511–524.

Hertz-Lazarowitz, R., Rosenberg, M., & Guttman, J. (1989). Children of divorce and their intimate relationships with parents and peers. *Youth and Society, 21*(1), 85–104.

Hodish, M.,, Sharabany, R., & Hertz-Lazarowitz, R. (1989, July). *Empathy and intimacy among juvenile delinquents.* Paper presented for International Society for the Study of Behavioral Development, Helsinki, Finland.

Jones, G. P., & Dembo, M. H. (1986, April). *The development of friendship and intimacy in childhood and adolescence.* Paper presented at the Annual Meeting of the American Educational Research Association, San Francisco.

Jones, G. P., & Dembo, M. H. (1989). Age and sex role differences in intimate friendships during childhood and adolescence. *Merrill-Palmer Quarterly, 35*(4), 445–462.

Kobak, R. R., & Sceery, A. (1988). The transition to college: Working models of attachment, affect regulation and perceptions of self and others. *Child Development, 88,* 135–146.

Kuhn, T. (1970). *Structure of scientific revolutions.* Chicago: University of Chicago Press.

Lamb, M. E. (1977). Father-infant and mother-infant interactions in the first year of life. *Child Development, 48,* 167–181.

Lamb, M. E., Thompson, R. A., Bardner, W. P., Charnov, E. L., & Estes, D. (1984). Security of infantile attachment as assessed in the "strange situation": Its study and biological interpretation. *Behavioral and Brain Sciences, 7,* 157–181.

Levinger, G., Rands, M., & Talaber, R. (1977). *The assessment of involvement and rewardingness in close and casual pair relationships* (National Science Foundation Technical Report DK). Amherst, MA: University of Massachusetts.

Levinger, G., & Raush, H. L. (Eds.). (1977). *Close relationships: Perspectives on the meaning of intimacy.* Amherst: University of Massachusetts Press.

Lev Ran, A., & Sharabany, R. (1981, August). *The development of intimate friendship among kibbutz children: A longitudinal study.* Paper presented at the 6th Biennial Meeting of the International Society for the Study of Behavioral Development, Toronto, Canada.

Levy, M. B., & Davis, K. E. (1988). Lovestyles and attachment styles compared: Their relations to each other and to various relationship characteristics. *Journal of Social and Personal Relationships, 5,* 439–471.

Main, M., Kaplan, N., & Cassidy, J. (1985). Security in infancy, childhood, and adulthood: A move to the level of representation. *Monograph of the Society for Research in Child Development, 50*(1–2), 66–104.

Main, M., & Weston, D. R. (1981). Security of attachment to mother and father related to conflict behavior and the readiness to form new relationships. *Child Development, 52,* 932–940.

Marris, P. (1982). Attachment and society. In C. M. Parks & J. S. Stevenson-Hinde (Eds.), *The place of attachment in human behavior* (pp. 185–201). London: Tavistock.

Mayseless, O. (1993). Gifted adolescents and intimacy in close same-sex friendships. *Journal of Youth and Adolescence, 22*(2).

Mayseless, O., Sharabany, R., & Sagi, A. (1992, July/August). *Internal working models, concurrent intimacy with husband and friend of mothers and their child's attachment.* Paper presented at the International Conference on Personal Relationship, Orono, ME.

Oppenheim, D., Sagi, A., & Lamb, M. E. (1988). Infant-adult attachments on the kibbutz and their relation to socioemotional development four years later. *Developmental Psychology, 24,* 427–433.

Osofsky, J. D. (1982, August). *The concept of attachment and psychoanalysis.* Paper presented at the American Psychological Association meeting, Washington, DC.

Osofsky, J. D. (1988). Attachment theory and research and the psychoanalytic process. *Psychoanalytic Psychology, 5*(2), 159–177.

Park, K. A. (1988, July). *A developmental model of the relationships between parent-child attachment and friendship.* Paper presented at the International Conference on Personal Relationships, Vancouver, Canada.

Paterson, R. J., & Moran, G. (1988). Attachment theory, personality development, and psychotherapy. *Clinical Psychology Review, 8,* 611–636.

Pine, F. (1988). The four psychologies of psychoanalysis and their place in clinical work. *Journal of American Psychoanalytic Association, 36,* 371–596.

Pine, F. (1990). *Drive, ego, object and self: A synthesis for clinical work.* New York: Basic Books.

Rakover, S. S. (1986). Breaking the myth that behaviorism is a trivial science. *New Ideas in Psychology, 4*(3), 305–310.

Reis, H. T. (1990). The role of intimacy in interpersonal relations. *Journal of Social and Clinical Psychology, 9*(1), 15–30.

Reis, H. T., Senchak, M., & Solomon, B. (1985). Sex differences in the intimacy of social interaction: Further examination of potential explanations. *Journal of Personality and Social Psychology, 48*(5), 1204–1217.

Reis, H. T., & Shaver, P. (1988). Intimacy as an interpersonal process. In S. W. Duck (Ed.), *Handbook of research in personal relationships* (pp. 367–389). London: Wiley.

Reusch, J., Block, J., & Bennett, L. (1953). The assessment of communication: I. A method for the analysis of social interaction. *The Journal of Psychology, 35,* 59–80.

Rubin, Z. (1973). *Liking and loving.* New York: Holt, Reinhart & Winston.

Sharabany, R. (1973, August). *The development of intimacy among children in the Kibbutz.* Paper presented at the Biennial Meeting of the International Society for the Study of Behavioral Development, Ann Arbor, MI.

Sharabany, R. (1974). Intimate friendship among kibbutz and city children and its measurement. *Dissertation Abstracts International, 35*(2), 1028B. (University Microfilms No. 74-17, 682)

Sharabany, R. (1980). *Intimate friendship in a society of peers: Kibbutz vs. city preadolescents in Israel.* Unpublished manuscript, University of Haifa, Israel.

Sharabany, R. (1993). *Intimate friendship scale: Review of measurement and construct.* Manuscript submitted for review.

Sharabany, R., Arnon, A., & Kav-Venaki, S. (1981, April). *Friendship among communal vs. family raised children.* Paper presented at the Biennial Meeting of the Society for Research in Child Development, Boston.

Sharabany, R., & Bar-Tal, D. (1982). Theories of the development of altruism: Review, comparison and integration. *International Journal of Behavioral Development, 5,* 49–80.

Sharabany, R., Friedman, U., & Eshel, Y. (1985, August). *Single, married and parents: Do women differ from men in levels of intimacy with same-sex friend vs. spouse?* Paper presented at the International Council of Psychologist, Newport, RI.

Sharabany, R., Friedman, U., & Eshel, Y. (1986, July). *Friendship across the lifespan: Adolescence to young adulthood.* Paper presented at the 21st International Congress of Applied Psychology, Jerusalem.

Sharabany, R., Gershoni, R., & Hoffman, E. J. (1981). Girlfriend, boyfriend, age and sex differences in intimate friendship. *Developmental Psychology, 17*(6), 800–808.

Sharabany, R., Hertz-Lazarowitz, R., & Hodish, M. (1993). *The role of parents and peers in empathy of juvenile delinquents and normal adolescents.* Manuscript submitted for review.

Sharabany, R., Mayseless, O., Tzur, S., & Treinin, O. (1992, July/August). *Similarity in concurrent relationship between spouse and parent of opposite sex.* Paper presented at the International Conference on Personal Relationships, Orono, ME.

Sharabany, R., & Rodgers, R. R. (1980). *The nature of intimate friendship: A focus on preadolescence and measurement.* Unpublished manuscript, University of Haifa, Israel.

Sharabany, R., & Wiseman, H. (1993). Close relationships in adolescence: The case of the kibbutz. *Journal of Youth and Adolescence 22*(6).

Shaver, P., Hazan, C., & Bradshaw, D. (1988). Love as attachment. The integration of three behavioral systems. In R. J. Sternberg & M. Barnes (Eds.), *The psychology of love* (pp. 68–99). New Haven, CT: Yale University Press.

Shechtman, Z. (1991). Small group therapy and preadolescent same sex friendship. *International Journal of Group Psychotherapy, 41*(2), 227–242.

Sternberg, R. J. (1986). A triangular theory of love. *Psychological Review, 93*(2), 119–135.

Sternberg, R. J., & Grajek, S. (1984). The nature of love. *Journal of Personality and Social Psychology, 47,* 312–329.

Sullivan, H. S. (1952). *The interpersonal theory of psychiatry.* New York: Norton.

Suppe, F. (1984). Beyond Skinner and Kuhn. *New Ideas in Psychology, 2*(2), 89–104.

Weiss, R. S. (1982). Attachment. In C. M. Parkes & J. Stevenson-Hinde (Eds.), *The place of attachment in human behavior.* London: Tavistock.

Wheeler, L., Reis, H. T., & Nezlek, J. (1983). Lonliness, social interaction, and sex roles. *Journal of Personality and Social Psychology, 45,* 943–953.

Wiseman, H., & Lieblich, A. (1993). *Loneliness and intimacy of young adults in transition: A comparison of Israeli students and overseas students in Israel.* Manuscript submitted for review.

Youniss, J., & Smollar, J. (1985). *Adolescents relations with mother, father and friend.* Chicago: University of Chicago Press.

# Chapter 9

# Stalking the Elusive Love Style: Attachment Styles, Love Styles, and Relationship Development

Keith E. Davis
*University of South Carolina*

Lee A. Kirkpatrick
*College of William and Mary*

Marc B. Levy
*Levy Counseling & Consulting, Salt Lake City, UT*

Robin E. O'Hearn
*St. Lawrence University*

The primary aim of this chapter is to provide a comparative analysis of the contributions that attachment theory (Hazan & Shaver, 1987, 1990, 1993; Shaver & Hazan, 1992) and love styles theory (Hendrick & Hendrick, 1986, 1990; Lee, 1973–1976, 1988) make to an understanding of relationship development among premarital heterosexual couples. One theme concerns conceptual clarification, because many elementary treatments of romantic love present these two approaches as essentially on a par with each and leave the impression that each is concerned primarily with individual differences in the experience of love relationships. We argue that such an impression is quite misleading, and that the potential range of phenomena relevant to love that may be explained by each theory is quite different in scope. To anticipate our conclusion, we argue that attachment theory is both potentially more powerful in its ability to integrate both normative and individual differences relevant to love than is love styles theory, and that empirically attachment theory has already shown its ability to generate both novel and integrative findings.

The second theme of the chapter is the empirical examination of three aspects of relationship development within the context of a 3-year study of unmarried couples. The three issues that we examine are (a) partner pairing and choice,

(b) predictors of relationship satisfaction, and (c) predictors of relationship stability versus breakup. In each case, we examine the potential and actual contributions of attachment styles and love styles to the prediction of these three aspects of relationship development.

## THE CAROLINA COUPLES STUDY

Throughout this chapter, we draw on data from a longitudinal study of dating couples conducted at the University of South Carolina over the past decade. Three hundred fifty-four couples from three different samples completed measures of adult attachment, the Love Attitudes Scale, and various characteristics of their relationship at Time 1. These individuals were interviewed by telephone 7–14 months later (Time 2) and then again 30–36 months (Time 3) after the initial phase to assess relationship status and stability. Here we briefly summarize the procedures and measures employed (see Davis, Levy, Kirkpatrick, & O'Hearn, 1993, for a more detailed presentation; Kirkpatrick & Davis, in press).

It is important to note that these interwave intervals are longer than most longitudinal studies of couple development. Hill, Rubin, and Peplau (1976) showed that breakups among student couples tend to cluster during natural breaks in the academic year, particularly during vacations. Thus, the short-term follow-ups often miss the time periods most likely to yield breakups. The transition from undergraduate life to work and/or further education is also likely to be a period that tests the viability of relationships. By the time of the third wave in our study, at least one member (and typically both members) of virtually all couples would have completed the undergraduate degree, begun a new job, or dealt with the process of moving to a new location.

Couples "in steady or serious dating relationships" were recruited from undergraduate courses in the psychology of marriage during 3 consecutive years and given course credit for their participation. Summing across the three samples—collected initially in 1986, 1987, and 1988—354 of the 414 couples who volunteered met the criterion in which both partners described the relationship as a serious dating relationship. Also, 86% of the men and 87.3% of the women described themselves as "in love with" their partners, and 94% were dating the partners exclusively. More than 84% of the couples had been dating at least 7 months prior to participation. The modal couple (64.1%) had gone together for at least a year. The majority (70.3%) of the sample was 21 years of age or younger, and the men were somewhat older than the women—41% of the men were 22 or older but only 18% of the women were 22 or older. The sample was predominantly White but 17% were African American and 3.4% were of Hispanic or Asian ethnic backgrounds.

At Time 1, respondents completed the Hazan and Shaver (1987) Attachment Style measure, the Hendrick and Hendrick (1986) Love Attitude Scale (LAS), the Davis and Todd (1985) Relationship Rating Form (RRF), and demographic and relationship history measures.

Unlike most previous studies, we asked participants to rate the self-descriptiveness of each of the three attachment descriptions separately on 5-point scales, and then assigned them to categories based on whichever style received the highest rating. Participants who completed the attachment measures twice were assigned to categories based on their mean ratings of each style across the two testings. Although this procedure rendered a number of subjects unclassifiable due to tied high scores, the lost subjects were presumably those who did not clearly fit into one of the categories. Therefore, we suspect that what was lost in sample size was gained in reliability of attachment classification. In all, 309 (89.3%) women and 275 (85.7%) men were assigned to an attachment category based on this procedure. For LAS analyses, we had no such subject loss.

At Time 2, a telephone interview was conducted to ascertain (a) whether the couple was "still together" (stability), and (b) the current status of the relationship, which ranged across eight options from "no longer dating" to "married." In those rare cases (less than 2%) where couple members disagreed about the state of their relationship, status was defined as the more negative of the two answers. A second follow-up telephone interview (Time 3) was conducted between 30 and 36 months after the initial assessment in all samples.

Attrition and couple stability rates for the three samples were good. At Time 2, we retained 317 of the 354 couples for a 10.4% attrition rate; and at Time 3, we retained 301 of the 354 for a 14.1% attrition rate. Analyses were undertaken to determine if dropout from the study was systematically related either to attachment style, LAS, or to original relationship characteristics as indicated by the RRF scales. At neither Time 2 nor Time 3 were any of the predictor variables significantly related to sample dropout. A pilot test for the couples' study was conducted in 1985 by Davis and Latty-Mann (1987) in which the LAS and RRF were the focal variables. We were able to add the attachment measures to the first wave of the study reported herein thanks to Hazan and Shaver (1987), who shared their prepublication results.

## ATTACHMENT THEORY

In Bowlby's (1969, 1973) formulation, attachment is conceived as an affectional bond between infant and caregiver, and attachments are taken to develop from an innate behavioral system that operates on control theory principles. The functions of the attachment system are to protect the infant from harm and to provide a secure base from which to explore the world. Thus, the attachment system is activated whenever the desired state or "set goal" is discrepant from the current state and deactivated when congruence is achieved. Discrepancies are taken to be unpleasant psychological states that normally are manifested in distress reactions and that generate behaviors such as crying, clinging, and calling, which are designed to bring the infant into closer proximity to the caregiver and hence to restore a state of felt security (Sroufe & Waters, 1977).

Individual differences in attachment style are derived theoretically from different histories of experiencing distress and coping with it. Ainsworth, Blehar, Waters, and Wall (1978) demonstrated that infants separated from their mothers in a standard laboratory situation (the Strange Situation) show three patterns of reactions consistent with Bowlby's clinical observations: secure, resistant (or anxious/ambivalent), and avoidant. In the case of the secure style, the caregiver is observed to be responsive to indications of distress and capable of comforting the infant rapidly. The typical mother of an anxious/ambivalent (or resistant) infant is characterized by poor timing in responding to distress and by intrusiveness in the child's play—interrupting an infant who is not showing distress nor a desire for parental attention. This type of infant openly exhibits his or her ambivalence in the Strange Situation, often crying to be picked up and then refusing to be comforted when the mother returns after a brief absence. An avoidant infant appears to have a caregiver who does not foster physical contact and who often rejects the infant's proximity-seeking behaviors. Such an infant tends to focus on the toys in the Strange Situation and shows little inclination to approach the mother for comfort when distressed.

Bowlby (1969, 1973) took the position that attachment patterns show a continuity across the life cycle, and argued that the stability observed is rooted in the internal working models of self and others that develop first within the infant–caregiver relationship. Through continued interaction, the infant (and then child) develops beliefs and expectations about whether the caregiver is caring and responsive and whether the self is worthy of love and attention. In taking this position, Bowlby agreed with other personality theorists who have held that enduring cognitive models of self and other are formed during early infant–caregiver relationships and carried forward in new personal relationships (Erikson, 1963). Several longitudinal studies of infants have demonstrated substantial temporal stability of attachment styles during childhood (Main, Kaplan, & Cassidy, 1985; Waters, Wippman, & Sroufe, 1979), and some evidence has been developed for the intergenerational transmission of attachment styles within families (Latty-Mann & Davis, 1993; Ricks, 1985). Furthermore, several longitudinal studies have shown that attachment classifications of infants made at 12–18 months are predictive of a wide variety of social behaviors during preschool and early elementary school years (see Bretherton, 1985; Sroufe, 1988).

## Adult Attachment and Romantic Love

Following Bowlby's (1969, 1973) argument that early infant–caregiver relationships become the model for subsequent adult attachment relationships, Shaver, Hazan, and Bradshaw (1988) argued that adult romantic love involves the integration of at least three behavioral systems: the attachment system (which serves the functions of proximity maintenance, safe haven, and secure base), the caregiving system (which provides for reciprocal ministering to needs and attempts to relieve distress), and the sexual mating system (which provides for reproduction and sexual play). It follows that reciprocity should be a central concern of lovers. Unrequited love provides no security of attachment. The dispositions to give one's utmost for the lover when he or she is in need and to expect the same follow as clear manifestations of caregiving. Sexual intimacy becomes a natural expression of the affectional bond combined with the reproductive and sexual mating system. Thus, the characteristics that are mentioned most often in descriptive accounts as central to romantic love (Davis & Todd, 1982; Rubin, 1970) can be derived from the conceptualization of romantic love as the integration of attachment, caregiving, and sexual mating.

Hazan and Shaver's (1987) second major accomplishment was the translation of the emotional dynamics of the three observed infant–caregiver patterns into the context of adult romantic relationships, and the generation of an assessment procedure for individual differences in attachment style. Respondents classified themselves by picking the brief paragraph that "best described your feelings." Their preliminary studies indicated that 95% of their adult samples could classify themselves into one of the three types, and that individuals so classified reported that their most important romantic relationships varied in ways predicted by the theory, and that they held views of others and of relationships consistent with hypothesized "internal working models." Secure lovers described their most important love relationships as happy, trusting, and friendly, and they were accepting of their partners' faults. Avoidant lovers reported fear of intimacy, emotional extremes, and jealousy as characteristic of their most important love relationships. Anxious/ambivalent lovers reported being obsessed with their lovers and having emotional extremes, jealousy, extreme sexual attraction, and a stronger desire for reciprocation and union than the other two types. Secure respondents reported longer lasting relationships and fewer divorces than the two insecure types.

As Hazan and Shaver (1993) showed, attachment theory offers general answers to five questions about close relationships: (a) What makes a potential relationship partner attractive? (b) How are relationships formed and how do they develop? (c) What makes relationships satisfying and enduring? (d) Why and how are relationships dissolved? and (e) What are the reactions to relationship breakup? Its power as a normative theory is perhaps even more marked than its predictions about individual differences.

## Partner Pairing

To the extent that individual differences in adult attachment influence the course of relationship development, we would expect to find relationship partners to be nonrandomly paired with respect to attachment style. Studies of both married and dating couples have suggested that secure partners not only prefer each other but tend to end up with each other (Collins & Read, 1990; Latty-Mann & Davis, 1993; Senchak & Leonard, 1992). However, the dynamics of internal working models of self and other for the two insecure styles suggest several reasons why dissimilar insecure attachment styles should be attracted to one another (i.e., avoidant subjects attracted to anxious/ambivalent partners and vice versa). For the anxious/ambivalent person, the central relationship issues are the dependability, trustworthiness, and commitment of his or her partner. An avoidant partner, who is concerned about too much intimacy and uneasy about commitment, displays an orientation toward the relationship consistent with the expectations of the anxious person. For the avoidant person, the distrust and demands for intimacy conveyed by the anxious partner likewise confirms his or her expectations of a relationship partner.

Several studies have offered modest support for these predictions. In both the Collins and Read (1990) and Simpson (1990) studies, anxious women were dating more avoidant men, and anxious men were more likely to be with less secure women.[1] Unfortunately, none of these data is adequate to determine at which point in the relationship development process attachment styles exert their influence: Attachment styles may influence either initial attraction, the early short-term stability of particular pairings, or self-reported styles may change as a result of being in a supportive relationship. However, in any case, evidence for nonrandom pairing of attachment styles would be supportive of the logic of internal working models that lies at the heart of attachment theory.

In a laboratory study, Pietromonaco and Carnelley (in press) asked subjects to imagine how they would feel in a relationship with a potential partner whose characteristics exemplified one of the three attachment styles. All subjects felt better with a secure rather than an insecure partner, but insecure subjects felt more comfortable with a dissimilar insecure partner than a similar one. That is,

---

[1]In contrast to the dimensional ratings employed in the Collins and Read (1990) and Simpson (1990) studies, Senchak and Leonard (1992) presented the $3 \times 3$ matrix of husband $\times$ wife attachment styles in a sample of newlyweds. Unfortunately, the small number of insecure subjects precluded any definitive conclusions about the relative frequencies of specific parings of avoidant and anxious partners, forcing the authors to collapse the two insecure styles into one category for most analyses.

avoidant subjects felt better imagining an anxious/ambivalent partner than an avoidant partner, whereas anxious/ambivalent subjects felt better imagining an avoidant partner than an anxious/ambivalent partner. These data support the conclusion that attachment style plays a role in the choice of partner, not merely in the early fate of the relationship.

## Attachment Style Relationship Satisfaction and Gender

The cross-sectional association between attachment styles and relationship characteristics is one of the most well-documented features of attachment research. Studies by Hazan and Shaver (1987), Feeney and Noller (1990), Levy and Davis (1988), and Simpson (1990) showed that an individual's evaluation of his or her relationships is related to attachment styles in theoretically consistent ways. Individuals with secure styles report higher levels of satisfaction, intimacy, trust, and commitment in their relationships, whereas individuals with avoidant styles report lower levels of these characteristics. Anxious relationship partners report less satisfaction and more conflict and ambivalence. The findings of Collins and Read (1990) suggest that gender moderates some of these associations. For men, security (i.e., comfort with closeness) was more predictive of positive relations than was their level of anxious attachment (i.e., concern about abandonment), but for women the opposite was true: The more anxious the woman, the less satisfied and the less trusting she was.

Both Collins and Read (1990) and Simpson (1990) extended these findings further to show that one's partner's attachment style is also predictive of one's own evaluation of the relationship. Collins and Read found that both partners were less satisfied with their relationship when the male was avoidant or distant (rather than secure) and when the female was anxious or preoccupied. The gender-conditioned pattern was also visible (although somewhat less striking) in Simpson's study, with female anxiety emerging as a particularly strong predictor of negative ratings by their male partners on virtually all relationship dimensions measured. These findings indicate a need to consider gender role issues for a complete understanding of how attachment style differences influence relationship functioning.

## Relationship Stability

In Hazan and Shaver's (1987) newspaper sample, secure individuals reported that their current relationships were of longer duration (10 years vs. 4.9 for anxious and 6 for avoidant) and that they were less likely to have divorced (6% vs. 10% and 12%) than either of the insecure styles. These retrospective data are suggestive of a straightforward secure-versus-insecure effect on couple breakup rates. However, prospective data are needed because of the possi-

bility that attachment styles may change over time and that the causal relationship between attachment and breakup is not as simple as the Hazan and
Shaver (1987) data suggest.

Several lines of research clearly have demonstrated that relationship satisfaction does not necessarily correspond to relationship stability. Research on
marriages has shown that some highly stable relationships are marked by relatively high levels of conflict and/or low levels of satisfaction (e.g., Cuber &
Harroff, 1965; Rands, Levinger, & Mellinger, 1981). Not all couples who stay
together are in fact happy together, nor do all dissatisfied couples break up.

The classic longitudinal studies of premarital couples (Burgess & Wallin,
1953; Hill et al., 1976; Levinger, Senn, & Jorgensen, 1970) have established
that (a) the longer a couple stays together the more likely they are to continue
together, and (b) the higher the level of commitment and/or satisfaction the
greater the likelihood of future stability. More recent longitudinal work also
supported the importance of these characteristics. Lloyd, Cate, and Henton
(1984) showed that 3-month and 7-month stability rates were positively related to prior commitment (specifically measured as involvement and prediction
of marriage) and satisfaction even when prior duration of the relationship was
controlled. Simpson (1987) showed that exclusivity of the relationship (an aspect
of commitment), satisfaction, and prior duration all contributed significantly
to a regression analysis of stability after 3 months.

These empirical correlates have been integrated into a coherent framework
by the Investment Theory (e.g., Rusbult, 1983). The investment model posits
that commitment to the relationship has two closely related aspects, a conscious
decision to stay together and a felt attachment to the partner, and that degree
of commitment is determined by the level of three intervening variables: satisfaction, availability of alternatives, and investment. To the degree that an individual is satisfied with the relationship, has no acceptable alternative partners,
and has invested heavily in the relationship, he or she will be highly committed to it and resistant to its breakup. The investment model clarifies why cases
exist in which an individual may be relatively unsatisfied with a relationship
and yet be highly committed to it. Either the lack of appropriate alternatives
or high degree of investment (time together, shared activities) or both could
account for the relatively high commitment. The ability of the investment model
to account for stay/leave decisions has been demonstrated both for romantic
relationships (Rusbult, 1983) and job commitments (Rusbult & Farrell, 1983).
Changes in level of commitment over time were more strongly predictive of
stay/leave decisions than were levels of satisfaction, alternatives, or investment.

However, another source of the stability of unhappy relationships may be
emotional needs that make the breaking of a primary relationship unthink-
able. In the popular and clinical literatures, various labels have been applied
to persons who remain in what appear to be unsatisfying relationships: love

addiction (Peele & Brodsky, 1975), neurotic dependency (Ackerman, 1958), or limerence (Tennov, 1979). All of these constructs are interpretable in terms of the anxious/ambivalent attachment style (Shaver & Hazan, 1988). This raises the interesting possibility that attachment styles might help us understand why some relatively dissatisfied couples would stay together. For example, the preoccupation with reciprocation of affection and the concern about abandonment that mark the anxious/ambivalent person could play a part in motivating special efforts to maintain a relationship, even though the relationship is not what the person had hoped for. In that case, anxious/ambivalent individuals could have just as stable relationships as secure individuals, but not be as satisfied with them. Another possibility is that avoidant partners would break up and not take any action to resist breakups, even though they are satisfied, out of a fear of becoming too dependent on another person. O'Hearn (1992) showed that both the anxious and the (fearful) avoidant styles are associated with the receipt of emotional abuse in intimate relationships.

## Attachment Style: Gender Roles and Stability

Although the distribution of attachment styles as measured by the Hazan and Shaver instrument appears to be independent of gender (Brennan, Shaver, & Tobey, 1991; Hazan & Shaver, 1987; Levy & Davis, 1988), the way in which attachment style relates to other variables may very well be dependent on gender role patterns.[2] Pietromonaco and Carnelley (in press) reported that avoidant males and preoccupied females experienced the most negative feelings when thinking about a relationship, irrespective of partner characteristics. Simpson (1990) found that avoidant men, but not avoidant women, were less distressed after a relationship breakup even when relationship quality and length were statistically controlled.

Traditional gender role patterns have long acknowledged women as the relationship specialists, and there is little evidence of change recently (Cancian, 1985). Women's thinking about moral and practical issues is guided more than men's by consideration of the impact on relationships (Gilligan, 1982). Women also tend to devote more effort than men to relationship maintenance efforts, particularly after early dating (Huston, Surra, Fitzgerald, & Cate, 1981), and are more likely to initiate breakups (Hill et al., 1976). Hence, females are the makers, maintainers, and breakers of relationships.

These gender differences may interact significantly with attachment styles in the prediction of relationship stability over time. For example, the traditional

---

[2]Gender differences in attachment-style distributions have been reported for Bartholomew's four-category classification system, with males disproportionately represented in the dismissing-avoidant category and females in the fearful-avoidant category (Bartholomew & Horowitz, 1991; Brennan, Shaver, & Tobey, 1991).

gender role patterns noted earlier suggest that it is the female's orientation to the relationship that should be most predictive of the maintenance of the relationship over the long term. Because an avoidant female would be less likely to engage in the relationship maintenance behaviors expected of women, this reasoning suggests the hypothesis that relationships involving an avoidant female would be less stable than relationships involving secure or anxious females. Although anxious females might be expected to exhibit relatively unstable relationships in light of their lower levels of satisfaction and commitment (Collins & Read, 1990; Simpson, 1990), they are also expected to exert the greatest efforts at relationship maintenance.

Given the role of females as the primary maintainers and breakers of relationships, the association between male attachment style and relationship stability is somewhat less straightforward. Secure males should make better relationship partners for females of any style and hence should exhibit the most stable relationships. Lower stability rates for avoidant males might be expected based on the low satisfaction ratings of avoidant males found in previous research (Collins & Read, 1990; Simpson, 1990). However, other research (Pietromonaco & Carnelley, in press) has shown that anxious females, who may work particularly hard at relationship maintenance efforts, are relatively comfortable with avoidant men. Thus, it is not clear whether the net effect of this pattern would lead to higher stability rates for anxious men or avoidant men. In the presentation of the results, we only hit the highlights and omit several important technical issues. A more detailed presentation may be found in Kirkpatrick and Davis (in press).

## RESULTS FROM THE CAROLINA COUPLES STUDY

### Partner Pairing

The relationship between partners' attachment styles was dramatic. The primary tendency was for everyone to be with secure partners. A secondary trend was clear among the insecurely attached—namely a tendency for oppositely insecure styles to be together. The most conspicuous aspect of the data is that there were no avoidant–avoidant or anxious–anxious pairs. Instead, avoidant participants tended to be paired with anxious partners and vice versa. For example, 25% of the anxious males had an avoidant female partner, and 42.9% of the anxious females had an avoidant male partner, compared with the respective marginals of 14.2% and 14.6%. Of course, the expected frequencies for these two zero cells, based on the marginals, were quite small (4.98 for avoidant–avoidant, 2.47 for anxious–anxious). However, the expected frequencies for the two anxious/avoidant cells were correspondingly low.

## Attachment Style and Concurrent Relationship Ratings

No significant interactions were found between male and female attachment styles for any of the relationship scales contained in the RRF. Males' attachment styles were strongly related to their own relationship ratings, with avoidant males displaying the most negative ratings and secure males the positive ratings, but were largely unrelated to their female partners' ratings of the relationship. Females' attachment styles were also related to both their own and their partners' relationship ratings. In contrast to the males, however, it was the anxious group (and their partners) that reported the most negative ratings of the relationship. These findings parallel those of Collins and Read (1990) and Simpson (1990) in all respects except that females with avoidant males rated the relationship just as favorably as those with secure or anxious males.

## Longitudinal Prediction of Relationship Stability

The most important question to be addressed is whether attachment styles contribute significantly to the longitudinal prediction of couple stability, particularly when classic predictors of relationship stability (e.g., prior duration and commitment) are controlled. The results are consistent with much previous research in that greater stability and status were associated with longer prior duration and with greater commitment and satisfaction for both partners. These univariate relationships were consistent across gender and follow-up time period. Subsequent regression analyses revealed that both prior duration and commitment made significant independent contributions to the prediction of stability, but that satisfaction did not. Although the failure of satisfaction to contribute to prediction above and beyond commitment is due in part to multicollinearity—satisfaction and commitment were highly intercorrelated among both men ($r = .81$) and women ($r = .78$)—the greater predictive power of commitment is consistent with an investment model perspective on relationship stability (e.g., Rusbult, 1983). In light of these findings, only prior duration and commitment were retained as control variables in subsequent analyses.

Anxious males displayed the lowest level of stability at Time 2, whereas avoidant males rated the relationship most negatively at Time 1. When the three attachment groups were statistically equated with respect to prior duration and commitment (the adjusted means in the lower panel), the stability of relationships of avoidant males was particularly high. The stability of avoidant males' relationships was surprisingly high when prior duration and commitment were taken into account.

For women, a different pattern emerged for stability—(significant only at Time 3)—anxious women's relationships were more stable (70%) than those of avoidant women (35%), with secure women (51%) in between. These high values for stability contrast markedly with the low satisfaction and high conflict/ambivalence displayed by anxious women at Time 1. Again, this seemingly paradoxical pattern was reflected in the adjusted means, the differences among which were exaggerated when prior duration and commitment were controlled. That is, if the three groups were statistically equated with respect to the covariates, the anxious females displayed the highest stability and status of all the groups. The pattern was similar at the first follow-up but was not statistically significant.

The relationships of avoidant males were surprisingly stable, despite their relatively negative ratings of the relationship at Time 1. Similarly, the relationships of anxious females were remarkably stable, despite the relatively negative ratings of the relationship by both partners in these relationships at Time 1. In contrast to Hazan and Shaver's (1987) retrospective data, couple stability was not merely a function of attachment insecurity. Rather, stability appeared to be moderated by gender and type of attachment style.


## ATTACHMENT THEORY AND THE RELATIONSHIP DEVELOPMENT PROCESS

The three main sets of findings from this study paint an intriguing and rather complex picture of the various roles that attachment styles may play at different points in the relationship development process. In each case—partner pairing, relationship satisfaction, and relationship stability—the results preclude any sweeping generalizations about which attachment styles are universally good or bad with respect to close relationships. Instead, the answer to this question depends on at least two factors, namely (a) the particular relationship stage or process under consideration and (b) gender.

The first phase of relationship development examined here involves the early stages of relationship formation. Our data suggest that certain pairings of attachment styles, namely anxious–anxious and avoidant–avoidant, are unlikely to appear among couples who identify themselves as being involved in a serious dating relationship. Pietromonaco and Carnelley (in press) demonstrated that avoidant subjects were uncomfortable imagining themselves in relationships with avoidant partners, and likewise for anxious subjects imagining anxious partners. However, these findings leave open the question as to how and when this discomfort influences the course of relationship development. Our results suggest that the effect occurs in the early stages of relationship formation: Anxious–anxious and avoidant–avoidant pairs either (a) are not initially attracted to one another, and hence never begin to develop a relationship; or (b) begin dating but feel uncomfortable with each other early on, leading to rapid dissolution of the relationship. We believe the problem is that a partner of a similar insecure style violates one's expectations of how an attachment figure or romantic partner should behave: Avoidant persons expect partners to be demanding, clingy, and dependent, whereas anxious persons expect partners to avoid intimacy, withdraw, and be rejecting. This clash of mental models in avoidant–avoidant and anxious–anxious pairs is sufficiently problematic, and occurs so early in the process of relationship formation that such relationships are unlikely to form or last very long.

Among the pairings that do make enough progress to identify themselves as in a serious dating relationship, attachment style is related concurrently to satisfaction, commitment, and conflict. Generally, attachment security is associated with greater satisfaction and commitment than is insecurity, but the specific pattern of effects is conditioned by gender. Consideration of traditional gender role issues seems important to the interpretation of this gender-conditioned pattern. For example, the possessiveness and demandingness of an anxious female partner may pose a threat to a male's concerns about autonomy and independence, whereas the behavior of an anxious male does not have a similarly threatening effect on his female partner. Male avoidance may be related to negative ratings of a relationship, particularly by the male partner, because these males are likely to be dismissive rather than fearful avoidants (Bartholomew, 1990), and thus fail to place a high value on the relationship in the first place. We found no evidence of any interactions between male and female styles in predicting RRF ratings. Avoidant males evidenced the most negative relationship ratings irrespective of their partners' attachment styles, as did anxious females. We suspect that this is because the two cells that would have contributed the most to a statistical interaction were empty in these analyses. In light of Pietromonaco and Carnelley's (in press) findings, we would expect to find the most negative relationship ratings among avoidant–avoidant and anxious–anxious pairs if such couples had been included in our sample, and such a pattern would be expected to result in a statistical interaction of male × female style. However, such pairings are evidently so unsatisfactory that they do not last long enough to appear in a sample such as ours.

The third phase of relationship development examined here concerns long-term stability. Again, the results are strongly gender dependent, but the pattern of findings differs dramatically from that of earlier relationship ratings and suggests the operation of different processes. These findings demonstrated the relationships of avoidant males and of anxious females—the relationships that generally received the most negative ratings at Time 1—were at least as stable as those of the relatively satisfied secure subjects. Instead, it was the anxious men and avoidant women who evidenced the highest breakup rates across time. We believe that the well-established observation that women are typically the maintainers and breakers of relationships is central to the understanding of this pattern. If avoidant women are both less inclined and less skilled in relationship maintenance than secure and anxious women, as would be expected from attachment theory, their relationships are likely to dissolve because no one is working to keep them together. Anxious women, for whom the abandonment and relationship loss are central concerns, would be expected to be more accommodating and more active in relationship maintenance efforts, and hence to have higher stability rates than their avoidant counterparts. Part of the success of anxious women in retaining partners may also be due to their tendency to pair with avoidant men, for whom their behavior in the relationship would confirm his working model of women in love.

The surprising long-term success of relationships involving avoidant men may also hinge largely on this same process. In our sample, all avoidant males were paired with secure or anxious partners. As a result, this group of males was the least likely group to suffer from the deficient relationship maintenance efforts of an avoidant female partner. Let us look at how this process may unfold.

First, the relationships of anxious/ambivalent women were significantly more stable than those of avoidant women (particularly at the second follow-up), despite relatively low levels of satisfaction and commitment at Time 1. Secure women evidenced intermediate stability rates. The lower stability rate of avoidant women was anticipated and follows from the ways in which avoidance of intimacy can undercut relationship maintenance activities typically expected of the female partner. Without her active relationship maintenance efforts, dissatisfaction and conflict undermine commitment and lead to dissolution of relationships involving an avoidant female partner. In contrast, we suspect that, despite relatively low levels of satisfaction early in the relationship, anxious women exert considerable effort toward relationship maintenance and succeed in keeping the couple together over time. Although they may wish for the perfect romantic relationship, this desire may be overridden by dependency on the current relationship, fear of being abandoned, and pessimism regarding their ability to attract another (perhaps more desirable) partner.

Second, avoidant men, who at the beginning of the study had the lowest levels of commitment and satisfaction, were just as likely to remain in their relationships as were secure men, who originally had the highest levels of satisfaction and commitment. This remarkable equivalence of stability rates for these two groups suggests the importance of the partners of avoidant men. In this sample, avoidant men were paired only with either anxious or secure women; there were no avoidant-avoidant pairs. Both secure and anxious women were assumed to have relationship maintenance skills, and hence to hold onto an avoidant partner if they so chose. Because male avoidance did not appear to adversely affect their female partners' levels of satisfaction in our sample, it seems reasonable to infer that the women did in fact work actively to maintain the relationship, and that these efforts were largely responsible for the couples' surprisingly high levels of stability across time.

Anxious males whose relationship stability was significantly lower than that of secure males were in relationships originally characterized as high in commitment and passion, but in which the female partners reported high levels of conflict/ambivalence and low levels of passion. The anxious males, then, had two factors working against the stability of their relationships. First, their intensely passionate involvement, jealousy, and demandingness could lead to overdependence and/or high levels of conflict within the relationship. Second, none of the anxious males had the "benefit" of an anxious female partner who would work especially hard at relationship maintenance efforts. Instead, many of these males were paired with avoidant females who, as we have already seen, were unlikely to exert the relationship maintenance efforts traditionally expected of the female partner.

Thus, attachment theory has provided a framework for the integration of findings about partner pairing and the possible bases of such pairing, relationship satisfaction, and relationship stability. Now it is time to turn to the other theoretical perspective—love styles theory—that guided our initial search for individual difference predictors of relationship quality and stability. In this case, the story is much different because the perspective does not turn out to have the conceptual resources for the kind of integration needed, and both conceptual and methodological problems plague the research on the love attitude styles.

## THE COLORS OF LOVE

Lee (1973–1976: 1976 edition used for direct quotations, 1988) was struck by the variety in how both writers and laymen seem to think about love. He read broadly in philosophy, psychology, and literature from the earliest periods of Western Civilization into the modern period, began to discern several distinct points of view, and found that he could represent these points of view regarding love on an analogy with the color solid. In this analogy, some viewpoints (colors) are taken to be primary, and other expressions are taken to be mixtures of the three basic love styles. Lee found that two kinds of mixtures were possible: compounds, in which the two ingredients combine to form a genuinely new style and which may have characteristics not shown by either ingredient; or mixtures, which are merely a blending of the two primaries so that the resultant reflects each primary but in a diluted form. Lee's scheme allowed him to identify numerous possible love styles. Twelve are mentioned in the first presentation, but he has given a priority to eight of these. He thought the ninth type—Agape—is too rare to be found often in the real world. What follows is a condensation of Lee's (1988) presentation of profiles of six of the eight love styles.

> *Eros.* Erotic lovers enjoy their work and lives, are ready for the risks of love. They know what kind of body type is most attractive to them. They expect to get to know the beloved quickly and intimately. They want an exclusive relationship. Erotic lovers consider that finding and living with their ideal beloved is the most

important activity in their lives. *Ludus.* Typical ludic lovers are unwilling to commit themselves to love. They delight in a variety of lovers and certainly do not fall in love. They avoid getting too involved. Sex is for fun, not for expressing commitment, and love is not the most important activity in life. *Storge.* Typical storgic lovers enjoy their friends and are satisfied with life. They expect love will be a special friendship in which more than the usual time and activities are shared. Storgic lovers are not anxious or preoccupied with an absent beloved. They recoil from passionate excess and want to get to know the partner first as a friend before getting into sexual relations. Mutual love is not a goal of life for itself but as an aspect of the greater goals of friendship and family. *Mania.* Typical manic lovers are usually lonely in adult life and often dissatisfied with their work. They feel a strong need to "be in love," but are also afraid that love will be difficult and painful. They are often surprised to find themselves in love with someone they don't even like. Manic lovers often appear to have lost their sense, are prone to extremes of jealousy, and demand more affection and commitment than partners are comfortable showing. Their partner finally ends the relationship. The manic lover will take a long time to get over it. *Pragma.* Typical pragmatic lovers feel they can master life and achieve goals through personal effort. Finding a compatible mate is a practical problem to be solved by sensible effort, and is often begun by looking among those at hand in office, club, or community. They carefully examine him or her for potential defects and generally disdain excessive emotional displays and jealous scenes . . . they appreciate reciprocal signs of thoughtfulness and increasing commitment. Sexual compatibility is important, but it is more a question of technical skill, which can be improved if necessary. No particular partner is worth sacrificing one's common sense for. *Storgic eros.* This loose combination of the primaries storge and eros is more common than agape. Such lovers consider that the act of loving is essential to a mature and fulfilled life, whether or not their love is reciprocated. They see love as a duty to respond to the need of others, to make sacrifices when necessary. Although pleased by reciprocation, they are not jealous or possessive. In fact they are willing to step aside when it appears that some other person would better meet the partner's needs. There is little emphasis on sexual intimacy. Loving another person is the central purpose and meaning of human life. (pp. 50–53; condensed by permission of Yale University Press)

Lee's (1988) preferred procedure for classification is based on a 1,500-item card-sorting task that allows a person to tell the story of his or her relationship and life history. In effect, the subject selects the alternatives that identify the scenario that their relationship exemplifies. Lee (1976) also developed two short-form procedures: Twenty Questions and the Profiles of Eight Lovestyles. In his description of the Twenty Questions procedure, he made it clear that although it may be useful for self-assessment, "results simply indicate your relative preference for various styles of loving, during the relationship in question. If you complete the test again using a different relationship you may obtain a quite different pattern of scores" (Lee, 1976, p. 206). However, in none of his published work did Lee describe studies that compare either of his briefer methods with the full card-sort procedure, nor did he report on the degree to which persons change in style when being assessed within the context of different relationship.

## THE LOVE ATTITUDE SCALE

One reason to describe the types in some detail is that a central question for current research is the degree to which the Hendrick and Hendrick (1986) LAS represents a faithful translation of Lee's model into assessment procedure.

### The Development of the LAS

The Hendricks began their work on the LAS by starting with a 50-item true–false instrument developed by Lasswell and Lasswell (1976). They modified these items by changing to a 5-point rating scale format and adding four new items (Hendrick, Hendrick, Foote, & Slapion-Foote, 1984). With a large sample ($N = 800$), they explored gender differences in item endorsement and the factorial structure of the items. Four clearly interpretable factors emerged: pragma, mania, agape, and ludus. However, the ludus factor contained only items that "seemed to reflect the secretive, nondisclosing aspect of the ludic style; [but not the items] reflecting skill and playfulness" (Hendrick et al., 1984, p. 187). Items intended to measure eros and storge appeared in various blends— sometimes with agape and ludus items—depending on gender. Hendrick et al. concluded that "though a start on scale development has been made, more work is needed" (p. 192).

The next step by Hendrick and Hendrick (1986) was to conduct two large-scale studies on a 42-item scale, with six 7-item scales for each love style. The 42 items represent items from the earlier 54-item pool, as well as some new items intentionally written to reflect Lee's distinctions and to clarify the factorial structure. Between the first and second study, six additional changes were made in item wording. The resulting internal consistency and pattern of factor loadings for the LAS has been replicated by both Hendrick and Hendrick (1988) and independent investigators (Davis & Latty-Mann, 1987; Richardson, Medvin, & Hammock, 1987).

## EMPIRICAL FINDINGS CONCERNING THE LAS
## SCALES AND RELATIONSHIP CHARACTERISTICS

Bierhoff (1991) and Hendrick and Hendrick (1992) both reviewed a considerable body of findings concerning LAS scales and gender, gender role orientation, ethnicity, and personality characteristics, such as sensation seeking, and so on. We do not review these data here because they do not have a direct

bearing on the ability of the LAS scales to predict and explain important issues in relationships, such as (a) partner pairing and selection, (b) relationship
satisfaction, and (c) relationship stability versus breakup. If the LAS scales
can predict any or all of these kinds of outcomes, it has much to offer to students of relationship dynamics. These are the same three issues investigated
with respect to attachment styles.

## Partner Pairing

Partners were found to be similar in all their love styles except mania, with
the largest correlations being on eros ($r = .49$, $p < .04$; Davis & Latty-Mann,
1987). Hendrick, Hendrick, and Adler (1988) also found positive correlations
among all the LAS scales, with the correlation between eros scores being the
highest at $r = .56$, $p < .05$. In their sample, mania scores were significantly
and positively correlated, whereas ludus scores were not significantly related.
Bierhoff (1991) reported somewhat higher intracouple correlations among two
samples of German couples. He also found that all of the incorrelations among
all LAS scales by partner were positive, even if a few were not statistically significant. In none of these studies was the design such that one could determine
whether pairs who were similar were more likely to stay together than pairs
who were dissimilar. However, Davis and Latty-Mann (1987) examined indices of absolute discrepancy and found that large discrepancies in agape were
predictive of poorer relationships for both men and women, that large discrepancies in eros were predictive of poorer relationships for women, and that large
discrepancies in ludus were predictive of poorer relationships for men.

The crucial issue is whether the love styles are the basis of choice or partner
selection versus being merely another variable along with partners that may
be shown to be more similar than randomly paired, artificial partners. The
most straightforward interpretation of the partner pairing data is that partners
in a relationship come to share views/descriptions/evaluations of that relationship. Thus, if one partner sees a lot of eros in the relationship, the other partner is also likely to see it as an erotic relationship. Thus, the correlations are
interpreted as being primarily a result of shared interaction, rather than as
a determinant of being selected as partners. One fact supporting this interpretation is that the level of correlation between partners of explicitly relationship
descriptive scales such as the RRF scales of Mutual Trust, Mutual Understanding, Mutual Enjoyment of Each Other's Company, and the degree of
Conflict/Ambivalence all tend to range between $r = .35$ and .50. The degree
of correlation between male and female partners' eros and agape scores also
falls in this range (but correlations between couples on mania, storge, and pragma tend to be somewhat lower), which is closer to that typically found for

personality traits such as those making up the Big Five model of personality (Shaver & Brennan, 1992). These data are also consistent with the interpretation (Hendrick & Hendrick, 1990) that the original LAS scales were largely made up of relationship-specific items, taping current relationship feelings and evaluations.

## Own and Partner Relationship Satisfaction

Bierhoff (1991); Davis and Latty-Mann (1987); Hendrick, Hendrick, and Adler (1988); Levy and Davis (1988); and Richardson et al. (1987) all examined this issue, and the findings are quite consistent. Eros and agape were positively associated with various measures of own satisfaction, and ludus was negatively associated. Among women but not men, mania was negatively correlated with satisfaction in some samples but not in all. Contrary to expectation, storge—except in one German sample and then only for males—did not predict relationship satisfaction, nor was pragma consistently related to satisfaction.

Among partners, the same three LAS scales—eros, agape, and ludus—were predictive of satisfaction, but one new variable emerged—partner mania was negatively related to own satisfaction for both the Richardson et al. (1987) study and for the Bierhoff (1990) sample. Another finding, replicated in two 1986 studies and extended in the Hendricks' (1988) paper, was that persons currently in love with their partners scored higher on eros and agape and lower on ludus than those not in love. An interpretation of these two patterns—of correlations with satisfaction and of mean differences as a function of being versus not being in love—is that the eros, agape, and ludus scales tap variables similar to those making up the major features of romantic love. Drawing on Kelley's (1983) analysis of Rubin's (1970) scale, on Fehr's (1988) prototype analysis, and on Davis and Todd's (1982) analysis of love as distinguished from friendship, one would argue that (a) depth of caring about the partner's welfare, (b) degree of passionate attachment, and (c) degree of conscious commitment to each other are three central characteristics of romantic love relationships. Indeed, Sternberg (1988), using slightly different labels—intimacy, passion, and commitment—argued that these three are the fundamental components of love. One implication of the family resemblances view of concepts or the "prototypicality" view is that even those characteristics taken to be fundamental need not be present to a significant degree in all cases of romantic love. Sternberg used this feature of the prototypicality view to identify variations in the degree and types of love. Taking this approach and applying it to a careful study of items of the agape scale show that it is heavily loaded with expressions of caring about the partner's welfare, willingness to make sacrifices for the partner, and giving a priority to the partner's welfare. The eros items reflect directly an intense attraction, an enjoyment of physical and psychological intimacy with the partner, and an appreciation of the partner's beauty—all of which are part of the passionate attachment factor identified by all theorists as part of love. Ludus reflects an explicit unwillingness to be committed to just one partner, and is thus a direct repudiation of a central premise of romantic love—faithfulness to one's partner. On this interpretation, one would expect that these LAS scales would load heavily on factors embodying these same distinctions when analyzed in relationship to other measures of love. The Hendricks led the way in such studies, completing one in 1989 with the original LAS, Hatfield and Sprecher's (1987) Passionate Love Scale, the Davis and Todd (1985) RRF, and Sternberg's (1988) Triadic Love Scales. Eros and agape loaded along with other measures of passionate love on one factor, and ludus loaded at the opposite ends of a dimension reflecting the degree of trust versus conflict in the relationship—caring and trust going together versus conflict, ambivalence, and ludic distrust. In 1991, the Hendricks replicated the major features of the pattern with the new, relationship-specific LAS.

### Relationship Stability versus Breakup

Bierhoff (1991) has had the most interesting samples, and because some of the couples were married with children, he was able to examine the issue of couple stability. His data are consistent with a path model of causal processes, in which eros primarily influences couple satisfaction, and agape and pragma influence couple stability and number of children. Hendrick et al. (1988) reported a small sample ($N = 57$, with 30 couples in the follow-up) study in which the ability of the LAS and other variables to predict breakup after 3 months was assessed. Commitment was the most powerful predictor, followed closely by dyadic satisfaction, eros, ludus, and self-esteem. The crucial issue not addressed in this study was the degree to which measures of the LAS scales added anything to the prediction of outcomes beyond what could be explained by measures of commitment, satisfaction, and investment in the relationship (such as duration of the relationship). If the interpretation of the LAS proposed earlier is correct, one would anticipate that it would not contribute much to the prediction of relationship stability once one had accounted for level of commitment and the other variables of the investment model (Rusbult, 1983). We address this issue in the three studies examined next.

### Theoretical and Conceptual Difficulties

Even for investigators who are initially taken by Lee's (1976) distinctions, one of the problems is what is conceptually central and what is a matter of empirical accident in his complex portrait for each type. The syndromes described are quite complex, and one might imagine that components or characteristics are not necessarily found together in everyday cases in the way that the pure case or ideal type suggests. Included are generalization about family history and work circumstances, about preferences for body types, about specific characteristics expected from relationships (e.g., "usually want exclusive relationships," "unwilling to commit," "feel a strong need to be in love"), about the temporal sequence of experiences (e.g., "getting to know the partner as a friend before getting into sexual relations"), and attitudes toward having other lovers at the same time. "Lovestyles are not things, but descriptions of the way lovers behave (including the way they think)" (Lee, 1988, p. 88).

Lee's theory was essentially a descriptive typology. In developing it, he did not appeal to any particular psychological theory or draw systematically on any framework. Rather, his approach was inductive. The results of Lee's inductive search is a set of types similar to the results of the conceptual exercise in generating all cases and only possible cases of love. But Lee gave little guidance about why some aspects of his complex profiles are central and others are not. As a prototype researcher might say, he did not make it clear which characteristics are prototypical. In principle, however, one must develop procedures for representing the degree of fit to the pure type, and for dealing with the possibility that persons, over their life histories, will exhibit different degrees of fit. In effect, one needs both a profile of degree of fit to each and all types, and longitudinal information about whether and under what circumstances one's love style changes. Lee took the very reasonable position that one's style can change, and that one's history of previous relationships and the love style of the current partner are influential in the process of change. But systematic principles of change and systematic descriptions of the influences of a partner's love style on the development of a relationship are not given. His theory is silent on these extremely important issues.

What is missing from Lee's theory? It does not provide answers to these questions: How do these types develop? Why do the types have the characteristics that they do? What is the basis for mutual attraction or mate selection? What is the basis for change of a person's type? How do pairings of types influence relationship stability? In short, almost all of the issues—other than the description of basic types and some informal observations on which types are more likely to be satisfied with each other—are not addressed in a systematic way.

### Validity of the LAS as an Operationalization of Lee's Theory

There are two ways in which questions about the validity of the LAS arise: First, three of the Hendrick and Hendrick scales—agape, storge, and ludus—appear to diverge in conception from Lee's model. Second, the LAS was never validated against Lee's fundamental criterion, namely patterns of responses to his 1,500-item card-sorting procedure. Failure to compare LAS scores to

Lee's preferred method leaves open the crucial question on criterion validity. Let us examine evidence for the three scales in question.

Agape "implies a duty or obligation to care about the other person, whether you want to care or not and whether the love is deserved or not. . . . [It] is 'gift love' . . . with no strings attached . . . completely altruistic and deeply compassionate" (Lee, 1976, p. 155). Lee followed up his description of the concept with the observation that he had "yet to interview any respondent involved in even relatively short-term affiliative love relationship which I could classify without qualification as an example of agape" (p. 156). Yet, when the items used by Lasswell and Lasswell (1976) and those ultimately retained by Hendrick and Hendrick (1986) in the LAS are administered, they are either the most popular or the next most popular items in the LAS. Everyone who claims to be in love with their current partner gives these items high ratings (means of 4.2 or so on a scale where 5 equals complete endorsement). The agape scale comes out as one of the first factors in any analysis of love domain items (Hendrick & Hendrick, 1986, 1989; Hendrick et al., 1984) and as one of the factors explaining the most variance among items. As Shaver and Hazan (1988) argued, what the LAS agape scale seems to measure is the caregiving component of love (both romantic and more general love). If the two items most reflective of Lee's extreme conception were softened to remove their masochistic flavor, the scale would correlate substantially with the eros items and more clearly reveal the connections among eros, agape, and traditional romantic love. In effect, Shaver and Hazan took the position that Lee's original formulation is biased and extreme, and that the version of agapic compassion and willingness to sacrifice embodied in the LAS is closer to a fundamental characteristic of love than Lee's formulation. We agree.

Storge "is love without fever or folly, a feeling of natural affection such as you might have for a favorite brother or sister" (Lee, 1976, p. 67). But as Richardson et al. (1987) noted, "storge is the most questionable [of the LAS scales] because scores on that scale were related to none of the other measures" (p. 650). Davis and Latty-Mann (1987) and Levy (1989) also failed to find any pattern of relationship between storge scores and scales measuring trust, confiding, depth of caring, presence of conflict, and relationship satisfaction. Thus, although the LAS contains a set of storgic items that are rather consistently answered, persons with high or low patterns of endorsement show none of the expected differences in how they relate to their partners in intimate relationships. Because of the ambiguity that exists for the criterion validity of the LAS, one cannot be certain whether the fault lies in Lee's conceptualization or in the LAS. Other researchers (e.g., Roberts, 1982, 1985) have found evidence for a type of man–woman relationship that is closer emotionally to friendship than romantic love, therefore one must keep an open mind about Lee's original theoretical distinction. Grote and Frieze (1993) recently addressed this issue and made a very persuasive case that it is the measurement of storge or friendship-based love that is at fault. With their revised measurement, storge shows just the patterns one might expect.

Ludic lovers "believe their childhoods were average but are often frustrated in adult life. . . . They are not ready to settle down . . . do not fall in love . . . see no contradiction in loving several partners equally . . . view sex as for fun, not for expressing commitment" (Lee, 1988, p. 50). As Hendrick et al. noted in their 1984 study, items reflecting the secretive, nondisclosing aspect of the ludic style hang together but not those getting at the playfulness and skill. Persons in love with their partners reject ludic items, and the mean value of the responses is at 3.8 (close to "disagree" in Hendrick and Hendrick's original item-response format, where "1" equals "agree strongly"). A strong negative correlation exists between the ludus and agape scale scores, so that in almost every factor analytic study these scales serve to define opposite ends of a factor (see Hendrick & Hendrick, 1988, 1989; Levy & Davis, 1988). This pattern of results raises the question of whether ludus is a distinct love style, or merely an aspect of the rejection of traditional romantic love with its emphasis on commitment, exclusiveness, sex as communion, and intimate sharing with one's beloved. Shaver and Hazan (1988) argued that Lee's original portrait of ludus as a happy game player is at fault. They assimilated ludus to their avoidant attachment type, where the avoidance of intimacy is associated with loneliness and unhappiness. In three separate samples, we found that ludus and degree of endorsement of the avoidant romantic attachment style are significantly related (Levy, 1989; Levy & Davis, 1988), but not strongly enough to support the conclusion that ludus and the avoidant style are essentially the same thing. Rather, it appears that ludus should be treated conceptually as a blend of dispositional avoidance of intimacy and an uncommitted current relationship status.

Thus, in at least three cases, the existing data suggest that the LAS is tapping something about people's attitudes toward love or love ideologies that is not quite what Lee intended. With agape and ludus, a case can be made that Lee's conception may be at variance with what other researchers can find. In the case of storge, the conception does not seem entirely faulty, but the items, which are internally consistent and face valid, do not connect to a pattern of conducting intimate relationships, at least not in any of the samples studied so far.

## Level of Analysis Issues: Traits, Attitudes, or States of the Current Relationship

In our view, both Lee and the Hendricks shared the tendency to blur fundamental conceptual distinctions about the status of the love style concept. Just what are the love styles? Sometimes they sound like enduring personality traits that one might expect to see manifest in each and every intimate relationship a person develops. In other cases, they sound like attitudes toward a specific partner; and in still other cases, they seem like descriptions of the current state of the relationship between two lovers, with no implication that it will remain that way over time. The clarification of these distinctions is critical in how one interprets empirical data from the numerous studies conducted so far. The Hendricks recently partially clarified their position. Talking about the styles as attitudes—as Hendrick and Hendrick (1986) did—provides little to clarify their conceptual status because attitudes may be conceived and assessed as dispositional or trait-like notions, or they may be conceived and assessed as current states. To illustrate the difference, we examine two items from the LAS (Hendrick & Hendrick, 1986): "Our lovemaking is very intense and satisfying" (an eros item); "I try to plan my life carefully before choosing a lover" (a pragma item). The first gives a description of experience in a current relationship. The second states a policy about the person's approach to lovers in general. This kind of contrast permeates the contrast between eros and pragma as assessed by the original 1986 LAS. Thus, in the LAS, some of the contrasts among scales are not just contrast in content but in the methodological status of the descriptions. Pragma and storge items express generalized expectations—general dispositions or attitudes—whereas eros items refer to how the respondent feels about a specific other, or with whom the respondent has a current relationship. (The standard instructions for the LAS are "Whenever possible, answer the questions with your current partner in mind. If you are not currently dating anyone, answer the questions with your most recent partner in mind.") When one takes into account the instructional set of the LAS, one finds that eros and agape items seem to be slanted toward assessments of current relationship feelings, whereas the pragma and storge items are slanted toward general dispositions toward relationships. The ludus and mania items are mixed in their dispositional versus current state focus. Levy (1989) examined the state-trait controversy in some depth, and developed an alternative measure that takes on a more clearly trait orientation.

What position has Lee adopted on the disposition versus relationship specific or current state view of love styles? He has not used these distinctions, at least not explicitly, and implicitly he seems to have argued as follows. The love story card sort technique obtains a retrospective scenario of one (or more) love affair. Although it is specific to a relationship, it serves as an indication of the style (in the sense of expectations, desires, policies, and preferences) with which he or she will approach another love affair. The result of experience may change these desires and expectations, and a new partner may elicit previously unknown feelings in a person, but a love style is more than just a report on how one love affair was experienced and how it turned out. "Once you have identified your preferred love-style for the present time in your life (remembering that preferences for love, as for color, may change with time and experience), you will naturally want to know that love-style 'matches' your choice" (Lee, 1988,

p. 53). For Lee, it seemed enough to get the complexity of different love relationships fixed within his descriptive typology. Thus far, he has shown little interest in relating the types to antecedent personality variables/types or to relationship outcomes.

For the Hendricks' (1986) program of research, a lack of attention to the distinction between dispositional love styles and love styles as current relationship states was a methodological flaw. Their aspiration was to connect Lee's theory to traditional scientific work within social and personality psychology and to demark the range of validity of Lee's observations. If all of the LAS scales had the status of dispositional measures, then correlations between the LAS scales and scales such as Rubin's (1970) Love and Liking scales have one significance—namely that of information about the degree to which traditional romantic love can be predicted from stylistic measures. But if the LAS scales are relationship-specific descriptions of the current status of the relationship, then correlations between these and Rubin's measures simply reflect the degree of agreement among measures of the same romantic relationships. As we judge the case, at least some of the scales are quite mixed, and one can draw no clear conclusions about what a love style is.

Since these concerns were first expressed by Johnson (1987) and Davis, Levy, and Latty-Mann (1987), the Hendricks (1990) have addressed part of the relevant issues. They have developed relationship specific measures for all of the love styles by rewriting the 19 items identified as general. The patterns of item means and variances, interitem correlations, gender differences, and factor structure of the two tests—the original LAS and the relationship specific LAS—are quite similar. Thus, one may reasonably conclude that most of the findings reported for the original version of the LAS are findings about love styles in the sense of the specific attitudes that have developed toward a specific partner. If one accepts this conclusion, it then raises the next issue.

## LOVE STYLES RESULTS
## FROM THE CAROLINA COUPLES STUDIES

The full results for the LAS in relationship to the RRF variables, to attachment styles, and to relationship outcomes were presented in Davis et al. (1993). In this presentation, we emphasize three questions that parallel our analysis for attachment styles. The questions concern whether LAS scores are relevant to partner pairing, to own and partner influence on relationship satisfaction, and to relationship stability. In the latter case, we adopted procedures to determine whether there are contributions of the love styles scales to the prediction of couple stability over and above that due to the correlation between love styles and couple commitment and duration—two well-established predictors integrated into the investment model of Rusbult (1983).

## Partner Patterns of LAS Scores

Consistent with other studies that have examined couple correlations among love styles, we found that partners tended to have similar scores on all love styles, with the largest correlations being for eros ( $+.35$, $p < .001$) and the smallest for ludus ( $+.16$, $p < .002$) and pragma ( $+.17$, $p < .001$). The components of the RRF, all of which were taken to be reports by each partner of the specific characteristics of the relationship, also had positive correlations that had a somewhat higher range of values, from $+.46$ and $+.38$ (both $p < .0001$) for commitment and satisfaction, respectively, to values of around $+.30$ for the other components of the RRF. There was no evidence for persons selecting partners because of love styles, therefore the most conservative interpretation of these small to modest correlations is that the two partners tended to see their relationship in the same way. Although not surprising, these data do little to illuminate the question of who gets together with whom and why.

## Relationship Satisfaction and LAS Scores

Consistent with the Hendricks' research, the eros, agape, and ludus scales were correlated concurrently with relationship satisfaction and commitment for both men and women. Neither mania, pragma, nor storge showed any significant correlations with partner's commitment or satisfaction.

The first step was to compute simple correlations of the love styles measures with indices of couple stability both short term (6–12 months) and long term (30–36 months). For males ($N = 317$), stability at both points in time was positively related to agape and negatively to ludus. For females ($N = 354$), stability was positively correlated with both eros and agape, and negatively with ludus (but only at the earlier point in time). The absolute magnitudes of these correlations were quite small—> $r = .20$ for all but two correlations. These findings contrast with the larger values reported by Hendrick et al. (1989) for a smaller sample and a much shorter time period (3 months).

We next ask whether these weak predictive relationships would remain significant after two classic predictors of stability were introduced as controls. The controls were duration of the relationship at Time 1 and the level of self-reported commitment (RRF) at Time 1. To answer this question, multiple regression analyses were conducted for each of the 12 (6 male, 6 female) LAS scales and each of the two follow-up measures, yielding 24 analyses in all. In each, the equation of the two stability measures were regressed on the LAS scale and on the two control measures. In each case, the regression weight for the LAS variables was not significant ($p > .05$), and the weight of commitment was highly significant ($p < .001$).[3] Thus, none of the LAS variables considered separately improved prediction of couple stability over and beyond the level already attained by the commitment and duration of relationship variables. However, when commitment was used as the predictor and LAS scales were used separately as control variables, commitment continued to have significant predictive power.

## CONCLUSIONS

We now look briefly at each theory and what each offers to the search for the elusive love style. Although these data, and consequently their interpretations, are somewhat complex, we regard these results as highly encouraging for the field of adult attachment research. First, the results go well beyond the relatively simplistic pattern reported in many published and unpublished studies— that secure attachment correlates with positive, desirable variables and insecure attachment correlates with negative, undesirable ones. If the truth were really that simple, there would be no need to call on such a rich and deep theory as Bowlby's (1969, 1973) attachment theory to explain it. The complexity of the data underscores, rather than undermines, the potential role of attachment theory for our understanding of adult relationships. Second, our results point to the importance of considering adult attachment within the context of traditional gender role issues, thus helping to build a bridge between attachment and another important (and obviously pertinent) domain of psychological theory and research. Third, and perhaps most important, the results force us to think carefully about relationship processes, rather than merely describing observed covariation. The dynamics of relationship initiation, satisfaction and conflict, and maintenance/stability across time are different, and attachment theory has the potential to help us understand these processes in a coherent way.

We believe that the data from our three longitudinal studies of relationship dynamics of unmarried couples raise questions about Hendrick and Hendrick's (1986) original LAS scales and about the viability of Lee's (1973–1976, 1988) conceptualization. At the conceptual level, Lee's model has too many serious limitations to be foundation for a theory of individual differences in romantic love. Among the most important are its failure to provide (a) a theory of the origins of the different love styles, (b) a theory of partner selection, (c) a theory of how and why individuals might change their love styles over the course

---

[3]Results for prior duration were as follows: significant at the .001 level in the twelve analyses predicting stability at the first follow-up; significant at the .05 level in the six analyses predicting stability at the second follow-up from male LAS scores, and approaching significance ($p < .10$) in the six analyses predicting stability from female LAS scores.

of the life cycle and of specific relationships, and (d) a framework that would integrate the large body of findings about relationship dynamics that currently exist. In contrast, attachment theory provides significant guidance on all four of the issues (Hazan & Shaver, 1993).

Empirically, the original LAS appears not to assess three of the love styles as Lee intended—agape, ludus, and storge. An argument has been made that Lee's conceptualization of both agape and ludus is problematic. Even if one grants that the Hendrick and Hendrick measure labeled "agape" might be better labeled "storgic eros" to make its label consistent with Lee's claims, it remains that neither love style measure quite behaves as Lee's theory would suggest. Rather, the Hendrick and Hendrick measures of these two styles appear to tap something quite important about romantic love—namely the caregiving/willingness to sacrifice dimension and reject traditional romantic commitment to or faithfulness to one partner. In the case of the storge, or friendship-based love, it appears that Lee was on the mark in his description of the syndrome, but that the Hendrick and Hendrick measure did not validly measure his distinction (Grote & Frieze, 1993).

Taken as a whole, the original LAS appears to reduce to three distinct clusters: (a) the romantic love measures (eros plus agape minus ludus); (b) the manic style, which shares a significant kinship with both Hazan and Shaver's (1987) anxious/ambivalent attachment style and Bartholomew and Horowitz's (1991) preoccupied style; and (c) the pragmatic, nonromantic approach to partner choice (Levy & Davis, 1988).

Thus, when one examines how the LAS measures behave as predictors of relationship stability and one controls for factors such as commitment and duration of the relationship (conceived as a measure of investment), one finds that the LAS scales have nothing to offer that is not already captured by measures of commitment to partner and duration of relationships. These data suggest that what the Hendricks discovered in their search for the elusive love style were three robust features of romantic relationships that form a loosely connected syndrome and two more dispositional ideologies toward love—one highly insecure, manic approach and one nonromantic, calm unemotional approach to partner choice. Although the LAS measure of mania shares some variance with the anxious/ambivalent style, it does not show the clear gender differentiated pattern of relation to couple stability that the self-classification measure of anxious/ambivalent attachment shows. In the context of our own data and those from other studies, there seems to be no question of which approach to the study of love styles offers the most promising leads—adult romantic attachment theory.

What accounts for the almost universal acceptance of the *Colors of Love* (Lee, 1973–1976) model by writers of social psychology, marriage and family, and personal relationships textbooks? We think that there are two aspects to the answer: First, until the mid-1980s, Lee had very little competition for a descriptive typology. Although there is a clinical and philosophical literature about types of love or close personal relationships, the empirical social science literature was largely restricted to dichotomous distinctions that clearly did not do justice to the variety of love relationships. The most commonly used distinction was between companionate and passionate (or romantic) love (Berscheid & Walster, 1978). Another was the distinction between limerance and mature-nonpossessive love (Tennov, 1979). Although each of these dichotomies captures something of importance and interest, no serious student of the topic thinks that they exhaust the relevant distinctions. Compared with these accounts, Lee's theory was a garden of theoretical delights that made the other accounts pale by comparison. Second, theories flourish within social psychology if they are accompanied by procedures that are easy to use and generate data. Although Lee did not get involved in providing a method of assessment that might do justice to his insights and also be relatively easy for other researchers to use, Hendrick and Hendrick (1986, 1990) provided this service for love styles theory. Soon a large number of studies appeared with interesting information about different love styles, so that secondary source writers could tell (a) a more interesting story about love using Lee than they could using any other available theory, and (b) they could cite data. In the competition between some theory and no theory, some theory will always win, even if it has major conceptual problems and has been subjected to no serious critical evaluation. Now we are ready for the next stage in the search for more about the elusive phenomena of love.

## ACKNOWLEDGMENTS

Study 1 was conducted by Keith Davis and Robin O'Hearn; Study 2 by Keith Davis, Marc Levy, and Robin O'Hearn; Study 3 by Marc Levy as part of his PhD dissertation, directed by Keith Davis. All of the 30–36 month Time 3 follow-ups were conducted by Lee Kirkpatrick and Keith Davis with funding from an NIH Biomedical Research support grant (#S07 RR 07160) from the University of South Carolina. Earlier versions of this chapter were presented at the Fourth (1988) International Conference on Personal Relationships in Vancouver, British Columbia, Canada, and at the Fifth (1990) International Conference on Personal Relationships, Oxford, England. The final chapter was written by Keith Davis and Lee Kirkpatrick, with editorial revisions by Marc Levy and Robin O'Hearn. The authors would like to thank Judy Beal, Mike Brondino, and Cathy Menne for their assistance in conducting the follow-up interviews and data collection. We also wish to thank George Levinger, Cindy Hazan, and Caryl Rusbult for their helpful comments on previous drafts of this chapter.

# REFERENCES

Ainsworth, M., Blehar, M. C., Waters, E., & Wall, S. (1978). *Patterns of attachment: A psychological study of the strange situation.* Hillsdale, NJ: Lawrence Erlbaum Associates.

Bartholomew, K. (1990). Avoidance of intimacy: An attachment perspective. *Journal of Social and Personal Relationships, 7,* 147–178.

Bartholomew, K., & Horowitz, L. M. (1991). Attachment styles in young adults: A test of a four-category model. *Journal of Personality and Social Psychology, 61,* 226–244.

Berscheid, E., & Walster [Hatfield], E. (1978). *Interpersonal attraction* (2nd ed.). Reading, MA: Addison-Wesley.

Bierhoff, H. W. (1991). Twenty years of research on love: Theory, results, and prospects for the future. *German Journal of Psychology, 15,* 95–117.

Bowlby, J. (1969). *Attachment and loss: Vol. 1. Attachment.* New York: Basic Books.

Bowlby, J. (1973). *Attachment and loss: Vol. 2. Separation, anxiety, and anger.* New York: Basic Books.

Brennan, K. A., Shaver, P. R., & Tobey, A. E. (1991). Attachment styles, gender, and parental problem drinking. *Journal of Social and Personal Relationships, 8,* 451–466.

Bretherton, I. (1985). Attachment theory: Retrospect and prospect. *Monographs of the Society for Research on Child Development, 50*(1–2, Serial No. 209), 147–166.

Burgess, E., & Wallin, P. (1953). *Engagement and marriage.* Chicago: J. P. Lippincott.

Cancian, F. M. (1985). Gender politics: Love and power in the private and public spheres. In A. S. Rossi (Ed.), *Gender and the life course* (pp. 253–264). New York: Aldine.

Collins, N. L., & Read, S. J. (1990). Adult attachment, working models, and relationship quality in dating couples. *Journal of Personality and Social Psychology, 58,* 644–663.

Cuber, J., & Harroff, P. (1965). *The significant Americans.* New York: Random House.

Davis, K. E., & Latty-Mann, H. (1987). Lovestyles and relationship quality: A contribution to validation. *Journal of Social and Personal Relationships, 4,* 409–428.

Davis, K. E., Levy, M. B., & Latty-Mann, H. (1987, November). *The role of Lee's love styles in courtship development.* Presented as part of a symposium entitled, ''New Developments in Love Styles Research'' at the Theory & Methods Workshop for the National Council on Family Relations annual meeting, Atlanta, GA.

Davis, K. E., Levy, M. B., Kirkpatrick, L., & O'Hearn, R. (1993). *Love styles and relationship stability.* Manuscript submitted for review.

Davis, K. E., & Todd, M. (1982). Friendship and love relationships. In K. E. Davis & T. Mitchell (Eds.), *Advances in descriptive psychology* (Vol. 2, pp. 79–122). Greenwich, CT: JAI Press.

Davis, K. E., & Todd, M. J. (1985). Assessing friendship: Prototypes, paradigm cases, and relationship assessment. In S. W. Duck & D. Perlman (Eds.), *Understanding personal relationships: An interdisciplinary approach* (pp. 17–34). Beverly Hills, CA: Sage.

Erikson, E. H. (1963). *Childhood and society* (2nd ed.). New York: Norton.

Feeney, J. A., & Noller, P. (1990). Attachment style as romantic relationships. *Journal of Personality and Social Psychology, 58,* 281–291.

Fehr, B. (1988). Prototype analysis of the concepts of love and commitment. *Journal of Personality and Social Psychology, 55,* 557–579.

Gilligan, C. (1982). *In a different voice: Psychological theory and women's development.* Cambridge, MA: Harvard University Press.

Grote, N. K., & Frieze, I. H. (1993). *Friendship-based love in intimate relationships.* Manuscript submitted for review.

Hatfield, E., & Sprecher, S. (1987). Measuring passionate love. *Journal of Adolescence, 9,* 383–410.

Hazan, C., & Shaver, P. (1987). Romantic love conceptualized as an attachment process. *Journal of Personality and Social Psychology, 52,* 511–524.

Hazan, C., & Shaver, P. (1990). Love and work: An attachment-theoretical perspective. *Journal of Personality and Social Psychology, 59,* 270–280.

Hazan, C., & Shaver, P. (1993). Attachment as an organizational framework for research on close relationships. *Psychological Inquiry, 4.*

Hendrick, C., Hendrick, S., Foote, F., & Slapion-Foote, M. (1984). Do men and women love differently? *Journal of Social and Personal Relationship, 1,* 177–195.

Hendrick, C., & Hendrick, S. S. (1986). A theory and method of love. *Journal of Personality and Social Psychology, 50,* 392–402.

Hendrick, C., & Hendrick, S. S. (1988). Lovers wear rose colored glasses. *Journal for Social and Personal Relationships, 5,* 161–183.

Hendrick, C., & Hendrick, S. S. (1989). Research on love: Does it measure up? *Journal of Personality and Social Psychology, 56,* 784–794.

Hendrick, C., & Hendrick, S. S. (1990). A relationship-specific version of the Love Attitudes Scale. *Journal of Social Behavior and Personality, 5*(4), 239–254.

Hendrick, C., Hendrick, S. S., & Adler, N. (1988). Romantic relationships: Love, satisfaction, and staying together. *Journal of Personality and Social Psychology, 54,* 980–988.

Hendrick, S. S., & Hendrick, C. (1992). *Romantic love.* Beverly Hills, CA: Sage.

Hill, C. T., Rubin, Z., & Peplau, L. A. (1976). Break-ups before marriage: The end of 103 affairs. *Journal of Social Issues, 32,* 147–167.

Huston, T. L., Surra, C. A., Fitzgerald, N. M., & Cate, R. M. (1981). From courtship to marriage: Mate selection as an interpersonal process. In S. Duck & R. Gilmour (Eds.), *Personal relationships: 2. Developing personal relationships* (pp. 53–88). New York: Academic Press.

Johnson, M. P. (1987, Nov.). *New directions in love style research.* Discussion of papers at the symposium conducted at the preconference theory construction and research methodology workshop at the annual meeting of the National Council on Family Relationships, Atlanta, GA.

Kelley, H. H. (1983). Love and commitment. In H. H. Kelley, E. Berscheid, A. Christensen, J. H. Harvey, T. L. Huston, G. Levinger, E. McClintock, L. A. Peplau, & D. R. Peterson (Eds.), *Close relationships* (pp. 265–314). New York: Freeman.

Kirkpatrick, L. A., & Davis, K. E. (in press). Attachment style, gender, and relationship stability: A longitudinal analysis. *Journal of Personality and Social Psychology, 66.*

Lasswell, T. E., & Lasswell, M. E. (1976). I love you but I am not in love with you. *Journal of Marriage and the Family, 38,* 211–224.

Latty-Mann, H., & Davis, K. E. (1993). *Attachment theory and partner choice: Preference and actuality.* Manuscript submitted for review.

Lee, J. A. (1976). *The colors of love.* Englewood Cliffs, NJ: Prentice-Hall.

Lee, J. A. (1988). Love-styles. In R. Sternberg & M. Barnes (Eds.), *The psychology of love* (pp. 38–67). New Haven, CT: Yale University Press.

Levinger, G., Senn, D. J., & Jorgensen, B. W. (1970). Progress toward permanence in courtship: A test of the Kerckhoff-Davis hypotheses. *Sociometry, 33,* 427–443.

Levy, M. B. (1989). *Integration of lovestyles and attachment styles: Cross-partner influences and a clarification of concepts, measurement, and conceptualization.* Unpublished doctoral dissertation, University of South Carolina, Columbia.

Levy, M. B., & Davis, K. E. (1988). Love styles and attachment styles compared: Their relations to each other and to various relationship characteristics. *Journal of Social and Personal Relationships, 5,* 439–471.

Lloyd, S. A., Cate, R. M., & Henton, J. M. (1984). Predicting premarital relationship stability: A methodological refinement. *Journal of Marriage and the Family, 46,* 71–76.

Main, M., Kaplan, N., & Cassidy, J. (1985). Security in infancy, childhood, and adulthood: A move to the level of representation. *Monographs of the Society for Research in Child Development, 50,* (Nos. 1 & 2), 66–104.

O'Hearn, R. E. (1992). *Dimensions of attachment and their relevance to issues of emtotional abuse in relationships.* Unpublished doctoral dissertation, Department of Psychology, University of South Carolina, Columbia.

Peele, S., & Brodsky, A. (1975). *Love and addiction.* New York: Taplinger.

Pietromonaco, P. R., & Carnelley, K. B. (in press). Thinking about a romantic relationship: Attachment style and gender influence emotional reactions and perceptions. *Personal Relationships, 1.*

Rands, M., Levinger, G., & Mellinger, G. D. (1981). Patterns of conflict resolution and marital satisfaction. *Journal of Family Issues, 2,* 297–321.

Richardson, D. R., Medvin, N., & Hammock, G. (1987). Love styles, relationship experience, and sensation-seeking: A test of validity. *Personality and Individual Differences, 9,* 645–651.

Ricks, M. H. (1985). The social transmission of parental behavior: Attachment across generations. *Monographs of the Society for Research in Child Development, 50*(1&2, Serial No. 209), 211–227.

Roberts, M. K. (1982). Men and women: Partners, lovers, friends. In K. E. Davis & T. O. Mitchell (Eds.), *Advances in descriptive psychology* (Vol. 2, pp. 57–78). Greenwich, CT: JAI Press.

Roberts, M. K. (1985). I and thou: A study of personal relationships. In K. E. Davis & T. O. Mitchell (Eds.), *Advances in descriptive psychology* (Vol. 4, pp. 231–258). Greenwich, CT: JAI Press.

Rubin, Z. (1970). Measurement of romantic love. *Journal of Personality and Social Psychology, 16,* 265–273.

Rusbult, C. E. (1983). A longitudinal test of the investment model: The development (and deterioration) of satisfaction and commitment in heterosexual involvements. *Journal of Personality and Social Psychology, 45,* 101–117.

Rusbult, C. E., & Farrell, D. (1983). A longitudinal test of the investment model: The impact of job satisfaction, job commitment, and turnover variations in rewards, costs, alternatives, and investments. *Journal of Applied Psychology, 68,* 429–438.

Senchak, M., & Leonard, K. E. (1992). Attachment styles and marital adjustment among newlywed couples. *Journal of Social and Personal Relationships, 9,* 51–64.

Shaver, P., & Brennan, K. A. (1992). Attachment styles and the ''Big Five'' personality traits: Their connections with each other and with romantic relationship outcomes. *Personality and Social Psychology Bulletin, 18,* 536–545.

Shaver, P., & Hazan, C. (1988). A biased view of love. *Journal for Social and Personal Relationships, 5,* 473–501.

Shaver, P., & Hazan, C. (1992). Adult romantic attachment: Theory and evidence. In D. Perlman & W. Jones (Eds.), *Advances in personal relationships* (Vol. 4, pp. 29–70). London: Jessica Kingsley.

Shaver, P., Hazan, C., & Bradshaw, D. (1988). Love as attachment: The integration of three behavioral systems. In R. Sternberg & M. Barnes (Eds.), *The psychology of love* (pp. 69–99). New Haven, CT: Yale University Press.

Simpson, J. (1987). The dissolution of romantic relationships: Factors involved in relationship stability and emotional distress. *Journal of Personality and Social Psychology, 53,* 683–692.

Simpson, J. A. (1990). Influence of attachment styles on romantic relationships. *Journal of Personality and Social Psychology, 59,* 971–980.

Sroufe, A. (1988). The role of infant-caregiver attachment in development. In J. Belsky & T. Nezworski (Eds.), *Clinical implications of attachment* (pp. 18–38). Hillsdale, NJ: Lawrence Erlbaum Associates.

Sroufe, A., & Waters, E. (1977). Attachment as an organizational construct. *Child Development, 48,* 1184–1199.

Sternberg, R. J. (1988). *Construct validation of a triangular theory of love.* Unpublished manuscript, Department of Psychology, Yale University, New Haven, CT.

Tennov, D. (1979). *Love and limerance: The experience of being in love.* New York: Stein & Day.

Vormbrock, J. K. (1993). Attachment theory as applied to wartime and job-related marital separation. *Psychological Bulletin, 114,* 122–144.

Waters, E., Wippman, J., & Sroufe, A. (1979). Attachment, positive affect, and competence in peer group: Two studies in construct validation. *Child Development, 50,* 821–829.

# Chapter 10

# Self-Evaluation Maintenance:
# A Social Psychological Approach
# to Interpersonal Relationships

Ralph Erber
*DePaul University*

Abraham Tesser
*University of Georgia*

In this chapter, we wish to look at interpersonal relationships from a self-evaluation maintenance perspective. Specifically, we try to show how a recent (e.g., Tesser, 1988) model of self-evaluation maintenance (SEM) can be applied to the initiation, maintenance, and termination of interpersonal relationships. We also compare our self-evaluation maintenance perspective with previous theoretical frameworks, and discuss the extent to which understanding self-evaluation maintenance processes can enhance our understanding of the dynamics of interpersonal relationships.

## THE SEM MODEL: A SYSTEMIC APPROACH
## TO RELATIONSHIPS

Bill and Ralph have been friends for years. Bill is a professional basketball player, and Ralph is a psychologist. Ralph frequently and proudly talks about his friend's accomplishments on the court. Similarly, Bill likes to brag about and takes pride in Ralph's papers and conference presentations.

Mary and Joe are a young couple blessed with fulfilling jobs and financial security. In addition, they share many common interests. Both like to travel, dine out, and go to the theater. However, chess is a passion for both. After all, that's where they met and fell in love. And while their relationship seems to benefit from going on trips and eating exotic foods, their passion for chess seems to get in the way sometimes. Every time Mary wins a match, Joe just doesn't seem the same. Similarly, Joe thinks that Mary is a little icy after he has won.

The previous examples illustrate a couple of phenomena not uncommon in close relationships such as marriages, friendships, or dating relationships. Bill and Ralph seem to bask in the reflected glory of each other's academic and athletic exploits, whereas Mary and Joe seem to be envious of each other's accomplishments. Why is this happening? Recently, Tesser (1988) introduced a self-evaluation maintenance model of behavior that can account for the phenomena illustrated by both of these examples.

The SEM model has at its core the assumption that people will behave in ways that will enhance or at least maintain their self-evaluation, and that their relationships with others can have a substantial impact on their self-evaluation. The term *self-evaluation* is not equivalent to *self-esteem*. The latter refers to a stable and global affective reaction toward the self. Self-evaluation refers to a more temporary and specific state of self-regard that is subject to fluctuation. The SEM model proposes two dynamic, complementary processes. One's self-evaluation may be enhanced through reflection, a process in which one basks in the reflected glory of a close other's outstanding performance (e.g., Cialdini et al., 1976; Cialdini & Richardson, 1980). However, the outstanding performance of a close other can decrease one's self-evaluation by comparison. If a close other performs very well, one's own performance may pale by comparison (for a more thorough discussion of the reflection and comparison process, see Tesser, 1988). Both the reflection and the comparison processes depend on the psychological closeness and the quality of the performance of the other. As closeness and/or performance goes down, the effects of reflection and comparison are attenuated. If the other person is psychologically distant (e.g., a stranger) or performs poorly, little can be gained via reflection or lost via comparison.

A close other's good performance can lead to an increase in self-evaluation through reflection or a decrease through comparison. Which of these occurs depends on the relevance of the performance dimension for the self. If a close other outperforms us on a dimension that is irrelevant to our self-definition, we tend to bask in the reflection of his or her accomplishments. This is the case in our first example. For both Bill and Ralph, the other's performance dimension is irrelevant to their own self-definition, thus enabling them to bask in the reflected glory of the other.

The picture changes when a close other performs on a dimension that is relevant to our self-definition. Under these conditions, comparison rather than reflection is likely to result. When the performance dimension is relevant, another's better performance is likely to result in a decrease in self-evaluation. This is the case in our second example. Joe and Mary are competing in a performance domain that is highly relevant for both of them, resulting in comparison. Thus, the relevance of another's performance to one's self-definition determines the relative importance of the reflection and comparison process. Psychological closeness to the other operates to intensify the comparison and reflection process.

The SEM model defines closeness in terms of the psychological proximity between a person and another from the perspective of the person. This definition is similar to Heider's (1958) notion of unit relatedness. To the extent that there is a unit relation between two people, they are close. Our definition of *closeness* differs in a couple of ways from *unit relatedness*, however. First, unlike unit relatedness, closeness is continuous (i.e., people can be more or less close). In this sense, friends are closer than casual acquaintances, who are closer than strangers. Second, closeness does not have to be symmetrical. Although Heider treated unit relations as symmetrical, the SEM model makes no assumptions about symmetry. Thus, Person A may be closer to Person B than B is to A (Tversky, 1977). Third, although the association between two people who are close will generally be positive, under some circumstances closeness may lead to friction and the experience of negative affect.

## SEM RESEARCH RELEVANT TO RELATIONSHIPS

Having outlined the processes of the SEM model, we turn to some research that is has generated. The studies look at the effects of relevance and performance on closeness, the effects of closeness and relevance on performance, and the effects of closeness and performance on relevance or self-definition.

### Relationships as a Dependent Variable

***The Effects of Relevance and Performance on Closeness.***    The SEM model predicts that when the performance domain is relevant to the self, a close other's better performance will result in a felt threat to self-evaluation via the comparison process. One way to deal with this potential threat is to decrease the psychological closeness to the other. On the other hand, when the performance domain is irrelevant to the self, increasing the psychological closeness to the other could promote reflection (i.e., basking in the reflected glory of the other's accomplishments).

To test these predictions, Pleban and Tesser (1981) had subjects compete against a confederate in a trivia game covering such areas as rock music, current events, hunting and fishing, and so on. Prior to that, subjects had indicated how important each of these areas was to their self-definition. The experimenter then picked a topic that was either self-relevant or not self-relevant to the subjects. After completing the question-and-answer period, subjects were informed that their performance was about average (near the 50th percentile). Subjects were further told that the confederate performed much better (at the 80th percentile), or about the same (at the 60th percentile).

The subjects and the confederate were asked to go to an adjacent room to fill out some questionnaires. Literally, the distance that subjects seated themselves from the confederate served as a behavioral measure of closeness. The results were consistent with the predictions derived from the SEM model. Consider first the high relevance conditions. Here another's better performance is potentially threatening via comparison. When relevance was high, subjects seated themselves farther away from the better performing confederate than the equal performing confederate. Now let us turn to the low topic relevance condition. Here the other's better performance should provide a basis for reflection. Indeed, subjects seated themselves closer to the confederate when he had clearly outperformed them than when he had done about the same. Similar results were obtained on a behavioroid measure of closeness ("Would you want to work with this person again?") and a cognitive measure of similarity ("How much are you and this person alike?"). However, subjects' responses on an affect measure ("How attracted are you to his person?") were not influenced by the performance of the confederate. In other words, subjects did not like the confederate any less when he had clearly outperformed them than when he had done about the same.

The results support the hypothesis that relevance and performance interact in affecting closeness. They also shed light on which aspect of closeness is affected by SEM processes. Because there was no effect of relevance and performance on the degree to which subjects liked the confederate, it appears that the comparison and reflection processes affect the unit aspect but not the sentiment aspect of closeness (Heider, 1958).

Recent research has suggested that relevance and performance also affect closeness in romantic relationships. Pilkington, Tesser, and Stephens (1989, Study 1) had subjects in a dating relationship scale the relevance of a number of activities, as well as their own performance and their partner's performance on these activities. What can we expect based on the SEM model?

Let us first focus on activities that the subjects rated as high in relevance to their self-definition. Because relevance is high, the comparison process should be important: A partner's better performance could be threatening. Thus, respondents should see themselves as outperforming their partners in these domains. Indeed, consistent with the SEM model, when relevance to the self was high, there were more activities on which subjects perceived themselves as outperforming their partner than activities on which they saw their partner as outperforming themselves. When relevance is low, the reflection process is important, and thus the partner's better performance is beneficial. Indeed, when relevance was low, subjects identified more activities on which the other outperformed the self than activities on which the self outperformed the other. Subjects also completed Rubin's (1970) Liking and Loving scales. Those below the median on liking for their partner showed a strong comparison effect and virtually no reflection effect. Consistent with the findings of Pleban and Tesser (1981), and the observation that relevance and performance primarily affect the unit aspect of relationships, differential comparison and reflection were not obtained when subjects were split on the median of Rubin's Love Scale.

The picture we have drawn so far sketches out the importance of SEM processes for individuals in relationships. But what about the SEM processes of their partners? After all, a concern for the welfare of one's partner is one of the unique features of close relationships (e.g., Clark & Mills, 1979). Thus, one might expect people who are romantically involved to show a concern for the other's SEM processes. To shed light on this issue, Pilkington et al. (1989, Study 2) had subjects rate the relevance of a number of activities to themselves and their partner, as well as their perceptions of how well they and their partner performed on those activities. If people are indeed concerned with their partner's self-evaluation maintenance processes, one would expect to find evidence of "empathic" comparison and "empathic" reflection (i.e., subjects should be sensitive to the relevance of the activity to the partner's self-definition). The results validated these expectations. First, as in their previous study, subjects indicated that they outperformed their partner on more activities relevant to the self, and that their partner outperformed the self on more activities low in relevance to the self. Moreover, there was evidence for both empathic comparison and empathic reflection. That is, when relevance to the partner's self-definition was high, subjects reported more activities on which their partner was superior than activities on which the self was superior. On the other hand, when relevance to the partner was low, subjects rated themselves as superior on more activities.

The emergence of empathic comparison and reflection processes suggests that the basic SEM model has to be extended in important ways when it is applied to close, intimate relationships. Specifically, it seems that people in such relationships may not only strive toward maintaining or maximizing their own self-evaluation but also the self-evaluation of their partner. This clearly has implications for the maintenance of close relationships and the experience of positive and negative affect. We return to this point later.

The findings that relevance and performance interact in affecting closeness has implications for the relative importance of similarity and complementarity in close relationships. Previous research has favored similarity, whereas the SEM model suggests a form of complementarity. If people reduce closeness when they are outperformed by their partner on a self-relevant dimension, then relationships in which both partners strive for excellence on the same performance dimensions will be unstable. On the other hand, when people complement each other by performing well on performance dimensions that are relevant to themselves but not to their partners, they will become closer via the process of reflection. Thus, from a self-evaluation maintenance point of view, there seems to be room for complementarity in close relationships, specifically with respect to the relevance of a performance dimension for one's self-definition.

The idea that complementarity may be important for the initiation and maintenance of close relationships seems to be at odds with the literature documenting the importance of similarity on attraction. However, the apparent inconsistency can be reconciled by distinguishing between performance dimensions and emotional dimensions (Campbell & Tesser, 1985). Performance dimensions are dimensions on which it is possible to outperform another (e.g., by being faster, more knowledgeable, more skilled). Emotional dimensions, such as attitudes and values, are dimensions that do not imply a "better" or "worse" performance. Thus, although it is possible to outperform one's partner when it comes to chopping an onion, there is nothing inherently better about being more or less liberal, religious, and so on than one's partner.

So far, the evidence we have for the importance of complementarity is based on self-reports about relevant and nonrelevant performance dimensions of dating couples (Pilkington et al., 1989). More sophisticated research on how attraction and relationship longevity are related to similarity on emotional dimensions and complementarity on performance dimensions is an important task for the future.

## Relationships as an Independent Variable

The previous sections looked at the effects of relevance and performance on closeness in relationships. In the following sections, we look at the closeness of relationships as an independent variable and review research on (a) how closeness interacts with relevance to predict performance, and (b) how closeness interacts with performance to predict changes in relevance or self-definition.

*The Effects of Closeness and Relevance on Performance.*    According to the SEM model, relevance and closeness should interactively affect relative performance. When relevance is high, the better the performance of a close other the greater the threat to one's self-evaluation through comparison. On the other hand, when relevance is low, the better the performance of a close other the greater the opportunity to enhance one's self-evaluation through reflection. One way to avoid the threat to self-evaluation posed by the better performance of a close other on a self-relevant dimension would be to inhibit the other's performance. Conversely, one way to enhance self-evaluation through basking in the reflected glory of a close other's better performance on a dimension not relevant to the self would be to facilitate the other's performance.

*Affecting Other's Performance.*    In a first test of these hypotheses (Tesser & Smith, 1980), two male friendship pairs reported to the lab, ostensibly to participate in a "password game." Three subjects in each session selected clues for the fourth who had to guess a target word. Because the experiment was set up so that every subject took a turn at being the guesser, subjects ended up giving clues to their friends as well as to relative strangers. To manipulate the relevance of the guessing task, subjects were told that the task was related to verbal ability and used as a selection and promotion device by many large companies (high relevance), or that the task did not reflect on any important ability of the guesser (low relevance). Subjects were given a list of clues that varied in terms of their difficulty. By choosing more or less difficult clues, subjects could either inhibit or facilitate the guesser's performance. The subject from each friendship pair who went first was informed that he did not do very well. The difficulty of the clues selected by this subject for his friend and a stranger served as the dependent variable. The results were quite supportive of the hypotheses. When relevance was high, subjects gave more difficult clues to their friends than to the strangers. When relevance was low, subjects facilitated the performance of their friends by giving them easier clues than they gave the strangers. Tesser and Cornell (1991) recently replicated these findings.

The two previous studies confirmed that people may alter their behavior to inhibit or facilitate another's performance to reduce possible threats to self-evaluation via comparison or increase opportunities for basking in the reflected glory of the other. Subjects also were actually kinder to the strangers than their own friends when relevance was high. Another way in which people avoid threats to their self-evaluation is by distorting the perception of the other's performance. Specifically, people should perceive the performance of a close other as more positive when the relevance of the task is low than when it is high. To test this hypothesis, Tesser and Campbell (1982) had subjects complete a number of items associated with two dimensions that differed in personal relevance to each subject. After receiving feedback regarding their own performance on each item, subjects were asked to guess the performance of either a friend (close other) or a stranger (distant other). The results were consistent with the SEM model: Subjects were more positive in their perception of a friend's performance on a low relevance task than on a high relevance task. The effect of relevance disappeared for the stranger. On the other hand, subjects were more charitable in their perception of the friend's performance than of the stranger's performance on the low relevance task. The friend's advantage disappeared when the task was high in relevance to the self.

*Affecting Own Performance.*   The previous research has shown that people will actively behave to affect another's relative performance, or will distort their perceptions of the other's performance. Another way to change the relative performance is by handicapping the self to make the other look better (when relevance is low) or to work harder at one's own performance (when relevance is high). Increasing one's own effort may be more difficult than distorting one's perception of performance. Therefore, the extent to which people choose a perceptual or a behavioral strategy should depend on the relative ease with which one's own and another's performance can be distorted.

To test this hypothesis, Dalhoff and Tesser (1987) had subjects compete with friends and strangers on a task that required a number of marketing decisions. The task was made self-relevant for all subjects by telling them that it was related to important abilities such as intelligence and decision-making quality. On average, subjects were always outperformed by their competitor. However, there was substantial variability in own and other's performance over trials. To reduce the ambiguity associated with this variability, half of the subjects were told the average level of their own performance over trials (unambiguous self) and half were not (ambiguous self). In addition, half of the subjects were given feedback on the other's average level of performance (unambiguous other) and half were not (ambiguous other). Subjects were then given an opportunity to prepare for another round of marketing decisions by looking at various pieces of information that were potentially useful for their decisions. These pieces of information were listed in a menu on a computer, and the number of items that subjects selected to look at served as the primary measure of task effort. The results supported the hypotheses derived from the SEM model. Specifically, subjects whose self-evaluation was threatened because they had been clearly outperformed (i.e., unambiguous self, unambiguous other condition) by a close other expended more effort preparing for the subsequent trials than subjects who had been outperformed by a distant other or subjects for whom performance was ambiguous in some way.

Taken together, the studies on the effects of relevance and closeness on performance suggest that people have two behavioral strategies at their disposal to avert threats to their self-evaluation resulting from the better performance of a close other on a self-relevant dimension. They can either try to inhibit the other's performance, or they can increase their own effort in an attempt to better their own performance. Although both strategies result in decreasing the discrepancy between own and other's performance, they are qualitatively quite different and may be triggered by different situations. The available experimental evidence suggests that people may be more inclined to inhibit another's performance when they know that they have done poorly on a task without knowing how the other will do. However, when the other has already performed better than oneself, increasing one's own effort may be the more suitable strategy.

The fact that an increase in effort is one way to deal with another's better performance has some interesting implications for close relationships. The threat posed on one's self-evaluation by the comparison process may not always be detrimental, as suggested by Tesser and Smith's (1980) findings. Instead, under some conditions, comparison may have a positively motivating effect, namely striving to be as good as the other. From this vantage point, the positive motivational effects of comparison may result in couples maximizing their joint outcomes. For example, take the case of dual-career couples. If income is a performance domain relevant to both partners and A earns less than B, A may increase his or her efforts so as to draw closer to, or surpass, B. Consistent with this speculation, there is evidence that married research psychologists are more productive than unmarried controls (Bryson, Bryson, Licht, & Licht, 1976) as indicated by the number of publications and research grants awarded. Based on what we know about the effects of closeness and relevance on performance, we would not be surprised if the increased productivity was at least partly due to self-evaluation maintenance strategies, particularly an increase in effort. However, the motivational advantage of comparison may be attenuated by its affective fallout, which we discuss shortly.

### The Effects of Closeness and Performance on Relevance.

The SEM model is straightforward in its predictions about how closeness and performance affect changes in relevance. Remember that the relevance of a performance domain determines whether the comparison or reflection process will be more important. When one has been outperformed by a close other, deemphasizing the relevance of the dimension to the self is one way to avert threats to one's self-evaluation. When another outperforms the self, if relevance is high the comparison process will be more important than the reflection process and the self will suffer, particularly if the other is close. Therefore, closeness and performance should interact in affecting relevance. The better another's relative performance, the lower the resulting self-relevance of a performance domain, particularly for close others.

In a study designed to test this hypothesis (Tesser & Paulhus, 1983), subjects were told that they had outperformed a close or distant other, or that they had been outperformed by the other on a fictitious task called cognitive perceptual integration (CPI). Subsequently, subjects indicated the relevance of the CPI on rating scales, through open-ended responses, and through a behavioral measure (time spent looking at the biographies of people believed to be high in CPI). The SEM predictions were supported on all three measures. Subjects rated the relevance of CPI to be lower when they had been outperformed, compared with when they had outperformed the other. This effect was more pronounced when the other was close. Data consistent with these findings have been reported by Tesser (1980) and Tesser and Campbell (1983).

Again we are able to draw some straightforward implications for close relationships. If people find themselves consistently outperformed by their partners, and reducing closeness is not an option, they may decide that the particular dimension is no longer important, or relevant, to them. Note that such a step not only lowers the threat to one's self-evaluation but also increases complementarity in the relationship.

We conclude our discussion of the research dealing with the three parameters of the SEM model and its possible implications for close relationships, and begin to compare the SEM model with previous approaches discussed earlier. We start this comparison by discussing another line of SEM research.

## SEM Processes and Emotions

In our previous discussion, we talked about a variety of consequences resulting from comparison and reflection. So far, we neglected to talk explicitly about the role that emotions play in self-evaluation maintenance. Intuitively, being outperformed on a dimension that is highly relevant to oneself should lead to negative affect, especially if the other is close. The kind of affect generated by the comparison process is akin to "social comparison jealousy" (Salovey & Rodin, 1984).

The reflection process should elicit positive affect, manifested perhaps in feelings of pride for the other. Evidence for this contention came from a study (Tesser & Collins, 1988) in which subjects recalled and described eight different situations that they had actually experienced: The subject and either a close or distant other were performing on a self-relevant dimension, and the self was either outperformed by the other or outperformed the other. For each situation, subjects described their feelings and rated the extent to which several emotion labels described the way they felt. The labels included jealousy, envy, pride, and pride in the other.

We focus first on the comparison emotions. Although closeness of the other had no effect, relevance and performance did have the expected effects. The threat of comparison resulted from being outperformed on a relevant dimension. As expected, the ratings of jealousy and envy were low and did not differ by relevance when self outperformed other. However, jealousy and envy were rated higher when other outperformed self, and this was particularly true when relevance was high. The results of pride were parallel to those for jealousy and envy. Pride was low, and there was little effect of relevance when other outperformed self. When self outperformed other, pride increased, particularly when relevance was high. On the other hand, pride in the other, the reflection emotion, was significantly affected by the closeness of the other and the relevance of the performance domain. When the other was close, pride in his or her accomplishments increased as his or her performance increased. Results consistent with these findings were obtained when subjects' facial expressions served as an indicator of their emotional experience (Tesser, Millar, & Moore, 1988, Study 3).

These results suggest that the affective concomitants of comparison and reflection provide one basis for the experience of emotion in close relationships. Positive comparison (having outperformed the other on a high relevance dimension) should result in positive emotions such as pride; negative comparison (having been outperformed on a high relevance dimension) should result in negative emotions such as jealousy and envy. On the other hand, reflection should result in positive emotions (Tesser et al., 1988, Study 2), such as pride in the other's accomplishments.

However, if we assume that people in close, intimate relationships are concerned with the SEM processes of their partners, matters become a bit more complicated. According to the extended SEM model (Tesser & Beach, 1988), the positive comparison and the resulting positive affect of one person could be associated with negative comparison and negative affect of the partner. If this is the case, and if people show empathic concern for their partners, the positivity of their own affect resulting from positive comparison should be attenuated. By the same token, the negativity of the affect resulting from negative comparison should be attenuated when one takes the partner's positive affect into account. Tesser and Beach are just now beginning to test these and other hypotheses about the role of comparison and reflection on the experience of emotions in close relationships.

## OTHER THEORETICAL FRAMEWORKS AND THEIR RELATIONSHIP TO SEM PROCESSES

### Exchange Theories

Exchange theory proposes that, regardless of type (e.g., friends, lovers, or parents and children), relationships are evaluated in terms of the ratio of what interactants put into them (costs) and what they receive from them (benefits; e.g., Levinger, 1979). What constitutes a benefit or a cost depends on individuals' subjective appraisals and is somewhat context specific.

Further, people evaluate the outcomes of a relationship in terms of the extent to which they fall above or below their expectations for that relationship, or what Thibaut and Kelley (1959; Kelley & Thibaut, 1978) called a comparison level (CL), and the extent to which they are attracted to relationships that exceed their CL. People also compare their outcomes to a comparison level for alternatives (CLalt), which is defined as the lowest level of outcomes they will accept in light of what they could get if they terminated the relationship. Although the discrepancy between actual outcomes and CL determines how attracted people are to a relationship, the discrepancy between outcomes and CLalt determines how dependent they are on the relationship, with the level of dependency increasing as the attractiveness of the alternatives decreases. In the early stages, relationships may often be characterized by attraction and relative independence. People may be attracted to each other but continue to date other people to ascertain that their outcomes not only fall above their expectations but also above what they could get elsewhere.

Exchange theory does not predict what kinds of rewards people give to each other in close relationships. Nonetheless, some data suggest a small number of universalities. When asked what they liked about each other and their relationship, couple members listed such things as display of affection, joint activities, mutual help and support (Levinger, Rands, & Talaber, 1977), along with commitment and sexual exclusivity (Davis, 1988; Levinger, 1974). Thus, it seems that people in a stable relationship exchange rewards whose value is specifically tied to the person providing them.

The idea that principles of exchange govern close relationships is perhaps the most controversial aspect of exchange theory. One objection to this idea is the implication of a tit for tat, with people keeping a running score on who owes what to whom. Although such record keeping may sound both counterintuitive and unromantic, there has been some evidence for it (Adams, 1965; Hatfield, Utne, & Traupmann, 1979; Walster, Walster, & Berscheid, 1978). More recent versions of the theory suggest that immediate reciprocity is less important in close relationships as the time perspective becomes extended (Levinger, 1979), and that benefiting the other may be rewarding in and of itself (Huesman & Levinger, 1976).

A more radical proposal does away with the notion of equity in close relationships. Clark and Mills (1979; Mills & Clark, 1982; see also Mills & Clark, chapter 2, this volume) distinguished between exchange relationships governed by equity principles and communal relationships in which benefits are given according to the perceived needs of the other. Exchange relationships are found among strangers, casual acquaintances, and business associates, whereas communal relationships are found among family members, romantic partners, and close friends. Exchange and communal relationships vary on a number of dimensions (Mills & Clark, 1982). In communal relationships, members have a special concern for the welfare of the other. In exchange relationships, there is no special concern for the welfare of the other. In communal relationships, benefits are given when the other has a need for the benefit or when a benefit might be particularly pleasing to the other. In exchange relationships, benefits are given in response to benefits received in the past and/or with the expectation that the other will return a comparable benefit. In communal relationships, giving a benefit specifically in response to a prior benefit is inappropriate and may compromise a relationship. Instead, to avoid the appearance of ''repayment,'' benefits following a previous gift should be noncomparable and delayed. In exchange relationships, giving a benefit specifically in response to a prior benefit is appropriate and strengthens a relationship. When one has been benefited in the past, giving a comparable benefit is more appropriate than giving a noncomparable benefit, and no delay before benefiting the other is more appropriate than a delay. Research has provided evidence for these and other hypotheses about communal and exchange relationships (e.g., Clark, 1984; Clark & Mills, 1979; Clark, Mills, & Powell, 1986; Clark, Ouellette, Powell, & Milberg, 1987; Clark & Waddell, 1985).

The implications of the communal/exchange distinction for the initiation, maintenance, and dissolution of relationships are clear. Initial encounters with another may be governed by exchange principles. As the relationship becomes closer and the time perspective is extended, exchange principles will be replaced by communal norms. In the very early stages of a relationship, benefiting someone without regard for reciprocation may make the other feel overwhelmed or create the feeling that "things are happening too fast." As a result, the relationship may never get off the ground. On the other hand, if one person in an ongoing relationship takes an exchange orientation while the other takes a communal orientation, conflict is almost certain to result, and the relationship may be terminated if the condition continues to exist.

## SEM Dynamics and Communal/Exchange Theory

The distinction between communal and exchange relationships bears a certain resemblance to the levels of the closeness variable (close/distant) in the SEM model. The findings from the SEM research manipulating both closeness and relevance of the performance domain suggest an important boundary condition for the rules applying to benefit allocation in communal relationships. Specifically, we have reason to suspect that people in a close (i.e., communal) relationship may be more likely to help another when the performance domain is irrelevant to their self-definition. On the other hand, based on the findings of Tesser and Smith (1980), we would expect that people may be disinclined to help a close other when the help would improve his or her performance on a task dimension relevant to the self. After all, such help may put the other into a position where he or she could outperform the self, and thus pose a threat to one's self-evaluation.

## Dissonance Theory

According to dissonance theorists, people strive toward maintaining consistency in their cognitions about another person. Attitude change occurs when two such cognitions are at odds with one another. For example, the cognition "I've paid $100 for this dinner" is incompatible with the cognition "My date didn't say a word all night." One way to reduce the resulting dissonance would be to consider the date a good listener rather than a dull and boring person, because such a cognitive maneuver would justify the expenses. Essentially, dissonance theory predicts that people are attracted to those for whom they suffer (Aronson & Mills, 1959). Interestingly, dissonance theory also predicts that people dislike those whom they make suffer. In an early study investigating this hypothesis (Davis & Jones, 1960), subjects were asked to harm another by giving a negative personality evaluation. Half of the subjects did so by "choice," whereas the other half had no choice about giving the evaluation. Furthermore, half of the subjects had a chance to subsequently explain that they did not really mean the evaluation, whereas the remainder did not have this opportunity. As it turned out, those subjects who gave a bad evaluation by choice and did not have an opportunity to explain themselves ended up disliking and derogating the other. If people think of themselves as basically kind, choosing to harm another should produce dissonance. Such dissonance can be reduced by convincing oneself that the other deserved the harm.

These principles have some interesting implications for the understanding of abusive relationships. The abused may be more likely to remain in the relationship because the principle of dissonance reduction may make them more attracted to the abuser. On the other hand, the latter may continue the abuse because it seems perfectly justified in light of the perceived worthlessness of the other. Ironically, the behavior of both may, at least to some extent, be a result of efforts to reduce dissonance.

## Dissonance Theory and SEM Dynamics

Both the SEM model and dissonance theory are motivational. As noted earlier, comparison and reflection are accompanied by positive and negative emotions, and these emotions are accompanied by arousal. In fact, a couple of studies from our lab (Tesser et al., 1988; Tesser, Pilkington, & McIntosh, 1989) showed that SEM processes are mediated by arousal, and Tesser (1991) argued that SEM arousal and dissonance arousal (Cooper & Fazio, 1984) may be similar in terms of how they motivate patterns of behavior directed toward self-evaluation maintenance and dissonance reduction. However, the similarities seem to end here. The antecedents of dissonance arousal (e.g., Cooper & Fazio, 1984) are qualitatively different from the antecedents of SEM processes. Further, unlike dissonance arousal, the arousal stemming from negative comparison does not seem to affect attraction (e.g., Pleban & Tesser, 1981).

## Individual Difference and Type Theories

None of the approaches reviewed so far has considered the elusive phenomenon of love. In fact, it has become commonplace to lament about the absence of serious attempts to account for love. However, attempts to treat love as more than a "second-hand emotion" date back as far as the early 1970s, when Rubin (1973) attempted to measure his concept of love as an attitude composed of attachment, caring, and intimacy. In the process, Rubin conceptually distinguished between liking and loving. In a similar vein, Berscheid and Walster (1978) distinguished between passionate love, referring to the feeling of intense emotion and absorption in the other, and companionate love, referring to respect and strong mutual commitment.

Recently, renewed efforts have been made to distinguish among different types of close relationships based on the kind of love that exists within them

(Hazan & Shaver, 1987; Hendrick & Hendrick, 1986; Kelley, 1983; Sternberg, 1986). Common to these approaches is the theme that there are different types of loving that vary systematically among people. The intellectual godfather of these approaches was Lee's (1973, 1988) "colors of love" typology, which distinguished between three primary types of love (passionate, game playing, and companionate) and three secondary types resulting from combinations of the primary types (possessive/dependent, logical/practical, and selfless). Berscheid (1983) proposed four types of love: eros, friendship, attachment-affection, and altruistic. Kelley (1983) distinguished between passionate, pragmatic, and altruistic love. As useful as such typologies may be to distinguish among different types of relationships, their applicability to the understanding of the actual processes inherent in those relationships is limited, because they are primarily descriptive accounts of love based on face validity (Clark & Reis, 1988). However, there are two notable exceptions.

Sternberg's (1986) triangular theory of love proposes that love consists of three components: intimacy, passion, and decision/commitment. The intimacy component refers to feelings that promote closeness, bondedness, and connectedness, and includes such feelings as concern for the welfare of the other, subjectively experienced happiness, positive regard, sharing, support, mutual understanding, and intimate communication. The passion component refers to sources of arousal that promote the experience of passion, such as sexual needs, needs for self-esteem, affiliation, dominance, submission, and self-actualization. The decision/commitment component refers to (a) the decision that one is in love with another, and (b) the decision to maintain that love. The presence or absence of each of these components yields eight different types of love, ranging from nonlove (where none of the components is present) to consummate love (where all three are present).

Hazan and Shaver's (1987; Shaver, Hazan, & Bradshaw, 1988) approach to the role of love in close relationships drew on Bowlby's (1969, 1973, 1980) theory of the development of attachment in infants. They conceptualized romantic love as an attachment process bearing striking similarities to the process by which infants get attached to their caregivers. Thus, like infants' attachment to their caregivers, adults can be securely, avoidantly, or anxiously attached to their romantic partners. Adults who are securely attached to their lovers should experience the relationship in terms of trust, friendship, and positive emotions, and they should believe in enduring love, the basic trustworthiness of others, and the likability of the self. Avoidantly attached adults should experience love as something marked by fear of closeness and lack of trust, and they should have doubts about the durability of love and its necessity for their own personal happiness. Finally, for anxiously attached adults, the experience of love should be a preoccupying and painful struggle, and they should fall in love frequently without finding true love. These and other hypotheses were confirmed by a couple of studies examining people's self-reports on the subjective experience of love in current and past relationships, and their general beliefs about the nature of love.

## Individual Difference Theories and SEM Dynamics

It is hard to draw straightforward comparisons between the SEM model and the individual difference approaches to close relationships. For one thing, they differ vastly in their epistemological nature: The individual difference approaches are structural and somewhat descriptive, whereas the SEM model is systemic. Furthermore, they differ in their theoretical focus: Individual difference approaches aim to distinguish many qualitatively different relationships (eight in Sternberg's case, three in Hazan & Shaver's case), whereas the SEM model is concerned with the quantitative dynamics of close relationships rather than qualitative distinctions among them. Finally, the SEM parameters of closeness, relevance, and performance have no equivalents in the triangular theory of love or the attachment-based approach to love in relationships. At the same time, passion, intimacy, and commitment, as well as attachment differences, are not directly relevant for the SEM model.

Having said this, we now offer a few speculations about possible connections between the SEM model and the individual difference theories. It seems that both comparison and reflection with their respective affective concomitants could influence the levels of some of the constructs in Sternberg's (1986, 1988) theory. For example, being at the "wrong end" of comparison might make it hard for passion to occur because the negative effect of comparison is incompatible with the positive emotions that surround passion. On the other hand, reflection may foster feelings of passion because of its contribution to the appearance of positive emotions. Intimacy may be similarly affected by comparison and reflection. Alternatively, high levels of passion may attenuate the importance of comparison processes in a close relationship, perhaps because it restricts the number of relevant performance dimensions, or because the additional arousal stemming from comparison adds to the arousal inherent in passion to enhance the experience (Clark, Milberg, & Erber, 1988).

## Emotion Theories

Yet another picture emerges when one looks at love as an emotion. On the basis of Schachter and Singer's (1962) seminal work on emotion, one can construe love as autonomic nervous system arousal that is labeled as love (Walster, 1971). The implication is that any type of arousal that does not have a clear, unambiguous source could be attributed to "being in love," or at least to being attracted to someone who just happens to be around. In fact, in Dutton and Aron's (1974) famous study, subjects were more attracted to a female confederate after walking across a shaky bridge (which supposedly increased their level of autonomic arousal), compared with subjects who had walked across a sturdy bridge prior to meeting the confederate.

Berscheid's (1982, 1983) work also was concerned with emotion in ongoing relationships. Drawing on Mandler's (1975) theory of emotion, she pointed to the interruptive qualities that others have on people's organized behavior sequences and higher order goals. In Mandler's framework, the interruption of ongoing behavior is causal for an increase in autonomic arousal and the experience of emotion. These interruptions can be caused by events in people's environment (a burst of lightning, the sudden appearance of an attractive member of the opposite gender) or by intrusive thoughts (Martin & Tesser, 1989; Simon, 1967) such as remembering a missed appointment or an upcoming date. Thus, initial attraction to someone might be caused by his or her ability to interrupt people's ongoing behavior in pursuit of higher order goals.

In ongoing relationships, people's goals and behavior are often tied to the other person. In Berscheid's terms, interconnections between people's sequences of behavior is what defines the closeness of a relationship. Closeness can be assessed by the frequency, strength, and diversity of the causal interconnections between two people's sequences or chains of behavior. If behavior sequences between two people are well meshed (Berscheid, 1983), that is, each person facilitates and augments the performance of the other's behavioral sequences, little observable emotion is hypothesized to occur. Instead, people experience strong emotions when the behavioral sequences become unmeshed. In other words, when some event in the other's chain prevents the remainder of a person's own behavioral sequence from occurring, or force him or her to modify it, he or she is likely to ruminate (Millar, Tesser, & Millar, 1988) and experience negative emotions (e.g., Simpson, 1987). Interruptions of ongoing behavior can also lead to positive emotions (i.e., that "loving kind of feeling"). Just imagine the interruptive qualities of unexpectedly being offered help while thinking depressing thoughts or folding laundry.

## SEM Dynamics and Emotion Theories

Berscheid's theory is specifically concerned with the conditions that bring about emotions in close relationships and Schachter's theory of the attribution of emotional arousal. In the SEM model, emotions are considered important mediators of behavior. Although the model has little to do with Berscheid's notion of meshed behavior sequences, Schachter's two-factor theory plays an important role. For example, Tesser et al. (1989) showed that if the arousal arising from SEM processes is misattributed to a pill or an ambient noise, SEM behavior patterns disappear. We suggest (e.g., Tesser, 1991) that arousal can come from being in a setting in which information potentially consequential to the self is anticipated. This autonomic arousal results in increased attention (Mandler, 1975) to those circumstances. In turn, increased attention to the situation leads to behavior that is more orderly and predictable from the situation. Thus, the predictions from the SEM model concerning close relationships seem to be intimately bound up with emotions.

## PHENOMENON-DRIVEN RESEARCH ON RELATIONSHIPS

We briefly address some ad hoc topics that, although not necessarily motivated by a specific social psychological theory, have taken a prominent place in the literature on attraction and interpersonal relationships.

### Physical Attractiveness

A number of reviews of the sizable literature on attractiveness (e.g., Berscheid & Walster, 1974; Hatfield & Sprecher, 1986; Huston & Levinger, 1978) have come to the not surprising conclusion that physically attractive people are liked better than physically unattractive people. Not only does this conclusion seem to hold for the early stages of relationships (e.g., Tesser & Brodie, 1971; Walster, Aronson, Abrahams, & Rottman, 1966), but the link between attractiveness and liking can get even stronger over time (e.g., Mathes, 1975).

Just why is physical attractiveness so important? People's perceptions of other people seem to be guided by a balance principle (Heider, 1958). People assume that good things go with good things and bad ones with bad. Thus, people believe that attractive people have positive characteristics, whereas unattractive people have negative characteristics (Dion, Berscheid, & Walster, 1972). Moreover, the attractiveness of one's partner may reflect on one's own attractiveness (Sigall & Landy, 1973).

### SEM and Physical Attractiveness

The physical attractiveness effect is so robust that undoubtedly there are a number of mechanisms sustaining it. The reflection process of the SEM model may be one of these mechanisms. Indeed, Sigall and Landy (1973) found that being with an attractive partner leads to more positive feelings about self. Thus, it seems that being with a physically attractive other allows people to bask in the reflected beauty of the other.

*Similarity Versus Complementarity.*   The importance of similarity for interpersonal relationships has been well documented in the literature, especially in the realm of attitudes (Byrne, 1971). Supposedly, attitude similarity is reinforcing. Positive affect is elicited by similar attitude statements, and negative affect is elicited by dissimilar attitude statements (Byrne & Clore, 1970; but see Ajzen, 1974, for a different explanation). Despite the robustness of the relationship between attitude similarity and attraction, a number of attempts have been made over the years to undermine it. For example, Meyer and Pepper (1977) tried to find evidence against it and in support of the contention that need complementarity (Winch, 1955, 1958; Winch, Ktsanes, & Ktsanes, 1954) is a crucial determinant for attraction in ongoing relationships. Hoffman and Maier (1966) tried to extend the similarity hypothesis to personality rather than attitudes. Both of these attempts were less than successful, although there is evidence that married couples tend to share a variety of attitudinal and personality characteristics. Yet there are other established conditions under which attitude similarity does not result in attraction. Specifically, attitude similarity has been shown to lose its impact on attraction when the other is believed to be emotionally disturbed (Novak & Lerner, 1968) or acts in an obnoxious and unpleasant fashion (Cooper & Jones, 1969). One of the more recent and severe attacks on the similarity hypothesis came from Rosenbaum (1986), who argued that attitudinal similarity does not lead to attraction but that dissimilarity leads to repulsion.

Our own belief is that similarity in some domains under some conditions and complementarity in some domains under some conditions are both associated with interpersonal attraction. Indeed, as we showed earlier, the self-evaluation maintenance model specifies some of the conditions under which some forms of complementarity and some forms of dissimilarity can be beneficial for a relationship.

## AN EPISTEMOLOGICAL NOTE

We discussed a variety of different approaches to relationships and compared them to a self-evaluation maintenance model on a case-by-case basis. However, it is also important to point to an overarching epistemological difference between the SEM model and previous approaches. Despite their differences in focus and theoretical orientation, each of the other approaches are basically recursive, linear cause–effect models. Most of them treat relationships as a dependent variable. Physical attractiveness, similarity, psychological consistency, and equity are hypothesized to affect a person's initial attraction to someone and the course the relationship may take. The communal/exchange approach (Clark & Mills, 1979) and Berscheid's (1983) emotion approach treat relationships as an independent variable. In the former case, the type of relationship determines the norms that will be applied to the interactions in that relationship. In the latter case, the closeness of the relationship determines the potential for the experience of strong emotions. As we showed, the SEM model is systemic (i.e., it treats the closeness of interpersonal relationships as both dependent and independent variables). We hope that, perhaps because of its extended theoretical focus, the SEM model adds something to previous approaches to relationships.

## ACKNOWLEDGMENTS

We gratefully acknowledge the support of NIMH grant #1R01MH41487-01 in preparing this manuscript, and we thank Theresa Luhrs for her help in finalizing it.

## REFERENCES

Adams, J. S. (1965). Inequity in social exchange. In L. Berkowitz (Ed.), *Advances in experimental social psychology* (Vol. 2, pp. 266–300). New York: Academic Press.

Aronson, E., & Mills, J. (1959). The effects of severity of initiation on liking for a group. *Journal of Abnormal and Social Psychology, 67*, 31–36.

Ajzen, I. (1974). Effects of information on interpersonal attraction: Similarity versus affective value. *Journal of Personality and Social Psychology, 29*, 374–380.

Berscheid, E. (1982). Attraction and emotion in interpersonal relations. In M. S. Clark & S. T. Fiske (Eds.), *Affect and cognition* (pp. 37–54). Hillsdale, NJ: Lawrence Erlbaum Associates.

Berscheid, E. (1983). Emotion. In H. H. Kelley, E. Berscheid, A. Christensen, J. Harvey, T. L. Huston, G. Levinger, E. McClintock, A. Peplau, & D. R. Peterson (Eds.), *Close relationships* (pp. 110–168). San Francisco: Freeman.

Berscheid, E., & Walster, E. (1974). Physical attractiveness. In L. Berkowitz (Ed.), *Advances in experimental and social psychology* (Vol. 7, pp. 157–215). New York: Academic Press.

Berscheid, E., & Walster, E. (1978). *Interpersonal attraction*. Reading, MA: Addison-Wesley.

Bowlby, J. (1969). *Attachment and loss: Vol. 1. Attachment*. New York: Basic Books.

Bowlby, J. (1973). *Attachment and loss: Vol. 2. Separation: Anxiety and anger*. New York: Basic Books.

Bowlby, J. (1980). *Attachment and loss: Vol. 3. Loss*. New York: Basic Books.

Bryson, R. B., Bryson, J. B., Licht, M. H., & Licht, B. G. (1976). The professional pair: Husband and wife psychologists. *American Psychologist, 31*, 10–16.

Byrne, D. (1971). *The attraction paradigm*. New York: Academic Press.

Byrne, D., & Clore, G. L. (1970). A reinforcement model of evaluative processes. *Personality: An International Journal, 1*, 103–128.

Campbell, J., & Tesser, A. (1985). Self-evaluation maintenance processes in relationships. In S. Duck & R. Perlman (Eds.), *Understanding personal relationships: An interdisciplinary approach* (pp. 107–135). London: Sage.

Cialdini, R. B., Borden, R. J., Thorne, A., Walker, M. R., Freeman, S., & Sloan, L. R. (1976). Basking in reflected glory: Three (football) field studies. *Journal of Personality and Social Psychology, 34*, 366–375.

Cialdini, R. B., & Richardson, K. D. (1980). Two indirect tactics of image management: Basking and blasting. *Journal of Personality and Social Psychology, 39*, 406–415.

Clark, M. S. (1984). Record keeping in two types of relationships. *Journal of Personality and Social Psychology, 47*, 549–557.

Clark, M. S., Milberg, S., & Erber, R. (1988). Arousal-state dependent learning: Implications for social judgments and behavior. In K. Fielder & J. P. Forgas (Eds.), *Affect, cognition and behavior* (pp. 63-83). New York: Hogrefe.

Clark, M. S., & Mills, J. (1979). Interpersonal attraction in exchange and communal relationships. *Journal of Personality and Social Psychology, 53*, 94-103.

Clark, M. S., Mills, J., & Powell, M. (1986). Keeping track of needs in communal and exchange relationships. *Journal of Personality and Social Psychology, 51*, 333-338.

Clark, M. S., Ouellette, R., Powell, M., & Milberg, S. (1987). Relationship type, recipient mood, and helping. *Journal of Personality and Social Psychology, 53*, 94-103.

Clark, M. S., & Reis, H. T. (1988). Interpersonal processes in close relationships. *Annual Review of Psychology, 39*, 609-672.

Clark, M. S., & Waddell, B. (1985). Perceptions of exploitation in communal and exchange relationships. *Journal of Social and Personal Relations, 2*, 403-418.

Cooper, J., & Fazio, R. H. (1984). A new look at dissonance theory. In L. Berkowitz (Ed.), *Advances in experimental social psychology* (Vol. 17, pp. 229-267). New York: Academic Press.

Cooper, J., & Jones, E. E. (1969). Opinion divergence as a strategy to avoid being miscast. *Journal of Personality and Social Psychology, 13*, 23-40.

Dalhoff, R., & Tesser, A. (1987). *Number two does try harder, but only sometimes*. Unpublished research data, University of Georgia. Athens.

Davis, K. E. (1988, November). *In search of a theory of love*. Paper presented at the 11th annual conference of the Society of Southeastern Social Psychologists, Greensboro, NC.

Davis, K. E., & Jones, E. E. (1960). Changes in interpersonal perception as a means of reducing cognitive dissonance. *Journal of Abnormal and Social Psychology, 61*, 402-410.

Dion, K., Berscheid, E., & Walster, E. (1972). What is beautiful is good. *Journal of Personality and Social Psychology, 24*, 285-290.

Dutton, D. G., & Aron, A. P. (1974). Some evidence for heightened sexual attraction under conditions of high anxiety. *Journal of Personality and Social Psychology, 30*, 510-517.

Hatfield, E., & Sprecher, S. (1986). *Mirror, mirror . . . The importance of looks in everyday life*. Albany, NY: State University of New York Press.

Hatfield, E., Utne, M. K., & Traupmann, J. (1979). Equity theory and intimate relationships. In R. L. Burgess & T. L. Huston (Eds.), *Social exchange in developing relationships* (pp. 99-133). New York: Academic Press.

Hazan, C., & Shaver, P. (1987). Romantic love conceptualized as an attachment process. *Journal of Personality and Social Psychology, 50*, 392-402.

Heider, F. (1958). *The psychology of interpersonal relations*. New York: Wiley.

Hendrick, C., & Hendrick, S. S. (1986). A theory and method of love. *Journal of Personality and Social Psychology, 50*, 392-402.

Hoffman, L. R., & Maier, N. R. (1966). An experimental reexamination of the similarity-attraction hypothesis. *Journal of Personality and Social Psychology, 3*, 145-152.

Huesman, L. R., & Levinger, G. (1976). Incremental exchange theory: A formal model for progression in dyadic interaction. In L. Berkowitz & E. Walster (Eds.), *Advances in experimental social psychology* (Vol. 9, pp. 192-229). New York: Academic Press.

Huston, T. L., & Levinger, G. (1978). Interpersonal attraction in relationships. *Annual Review of Psychology, 29*, 115-156.

Kelley, H. H. (1983). Love and commitment. In H. H. Kelley, E. Berscheid, A. Christensen, J. H. Harvey, & T. L. Huston (Eds.), *Close relationships* (pp. 265-314). New York: Freeman.

Kelley, H. H., & Thibaut, J. W. (1978). *Interpersonal relations: A theory of interdependence*. New York: Wiley-Interscience.

Lee, J. A. (1973). *The colors of love: An exploration the ways of loving*. Don Mills, Ontario: New Press.

Lee, J. A. (1988). Lovestyles. In R. J. Sternberg & M. L. Barnes (Eds.), *The psychology of love* (pp. 38-67). New Haven, CT: Yale University Press.

Levinger, G. (1974). A three-level view on attraction: Toward an understanding of pair-relatedness. In T. L. Huston (Ed.), *Foundations of interpersonal attraction* (pp. 99–120). New York: Academic Press.

Levinger, G. (1979). A social exchange view on the dissolution of pair relationships. In R. L. Burgess & T. L. Huston (Eds.), *Social exchange in developing relationships* (pp. 169–193). New York: Academic Press.

Levinger, G., Rands, M., & Talaber, R. (1977). *The assessment of involvement and rewardingness in close relationships*. Unpublished technical report, University of Massachusetts, Amherst.

Mandler, G. (1975). *Mind and emotion*. New York: Wiley.

Martin, L. L., & Tesser, A. (1989). Toward a motivational and structural model of ruminative thought. In J. F. Uleman & J. A. Bargh (Eds.), *Unintended thought* (pp. 306–326). New York: Guilford.

Mathes, E. W. (1975). The effects of physical attractiveness and anxiety on heterosexual attraction over a series of five encounters. *Journal of Marriage and the Family, 37*, 769–783.

Meyer, J. P., & Pepper, S. (1977). Need compatibility and marital adjustment in young married couples. *Journal of Personality and Social Psychology, 35*, 331–342.

Millar, K., Tesser, A., & Millar, M. (1988). The effects of threatening life event on behavior sequences and intrusive thought. *Cognitive Therapy and Research, 12*, 441–457.

Mills, J., & Clark, M. S. (1982). Exchange and communal relationships. In L. Wheeler (Ed.), *Review of personality and social psychology* (pp. 121–144). Beverly Hills: Sage.

Novak, D. W., & Lerner, M. J. (1968). Rejection as a function of perceived similarity. *Journal of Personality and Social Psychology, 9*, 147–152.

Pleban, R., & Tesser, A. (1981). The effects of relevance and quality of another's performance on interpersonal closeness. *Social Psychology Quarterly, 44*, 278–285.

Pilkington, C. J., Tesser, A., & Stephens, D. (1989, April). *Self-evaluation maintenance in romantic relationships: Considering your partner's welfare*. Paper presented at the annual meeting of the Midwestern Psychological Association, Chicago, IL.

Rosenbaum, M. E. (1986). The repulsion hypothesis: On the nondevelopment of relationships. *Journal of Personality and Social Psychology, 51*, 1156–1166.

Rubin, Z. (1970). Measurement of romantic love. *Journal of Personality and Social Psychology, 16*, 265–273.

Rubin, Z. (1973). *Liking and loving: An invitation to social psychology*. New York: Holt, Rinehart & Winston.

Salovey, P., & Rodin, J. (1984). Some antecedents and consequences of social comparison jealousy. *Journal of Personality and Social Psychology, 47*, 780–792.

Schachter, S., & Singer, J. E. (1962). Cognitive, social and physiological determinants of emotional state. *Psychological Review, 69*, 379–399.

Shaver, P., Hazan, C., & Bradshaw, D. (1988). Love as attachment: The integration of three behavioral systems. In R. J. Sternberg & M. L. Barnes (Eds.), *The psychology of love* (pp. 68–99). New Haven, CT: Yale University Press.

Sigall, H., & Landy, J. (1973). Radiating beauty: Effects of having a physically attractive partner on person perception. *Journal of Personality and Social Psychology, 28*, 218–224.

Simon, H. A. (1967). Motivational and emotional controls of cognition. *Psychological Review, 74*, 29–39.

Simpson, J. A. (1987). The dissolution of romantic relationships: Factors involved in relationship stability and emotional distress. *Journal of Personality and Social Psychology, 52*, 1061–1086.

Sternberg, R. J. (1986). A triangular theory of love. *Psychological Review, 93*, 119–135.

Sternberg, R. J. (1988). Triangulating love. In R. J. Sternberg & M. L. Barnes (Eds.), *The psychology of love* (pp. 118–138). New Haven, CT: Yale University Press.

Tesser, A. (1980). Self-esteem maintenance in family dynamics. *Journal of Personality and Social Psychology, 39*, 77–91.

Tesser, A. (1988). Toward a self-evaluation maintenance model of social behavior. In L. Berkowitz (Ed.), *Advances in experimental social psychology* (Vol. 21, pp. 181–227). San Diego, CA: Academic Press.

Tesser, A. (1991). Emotion in social comparison and reflection processes. In J. Suls & T. A. Walls (Eds.), *Social comparison: Contemporary theory and research* (pp. 115–145). Hillsdale, NJ: Lawrence Erlbaum Associates.

Tesser, A., & Beach, S. (1988). *Emotion in marriage: The role of social reflection and comparison processes.* Unpublished research proposal, University of Georgia, Athens.

Tesser, A., & Brodie, M. (1971). A note on the evaluation of "A computer date." *Psychonomic Science, 23,* 300.

Tesser, A., Campbell, J. (1982). Self-evaluation maintenance and the perception of friends and strangers. *Journal of Personality, 59,* 261–279.

Tesser, A., & Campbell, J. (1983). Self-definition and self-evaluation maintenance. In J. Suls & A. Greenwald (Eds.), *Social psychological perspectives on the self* (Vol. 1, pp. 1–31). Hillsdale, NJ: Lawrence Erlbaum Associates.

Tesser, A., & Collins, J. (1988). Emotion in social reflection and comparison situations. *Journal of Personality and Social Psychology, 55,* 695–717.

Tesser, A., & Cornell, D. P. (1991). On the confluence of self processes. *Journal of Experimental Social Psychology, 27*(6), 501–526.

Tesser, A., Millar, M., & Moore, J. (1988). Some affective consequences of social comparison and reflection processes: The pain and pleasure of being close. *Journal of Personality and Social Psychology, 54,* 49–61.

Tesser, A., & Paulhus, D. (1983). The definition of self: Private and public self-evaluation maintenance strategies. *Journal of Personality and Social Psychology, 44,* 672–682.

Tesser, A., Pilkington, C. J., & McIntosh, W. D. (1989). Self-evaluation maintenance and the mediational role of emotion: The perception of friends and strangers. *Journal of Personality and Social Psychology, 57,* 442–456.

Tesser, A., & Smith, J. (1980). Some effects of friendship and task relevance of helping: You don't always help the one you like. *Journal of Experimental Social Psychology, 16,* 582–590.

Thibaut, J. W., & Kelley, H. H. (1959). *The social psychology of groups.* New York: Wiley.

Tversky, A. (1977). Features of similarity. *Psychological Review, 84,* 327–352.

Walster, E., Aronson, V., Abrahams, D., & Rottman, L. (1966). Importance of physical attractiveness in dating behavior. *Journal of Personality and Social Psychology, 5,* 508–516.

Walster, E., Walster, G. W., & Berscheid, E. (1978). *Equity: Theory and research.* Rockleigh, NJ: Allyn & Bacon.

Winch, R. F. (1955). The theory of complementarity needs in mate-selection: Final results on the test of the general hypothesis. *American Sociological Review, 20,* 552–555.

Winch, R. F. (1958). *Mate-selection: A study of complementary needs.* New York: Harper.

Winch, R. F., Ktsanes, T., & Ktsanes, V. (1954). The theory of complementary needs in mate-selection: An analytic and descriptive study. *American Sociological Review, 19,* 241–249.

# Chapter 11

# The Theory of Mental Incongruity, With a Specific Application to Loneliness Among Widowed Men and Women

Pearl A. Dykstra
Jenny de Jong Gierveld
*NIDI, The Netherlands*

Widowhood is one of the most painful experiences a person is likely to endure. It not only involves the loss of a loved one, but means the end of a way of life shared with that person. There are many similarities in the manner in which widowed men and women adapt to life without their former spouses, but there are also many differences. Some prefer to remarry, whereas others want to remain single. Some desire to remarry within a relatively short period of time, whereas others prefer to wait. Some find a new partner relatively soon, whereas others, despite repeated efforts, do not. After a while, some become content with life as single people, whereas others continue to experience stress. Why are there such differences in the adaptation to widowhood? What factors influence the adaptation?

The adaptation to widowhood requires a reorganization of daily activities, the network of personal relationships, and so on. Processes of reorganization are not unique to widowhood, however. They are also required by events such as unemployment, retirement, relocation, the birth of a child, and divorce. For that reason, to answer questions about differences in adaptation to widowhood, it is helpful to make use of a general theory about the manner in which people react under restrictive circumstances. "General" means that the propositions used in the explanation do not refer to specific events or specific categories of individuals. The propositions have a higher level of generality than the phenomena under investigation. When applying a general theory, the propositions must be tailored to the problem at hand.

In the present chapter, it is our objective to illustrate some of the possibilities of working with a general theory, a theory that explains why certain people make life transitions with greater ease than others. The general theory of interest is the theory of mental incongruity (TMI). The TMI is a structural-individualistic theory, meaning that two types of factors are used to explain and predict behavior: (a) the structural and normative opportunities and constraints to behave in a certain way, and (b) the individual disposition to behave in a certain way. The TMI assumes that circumstances alone do not necessarily explain behavior: Some people manage to do things despite considerable constraints, whereas others do not, not even if there are ample opportunities to do so. Given the opportunities, the theory specifies that for particular behavior to occur, people must have the disposition to do so. Contrary to classical attitude theory, the behavioral disposition is not conceived in terms of a single attitude, but rather in terms of a complex of mental elements, the so-called "mental system."

In the next section, we provide a description of the theory of mental incongruity. First, we describe the most important elements comprising the theory, then we present the general theoretical propositions. We decided to devote relatively much space to the presentation of the theory of mental incongruity because English audiences are generally unfamiliar with it. Since the TMI was first introduced (Münch, 1972), it has undergone a number of revisions (Tazelaar, 1980, 1983; Tazelaar & Wippler, 1982, 1985). Our description of the theory is largely a condensation of these writings. A model of the TMI (adapted from Tazelaar, 1982) is provided in Fig. 11.1.

As the reader discovers, the TMI is highly abstract and complex. To help judge its usefulness, we discuss the similarities with and differences between the TMI and other attitude-behavior approaches. We also consider what we feel are the benefits of using such a complex theoretical model. In the last part of the chapter, we show how the theory was applied in our study of widowhood. We used it to specify the conditions contributing to experiences of loneliness. Our intention is to illustrate the possibilities and the potential usefulness of the TMI in relationship research.

## THE THEORY OF MENTAL INCONGRUITY: GENERAL VERSION

Mental elements and their interrelations together form the mental system. Two classes of mental elements can be distinguished: standards and cognitions. Standards are expressions of what one wants or desires, or of what should be, whereas cognitions refer to what one experiences, perceives, knows, or expects. Mental incongruity exists when there is a discrepancy between standards and their related cognitions, that is, when a person experiences not being in the desired situation (not behaving as desired) or, alternatively, when a person

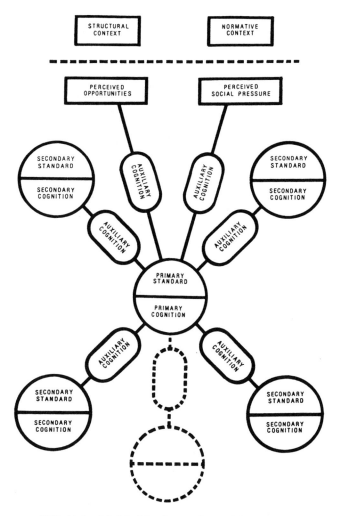

FIG. 11.1.   Model of the theory of mental incongruity.

experiences being in a situation (behaving in a way) that is not desired. The incongruity is greater (a) the more dominant the standard is, that is, the greater the desire for a particular situation (or to behave in a certain way), and (b) the more the standard relates to the individual specifically, that is, not only to the social category to which the individual belongs (e.g., "the widowed"), but also to the "self."

Further, the mental system can be distinguished according to the primary, secondary, and tertiary domains. The primary domain is defined as such by the researcher: It refers to the research problem, the incongruity reduction to be explained. Secondary domains are assumed to be affected by changes in the primary domain, whereas tertiary domains are not. For that reason, second-ary domains are and tertiary domains are not considered to be relevant to the explanation of the problem at hand.

In addition to "fixed" secondary domains, a number of "nonfixed" second-ary domains, which vary from research problem to research problem, can be specified. The fixed domains are assumed to be relevant to every explanation. They are: (a) money or income, (b) time, (c) prestige, and (d) social contacts. Additional fixed elements are (e) perceived social pressure, and (f) perceived opportunities for change. The latter two elements explicitly posit that people's behavior cannot satisfactorily be explained in terms of the circumstances in which they find themselves, but that it is necessary to consider the manner in which the circumstances are perceived. A central theoretical assumption is that perceived social pressure and factual social pressure are rather weakly relat-ed, as are perceived opportunities and factual structural opportunities. Em-pirically, this assumption has received considerable support (Tazelaar & Wippler, 1985). Further, these perceptions are assumed to play a crucial role in the explanation of incongruity reduction. The nonfixed elements are problem specific, and can be identified on the basis of previous research.

The primary domain is connected with the secondary domains by means of auxiliary cognitions. Incongruity can exist in the primary domain as well as in the secondary domains. Auxiliary cognitions are the perceptions, knowledge, or expectations that people have about the consequences of changes in the primary domain for the cognitions in the secondary domains, and there-fore for the incongruity in the secondary domains. For example, people ex-periencing marital problems (primary incongruity) have expectations about the consequences of divorce for the relationship with their children (possible production of incongruity in the secondary domain of social contacts).

## Theoretical Propositions

So far, only the elements comprising the TMI have been described. The next section considers the theoretical propositions regarding when incongruity reduc-tion is likely to occur, and how a particular incongruity is likely to be reduced. Central to the theory is the proposition that in mental systems there is a tend-ency toward maximal incongruity reduction. Total incongruity is determined by the sum of all the incongruities in the primary as well as in the secondary domains. Reduction of a primary incongruity can lead to a reduction of a secondary incongruity but it can also result in the production of incongruity in a previously congruent domain. The theory posits that reduction of a primary incongruity occurs only if the expected increase in secondary incongruities is smaller than the primary incongruity to be reduced.

The situation of an unmarried person who would like to have a partner can serve as an example. Suppose that, at present, this particular individual is very satisfied with his or her friendships and attaches great importance to them. If he or she becomes involved in a partner relationship, interactions with friends are likely to change. There may be conflicting demands, less time for servicing friendships, and so forth. It is conceivable that the involvement in a partner relationship (a means of reducing the primary incongruity) is perceived to have such serious and negative ramifications for existing friendships (production of secondary incongruities) that the person decides to remain single (i.e., nonreduction of primary incongruity).

The TMI specifies when incongruity reduction is likely to occur and when it is not: If reduction of a primary incongruity is expected to produce greater overall incongruity in the mental system, it will not occur. Nonreduction in the mental system is either stable, referred to as zero reaction, or nonstable and temporary. In the latter case, the individual is likely to experience stress, as indicated by psychosomatic complaints.

What makes the theory interesting is that it not only specifies when congruity reduction is likely to take place but also how it is likely to do so. There are several ways to reduce incongruity. The cognition can be adapted in the direction of the standard either by actual changes in situation or in behavior, or by perceived changes. The latter is referred to as "as if" behavior or cognitive trickery; actual behavioral changes do not take place. An example of cognitive trickery is the situation of a widow who "fails" to accept the loss of the spouse and continues to engage in behavior such as setting the dinner table for two instead of for one, reserving his armchair in front of the television, and so forth. Cognitive trickery tends to be pathological.

Incongruity reduction can also take place by adapting the standard in the direction of the experienced situation: attitudinal change or resignation. Thus, the theory considers adaptation in the form of behavioral changes, as well as mental changes such as cognitive trickery or resignation.

According to the theory, behavioral changes are more likely the more dominant the primary standard is (i.e., the greater the desire for a particular nonexisting situation). Behavioral changes are also more likely the more central the secondary and auxiliary cognitions are. "Centrality" refers to the relative advantages and disadvantages the desired situation is expected to have (e.g., financial gains or costs, more free-available time or less, more prestige or less, improvement or deterioration of social contacts) and to the favorability of the perceived opportunities for bringing about behavioral changes.

The previous conditions determine the strength of the behavioral disposition. Whether the behavioral disposition is carried out successfully depends on actual opportunities and constraints, which can be structural or normative. Given the behavioral disposition, the theory specifies that behavioral changes are more likely the more opportunities and fewer constraints provided by the structural context (e.g., transportation facilities, health condition, financial resources). Behavioral changes are also more likely the more opportunities and fewer constraints provided by the normative context (i.e., the greater the extent to which the individual's standards are shared by relevant others).

Changes in standards are more likely the less central the secondary and auxiliary cognitions are. In other words, changes in standards are more likely the fewer advantages and the more disadvantages the desired situation is expected to have, the less favorable the opportunities for a change in situation are perceived to be, and the less the desired situation is expected to be in accordance with the perceived standards of relevant others.

## The Complexity of the Theory of Mental Incongruity

The TMI is a complex theory, integrating and extending different lines of theorizing on the attitude-behavior consistency. A number of theoretical elements are not unique to the TMI, but what makes it valuable is that the various elements are brought together in one theoretical framework. The result appears to be a rather unwieldy and nonparsimonious model. One can question the benefits and raise doubts about the necessity of using such a complex model. In our view, the complexity is necessary to adequately explain why people so often are found to act differently than they are expected to given the attitudes they have. The TMI specifies conditions under which people are not likely to act in accordance with their attitudes: (a) if performance of the behavior is expected to lead to greater net incongruity in the mental system, and/or (b) if the factual opportunities for performing the behavior are perceived as unfavorable.

Part of the theory's complexity stems from the distinction that is made between secondary standards, secondary cognitions, and auxiliary cognitions. The terminology is different from what is common in the research literature. Yet, obvious similarities exist, for example, between auxiliary cognitions and the concept of beliefs (i.e., the perceived consequences of performing a particular behavior) from Fishbein and Ajzen's (1975; Ajzen & Fishbein, 1980) theory of reasoned action, and between secondary standards and Fishbein and Ajzen's concept of evaluations (i.e., the desirability/noxiousness of these consequences). Secondary cognitions, conceptualized as the degree to which a person has free-available time, money, prestige, social contacts, and other problem-specific attributes, do not have an obvious pendant in the theory of reasoned action. However, it is precisely this concept that makes it possible to examine marginal utility. Thus, on the basis of the TMI, one can predict that, despite having (a) a relatively strong belief that the performance of a particular behavior will lead to more money and (b) a relatively positive evaluation of money, a person may have only a weak behavioral intention because he or she already has relatively much money and performance of the behavior has small marginal utility. We point out that Bagozzi (1986) had a similar conceptualization. His theory of purposeful behavior includes the concept of conditional approach/avoidance responses. These indicate the subjective conditional likelihood that a person will perform a particular behavior, given the belief that such a performance will lead to a particular consequence.

The complexity of the TMI also stems from the specification of six fixed secondary domains (the four domains of money, time, prestige, and social contacts, in addition to the domains of perceived social pressure and perceived structural constraints) and a variable number of nonfixed or problem-specific secondary domains. The specification of multifold domains makes it possible to identify contingencies in the considerations that people have: Some may be primarily guided by the "economic" principles of time and money, whereas others may be more likely to follow the "social" principles of prestige and social contacts.

The elements regarding perceived social pressure and perceived structural constraints are similar to those of other theoretical approaches. For example, Bandura's (1977, 1982) self-efficacy concept and Ajzen's (1985) concept of perceived behavioral control correspond to the auxiliary cognition with respect to the perceived opportunities for change. Fishbein and Ajzen's (1975) concept of normative belief parallels the auxiliary cognitions with respect to perceived social pressure, whereas their concept of the motivation to comply parallels the secondary cognition with respect to conformity in behavior. However, the TMI explicitly takes the actual opportunities and constraints into account, which the other theories do not. Thus, the TMI is able to explain why some people successfully perform certain behaviors, despite the existence of considerable objective restrictions (e.g., friends who continue to keep in close and frequent contact despite living at long distances from one another). It also explains why some people do not perform certain behaviors even though, objectively speaking, they have considerable opportunities to do so (e.g., do not remarry despite the existence of many eligible mates).

## Applications of the Theory of Mental Incongruity

Processes of adaptation as regarded by the TMI concern mental and behavioral changes aimed at achieving cognitive balance (or reducing incongruity). The theory can be used to explain (a) changes that take place from one point in time to another, and (b) the outcome of changes that have or have not taken place. The first requires a longitudinal design: Data gathered at Time 1 are considered to be the starting point of a continuing process of adaptation. Predictions can be formulated about the manner in which incongruity at Time 1 is likely to be reduced, and data gathered at Time 2 can be used to test them. The second explanation problem requires a cross-sectional design: Data collected at a single point in time are viewed as the temporary outcome of an ongoing process of mental incongruity reduction. Thus, depending on the type of research design, the theory can be used to explain differences in existing in-congruity (cross sectional) or differences in incongruity reduction (longitudinal).

The TMI has been tested successfully in a number of studies: participation in the labor force by married, university-educated women (Tazelaar, 1980), housing (dis)satisfaction of inner-city dwellers (Tazelaar, 1985), and long-term unemployment experienced by middle-aged men (Tazelaar & Sprengers, 1985). However, it has hardly been applied to research in the area of personal rela-tionships. A noteworthy study was one reported by Stevens (1989), who em-ployed the TMI as a general framework for explaining differences in well-being among older widows. Largely using material from open-ended interviews, Stevens analyzed the ways in which widows fulfilled their relationship needs (behavioral changes) and relationship desires (changes in standards) in their husbands' absences, thereby reducing the incongruity that was created by their loss. Dykstra (1990) used the TMI in a study of loneliness among older adults. That study identified conditions under which a discrepancy between available levels of support and desired support levels was particularly stressful. Under those conditions, older adults were severely lonely. Applications of the TMI in studies of the aftermath of divorce can be found in Broese van Groenou (1991) and de Jong Gierveld and Dykstra (1993).

In our view, the TMI is potentially of use to relationship researchers for both substantive and methodological reasons. The field of personal relationships tends to be dominated by psychological explanations. The TMI links psychological (dispositional) factors with structural/normative factors. In that way, it opens the door to sociological explanations. The theory can guide relationship researchers to new questions that address the interplay of dispositional and structural/normative factors. Furthermore, the manner in which relationship phenomena are examined can also benefit from applications of the TMI. Because the theory provides a systematic and coherent framework, its application should encourage methodological sophistication. By methodological sophistication we do not mean a refinement of measures. Rather, we mean an orderly and systematic treat-ment of the phenomena at hand, and the testing of more complex hypotheses—hypotheses of the form "under what conditions is what type of relationship behavior likely or not likely to be observed?" This way the TMI opens the door to greater depth in the explanation of relationship phenomena.

## SPECIFIC APPLICATION OF THE TMI
## TO A CROSS-SECTIONAL STUDY OF
## LONELINESS AMONG WIDOWED MEN AND WOMEN

In the next part of this chapter, we demonstrate, using data from a cross-sectional study of widowed men and women, how the TMI was used in the explanation of loneliness. Using cross-sectional data, it is possible to approxi-mate the adaptation to widowhood, as it occurs over time, by drawing a comparison between those who have experienced the loss (i.e., widowed respondents) and those who have not (i.e., respondents living with a partner). Presumably, the widowed have recovered from the loss they have suffered if there are no differences between them and their cohabiting counterparts in terms of loneliness. Although the emphasis in this chapter lies in the explanation of loneliness among the widowed, data on differences between the widowed and the cohabiting are presented to provide an indication of the degree and nature of the adaptation to the loss of the partner that has taken place.

Loneliness can be seen as an incongruity in personal relationships: the unwanted discrepancy between the relationships a person has and the relationships he or she desires (de Jong Gierveld, 1987; Perlman & Peplau, 1981). The discrepancy can refer to situations where the number of existing relationships is smaller than desired, as well as to situations where the quality one wishes for has not been realized. We show in consecutive steps, starting with a simple one-factor explanation, how the introduction of secondary domain elements leads to greater depth of the explanation of loneliness. Our treatment of the secondary domain elements illustrates the manner in which it is possible to enter structural/normative factors into the explanation of loneliness. At each of the consecutive steps, the general hypothesis used in the explanation of incongruity is presented before describing the operationalization of the general hypothesis and the resulting specific prediction that was used in the explanation of loneliness.

It is not our intention here to put the entire theory to the test. The theoretical elements are not dealt with in every possible detail, and in that sense we do not do justice to the full potential of the TMI. Our purpose here is only to illustrate some of the possibilities of working with the TMI, and to suggest avenues for future research.

## Design of the Study

The data were from a friendship survey that was completed in January 1987. The names and addresses of the respondents were obtained by taking random sample stratified according to age, gender, and marital status from the population registers of two cities in The Netherlands: Haarlem (population approximately 150,000) and Hilversum (population approximately 85,000). The men and women who participated in the study belonged to two age cohorts: people between the ages of 30 and 40 inclusive, and people between the ages of 65 and 75 inclusive. Within each age cohort, the numbers of men and women officially registered as never married, married, divorced, or widowed were approximately equal.

A respondent's official marital status did not necessarily coincide with his or her partner status. Some of the respondents who were officially registered as widows or widowers were living with a partner without having remarried.

Conversely, some of the respondents who were not officially registered as widows or widowers no longer had a (homosexual) partner because that person had died. Widowed respondents in the present analysis were respondents who had lost a partner (spouse or cohabitant) through that person's death and who were living on their own. In our sample, 75 respondents met these criteria; 25 were between the ages of 30 and 40 inclusive, whereas 50 were between the ages of 65 and 75 inclusive. Of the younger widowed, 12 were men and 13 were women. Of the older widowed, 26 were men and 24 were women. For the younger respondents, the median duration of widowhood was 2 years, whereas it was 6 years for the older widowed.[1] The comparison group was formed by 120 respondents who were living with a partner, either officially married or not. Of the 60 younger respondents who were cohabiting, 30 were men and 30 were women. Of the 60 older respondents who were cohabiting, 37 were men and 23 were women.

The respondents were interviewed in their own homes. The semistructured interviews lasted from 2 to 3 hours. Special care was taken to create a research situation in which the respondents would feel free to disclose their experiences and ideas. The interviewers who were selected had extensive prior experience in conducting lengthy semistructured interviews on personal and emotional topics. Close attention was paid to the order in which the questions concerning the central theoretical concepts were presented. The interview involved a progression from less to more intimate inquiries as the relationship between the respondent and the interviewer developed.

## EXPLANATION OF LONELINESS: PRIMARY DOMAIN ELEMENTS

Given the tendency to achieve cognitive balance, primary incongruity at one point in time is generally not expected to exist. According to the TMI, primary incongruity at Time 1 exists only under very specific conditions, namely only if the reduction of the primary incongruity is expected to lead to the production of greater secondary incongruities, thus resulting in greater net incongruity in the mental system. The general hypothesis, based on primary domain elements, is this: Given the centrality of the primary cognition, (a) the more dominant the primary standard, and/or (b) the more the primary standard relates to the individual specifically, the greater the primary incongruity. That

---

[1]Before testing the predictions derived from the TMI, we examined whether possible differences in loneliness among the widowed could be attributed to our sampling criteria. A two-way analysis of variance (ANOVA) showed no significant age and gender differences ($F = .5$, $p > .05$, and $F = .7$, $p > .05$, respectively). The two-way interaction was not significant either ($F = .1$, $p > .05$). The results indicated that it was not necessary to control for age and gender in subsequent analyses.

is, given the perception of the situation that the person is in, the greater the desire for (or the greater the value placed on) a situation different from the existing one, the greater the primary incongruity.

The specific prediction about the primary domain elements contributing to loneliness was derived in the following way. We started with the operationalization of loneliness. The measure of loneliness, an 11-item scale, was based on the conceptualization of loneliness as an incongruity in personal relationships (for details on the development of the scale and its psychometric properties, see de Jong Gierveld & Kamphuis, 1985). The scale consisted of items describing perceptions of, and feelings associated with, the presence or absence of a discrepancy between the relationships one has and the relationships one wants. Both positive and negative items were included. An example of a positive item is "There are enough people that I feel close to."[2] An example of a negative item is "I miss having people around." The scale scores ranged from 0, indicating the absence of loneliness, to 11, indicating severe loneliness.

Common to the widowed is the loss of the partner. Although people without a partner are generally found to be more prone to loneliness than people with a partner (de Jong Gierveld & van Tilburg, 1987; Perlman, 1988), the absence of a partner should not be equated with a situation of loneliness. For example, the presence of supportive relationships with friends or family members can compensate for the absence of a partner relationship (Dykstra, 1990, 1993). For that reason, two measures of the primary cognition were used: the absence of the partner and the support from other types of relationships. The support scores were based on the total support derived from the respondents' most important relationships (i.e., their "top six" relationships, or fewer, if fewer were nominated). The support questions concerned either unconditional positive regard (e.g., "He or she cares about me") or validational support (e.g., "He or she helps me be honest about myself"). The maximum support score was 60; the minimum score was 0. Details about the procedure, which was followed to compute the support scores, can be found in Dykstra (1990).

Incongruity exists when the standards one has do not match the situation one is in. In other words, the absence of a partner is only a situation of incongruity (i.e., loneliness) if the widowed individual has a dominant partner standard. However, possible discrepancies between the standards and cognitions with respect to a partner are not the only sources of loneliness. The widowed person can experience deficits in other types of relationships, such as relationships with friends, siblings, children, or neighbors. For that reason, two different relationship standards were measured: the partner standard and the standard with respect to relationships other than the partner. The partner standard was

---

[2]This and all subsequent items have been translated from the actual items that were administered in Dutch.

based on the rating of the importance attached to a partner relationship. Rating scores ranged from 1 to 6; the higher the rating, the more dominant the partner standard. The measure of the standard for relationships other than a partner was based on a summation score of the number of times same-gender friends, neighbors, siblings, and children were considered to be "absolutely essential." The scores ranged from 0 to 4; the higher the score, the more dominant the standard for other relationships. For the sake of clarity, the relationship standards are referred to as (a) the importance attached to a partner, and (b) the importance attached to other ties. These operationalizations bring us to the following specific prediction: Given the absence of a partner, given the support from the most important relationships,

- the greater the importance attached to a partner,
- the greater the importance attached to other ties, and/or
- the greater the intensity of loneliness.

The predictions emphasize that the intensity of loneliness, given a particular availability or quality of relationships, depends on the relationship standards. At a given level of support, the more dominant the standards, the greater the discrepancy between what one has and what one wants and, therefore, the greater the intensity of loneliness. Someone without a partner is not expected to be very lonely if he or she attaches relatively little importance to that relationship. Similarly, someone with relatively little support is not expected to be very lonely if he or she attaches relatively little importance to having relationships. Furthermore, someone with relatively much support is expected to be lonely only if he or she attaches extreme importance to having relationships. The test of the specific prediction is described in the following section.

## Comparison Between the Widowed and Their Cohabiting Counterparts

First we compared the mean loneliness score of the widowed with that of cohabiting counterparts. The purpose was to find out whether the absence of a partner was an incongruity producing situation. On average, the widowed were significantly more lonely than were the cohabiting ($t = -5.3, p < .001$). The means were 3.7 ($SD = 3.0$) and 1.7 ($SD = 1.9$), respectively. Thus, the absence of a partner was generally found to be a situation that produced incongruity. However, the magnitude of the standard deviation indicated that the extent to which widowed men and women suffered negative consequences after the death of the spouse (as indicated by the intensity of loneliness) varied widely.

According to the TMI, variations in loneliness among the widowed are determined by the extent to which compensation for lost support has been found in other types of relationships (behavioral changes) and/or the extent to which the importance attached to relationships has been lowered (changes in standards). A comparison between the widowed and the cohabiting respondents provides an indication of the extent to which such changes have taken place. Table 11.1 shows differences between the widowed and the cohabiting respondents with respect to (a) the primary cognition (i.e., the support received from the most important relationships), and (b) the primary standard (i.e., the importance attached to a partner relationship and that attached to other ties). As the table shows, on average the widowed received significantly less support from their most important relationships than did the cohabiting. The difference suggests that, on average, the widowed had not "fully" compensated for the loss they had suffered.

A significant difference also emerged for the partner standard. On average, the widowed attached less importance to that relationship than did the cohabiting. This finding suggests that in the process of adapting to life as single people, the widowed, on average, reduced the importance of having a partner relationship. Interestingly, no differences between the widowed and the cohabiting were observed with respect to the standard for other relationships. Apparently, the importance attached to relationships such as those with same-gender friends, neighbors, children, and siblings was generally not affected by widowhood.

## Test of the Specific Prediction

Previously, in comparing the loneliness scores of the widowed and their cohabiting counterparts, it was shown that, on average, the absence of a partner was associated with greater loneliness. However, the absence of a partner was

TABLE 11.1
Differences Between Widowed and Cohabiting Respondents
with Respect to the Primary Domain

| Primary Domain | Widowed (n = 75) | | Cohabiting (n = 120) | | |
|---|---|---|---|---|---|
| | M | SD | M | SD | t |
| Primary cognition | | | | | |
| Support partner (range 0–10) | — | — | 8.1 | 2.3 | — |
| Support other ties | 31.2 | 14.2 | 27.7 | 12.7 | — |
| Support top six (range 0–60) | 31.2 | 14.2 | 35.9 | 13.3 | −2.1* |
| Primary standard | | | | | |
| Importance partner (range 1–6) | 4.4 | 1.5 | 5.3 | 1.0 | −4.5** |
| Importance other ties (range 0–4) | 1.7 | 1.0 | 1.7 | 1.0 | .1 |

Note. *p < .05.
**p < .001.

not assumed to affect the widowed uniformly. As the TMI predicts, given the absence of a partner, the more dominant the partner standard, that is, the greater the importance attached to a partner relationship, the greater the intensity of loneliness. Our findings were consistent with this prediction. The pearson correlation between the importance attached to a partner and loneliness was .25 ($n$ = 75, $p$ < .05).

The results showed that the more support the widowed received from their most important relationships, the less likely they were to experience loneliness. The pearson correlation between support and loneliness was $-.41$ ($n$ = 75, $p$ < .001). However, the TMI predicts that, given the total support from their most important relationships, the more dominant the standard for other relationships, that is, the greater the importance attached to other ties, the greater the intensity of loneliness. Again, the results were consistent with the theoretical predictions. The partial correlation (i.e., controlling for support) between the importance attached to other ties and loneliness was .21 ($n$ = 75, $p$ < .05).

In summary, by using the TMI we demonstrated that although the absence of a partner generally made the widowed more vulnerable to loneliness, the degree to which they experienced loneliness depended, among other factors, on their partner standard. Given the absence of a partner, the more importance placed on having a partner, the more lonely the widowed were. Similarly, we demonstrated that although a relative lack of support from close ties generally contributed to loneliness, the degree to which this occurred depended, among other factors, on the standard for relationships such as the relationships with same-gender friends, neighbors, children, and siblings. The more the widowed valued such relationships (given the support they received), the more lonely they were.

## EXPLANATION OF LONELINESS: SECONDARY DOMAIN ELEMENTS

Up to this point, the explanation of loneliness has not been very different from one based on a cognitive processes approach (de Jong Gierveld, 1987; Perlman & Peplau, 1981). That approach also emphasizes the discrepancy between the relationships a person has and the one he or she desires. Admittedly, few loneliness researchers have actually measured relationship standards and contrasted them with existing relationships. However, the necessity of doing so has been pointed out by several authors (Marangoni & Ickes, 1989; Peplau, Miceli, & Morasch, 1982; Rook, 1988; Solano, 1986). What makes the TMI interesting is that the explanation of loneliness does not stop at an account of relationship standards and the quality of relationships. The explanation is carried a step further, by taking elements from the so-called "secondary domain" into consideration. These elements identify conditions under which the degree of loneliness is intensified.

The general hypothesis for the explanation of incongruity, taking into account both primary and secondary domain elements, is this: Given the primary cognition, the more dominant the primary standard, the greater the incongruity, and the more so, (a) the more central the auxiliary cognitions with respect to the fixed secondary domains of time, money, prestige, and social contacts; (b) the more central the auxiliary cognitions with respect to the nonfixed secondary domains; (c) the more central the auxiliary cognitions with respect to perceived social pressure, and/or (d) the less central the auxiliary cognitions with respect to the perceived opportunities for change. In other words, incongruity depends on more than the discrepancy between the primary cognition and the primary standard. It also depends on conditions such as the expected advantages and disadvantages of the desired situation, the perception of the degree to which the desired situation is in accordance with the standards of others, and/or the perception of the opportunities for change.

In operationalizing the secondary domain elements, we made the distinction between secondary elements concerning the partner and those concerning relationships more generally. This is consistent with the manner in which the primary domain elements were operationalized. We started with the auxiliary cognitions involving the advantages and disadvantages of having a partner or of being without one. According to the TMI, the intensity of loneliness that exists when a person has a dominant partner standard but does not have a partner is even greater when that person perceives the partner relationship as having relatively many advantages and relatively few disadvantages. The intensity of loneliness is also expected to be greater when that person perceives being without a partner as having relatively few advantages and relatively many disadvantages.

The TMI specifies four fixed secondary domains, namely money, time, prestige, and social contacts, from which to view the relative advantages and disadvantages of having a partner relationship or of being without one. To limit the length of the questionnaire, we did not measure the auxiliary cognitions with respect to the fixed mental elements.[3] Instead, we assessed the relative advantages of having a partner in terms of nonfixed secondary domains. We developed a scale consisting of eight items. The items expressed the positive (or negative) consequences of having a partner (or of being single) either in terms of one's meaning of life or in terms of one's individuality. The focus

---

[3]To provide the reader with an idea of how fixed mental elements could possibly be measured in future studies, the following sample items are presented: "If I have a partner, I can share my living expenses" (money); "If I have a partner, I will have less time to myself" (time); "If I have a partner, I will no longer feel I am a failure" (prestige); and "If I have a partner, I will have someone to keep me company" (social contacts). These are examples of auxiliary cognitions. The secondary standards concern the desires and values associated with the fixed domains (i.e., the values placed on free-available time, prestige, etc.), whereas the secondary cognitions concern the degree to which individuals perceive having free-available time, prestige, and so on.

on the consequences of a particular partner status differentiates this measure from the partner standard measure. Of course, conceptually, the two measures are closely related. The items are presented in Table 11.2. The higher the score on the scale, the more a respondent agreed with the positive consequences and disagreed with the negative consequences of having a partner, and the more he or she agreed with the negative consequences and disagreed with the positive consequences of being without a partner. To avoid the use of lengthy descriptions, this scale (with scores ranging from 0 to 8) is referred to as the measure of the advantages of having a partner relationship.[4]

According to the TMI, the intensity of loneliness that exists when a person has a dominant partner standard but does not have a partner depends further on the (perceptions of) the normative context. More particularly, it depends on the (perceived) social pressure to be involved in a partner relationship. If the dominant partner standard is (perceived to be) shared by significant others, the intensity of loneliness among the widowed is expected to be greater. Because only the widowed were interviewed, and not any of their network members, we had no direct measures of the partner standard of significant others. Neither did we ask the widowed about their perceptions of the partner standard of those who were close to them. However, information was collected on the partner status of the top six persons, providing us with a measure of the (dis)similarity in partner status between the widowed and their most important ties. Partner status was the presence or absence of a cohabitant. We assumed that the (dis)similarity in partner status was an indication of social pressure. The greater the number of same-age persons among the top six who were living with a partner, presumably, the more couple oriented the social involvements of the widowed were and the less support there was for the situation of the single, bereaved person. (Top six members were considered to be of the same age as the respondents if there was no more than a 16-year age difference.)[5]

The next operationalizations of the secondary elements concern relationships more generally, not just the partner relationship. Given the primary domain elements, the TMI posits that people experience greater incongruity the less favorable their perceptions of the opportunities for change in the direction of the primary standard are. In the present study, perceived opportunities for change concerned the opportunities to establish and maintain relationships. Two measures were used: experienced health problems and social anxiety. Both

---

[4]The degree to which the respondents valued having or perceived having a meaning in life or their individuality (i.e., the secondary standards and the secondary cognitions with respect to these nonfixed domains) were not measured specifically. Thus, we assumed that people's standards and cognitions in these domains generally do not differ.

[5]We assumed that individuals generally strive toward normative conformity with those who are close to them. In other words, the secondary standard with respect to conformity in behavior was not measured specifically.

TABLE 11.2
Items Measuring the Advantages and Disadvantages of Having
a Partner Relationship or of Being Single, Respectively

| *List of Items* |
| --- |
| 1. With a partner life becomes meaningful |
| 2. Without a partner one develops a strong personality |
| 3. With a partner one loses one's identity |
| 4. Without a partner one is incomplete as a person |
| 5. A partner imposes restrictions on one's life |
| 6. A partner enriches oneself |
| 7. Without a partner one is free to do as one chooses |
| 8. Life is empty without a partner |

factors influence the perceived control individuals have in relationships. Experienced health problems (yes/no) were indicated by an affirmative answer to either the question "Do you feel you are physically restricted in establishing and maintaining personal contacts?" or "Do you currently have health problems?" A scale consisting of five questions was used to assess social anxiety. An example is: "Do you generally feel comfortable when you are with people whom you do not know well?" Scale scores ranged from 0, indicating the absence of social anxiety, to 5, indicating extreme social anxiety.

The operationalizations of the secondary domain elements bring us to the following specific prediction: Given the absence of a partner, given the support from the most important relationships,

- the greater the importance attached to a partner,
- the greater the importance attached other ties,
- the greater the intensity of loneliness,
- the greater the perceived advantages of a partner relationship,
- the greater the number of most important persons who are living with a partner,
- the greater the experienced health constraints, and/or
- the greater the experienced social anxiety.

## Comparison Between the Widowed
## and Their Cohabiting Counterparts

Before providing results pertaining to the tests of the specific prediction, we present data on differences between the widowed and the cohabiting respondents with respect to elements from the secondary domain (see Table 11.3). The differences concern (a) the auxiliary cognition with respect to nonfixed

TABLE 11.3
Differences Between Widowed and Cohabiting Respondents
with Respect to the Secondary Domain

| Secondary Domain | Widowed (n = 75) | | Cohabiting (n = 120) | | t |
|---|---|---|---|---|---|
| | M | SD | M | SD | |
| Nonfixed elements | | | | | |
| Advantages partner (range 0–8) | 4.1 | 2.1 | 4.3 | 1.7 | – 1.0 |
| Social pressure | | | | | |
| Top six with partner | 1.3 | 1.6 | 2.0 | 1.9 | – 1.8* |
| Perceived opportunities | | | | | |
| Health problems (% yes) | 20.0 | 40.0 | 19.0 | 39.4 | .2 |
| Social anxiety (range 0–5) | 1.9 | 1.7 | 1.7 | 1.4 | 1.0 |

Note. *p < .05.

domains (i.e., the perceived advantages of a partner relationship in terms of one's meaning of life and one's individuality), (b) the normative context (i.e., the number of most important persons who are living with a partner), and (c) the perceived opportunities (i.e., experienced health problems and social anxiety). Inspection of the table reveals that the widowed and the cohabiting did not differ in terms of the perceived advantages of a partner relationship. This finding is unlike that for the importance attached to a partner. As was shown previously, the widowed, on average, attached less importance to a partner relationship than did the cohabiting. Apparently, the difference in the partner standard is not necessarily accompanied by a difference in the perceived advantages of a partner. A significant difference was found with respect to the mean number of relationships with people who were living with a partner. (To avoid confounding, the relationship with the cohabitant was excluded from this analysis.) On average, the widowed nominated fewer persons with a partner among their top six relationships than did the cohabiting. This finding suggests that, among the widowed, a reduction takes place in the number of close ties with people whose partner status is different from their own. No significant differences between the widowed and the cohabiting were found with respect to health problems and social anxiety.

## Test of the Specific Prediction

Table 11.4 provides specific illustrations of the manner in which elements from the secondary domain influenced the primary incongruity. The top part of the table shows first of all (and repeating a point made earlier) that the widowed who attached relatively little importance to a partner relationship were, on average, less lonely than those who attached relatively much importance to that

TABLE 11.4

Mean Loneliness Scores for Widowed Respondents Broken Down
by Elements from the Primary and Secondary Domains

| *Domains* | *Scores* | | | |
|---|---|---|---|---|
| Primary domain | | | | |
| Importance partner | low (*n* = 30) | | high (*n* = 45) | |
| | 2.8 (2.1) | | 4.3 (3.3) | |
| Secondary domain | | | | |
| Advantages partner | few (*n* = 20) | many (*n* = 10) | few (*n* = 22) | many (*n* = 23) |
| | 2.1 (1.5) | 4.2 (2.5) | 3.9 (3.1) | 4.6 (3.5) |
| Primary domain | | | | |
| Support | high (*n* = 37) | | low (*n* = 38) | |
| | 2.5 (2.4) | | 4.8 (3.0) | |
| Importance other ties | low (*n* = 16) | high (*n* = 21) | low (*n* = 26) | high (*n* = 12) |
| | 1.9 (1.9) | 3.0 (2.1) | 4.4 (2.8) | 5.8 (3.3) |
| Secondary domain | | | | |
| | low (*n* = 10) | low (*n* = 10) | low (*n* = 10) | low (*n* = 6) |
| Social anxiety | 0.8 (0.4) | 2.5 (2.5) | 3.3 (2.8) | 4.7 (2.6) |
| | high (*n* = 6) | high (*n* = 11) | high (*n* = 16) | high (*n* = 6) |
| | 2.5 (2.2) | 3.4 (3.0) | 5.5 (2.6) | 6.8 (3.9) |

*Note.* The standard deviations are provided in parentheses. The variables were recoded as follows. Support: low (score 0–32), high (score 33–60). Importance partner: low (score 1–4), high (score 5–6). Advantages partner: low (score 0–4), high (score 5–8). Importance other ties: low (score 0), high (score 1–4). Social anxiety: low (score 0–1), high (score 2–5). The partial *r* (controlling for support and the importance attached to a partner) between loneliness and the perceived advantages of a partner was .25 (*p* < .05). The partial *r* (controlling for support and the importance attached to other ties) between loneliness and social anxiety was .25 (*p* < .05).

relationship. Second, it shows that the intensity of loneliness in the two partner standard groups depended on a secondary domain element, namely the perceived advantages of having a partner. For example, the widowed who attached relatively little importance to a partner were even less lonely, on average, if they perceived a partner relationship to have relatively few advantages (*M* = 2.1). On the other hand, the widowed who attached relatively much importance to a partner were even more lonely, on average, if they perceived a partner relationship to have relatively many advantages (*M* = 4.6).

The bottom part of Table 11.4 shows results similar to the top part, but they are based on different primary and secondary elements. First it shows (repeating a point made earlier) that the widowed who received relatively much support from their top six relationships were, on average, less lonely than those who received relatively little support. Next it shows (again repeating a point made earlier) that within the two distinguished groups, the intensity of loneliness differed according to the relationship standard (i.e., the importance attached to other ties). The bottom line shows the mean loneliness scores after having taken a secondary domain element into account, namely social anxiety.

The lowest degree of loneliness ($M$ = 0.8) was observed among the widowed men and women who (a) received relatively much support, (b) attached relatively little importance to other ties, and (c) had relatively little social anxiety. The highest degree of loneliness ($M$ = 6.8) was observed among those who (a) received relatively little support, (b) attached relatively much importance to other ties, and (c) had relatively much social anxiety. In other words, relatively strong loneliness feelings were found among the widowed who expected more from relationships than what they actually received. Their loneliness was exacerbated if they were socially anxious and, presumably, perceived few opportunities for improvement.

To avoid redundancy, the findings for the other two secondary domain elements, namely social pressure and health problems, have not been summarized in a table. The results for those secondary elements were also consistent with the theoretical predictions, which can be shown by means of partial correlations. The partial correlations were controlled for the primary domain elements, namely the support received from the most important relationships, the importance attached to a partner, and the importance attached to other ties. As predicted, the greater the social pressure, as indicated by the number of persons among the top six who were living with a partner, the greater the intensity of loneliness (partial $r$ = .21, $p$ < .05). Furthermore, as predicted, health problems were found to be positively associated with loneliness (partial $r$ = .33, $p$ < .01).

So far, the specific prediction involving both the primary and the secondary domains has not been tested in its entirety. An analysis of variance (ANOVA) was performed to examine whether each of the distinguished factors would continue to produce a significant effect once all the factors were entered into an analysis together.[6] The support received from the most important relationships was introduced as a covariate. In other words, the effects of the independent factors were adjusted for differences in support. Experienced health problems were excluded because the analysis allowed no more than five independent variables. The independent variables were dichotomized at the median (as far as this was possible). The hierarchical procedure was used, meaning that the effect of a particular variable was computed after the effects of preceding variables had been taken into account. As can be seen in Table 11.5, each of the factors had a significant effect on loneliness. The effects were all in the direction predicted by the TMI.

The table shows how much each of the factors independently contributed to the variation in loneliness scores. Using the information from the table, it

---

[6]The factors were largely uncorrelated. Only three pearson correlations were significant at the .05 level: top six support with the importance attached to other ties ($r$ = .20); top six support with the number of top six persons living with a partner ($r$ = .42); and the importance attached to a partner with the perceived advantages of having a partner ($r$ = .20).

TABLE 11.5

Summary of Hierarchical Five-Factor ANOVA of the Mean Loneliness Scores
of Widowed Men and Women

| Variable | n | adj. dev.* | F | p |
|---|---|---|---|---|
| Support top six | | | 19.8 | < .001 |
| Importance partner | | | 6.0 | < .05 |
|   Low (score 1–4) | 30 | – .8 | | |
|   High (score 5–6) | 45 | .5 | | |
| Importance other ties | | | 4.0 | < .05 |
|   Low (score 0) | 42 | – .4 | | |
|   High (score 1–4) | 33 | .5 | | |
| Advantages partner | | | 4.3 | < .05 |
|   Few (score 0–4) | 42 | – .8 | | |
|   Many (score 5–8) | 33 | 1.0 | | |
| Top six with partner | | | 7.8 | < .01 |
|   0 members | 32 | – 1.0 | | |
|   > 0 members | 43 | .7 | | |
| Social anxiety | | | 5.4 | < .05 |
|   Low (score 0–1) | 36 | – .7 | | |
|   High (score 2–5) | 39 | .6 | | |

Note. Support was introduced as a covariate. Two-way and three-way interactions were not significant.

*Deviation from the grand mean (3.7) adjusted for the effects of the covariate and the other factors.

$r^2$ = .41.

is possible to identify the conditions under which widowed men and women were likely to experience stronger feelings of loneliness, and the conditions under which they were relatively free from loneliness. For example, given a particular level of support, if a widowed respondent attached relatively little importance to a partner relationship, his or her loneliness score dropped .8 scale points, resulting in a mean score of 2.9. In addition, if that respondent had no top six members living with a partner, his or her loneliness score dropped 1.0 scale point to 1.9. The latter mean score hardly differed from that found for the group of cohabiting respondents, namely 1.7.

In summary, we were able to demonstrate that by taking elements from the secondary domain of the TMI into consideration, greater depth in the explanation of loneliness was reached. Through the introduction of the secondary domain elements, the explanation of loneliness went beyond an explanation in terms of a perceived discrepancy between achieved relationships and desired relationships. The secondary domain elements identified conditions under which the degree of loneliness was intensified. We were able to show that the widowed became even more vulnerable to loneliness if, for example, they perceived that having a partner had relatively many advantages (and that being single had relatively many disadvantages). Loneliness was also likely to be aggravated if the widowed had relatively many people among their closest relationships whose partner status was different from their own. Another condition under which loneliness was likely to be intensified was if there were relatively few opportunities for establishing and maintaining personal relationships, for example, as the result of health restrictions or personal inhibitions.

## DISCUSSION

In this chapter, the theory of mental incongruity was used to explain the intensity of loneliness among people who have had the painful experience of losing their partner. Our study was a specific application of the TMI in a specific context. Our aim was to provide the reader with ideas about how to apply the TMI to other problems in relationship research, as well as with insights about the potential usefulness of the TMI.

The problems to which the TMI can be applied are those concerning the general question of why certain people make transitions with greater ease than others. These transitions may be in response to events that were imposed on the people involved, such as the death of a loved one. Alternatively, they may be linked with changes that people bring about themselves, such as the birth of a child or the breakup of a marriage. The answer to the general question of why people react differently under similar circumstances is sought in an analysis of the manner in which people attempt to achieve congruity between their standards (i.e., their desires or expectations) and their cognitions (i.e., their perceptions of the situation they are in).

The TMI is an attractive theory because it offers a coherent framework—a framework that integrates dispositional as well as structural/normative factors. We argued that application of the TMI should encourage the search for sociological explanations in relationship research. This was illustrated in the present study: The (dis)similarity in partner status between the widowed individual and the members of his or her social network was one of the factors that was introduced as a sociological determinant of loneliness. This particular factor served as an indication of the social pressure to be involved in a partner relationship.

We also argued that application of the TMI should encourage greater depth in the explanation of relationship phenomena. Our treatment of the determinants of loneliness was such that we started with a relatively simple explanation of loneliness in terms of the quality of achieved relationships and relationship standards. Subsequently, at successive steps we introduced other factors into the analysis, revealing conditions under which the widowed were likely to experience even stronger feelings of loneliness. These conditions concerned the perceived advantages of being partnered (and the perceived disadvantages of being single), the social pressure toward involvement in a partner relationship, poor health, and social anxiety. That factors such as reported health problems and social anxiety were associated with loneliness was not a new finding. What was new was that these factors were incorporated into a broader theoretical framework. Application of the theory directed the attention toward the examination of hypotheses of the form: Given the loneliness that arises from the perceived discrepancy between available relationships and relationship standards, under what conditions are widows and widowers likely to experience even stronger feelings of loneliness and under what conditions are they likely to be free from feelings of loneliness?

Although we consider the TMI to be potentially useful to relationship researchers, one should keep in mind what the theory can and cannot do. The TMI is not a psychological theory. It does not aim to provide insight into cognitive and perceptual processes. For example, although it specifies the conditions under which mental changes such as changes in standards are or are not likely to occur, it does not specify the nature of these changes or the mechanisms underlying them. Thus, although the TMI predicts when widowed men and women are likely to adapt to their partner standard, it does not unfold how the process takes place. To gain insight into how people come to have the standards they do, one must turn to other theories (e.g., psychological coping theories). As said, the usefulness of the TMI lies in the fact that it provides a general framework—a framework with which it is possible to methodically analyze relationship phenomena. The general framework must be tailored to the specific problem at hand, and this can only be done if one has substantive knowledge about the specific problem.

We find it exciting to work with the TMI because it calls for a focus on different kinds of behaviors and their outcomes: overt, observable activities and covert, mental activities as different means of adapting to or overcoming unwanted situations. This multifaceted focus makes it different from most theories. In our view, the challenge for new relationship research lies in such an approach. More studies should examine the ongoing interdependence between what people expect from others, what people do to have their expectations met, and what the upshot of their endeavors is.

## ACKNOWLEDGMENTS

Work on this chapter was supported by grants from the Netherlands Organization for Scientific Research (N.W.O.) and the Queen Juliana Foundation (K.J.F.). The authors wish to thank Frits Tazelaar for his helpful comments on an earlier version of the manuscript.

# REFERENCES

Ajzen, I. (1985). From intentions to actions: A theory of planned behavior. In J. Kuhl & J. Beckmann (Eds.), *Action control: From cognition to behavior* (pp. 11–39). Berlin: Springer.

Ajzen, I., & Fishbein, M. (1980). *Understanding attitudes and predicting social behavior.* Englewood Cliffs, NJ: Prentice-Hall.

Bagozzi, R. P. (1986). Attitude formation under the theory of reasoned action and a purposeful behavior reformulation. *British Journal of Social Psychology, 25,* 95–107.

Bandura, A. (1977). Self-efficacy: Toward a unifying theory of behavioral change. *Psychological Review, 84,* 191–215.

Bandura, A. (1982). Self-efficacy mechanisms in human agency. *American Psychologist, 37,* 122–147.

Broese van Groenou, M. I. (1991). *Gescheiden netwerken: De relaties met vrienden en verwanten na echtscheiding* [Separated networks: The relationships with kin and nonkin after marital separation]. Unpublished doctoral dissertation, University of Utrecht, The Netherlands.

de Jong Gierveld, J. (1987). Developing and testing a model of loneliness. *Journal of Personality and Social Psychology, 53,* 119–128.

de Jong Gierveld, J., & Dykstra, P. A. (1993). Life transitions and the network of personal relationships: Methodological and theoretical issues. In W. H. Jones & D. Perlman (Eds.), *Advances in personal relationships* (Vol. 4, pp. 195–227). London: Kingsley.

de Jong Gierveld, J., & Kamphuis, F. (1985). The development of a RASCH-type loneliness scale. *Applied Psychological Measurement, 9,* 289–299.

de Jong Gierveld, J., & van Tilburg, T. G. (1987). The partner as source of support in problem and non-problem situations [Special issue]. *Journal of Social Behavior and Personality, 2,* 191–200.

Dykstra, P. A. (1990). *Next of (non)kin: The importance of primary relationships for older adults' well-being.* Amsterdam: Swets & Zeitlinger.

Dykstra, P. A. (1993). The differential availability of relationships and the provision and effectiveness of support to older adults. *Journal of Social and Personal Relationships, 10,* 355–370.

Fishbein, M., & Ajzen, I. (1975). *Belief, attitude, intention and behavior: An introduction to theory and research.* Reading, MA: Addison-Wesley.

Marangoni, C., & Ickes, W. (1989). Loneliness: A theoretical review with implications for measurement. *Journal of Social and Personal Relationships, 6,* 93–128.

Münch, R. (1972). *Mentales System und Verhalten: Grundlagen einer allgemeinen Verhaltenstheorie* [Mental system and behavior: Foundations for a general behavior theory]. Tübingen, West Germany: Mohr.

Peplau, L. A., Miceli, M., & Morasch, B. (1982). Loneliness and self-evaluation. In L. A. Peplau & D. Perlman (Eds.), *Loneliness: A sourcebook of current theory, research and therapy* (pp. 135–151). New York: Wiley.

Perlman, D. (1988). Loneliness: A life-span, family perspective. In R. M. Milardo (Ed.), *Families and social networks* (pp. 190–220). London: Sage.

Perlman, D., & Peplau, L. A. (1981). Toward a social psychology of loneliness. In R. Gilmour & S. W. Duck (Eds.), *Personal relationships: 3. Personal relationships in disorder* (pp. 31–56). London: Academic Press.

Rook, K. S. (1988). Towards a more differentiated view of loneliness. In S. W. Duck (Ed.), *Handbook of personal relationships: Theory, research, and interventions* (pp. 571–611). New York: Wiley.

Solano, C. H. (1986). People without friends: Loneliness and its alternatives. In V. J. Derlega & B. A. Winstead (Eds.), *Friendship and social interaction* (pp. 227–246). New York: Springer-Verlag.

Stevens, N. (1989). *Well-being in widowhood: A question of balance.* Unpublished doctoral dissertation, University of Nijmegen, The Netherlands.

Tazelaar, F. (1980). *Mentale incongruenties—sociale restricties—gedrag. Een onderzoek naar beroepsparticipatie van gehuwde vrouwelijke academici* [Mental incongruities—social restrictions—behavior. A study on the labor force participation of married university-educated women]. Unpublished doctoral dissertation, University of Utrecht, The Netherlands.

Tazelaar, F. (1982). From a classical attitude-behavior hypothesis to a general model of behavior via the theory of mental incongruity. In W. Raub (Ed.), *Theoretical models and empirical analyses: Contributions to the explanation of individual actions and collective phenomena* (pp. 101–128). Utrecht, The Netherlands: Explanatory Sociology Publications.

Tazelaar, F. (1983). Van een klassieke attitude-gedragshypothese naar een algemeen gedrags-theoretisch model [From a classical attitude-behavior hypothesis to a general theoretical model of behavior]. In S. Lindenberg & F. N. Stokman (Eds.), *Modellen in de sociologie* (pp. 112–138). Deventer, The Netherlands: Van Loghum-Slaterus.

Tazelaar, F. (1985). *De kwaliteit van het stedelijk leefmilieu* [The quality of city living conditions]. Utrecht, The Netherlands: Explanatory Sociology Publications.

Tazelaar, F., & Sprengers, M. (1985). Arbeitslosigkeit und soziale Isolation: Ein vergleichender Test der Statusinkonsistenztheorie und der Theorie mentaler Inkongruenzen [Unemployment and social isolation: A comparative test of the status inconsistency theory and the mental incongruity theory]. In G. Büschges & W. Raub (Eds.), *Soziale Bedingungen—Individuelles Handeln—Soziale Konsequenzen* (pp. 181–222). Frankfurt am Main: Lang.

Tazelaar, F., & Wippler, R. (1982). Die Theorie mentaler Inkongruenzen und ihre Anwendung in der empirischen Sozialforschung [The theory of mental incongruity and its application in empirical social research]. *Angewandte Sozialforschung, 10,* 237–275.

Tazelaar, F., & Wippler, R. (1985). Problemspezifische Anwendungen der allgemeinen Theorie mentaler Inkongruenzen in der empirischen Sozialforschung [Problem-specific applications in empirical social research of the general theory of mental incongruity]. In G. Büschges & W. Raub (Eds.), *Soziale Bedingungen—Individuelles Handeln—Soziale Konsequenzen* (pp. 117–179). Frankfurt am Main: Lang.

# Author Index

# L

# M

# Subject Index

269